NOISE FROM THE NORTH END

The Amazing Story of
The UGLY DUCKLINGS

Dave Bingham

 FriesenPress

Suite 300 - 990 Fort St
Victoria, BC, Canada, V8V 3K2
www.friesenpress.com

ISBN
978-1-4602-6650-2 (Paperback)
978-1-4602-6651-9 (eBook)

1. Biography & Autobiography, Composers & Musicians

Distributed to the trade by The Ingram Book Company

SET LIST

FOREWORD & DEDICATION

This book is the truth, as I recall it. Where there was any question as to the validity of certain facts, they have been left out. I realize that with the passage of time some memories can become enhanced, so I've tried to avoid exaggeration.

Sometimes I could not remember specific dates or complete names, so I have stated what I *can* remember as accurately as possible.

Since 1998 and the re-release of The UGLY DUCKLINGS back catalogue, I've been reliving the experience of being in a rock 'n roll band in the 1960s.

The "DUCKS" were not one of the most successful bands in Canada, but we were definitely one of the most notorious. We were Canada's answer to The Rolling Stones. We delighted in being as badass as we could be. "Every mother's nightmare" was a common phrase used to describe us at the time, and we took great pride in trying to live up to our reputation.

We exploded on the scene in Toronto in 1966 at the same time as the British Invasion really began to take hold of the charts in the U.S. and Canada. Our story is similar to the story of hundreds, if not thousands of bands in North America and beyond, who started musical careers at that time by trying to emulate their musical heroes from the other side of the Atlantic.

We simply loved the music! When the Stones first made it to the charts we were already ahead of the game because of our slavish addiction to Bo Diddley and Chuck Berry. All we had to do was grow our hair and get an attitude.

Eventually, out of an intense desire to play, a unique "Ugly Ducklings Sound" was born. Because we weren't the greatest players around, we ended up writing our own material. It was easier that way. The necessity to create music that we *could* play forced us to be innovators. We didn't have time to become schooled players so we let our personalities carry the weight, and somehow the total character of those personalities created our own individual sound.

That's how it was with the "Ducks". We had no concept of our own musical identity. It was all just sort of a crazy feeling that we had, collectively. We put it out there, then we jammed until we got in the zone, and then we let the people be the judge.

I guess it's just the law of probabilities that sometimes the sum of the parts can turn out to be a little bit bigger than the whole!

DEDICATED TO

Roger Mayne, Howie Smith, Domenic Troiano, Jim Franks, Rick James, Bruce Palmer, Ray Nowak, Rick Lamb, John Hughes, Brian Maxim, Buzz Shearman, Pinky Dauvin, Richard Newell (King Biscuit Boy), Norm Wellbanks, Willie P. Bennett, Jeff Healey, Ritchie Oakley, Paul Naumann, Steve Propas, Phil Marshall, Ken Crabtree, Ron Scribner, Bob MacAdorey & Jungle Jay Nelson.

Friends and fellow musicians who shared my passion and changed my life.

Photo: Villiam Hrubovcak

FOR

My wife Jane, my son Sean, and all of the fans who have suggested to me over the years, that there are people out there who would be interested in reading my story.

CHAPTER I

INITIATION

I was always terrified of public speaking.

For me, the prospect of deliberately engaging a room full of people had always been a recipe for disaster. Immediately I would suffer from hyperventilation, heart palpitations and sweaty palms; while fear vibrated through my very core. I would stare at the floor in front of my feet and avoid making eye contact with even a single solitary member of the audience.

And, as if that wasn't enough, sweat would bead up and run down the small of my back and my tongue would righteously glue itself to the roof of my mouth.

So why was I here?

What had made me think that I could stand up on that auditorium stage in there, and *sing* in front of 450 people? I must have been mad!

Now, as I walked shakily up the grey concrete steps to the front entrance of the school, I was having second thoughts. Was this something I really wanted to do? All those evenings in the basement playing air guitar and lip-synching the words to "Not Fade Away" or "Bo Diddley" hadn't really prepared me for this. The show was still hours away and my stomach felt like I'd just swallowed a whole can of pickled oysters!

Just inside the door I looked around to see if any of the other guys had arrived. There were no signs. I headed up the hall to the rear entrance of the auditorium. Inside I could hear voices and laughter. The laughter helped. I could feel my stomach relax a little bit as I pushed open the door and walked backstage. John Read turned around and smiled as I slashed my way through the curtains and out onto the stage.

"Roger's on his way," he said, "he had to pick up some clothes at the dry-cleaners or something."

"What about Glynn," I asked.

"I don't know," said John, "his amp's here but he's not around."

Bill Huard was with John. He was "Mr. Cool", decked out in his corduroy Beatle jacket and black stovepipes and a genuine pair of imported Beatle boots that someone had sent him from England. Every girl in school literally swooned when Huard walked by in the halls. They all commented on how much he looked like Paul McCartney.

I nervously asked him, "Do you think we can pull this off, Bill? It's gonna be a pretty tough go without Rob playing the drums."

I hated not having control of every aspect of what was going to happen. The fact that the school wasn't going to let Rob play just because he went to Westhill Collegiate, was a total downer and had definitely played on my mind; my stomach too, for that matter.

Huard piped up, "Don't worry Dave, Marty will be just fine. He's played this kind of stuff before with Dave Ellis and Scotty Kessler."

Bill was the eternal optimist, always positive. It was nice to have him around. After the school committee had informed us that Rob wouldn't be allowed to play, Glynn had suggested we call up Marty Ranger and ask him to sit in, so Bill obliged. Marty jumped at the chance. Apart from the fact that he was a tried and true greaser, he was definitely a real R&B guy, and fit in nicely.

The plan was that we would all meet at the school, set up and test the gear and then go over to the plaza and hang out until around the time we were supposed to go on. This was because all of our friends and family would be arriving early to get good seats for the show and it would be awkward seeing everyone in the halls and having to meet and greet. Besides, it would be nearly impossible to sneak a few swigs of really good scotch in the hallways of the school, and the consequences of getting caught doing so would be disastrous.

John was busy turning over the top of his Ampeg Portaflex Bass Amp. It looked really cool with the exposed transformer and components gleaming under the overhead stage lights. He snapped it together, plugged in his chord and hit a few notes. It was deep. Deep, deep bass. John was a Donald "Duck" Dunn fan; along with Booker "T" Jones, Otis Redding, and Wilson Pickett. He was going to lay down a real pulse for us tonight!

He looked up at Huard, "I hope one rehearsal is enough!"

"Don't worry," Bill said, "You guys have been playin' a lot, and Marty knows all these tunes anyway."

It was true, Marty was really into it already. He was so wound up at rehearsal he didn't want to stop. We'd get through this just fine; I had a good feeling about it. Hell, even my dad was coming, this was really going to be something special.

John sat on the corner of his Portaflex and started playing his bass part for "Mona". He laid it out slowly, gradually building a rhythm into the repetition of the notes, rocking backwards and forwards, shifting his weight alternately from the heels of his Clarke's "winkle picker" shoes, to his toes. Suddenly, a flash of long blond hair swirled around behind him, and Glynn slithered his way between the curtains and into the centre section of the stage, where the gear was set up.

"Where's Roger?" he asked, with a faint accent.

"On his way," replied John. "He had to pick up his clothes,"

Glynn was wearing cords. Thick heavy cords. And a tangerine coloured shirt on which I had sewn a row of ruffles down the front. I had on my houndstooth pants and a black and orange button-down collared shirt. Quite a contrast with John's downtown "rounder" look. With his black suede "winkle-pickers" and mohair pants, he was a dead ringer for Ed "Kookie" Byrnes from 77 Sunset Strip.

Glynn, on the other hand, was a dead ringer for Brian Jones of The Rolling Stones. He was one of the coolest guys in the halls at school. Girls started yipping and yammering whenever he walked by. They fell apart just looking at him.

He sized me up with one quick glance. "You got nerves, or somethin', Dave?" he asked.

"No, it's just the same old anticipation," I murmured, "I almost feel like I'm going to float away."

We had commented recently about how everyone in the band just dug playing so much! We actually felt a physical reaction when we were going to play. Music was a revelation. It was our first spiritual experience; sort of like glimpsing something from another realm. The sound of Howlin' Wolf singing "Evil", had made the hair stand up on the back of our necks and drew us in, like a fish to water. Now we were going to find out if we could pull off the same trick with the audience tonight.

I was feeling lucky. And a little bit cocky, too! I had a brand new Hohner "A" Marine Band harp for the evening. It was so cool playing a new harp. The reeds were so loose, and the tone was so sinister and sweet at the same time! Now, if I could just get these jitters to go away.

A loud thud grabbed everyone's attention as the rear stage door burst open and Roger sashayed onto the stage using his amp to hold the door open as he held a dry cleaner's clothing bag high over his left shoulder. He put everything down and went back out into the hall to bring in his guitar. He came back in, looked around at everyone and said, "Well, is everybody ready? Where's Marty, he didn't chicken out did he?"

"No, Roger, I think he had to go over to the Elaine Plaza to get some new sticks," piped up Huard.

"O.K. then," said Roger, "Let's get everything ready for when he gets here!" He took the clothes over to a counter at the side of the stage and set them down, opened his guitar case and took out his beautiful '63 Gibson Les Paul Junior and leaned it up against his amp.

"Anybody got butterflies?" Roger asked, glancing my way.

I mumbled something negative along with everyone else. No one was going to admit that they might be a bit shy. Even if we all felt it, it was only going to make us more determined.

We set all the amps in a straight line leaving a space for the drums, and then set about tuning up. We'd probably have to do it again later on, but it was necessary because everyone had recently bought new strings.

As soon as we were reasonably tuned Roger and Glynn started working up "Mona". I grabbed my maracas in one hand and improvised with my new "A" harp in the other. It was like magic! Even without the drums it felt like some kind of transformation took place. There was just something about that Bo Diddley beat that hypnotized and transfixed us.

Roger was loosely strumming while Glynn punctuated the rhythm with a little bit of wide vibrato on his amp. John just locked into the rhythm. This was the kind of thing that would go on for hours in the basement at Roger's place. It was where we all loved to be.

After five minutes or so we called it quits. Time to go. Marty could get the drums set up on his own time. We agreed to meet backstage in an hour and fifteen minutes. But right now it was time to head over to the mall and loosen up!

Hopefully by the time we were finished getting the bugs out of our brains and gulping a few swigs of courage,

Marty would be set up and we could do a final tuning and sound check.

An hour later following our little sojourn to the plaza, we were on our way into the auditorium via the rear entrance to the school, after sliding down the incline of the football field behind the plaza. As we arrived we could hear the familiar sound of bass drum and snare, hi-hat and symbols all smashing and rumbling together in a mad cacophony of jungle rhythms. Marty had definitely arrived.

On the way into the school we'd seen dozens of cars arriving and parking out around the football field and at the side parking lot. Once inside we could hear the voices of students, moms and dads all making their way down the halls to the auditorium to get seated.

We slipped in the stage door entrance and into the dressing room at stage left. No one was around. Huard went out to see Marty and stuck his head out between the curtains to check out the scene. He came back in to report, "There's about fifty people out there already!" We checked our tuning to my brand new "A" Marine Band Harmonica and then got cleaned up. Glynn had a nice soft polishing cloth to shine up his Gretsch, which he passed over to Roger and John. Marty breezed into the dressing room and started combing his pompadour, gazing intently at the dressing room mirror. Roger changed into his red and black plaid shirt with his black leather vest and grey stove pipes. We were lookin' good and starting to sweat. John passed around his little box of Sen-Sens for anyone who felt a little self-conscious about their alcohol-tainted breath and then we started working on a set list out loud amongst ourselves.

By eight o'clock the noise from out in front was really getting noticeable. The school principal, Mr. Campbell, was pacing back and forth behind the first curtain trying to decide when to put the show in motion.

After a quick walkabout to check on the readiness of all the participants he slid through the part in the front curtains and stepped up to the mike to make the announcement to commence the fourth annual Cedarbrae Collegiate Talent Night. First up there were a couple of girls doing baton tricks and next a sweet young thing performed a piano and voice recital. Then after a short interlude while we primped and straightened our shirts, Mr. Campbell came back to the mike and introduced in a booming voice, "And now from Cedarbrae Collegiate and all hailing from Scarborough, Ontario, ladies and gentleman, The Strolling Bones!"

The curtains parted as we started the opening chords to "Mona". We went through the "head" once and then Marty came in with that thundering Bo Diddley beat. One more time around and John boomed in with a pulsating bass line matched by my shaking maracas. Before I could even sing the first line there were muffled little screams and whoops from the audience. I slid sideways across the stage alternately rotating my feet with a James Brown stance 'n dance. Roger planted his left foot hard on the stage and wound up with a little Keith Richard fill here and there interspersed between the chords. Glynn straightened up his shoulders and shook his long blond hair while swinging his right hand across the strings of his guitar in a wide arc. My voice reverberated around the cathedral-like ceiling of the auditorium. It was absolute heaven. We were spellbound.

As if in a dream we finished "Mona" to thunderous applause and slid gracefully into the next tune, "I'll Follow the Sun", by the Beatles. When we reached the first bridge of the song Glynn joined me in harmony with, *And now the time has come and so my love I must go,* and at that instant all hell broke loose and girls started screaming and squealing in the audience. It was so much more than we expected that it temporarily un-nerved us. John looked over at the two of us and smiled. Roger just whirled around strumming his Les Paul and grinned a humongous grin that washed all our nerves away. When we finally finished, the audience went nuts. I looked out and saw my mom and dad clapping furiously. It was time to up the ante.

Marty yelled the count and we laid in to the very dramatic intro to "Not Fade Away". Right off the top in the first verse I was wailing on my harp. The hair stood up on the back of my neck and shivers convulsed down my spine. I started singing the first line, *I'm gonna tell yah, how it's gonna be.*

Screams, whistles, whoops!

You're gonna give your love to me, pandemonium! Roger wailed mercilessly on his guitar, egging me on. I answered with my harp wailing right back at him. We ran across the stage and inspired each other to ever greater and louder jams. Glynn listened intently and filled every pause and respite with clamorous rhythms culminating with his favourite embellishment, which was a long drawn out slide starting at the twelfth fret, moving down slowly, ending on the open "E" chord.

The crowd were right with us and followed every nuance of the performance, yelling and shrieking their encouragement. We extended the song. One extra verse, then two, then a final gut-wrenching vampire wail from Roger's little Les Paul and my flailing harp and a shuddering stomp of an ending that built to a mind-blowing gasping climax! On the last note I smashed my maracas into the stage floor with such force that they vanished into a thousand pieces. Corn kernels and gourd splinters danced across the stage landing in the laps of the people in the front row.

It was pure psychedelia and the audience loved it. They whooped and hollered and screamed out loud for more, but alas it was not to be. We had already passed our allotted time and none of the acts were allowed an encore. We waved goodbye to the audience. I stumbled forward and thanked them one more time as the clamoring and whistling died down.

The curtains closed.

It was hard to move our gear. All of us were totally exhausted and drenched with sweat. To me it felt like I had just experienced the most intense twenty minutes of my life. We just shoved the equipment off to one side into a backstage corner and then ducked into the left stage dressing room to regroup.

We were all high and we knew it. It was addictive.

I looked at Roger, "What'd you think?" I asked.

"Sure felt good out there," he said. "Were we really that good?"

"I don't know," I said. "But I don't care, it just *felt* so good!"

Glynn was grinning; the sort of grin that had a scary slant to it. "I think maybe we should keep on doin' this for a while, what do you think, Dave?"

"Yeah, yeah, we got nothin' to lose. Those people were freakin' out, right? I mean, our families only amount to twenty or thirty people. The rest of the crowd were just as worked up as our friends. There must be something to it."

Just then Mr. Robin Boers slid through the side door entrance to the dressing room.

"That was amazing you guys! Too cool! Everybody around me was just stunned." He looked over at Marty and congratulated him on a great show. Marty was a bit shy and flushed a wee bit, his face growing a little pink.

"Yeah, Marty," everyone chipped in, "That was great!" Rob was shaking Marty's hand.

John still had his bass strapped on and suddenly ripped in to the surf-frenzied intro to "Wipe Out". The rolling bass line to the song became the soundtrack for a discussion about the longevity of the band and our chances of success. Bill Huard suggested that a really good strategy would be to play downtown in Yorkville in one of the newly emerging coffee houses. If we could make it there who knows what might happen!

We were all so pumped. It was agreed that that would be the ultimate goal. We'd have to rehearse our asses off to get enough tunes to play a full night, but summer was coming and The Village, as it had been christened, was just waiting for us. All we had to do was find the appropriate place to play. It was a lead pipe cinch!

We all shook hands on it in a self-congratulatory sort of way and then set about packing up our gear so that we could get out front with our families and friends and enjoy the rest of the night.

It was going to be a long hot summer!

Two weeks after the talent show at Cedarbrae I was in a sweet little '59 VW bug heading down to The Village with one of my best school buddies, Dennis Cook. He had volunteered to be my chauffeur for the exploratory mission to check out all of the coffee houses and clubs that had "live" music. We were late heading out but determined to find out for ourselves what was causing all the fuss in the papers and through the grapevine.

Toronto had long been a magnet for music and night-life, but something as off the wall as The Village had never been seen before. It was like a little mini "French Quarter" à la: New Orleans. Restaurants, shops, coffee houses and music clubs: all crammed into a five or six square block area in the middle of downtown Toronto.

Yorkville in its heyday had been a genteel neighborhood on the fringes of the city in the late 1800s. In the early sixties its proximity to downtown and to the University of Toronto, created a golden opportunity for it to develop as a cultural hub, as the local homeowners sold off their homes with the encroachment of the city and moved out to the surrounding suburbs. Rooming houses proliferated all over the surrounding neighbourhoods north of Bloor Street near the university, as enrolment increased to accommodate the baby boomer generation. The next logical step was for entertainment businesses to open in the area to satisfy the students' desires for a social scene. By 1965 things were really humming!

Dennis was an intellectual of a special sort. He was very down to earth and humble. He liked contradictions and enjoyed trying to work them out. The chance to see such a new expression of our own generation had him excited and filled with anticipation. The scuttlebutt about The Village at school was filled with obvious inaccuracies and speculation and didn't represent reality at all. Hardly anyone from Cedarbrae had been down there and shared their experiences with us. Our only connection to The Village was the fact that Klaus Kassbaum (aka: Nick St. Nicholas), who was one year ahead of us, had left school in the fall of 1964 and moved down to Yorkville to play with Jack London and The Sparrows.

We drove across Lawrence Ave. heading west and then down Victoria Park to Danforth Avenue. From there it was a straight line over to Bloor and Yonge Street and Yorkville Avenue.

By the time we reached Bay Street it was almost ten o'clock. We turned right and headed north to Yorkville. We got about twenty yards and then joined the line-up of cars waiting to turn left onto "the strip". They were turning from the north and the south. The weather was unusually warm for an April night and a few of the cars in the line had their convertible tops down so as to get a better handle on the sights and sounds as they drove through the strip.

We rounded the corner and then rolled the windows right down. On both sides of the street couples were walking arm in arm taking in the human spectacle and the warm spring air. The first club we saw was the Chez Monique on the north side of the street just after Bellair Street butted into Yorkville. It looked funky and greasy at the same time. We could hear loud twang-y music wafting out the front door as we passed by. It sounded to me like someone was playing a Rickenbacker guitar.

As we slowly moved along we approached an apartment building on the right. There were people sitting out front at picnic tables drinking and smoking and laughing and generally having a good time. On the left was a clothing store lit by "black" light, so that all the pure white and pastel clothing inside glowed purple-y white and shimmered in the incandescent light of the overhead street lamps.

Ahead on the right was a rather large patio in front of a house that was decorated with dull wood paneling and barn board beams. A railing separated the evening strollers from the customers outside as they sat slightly elevated above the sidewalk. This place was quite special as it was lit with numerous lights and seemed to have drawn a large crowd of students and music fans alike. From inside the sounds of a jazz-blues trio heated up the still night air. I could have sworn it was Jimmy Smith playing the organ, but I knew it wasn't. There was no poster out front announcing the band, just big wooden cut out letters spelling out The Penny Farthing. Sort of odd I thought.

Dennis pointed out the next club which was almost next door. Bold floodlights lit up the front of the house and a Go-Go Girl in white boots danced in the upstairs front bay window! The place was called The Myna Bird. I didn't dig it at all. Too plastic and phony. Dennis concurred.

Across the street and off to the left was a doorway leading down to a basement club called the El Patio. This one really appealed to me. It had all the right features. The sign out front was large and well lit, announcing, Next week: The Sparrows.

The stairway was only fifteen feet from the street so that the sound of music coming from below confronted anyone walking by. I made a mental note.

Up ahead to the right, again Dennis pointed out The Riverboat. Definitely the classiest club on the strip. It had a Marquee-style sign with little lights surrounding it and was painted up to look like a cottage. The patio out front was tiled with terra cotta tiles and shaded by a small maple tree that sprouted out from between the tiles and the corner of the wall. The sign in the marquee announced, Gordon Lightfoot. We crawled on.

When we got to the corner of Avenue Road we had a slight debate over which way to turn. In the end it was fortuitously to the right!

Just around the corner was The Purple Onion. Set back a few feet from the houses on either side, it was a bit shabby and unkempt. The old front window of a long disappeared living room was painted over to add some mystery to the pulsing high energy music that was shaking the place to its very foundations. The sign outside read To-Night, Luke and The Apostles! This was definitely on my list to be checked at a later date. And the music as well. The incredibly loud sound reverberating out onto the street was raw and primitive and easily grabbed my attention.

After the experience of the "Onion" we were on a high and looking for more, but stymied by the lack of places to be discovered on Avenue Road. We headed north and turned right to circle around for another pass. When we got back to the strip the cars were still lining up so we decided to make a detour down to Bloor Street and come at the Village from the south on Cumberland St. Maybe we could find a parking spot and walk around. Right after we turned right we lucked out and spotted a car pulling out of a parking lot about a hundred feet from the corner. We pulled in and jumped out of the bug in a hurry. We wanted to check out as much as we could in an hour and then get back to Scarborough before midnight.

As soon as we were out of the car the sound hit us. It was loud and impulsive and seemed to be vibrating the wall right next to where we parked. We doubled back around to the front of the building and came upon a line-up at the door. Above the door was a sign that read, The Inn-On-The Parking Lot. We had to check it out.

The cover was a buck fifty and after paying we squeezed through the narrow front hall and into the main room of the club. The stage was in the front of the former living room of the old house, set into the valance of the front bay window. On stage the band were thumping out an incredible sustained R&B rhythm and sweating like professional wrestlers in a steam bath. There was hardly any ventilation in the claustrophobic tiny space and there had to be fifty people crammed into three rooms that would easily fit into the recreation room at my parents' place in Scarborough.

We made our way to the rear and to a short snack bar where a woman in her forties was doling out chips and cold drinks. No alcohol; just lemonade, pop, grapefruit juice and coffee. We grabbed a couple of coffees and checked out the band for a few tunes. They were called The Power, from the Kitchener-Waterloo area and featured a singer with intense compassion and incredible range. We sat spellbound for the duration of the set and felt exhausted. When the band finished I asked the woman behind the counter if we could speak to the owner, whereby we were told he was out and given a business card and told to call during the day.

The ride home to Scarborough was cool and smooth after such a mind-blowing experience and the hints of musical adventure that we'd previewed. All in all we decided we had enough information to a least make a stab at getting in the door at one of the clubs.

The prospect of breaking into the scene in Yorkville was no longer intimidating, but more exciting than ever and we were sure it would only be a matter of time.

Dennis was full of optimism and certainty after seeing our performance at the school show. One thing he did suggest though, was that we would have to come up with an appropriate name for the band that wasn't an advertisement for any other group on the planet. He suggested we think long and hard. And keep it simple. Make it something that people would hear once and never forget. Just like The Stones or The Beatles.

That was definitely a challenge that I felt we were up to. The kind of warped humour and repressed logic that permeated our conversations at rehearsals gave me every confidence that we'd be up to the task. I couldn't wait for our next rehearsal to inform the rest of the guys.

Dennis dropped me off at home and I thanked him profusely and then made my way to my bed and crashed dreaming of hot gigs and musical mayhem in the clubs of Yorkville. Nothin' was gonna stop us now; nothin'.

It was a given.

CHAPTER 2

CONCEPTION

The following weekend after Dennis and I had our little adventure in Yorkville, the band got together at Roger's place to rehearse and plan our strategy. Bill Huard came along to lend us encouragement and give advice. By noon everyone had arrived and we ran through the six songs that we knew and then sat in silence for a few seconds wondering where we should go from there.

Roger led the charge, "We're gonna have to come up with a list of tunes to try out. Anybody got any ideas?"

The room was filled with anxious voices, all reciting lists of favourite tunes by favourite artists. With each song suggestion a chorus of voices shouted out yeahs, or nays. There had to be a better way.

Huard stood up in the centre of the room and took charge. "Look you guys, it isn't going to work out like this. We'll have to get organized. Let's just pick a couple of tunes for today and then bring in lists of favourites to the next rehearsal. Then we can lay them all out and vote on them. We're probably going to need thirty-five tunes, so everyone should be able to get their two cents worth!"

We all agreed. We picked "Around and Around", a Stones/Chuck Berry tune, and "If You Need Me", a slow burner by Solomon Burke as the featured songs for the day and proceeded to tear it up for the next hour and a half.

When break time came around the conversation turned to our prospects for gigs and how we were going to get them.

Everyone but me was still in school. I had left in January, totally dejected with the learning process and determined to get a job downtown. As it turned out it was easier than I'd expected and I landed a job within two weeks. Because I had left, the school had been quite gracious in allowing me to perform with the rest of the guys at the talent show.

Huard had just made the decision to pack it in as well, although he hadn't made it official just yet. He came trundling down the stairs with a coke in his hand and walked into the centre of the room, surrounded by all the equipment. "Look you guys, I got an offer to make. I'll do all the leg work. I can do the management thing for the band and that way you guys can just concentrate on doing the music part. I'm quitting school anyway, so there's no big deal. I can check out the clubs in The Village and contact all the schools and community centres in Scarborough. I know I can do it, it can't be all that difficult."

Everyone stared at him. Glynn stood up and leaned his guitar against his amp, "It sounds O.K. to me, Bill, but what about the split? We can't do the standard percentage thing, you know? You don't really have any experience and we can't afford it anyway. We're just getting started."

It was my turn. "What about an even split, then, six ways? We can't be much fairer than that. Everybody pulls their own weight, and we split the money six ways after all the expenses are paid."

John interjected, "How soon are we going to play? 'Cause I need some money to pay for this damn amplifier."

"Yeah? I'd like to get some more new harps, too."

Rob, who had been silent up to this point, did a drum roll and hit the bass drum hard, "Yeah, and I've gotta make the payments on these new cymbals at the end of the month."

Huard stepped in, "O.K. so we've got to play soon. We'll try the folks at Club Cedar first and see what they say. Meanwhile you guys have to learn a bunch of tunes; and fast."

"And there's still the name," John said. "We gotta pick a name!"

"Glynn and I have a list that we made up in the cafeteria one day," I said. "We'll bring it in to the next rehearsal."

The next rehearsal was on Wednesday night. Roger's mom was out doing some mid-week socializing. We all showed up with our lists of songs. And of course Glynn and I had brought our list of potential names.

Each of us read off our list of tunes. Huard wasn't allowed a vote. That way there wouldn't be any ties. Glynn and I favoured a lot of Stones tunes, including their recent hit "It's All Over Now". John was high on Motown, suggesting that it would be a travesty to not do at least one Marvin Gaye or Sam Cooke tune. When Rob's turn came he was a little more into the more obscure British stuff like Them, featuring Van Morrison and The Spencer Davis Group. Roger was quite eclectic, picking tunes by Garnett Mimms, James Brown and Bo Diddley.

Within half an hour we had a comprehensive list figured out. The task of learning the tunes would be a labour of love. That was a given.

The choice of a name was another matter. Glynn and I had compiled a list of approximately forty names one afternoon during a spare in the cafeteria. We chose names incorporating favourite tunes (The Roadrunners, The Youngbloods), favourite clothes (The Shades, The Chaps) to favorite stories (Call of the Wild, The Saints). They were all pretty standard and not much of an inspiration.

In our frustration, at the end of the spare period we had written down a bunch of really off the wall things, just for a laugh. After plodding through so much that didn't inspire us, we started rhyming off the odd-ball names. The Doubting Thomases, The Look, The Downbeats, The Bad Apples, The Ugly Ducklings...woah! When we got to the Ugly Ducklings John mockingly interjected, "Who turned out to be beautiful swans!"

Everybody moaned. But then a light bulb started lighting up in everyone's head. What a perfect way to get attention for ourselves. CALL ourselves ugly! It made more and more sense every minute. One of our favourite bands from England was called The Pretty Things. A lot of people were astounded when they came out, amazed that a band would actually call themselves pretty. Well, how about one who called themselves ugly? It was too cool. In a few short minutes the choice was made. We shook hands on it and chuckled to ourselves knowing the reaction that we were bound to get. We loved the very thought of it!

The next weekend we were deep into our rehearsal when Huard showed up with the good news that we were booked for a Saturday night at Club Cedar in the community centre beside the school. He was also working on a couple of dates in the fall after summer break at David and Mary Thompson Collegiate and Woburn High School. The David and Mary Thompson thing was a "sock hop" and the Woburn High School gig was a "Sadie Hawkins" dance.

After filling us in on the gigs he pulled out a small Kodak Brownie camera and said, "We're going to take some pictures after rehearsal, we have to have something to put up for these gigs." What a downer. None of us were wearing half decent clothes!

"Aw, come on Bill," said Glynn, "We'll look like a bunch of 'Maynard G. Crebbs' or something," referring to the popular character on T.V's Dobbie Gillis show.

Huard shot back, "No we won't. I'll get close up shots that don't focus on your clothes."

There was a bit more grumbling and whining but in the end it was decided that it was necessary, so we did it. Right in Roger's yard, in front of a telephone pole. Eventually in a fit of creative genius we even climbed the pole, grabbing a hold of the lineman's "L" brackets that jutted out starting at about six feet, and pulling ourselves up to pose in pyramid like fashion, our arms outstretched. We would have to wait until we got the photos back to see how dorky we really looked!

Ten days later we were setting up at Club Cedar in the main lounge area in the centre building of the community centre. Glynn and I had recently been to Kramer's Music on Danforth Road, and found a very interesting guitar.

It was a teardrop shaped Danelectro, very similar to the white Vox teardrop that Brian Jones of the Stones had been playing on tour recently in Europe. We knew we had to have it, so the down-payment was made and the commitment was now there to pay it off, along with all the other essential gear we were slowly accumulating.

Glynn gingerly removed it from its case and started tuning it up. It was a stunning departure from a standard electric guitar. The body was a stretched out teardrop painted with a purple to light-pink sunburst effect. The neck wasn't especially good for lead playing but as a rhythm guitar it was more than adequate and it was sure going to turn a few heads.

I had also purchased various maracas and a nice heavy maple bodied tambourine to add a little punctuation to our percussion. At times when I was playing harp or dancing around in a James Brown fit, Huard would pick up his shaker of choice and play along with the band. They all added nicely to that simple Bo Diddley beat that we seemed to be so hooked on. We had even added "Diddley, Diddley Daddy" to our repertoire recently, to round out our patently idolatrous homage to the man. At this point we did six of Bo's tunes.

Rob had cleaned and polished his drums and made up some nice stick-on letters for the front skin of his bass drum that spelled out, The UGLY DUCKLINGS in big bold capitals that could be seen at the back of the club. When we all saw them it was a revelation. A turning point. We had arrived as a band. There was now a commitment to make this work and to indelibly imprint ourselves into the hearts and minds of our audience. Roger said it best when he implored us, "Make sure they remember us!"

It wasn't going to be just the music. It was going to be the *Show* as well. "Entertain them", Roger said. "Make them remember, that's the key!"

Outside the main room next to the oak entrance door was a brand new 8" x 10" glossy photo of The UGLY DUCKLINGS, made up especially for the occasion. By the end of the evening it would vanish without a trace. A good sign.

At Roger's Place – April 1965

On stage at "Club Cedar"- Spring '65. Note: Roger playing his "Les Paul Junior". Glynn plays the "Danelectro" & John, a "Kay" Bass!

That night was sweat night. I must have lost five pounds. All five of us did our level best to put on as much of a show as we could muster. We tore through all the Stones' tunes with a reckless abandon and then hung ourselves up in the Bo Diddley repertoire until we could barely stand, our legs buckling and shaking involuntarily with the incessant rhythm.

After two one-hour sets we were totally spent and wound it up with a ten minute version of "2120 South Michigan Avenue" from the first Stones album. The audience were pretty well done too and showed little resistance to letting the night end gracefully. Amid whoops and whistles and deafening applause we bid everyone goodnight with a promise to return again in the summer. Chalk one up for the team! The best was yet to come!

By the end of May we had already played our second gig as The Ugly Ducklings at a local drop-in centre in Scarborough. It was billed as a "sock hop" and was a major success.

The effects of the gigs on my psyche were more than I had anticipated.

I was still living at home with my parents and driving downtown to work every morning with my dad in our beautiful black '64 Plymouth Fury. My dad had tried to talk me into getting my learners' permit so that I could learn to drive but I had little interest and balked at every opportunity that he presented to me. Once the band had started to play and we began to take ourselves seriously, the daily drive became more and more of a hassle. The conversation would always come around to work and life issues that I just didn't want to deal with at that point in my life. The same thing began happening at work in the Customs Department at Simpson's Sears.

I just couldn't take everything seriously. Although I was scrupulously on time and dutifully efficient my heart just wasn't in it. My boss Jake Moll was starting to notice a change in my demeanour. I had been working there since the end of January and for sure my attitude had been changing. Jake was very perceptive and I noticed little changes in the way he asked me to perform my duties. He wasn't confrontational for now though, and I was still saving my money for my eventual departure.

By the middle of May we had our first major gig. The Club Trocadero on Bloor St. West agreed to try us out for a Friday night gig on the strength of a very positive recommendation from Luba Klachok, the president of the

Toronto Rolling Stones Fan Club. This was definitely a classy gig. The Troc' was a large hall with a similarly large stage, complete with a real lighting system that included multi-coloured pots and genuine spotlights. They also advertised in the Toronto newspapers, so it was the first time we saw our name advertised beside all the other bands of the day. The initial excitement of securing the gig was tempered by our fear that the R&B crowd that frequented the club might not take to our particular brand of their music. It was our first test; our first exposure to a tried and true R&B audience.

When four thirty arrived on Friday I ducked out of the office and walked across the covered bridge to the second floor of Simpson's. I headed straight to the record department and started browsing through the "Blues" section and almost immediately found the prize I was looking for. "Big City Blues" by John Hammond Jr. On previous visits I had purchased his first album and subsequently seen posters announcing the second.

I paid my $2.89 to the cashier and headed out the door clutching the album under my arm. The front cover of the album was a photo of John Hammond Jr. seated on a nameless motorbike in front of a view of the New York skyline dressed in funky leathers and shades. He was an American version of Mick Jagger with an even greater knowledge of the Blues than Mick, and this was his first recording with a band! I was full of great expectations. On the subway ride up to Eglinton Station I read the liner notes and tried to imagine the sound that he might produce with a full band. His first record had filled me with confidence that white boys sure could sing the blues! I arrived home by six o'clock and headed downstairs to try out Mr. Hammond on my turntable. I wasn't disappointed as I heard the first few bars of "Love the Life I Live". It was an anthem for the way we all felt. Another good source for tunes.

After listening to a couple more tracks, I showered and got dressed, grabbed my harps and headed out the door to John Read's place, which was a good ten minute walk. Roger picked us up at seven in his mom's '64 Parisienne and we headed into the unknown.

When we got to the Trocadero the first thing we noticed was the damp wood smell. The place was old.

We walked in the front door like we owned the place, instruments in hand. Roger saw someone in the backstage area and shouted out, "Yo!"

Bill Huard yelled back, "We're all here, we're parked out back." As we got closer we saw Glynn and Rob and Bill's good friend Ken Crabtree lunging through the back door, toting drum cases and amps. In a very short time we had everything unloaded except the P.A. System that we had rented.

"Come on Dave," chided Glynn, "Once we get these stupid columns in we'll almost be done." He had lifted up one end of the grey monstrosities and glanced at me with a pleading look on his face.

The columns were each five feet long and fourteen inches wide and each held eight, eight-inch speakers. Along with a sixty-amp Bogen Mixer they packed quite a punch as a vocal system. We needed as much power as we could get to overcome the output of the guitars and bass.

Set up took all of half an hour and then Rob quickly tuned his snare and toms. Afterwards we all sat around and discussed our strategy for the night.

Glynn lead off, "I think we should start with 'Everybody Needs Somebody' and then keep punchin' out fast stuff for a while. Let's not do any slow tunes 'till near the end of the first set. And we probably shouldn't even do The Beatles tune."

Huard and I both replied with a "yeah" at the same time.

Rob asked politely, "Are we gonna do the new version of 'It's Alright' tonight?"

Everyone had to think about that one. We'd only done the song twice at rehearsal, but what a vibe!

"It sure would be a great way to end the first set," I said.

It was agreed. Throw caution to the wind!

We planned out the rest of the sets and then hung out backstage listening to the sounds of people wandering into the room. We could hear folks talking and speculating about the band. Rude comments about the name; real uncertainty about our abilities. It was just what we needed to hear. The more people doubted us the more fun it was going to be to really sock it to them when we went out on stage.

When we were introduced that night and the stage lights came on, we came alive. We were a well-oiled machine. Solomon Burke himself, would have been proud of our performance. Rob was especially "on", a real driving force.

With every round of applause we got hotter and hotter, both physically and musically. Roger literally wailed on his little Les Paul Jr. and shook his whole body in a curious sort of way. If one were to watch him closely, you could see his whole lower body held perfectly rigid; anchored by one foot that seemed glued to the floor, while his shoulders and arms moved rhythmically to the beat. His Nordic blond locks swung back and forth and side to side with the tempo of the song. It was a strange kind of musical communication that was going on that night, but the audience was in on it too, and spurred the band on to even greater heights. All our earlier worries evaporated and were replaced by a new-found confidence.

Late in the second set we did "Here Comes the Night", by Them and got a standing ovation. Whenever that happened I got shivers down my spine. At the same time Glynn would smile a smile that would light up a Christmas tree and John's grin would part the Red Sea!

That night was our first big paycheque, one hundred and thirty five dollars! Quite a princely sum considering that I was only making forty-four bucks a week at Simpson's. It was cause for celebration. The next step in our plan was to get into The Village.

As we tore down the equipment that night all our conversation centred on the necessity of finding a gig in Yorkville. We wanted a home base that we could operate from. Somewhere we could rehearse and play and get known.

Huard kept on exclaiming he was up for the task and we all put our confidence in him and gave him an extra twenty bucks to spend on phone calls and transportation in order to get the job done. We drove home tired but determined.

Bill was a pretty confident guy by now and would walk right into any situation without giving it a second thought. He spent the most part of the following week going from club to club in The Village sussing things out. For the first part of the week he had come up against a brick wall at most of the clubs. "Yes, it was wonderful that we had such a great reaction at 'The Trocadero', yes we've heard the word of mouth about the band, but we're sorry, we already have a house band and we're booked for six weeks in advance!" He was really getting discouraged and losing faith, but then on the Thursday morning something strange and wonderful happened. One of Glynn's friends, Jim Haines had told Bill that he had heard that a new club was going to open where the Inn On The Parking Lot had been, and he had met the owner. He sent Bill to meet with him.

When Bill knocked on the door of the old Inn on The Parking Lot he was met by the new owner of the building, who had shut down the club immediately after buying the property. Bill engaged him in conversation, described our situation and the buzz about the band and he responded favourably!

The owner's name was Robert (Bob) Johnston, but everyone called him "Charlie". It was a nickname from his navy days. "Charlie" was about five foot eight, quite skinny although elegant and sported a greyish blond goatee and slightly long golden locks. He was the spitting image of the Sheriff of Nottingham from the fifties British T.V. series "Robin Hood". Bill chatted with him for a couple of hours and worked out all the details of our future arrangement as Charlie's new house band.

To start fresh "Charlie" wanted a new name for the club and the first probable name that Huard put forth was "Charlie's Place". But it was decided that was too static. "Charlie" said he wanted it to be a kind of a drop-in place and on a whim Bill suggested "Charlie Brown's Place" after his favourite "Peanuts" character by Charles Shultz.

And "Charlie Brown's" was born.

Bill called everyone early Saturday morning to give us the news.

Our first gig would be in June, very close to my birthday. There was lots to plan and lots to look forward to. I decided to move out of my parent's place and get a room in The Village.

I took the whole day, Saturday and checked out ten or fifteen rooming houses within a three block area of Yorkville Ave. I wasn't having much success and later on in the afternoon I stopped for a drink at the Mousehole, a tiny little restaurant/club tucked away under an art gallery in the middle of Yorkville. There I met a tall dark haired waitress with an ultra-friendly personality and a winsome smile who listened to my complaints and told me I should check out the house that she and her girlfriend lived in at 16 Admiral Rd. Her name was Tannis Neiman. I took her up on her advice and found a super large room on the main floor of an old mansion for eight bucks a week. It had been the sitting room in the original old house and possessed four six foot high bay windows on the north side. It was going to be available at the end of the next week, so I had plenty of time to pack things up and get prepared. Suddenly everything in my life was looking up.

As soon as I got home that night I phoned Glynn and Roger to tell them my plans. I happened to mention that I'd seen the marquee on The El Patio announcing, Jack London and The Sparrows for Sunday night. We decided to check out our first band in Yorkville. It was time to get to know the competition.

We arrived the next night at around quarter to nine, too late to get a seat in the club. Luckily they were allowed ten people for standing room only and we lined up at the back, next to the bar.

The club was dark and cozy. The west wall was lined with a dark cork-like material that looked organic and funky and obviously helped soak up some of the sound. The chatter was constant and loud. An air of anticipation filled the club.

Jack London and The Sparrows had charted two singles on radio in Toronto and released an album on Capital Records. Their look fitted the mold of the British invasion but their sound was a little bit bubble-gum, on record. My opinion was that Jack's vocal style was a bit put-on and too fluffy. Not much soul.

On the dot at nine the band appeared from the dressing room and made their way to the stage. From the beginning they played with feeling and finesse. The drummer Jerry Edmonton was absolutely cool. So in control. And the bass player Nick St. Nicholas (our old school chum from Cedarbrae, Klaus Kassbaum) was a killer groove monster. The keyboard player, Art Ayers was slightly older than the rest of the group and very experienced. He filled all the holes quite nicely. Jerry's Brother Dennis played the guitar and wrote most of the material and sang great harmonies. We loved everything about the band except the singer.

He was the wrong guy for the band. He had a good voice but no dynamics. These guys needed someone like Wilson Pickett or Eddie Floyd. When they played hard driving music the audience was floored. We were learning about presentation. Sometimes sweetness and honey were the wrong hooks to grab the audience. The music had to fit the character of the players and flow from a natural source. It had to be true to the heart. We chalked up another lesson learned and put it in the memory vault.

On Monday night I phoned Ken Crabtree and Glynn and made all of the arrangements for the big move the following weekend. Ken was going to bring his little Austin wagon and we would load up all my worldly possessions and head downtown. I couldn't wait. There was something about leaving the nest that made all my perceptions of the world change overnight. Freedom was the obvious catalyst for the new awareness, but it was more than that. Adventure was our creed. Playing in a band and traveling around was going to be so much more exciting than working inside a dull grey office, or facing an eight-hour day of unending repetition. We certainly didn't want our daily lives to embrace anything that resembled school.

My mom and dad had expected that sooner or later I would move out after I got the job at Simpson's, but the success of the band even though it was very minor at this point was a concern for them because of all the unknowns involved. They had known the paths they took after school would lead to predictable outcomes. Music on the other hand was an unknown and certainly all of the rumours about the debauchery and decadence that went on in The Village, weren't totally unfounded!

On Sunday afternoon Glynn, Rob and Ken arrived after lunch and we got down to the basic task of loading up. I grabbed my Kodak Brownie and shot a few pictures. Mom had given me a few extras, such as some sheets and pillow cases, some old towels and face cloths from the cottage. At least I would be comfy and clean where I was going. I was more concerned with loading all of my records and my little Sea-Breeze record player. I had to have music. My clothes filled two enormous garbage bags.

By two-thirty we were set to go. The good-byes were mostly hugs and handshakes. Dad smiled as he pumped my hand and arm vigorously. A few tears escaped the corner of mom's eyes as her oldest slid into the rear seat of Ken's funky little Austin, ready to back out of the driveway. My brothers stood at the front door and waved and my sister Kathy kissed me on the cheek and then ran into the house.

Glynn & Rob in Ken's '59 Austin

We were off! The long ride downtown seemed to take forever. Arriving at

16 Admiral Road we were greeted by a tall skinny dude running around the house in black bathing trunks. He was quite muscular and moved like a dancer up and down the stairs. I had certainly not seen him when I came to rent the room. As we approached the door he introduced himself.

"Hi, I'm Woody Comeau," he said. "You're the new guy aren't you?"

"Yes," I replied. "I'm moving into number 2."

"Well, I guess we should all give you a hand." His voice had a slight lisp to it. He disappeared into the house and came out momentarily with two dark haired girls.

One of them was Tannis, the girl I had met at The Mousehole.

"Hi guys, welcome to sixteen!" She walked down the porch stairs and looked directly at me. "Who are your friends Dave?"

"Uh, this is Glynn our rhythm player and Rob, our drummer and our driver here is Ken, he sort of does the roadie thing for some of our gigs."

"Well pleased to meet you," Tannis replied, "This is my friend and room-mate Jeannine."

"Well, let's get your stuff into the room. I'm makin' spaghetti sauce this afternoon, you guys are invited for dinner if you'd like."

Woody grabbed a garbage bag of my clothes and said with an obvious lisp, "Come on in and I'll show you to your room."

With everyone's help we unloaded the car and had the room arranged and tidy in half an hour. Woody was impressed with the way I made the bed, hospital style, with corners neatly folded under, etcetera.

"Where did you learn that?" he queried.

"Oh, I had polio when I was a kid. After I learned how to walk again, I had to make my own bed every day."

"You had polio? Well then, you're a survivor. Congratulations!" He pranced out the doorway and down the hall to his own room. Ken, Rob and Glynn left at about four-thirty to get home in time for dinner and I went into the kitchen to see how Tannis's spaghetti dinner was coming. Woody was there, still in his black bathing trunks but also sporting a long black cape with a greyish silver lining. I'd never seen anything like it before. He noticed my reaction.

"Isn't it lovely?" He said. "I got it at the CBC costume department." He didn't elaborate and he didn't try to hide his lisp.

Tannis was busy stirring the pasta, and a big grin came across her face. She was tacitly enjoying my reaction.

Woody sat at the head of the table and motioned to the place set beside him. "Have a seat, Dave." He patted the chair-seat delicately.

At that moment Jeannine entered the room and sat down opposite me at the table. Tannis brought the bowls of sauce and pasta to the table and dinner was served. I was duly impressed. Tannis's spaghetti was just as good as mom's home cookin'. I was already feeling right at home

CHAPTER 3
LIBERATION

After a spectacular dinner I helped Tannis & Jeannine do the dishes and retreated to my room to do some organizing. I found appropriate places to stash all of my clothes and set up my little Sea-Breeze record player on an old tea-caddy that was parked at the centre of my magnificent bay window on the north side of the room. There were two shelves beneath the caddy that held all of my precious 45's perfectly. The LP's I arranged on the top of my bureau between two antique bookends that had been left by a previous tenant.

The room was starting to feel homey but was still in need of some more human touches. As I looked around it dawned on me that one of the first things that would have to be done would be to get some curtains for that window. It was humungous. I foresaw scenarios where too much light was going to come streaming in there.

Next, a table; I needed some kind of a table for the centre of the room. It wasn't going to be party central here, but it was still a matter of convenience. I certainly needed somewhere to eat. There was a small electric kettle and a grungy hot plate sitting on a small table in one corner that teetered ominously when the kettle was filled with water and set on top of it. One leg of the table was a half inch shorter than all the rest. I made another mental note.

I sat in one of my two 1940's plush arm chairs and surveyed my castle. Not bad for eight bucks a week. With a little TLC and some imagination it would be more than adequate. For now though I was more interested in what was happening outside. Just a block and a half away the world was coming to order.

I shaved and changed into some old jeans and the striped sports jacket that I'd bought on Queen Street a week earlier. I grabbed my little Kodak Brownie and headed out the door. The night was young and I was a free man. As I walked south on Admiral Road I could hear the clamour of car horns, music, and people permeating the warm June air. As I turned left onto Lowther Avenue I could see a hub of activity by Webster's Restaurant and The Purple Onion. It was still the weekend at The Village.

My first stop was The Purple Onion. I walked up the steps and inside the front door to check the place out, but I was too early. It was only about eight-thirty. An older guy was taking chairs down off of the tables and setting them up along the wall opposite the bandstand. I checked out the band's gear. It was some pretty beat-up lookin' stuff. On the right side was a Hammond organ of some ilk. (I couldn't tell what model it was because the stage was just a bit too high to manage a peek). Just to the left of the organ was a beautiful Fender Concert amp. It was a caramel/beige colour and had four ten-inch speakers. In the middle of the stage was a set of silver-grey Ludwig drums. They looked well-played, the skins sporting lots of brown stick marks and scuffing.

Off to the left was a strange-looking bass amp that really piqued my interest. The cabinet was a dark charcoal colour and looked large enough to accommodate a twenty- inch speaker. There was an accompanying head sitting on top, but neither sported any identifying name plates. I was intrigued.

I asked the guy when the band was going to go on and was told that the usual start time was about nine-thirty. I headed out the front door and made a quick left onto Yorkville to check out the rest of the scene.

As I strolled along the north side of the street I spotted a group of guys hanging out on the south side in front of a couple of old three-story apartment buildings. One particular guy caught my interest. He was tall and lanky and had shoulder-length black hair like Phil May of The Pretty Things. I crossed the street and approached the crowd and asked if anybody was going to be going to The Onion to see Luke and the Apostles. The tall lanky guy responded, "Yeah, me and my buddy here were thinking of going. What's it to ya?" I asked if they'd ever seen them before. "Yeah, lots," was the reply.

"My name's Dave," I said, "and I'm into it too. Are either of you guys musicians?"

"I'm Bob," said the tall guy, "Bob Melbourne. This is my friend Dave Tygeson. We're both into commercial art, but we wish we could play. Haven't you seen these guys before?"

I said no and then told them about the Ducklings and about my big move to The Village. They were both impressed. Neither one of them lived down here. They both came in from the outskirts to check out the action.

Dave Tygeson was about the same build as me with thinning dirty blonde hair in a slight bowl-cut. He looked like he was constantly shrugging his shoulders and had a wry smile. We all sat down on the short brick wall that ran across the front of the apartment courtyard.

Max Brown, Woody Comeau & Bob Melbourne at 16 Admiral

Bob lit a cigarette, took a drag, and then blew a perfectly formed smoke-ring out into the stream of traffic that was moving eastward on Yorkville Avenue.

"You won't believe these guys Dave," Bob said. "They've got the best groove of any of the bands in the village! And their guitarist is a killer."

"Plays bottleneck with his mic-stand." Dave added.

I asked them about that intriguing black bass amp with the no-name mystique.

"Oh, that's Jonesy's homemade job." Bob replied, "He's a real techno-nut, built it himself."

"Jonesy?" I asked.

"Jim Jones." Bob said. "He's definitely the coolest bass player in the village. He does a lot of technical work on the band's gear and everything. And he's really a punchy and smooth player. You'll see later on."

I was thinking how cool this was going to be, and starting to get antsy.

Dave stood up and suggested that we take a stroll down to the Chez Monique to see what was happening. Evidently they started a bit earlier there and we might get a glimpse of another band before we headed to the Onion.

A few minutes later we arrived in front of a grubby looking building on the north side of the street. Dennis Cook and I had passed it several weeks before.

Sure enough there was a band rattling the rafters and music was drifting out into the street. They were called Just Us, and had a hard-edged R&B kinda feel that was softened by the Rickenbacker guitar that one of the guitarists was playing. The singer on stage was a cool-looking black dude who sang and danced like Mick Jagger. He had a potent delivery and exuded confidence, connecting with the audience like no-one I had ever seen before.

The area in front of the stage was thick with girls who watched his every move and even sang along with some of the lyrics to the tunes.

"That's Ricky James Matthews," Bob shouted in my ear. "He's originally from Buffalo. Pretty good, eh? He and the guy on the Rickenbacker play in a band called the 'Mynah Birds', just up the street at The Mynah Bird Club."

"Oh Yeah?" I chimed in, "What's the guitar player's name?"

"Neil Young, he's from Winnipeg. He moved into town a while ago and hooked up with Ricky."

I was really impressed, but eager to get over to the Onion to hear The Apostles. The memory of that sound as Dennis and I had driven by a few weeks before was still clear in my mind and I didn't want to miss a lick! I shouted in Bob's ear, "Do you think we'd better get over to The Onion? If we don't get there soon we might not get very good seats!"

"Yeah, maybe," Bob yelled back, he turned and nudged Dave.

"O.K. let's went," was my reply.

We squeezed through the crowd and out onto the street, quickening our step as we headed west towards Avenue Road. When we walked past the coffee houses and shops we could see people sitting around tables, shrouded under black lights and dancing to canned music. Out on the street there were a few patios where folks sat and sipped coffee or soft drinks, conversing and flirting in the warm summer breeze.

We passed the Upper Crust at Hazelton Avenue and then the Grab Bag Variety and the Riverboat. A few more minutes and we were there.

What a difference an hour made. When we made it through the door I was dumbfounded. The joint was packed. All of the tables were taken and there were people standing near the back and anywhere else along the walls where they could squeeze in. There was a certain amount of tension in the air and a constant buzz of conversation rising and falling.

On the stage was a standard looking cream-coloured Telecaster set on a brand new guitar stand, and next to it, a blue-grey Moserite Bass that leaned against that sinister black-box bass-amp that had so intrigued me. There was a feeling of anticipation. Everyone was waiting and constantly gazing around the room, watching for the band.

Finally, after a five or ten minute wait the band streamed into the room from a rear side door. They were led by a debonair dude with an art-school look wearing a black turtle neck and a friendly grin. Behind him strolled a mad-professor type guy with hair that skewed out from his head in every direction, topped by the biggest cowlick that I had ever seen. He immediately sat down at the Hammond, looking right at home. He reached down somewhere to his left and hit a switch. I heard a small whirring sound and saw the rotating speaker in the Leslie tone cabinet behind him come to life. He scratched his head and rubbed a stubbly beard and adjusted the pre-sets on the Hammond.

Just then the other three members of the band appeared from the back door and made their way through the crowd. They were led by a smallish skinny dude in a black and white striped long sleeve T-shirt. He moved quickly to the stage and surveyed the crowd, acknowledging regular patrons with a smile and a nod. The drummer and guitarist followed and started readying their gear. Electric amps came to life; clicks and pops jolted the speakers as the current passed through coils and capacitors and began warming scads of cathode tubes and transformers.

The guitarist looked pumped as he removed a glass tube from his jeans pocket and set it on top of his amp, for easy access. He was tall and lanky and wore heavy horn-rimmed glasses that gave him a kind of Buddy Holly look, but without the impish choir-boy face and wavy hair.

The drummer sort of reminded me of my new-found pal, Dave Tygeson, except that his dirty blond bowl cut was much longer, his upper body was very muscular, and he smoked what looked like a cigarillo. It dangled from his lips precariously as he tuned his toms and made a final adjustment to his snare.

After a few confirmative glances around the stage we heard one heavy thud on the bass drum and then heard a four-count under someone's breath and out of the side of their mouth.

Immediately the room was filled with the most thunderous, glorious sound! The five men up on stage seemed to fill the room like a symphony orchestra. The tune was "Steppin' Out", a Freddy King standard that the band attacked with reckless abandon. I was in heaven. I looked around at the boys. Heads were nodding in appreciation, all eyes were glued to the bandstand. Each member of the group had a shot at eight bars of soloing as their personal introduction to the audience and each of them excelled at getting the crowd's attention and keeping it. When the tune ended the audience broke out in spontaneous applause, stomping and whistling encouragement.

Then came the first vocal of the night. It was a tour de force, a rabble-rousing performance of "Good Morning Little Schoolgirl" that was sensuous and passionate, and filled with sexual innuendo and humour. Luke Gibson was an amazing interpreter of the blues. He wasn't aping any of the singers of the day, or any of the blues greats that he so obviously loved. No, his voice was his. He understood the feeling and the cadence and energy in the music. The audience responded to it, too. It was an energy and passion that hooked them and immediately pulled them in.

"Luke and The Apostles" onstage at The Purple Onion, May 1965

As Luke performed, he moved almost spastically on stage, dancing in one spot; moving his body subconsciously, locked in a James Brown trance. At times both of his feet would be off of the stage and he'd be suspended in mid-air, held there for a split- second by the energy in the music. He would punctuate the song with deft microphone work, writing and twisting the mike cord around his arms and over his shoulder, never missing a beat or fumbling a lyric. It was like he was releasing all of the pent-up energy of the day in every performance and the audience loved it.

For the next hour the band worked through many blues classics and some not- so-well-known R&B standards. Every tune benefited from their intense commitment to the music and their personal arranging skills. The organist and guitar player constantly played off of each other and kept an ear to the bass and drums, so that the overall syncopation and feel of the music lifted the audience and was never boring. They understood the secret of the blues. I was totally enamoured. When the first break came I approached the guitarist with the Buddy Holly specs, determined to make a real connection. I walked to the front of the stage as the band descended into the audience.

"Hi, my name's Dave Bingham. That was really amazing!" I couldn't think of what else to say. I extended my hand. He reached out and shook it. "Mike McKenna," he said. "Have I ever seen you before?"

"No, I don't think so. It's the first time I've seen you guys."

He turned slightly and moved off to one side as the organist jumped down from the stage. Then he turned to me and brought us face to face. "This is Peter Jermyn, our keyboard player."

I shook hands with Peter and introduced myself and then turned to the both of them and asked, "Where do you guys get so much energy?" They looked at each other and then back at me. Mike spoke. "I don't know, it just sort of happens."

"Yeah, I know what you mean," I added.

"Do you play?" Mike asked.

"Yeah, I'm in a band called The Ugly Ducklings; we're going to be the new house band at Charlie Brown's where the Inn On The Parking Lot used to be."

"Oh yeah, I heard something about that," Peter nodded. "When's the opening going to be?"

I filled them in on the details of The Ducks impending debut in The Village and then they begged off to go get some fresh air before the next set. Likewise, Bob and Dave and I headed outside to cool off and people watch. Out on the street longhaired girls in faded blue jeans strolled past us giggling and cajoling each other as they cast us a passing glance.

Bob lit up a smoke. "Well Dave, what'd you think?"

I didn't hesitate. "They've got it, man." I couldn't really say what *it* was, but they definitely possessed it. "There's a lot of passion there, eh Dave?"

Mr. Tygeson had been quiet after we got outside. He turned and looked squarely at the Bob and I. "They should be on record, man. They could give The Stones a run for their money!" The two of us agreed. I suggested we should get back in the club before the second set started and get a seat across from the stage. It was a done deal.

When the band came on for the second set we were pumped and sitting directly across from Luke, against the south wall of the room. It was loud! Much louder than where we had stood for the first set.

The set opened with "Spoonful", in a very dramatic fashion. Starting with the Hammond, the bass and drums built gradually to accent that *oh-so-perfect* guitar riff until the repetition was burned into the audience's collective memory and we could all feel it pulsing through our bodies with every strike of the bass drum. Then quite suddenly with a slash of the snare the volume dropped like a stone and Luke started singing. *Could be a spoonful of coffee, could be a spoonful of tea.*

I heard a few feminine squeals and then noticed everyone holding their breath. People were listening. Intently. Luke guided the audience through the whole tune, sharing all the imagery with them, making them believe every word.

The band cart-wheeled right along with him accenting every anticipated beat and extending every whispered syllable or punching out each wailing holler. The audience was transfixed, wanting more; whistling and stomping their feet.

For forty five minutes the whole place rocked and rolled ecstatically, following every cue without question. Then for the last tune Peter announced, "O.K. folks, some Willie Dixon, 'You Can't Judge a Book by the Cover!'" The audience started to applaud. Then he added, "Oh, and we're going to feature Mike on the guitar! Everybody up!"

The whole club rose to their feet.

By the time the band was half-way through the song the audience was all clustered in front of the tiny stage moving joyously to an incredible Bo Diddley beat. Peter was punching and stabbing at the Hammond's keyboard. Jonesy and the drummer stunned us all with a trance inducing bottom end; all toms and back beat, and Mike's guitar cut through like a knife. He stretched the strings of his Tele mercilessly and occasionally hit the treble switch at just the right second causing the strings to heterodyne; creating an all-together different note with the ensuing feedback. At the end of his solo as the song was heading for the grand finale he removed the little glass bottle neck from his left pinky and set it on the top of his amp. He turned and grabbed the mike stand in front of him, pulling it back towards the Telecaster. Everyone cheered. With the volume maxed right out on his old Fender Concert he gently placed the strings against the mike stand and started a slow slide; keeping an even pace and building with the intensity of the music behind him. Together, the band and Mike reached a perfect climax as the drums and bass sustained a final chord and Peter's Hammond groaned and vibrated in perfect unison.

Everything stopped and the audience came to life, erupting in spontaneous applause and whooping with incredible enthusiasm.

Bob and Dave and I looked at each other and grinned. Sweat was slowly dripping down the hollow of my back. I took my jacket off and wiped sweat from my forehead on my shirtsleeve. How was I going to explain this to the guys in The Ducks? They were going to have to come and see for themselves. There was no other way.

After complimentary conversation and congratulations all around, the audience slowly drifted off. Bob and Dave and I hung around to see when the band was going to be performing again at The Onion. I shook hands with everybody and invited them all over to The Duckling's debut at Charlie Brown's the following weekend.

More lessons learned, more revelations. I walked back to Admiral Rd. in a state of grace.

Oh! What a night.

CHAPTER 4

INTRO"DUCK"TION

On Monday I called Huard to find out about rehearsing for our first gig at Charlie's. He was still busy with organising the food and drink thing as well as trying to find some small tables and chairs for the club. He had already put an ad in The Toronto Telegram's "After Four" section announcing our debut on Friday night. We were slated to play the whole weekend; Friday, Saturday & Sunday. Because I was still working at Simpson Sears we were going to have to rehearse at night. It was a hassle, but there was no way around it. I had already promised the guys that I was only going to stay on until I had a good bank-roll for the summer. I had no intention of screwing up a perfectly good time in The Village in order to become a customs clerk!

Wednesday was rehearsal night. Everybody was stone-cold serious about it and arrived right on time. We were hopeful that this would be the last time we would be disturbing Roger's next door neighbours. Everything went satisfactorily. We ran through all the tunes that we had learned up to that point and then added "The

Spider and The Fly", "That's How Strong My Love Is" and "Get Off Of My Cloud". When we got right down to the nitty-gritty in "That's How Strong My Love Is" I got goose-bumps.

It felt that good.

Afterwards we sat around discussing set lists, door charges, starting times and all the other bullshit that went with getting a club up and running.

"We're sort of at a disadvantage." Huard said. "The club's been shut down for two months now and nobody on the street really knows what's going on."

Roger was optimistic. "So we'll play as loud as we can and leave all the windows open!" There were a few chuckles and guffaws.

Glynn wasn't laughing; a serious look came over his face. He was deep in thought and drumming his fingers on his guitar case. A light-bulb went on suddenly in his head.

"I've got it! We get some flyers printed up and get all our friends to hand them out on the strip!"

"Yeah, that'll do it." Huard was thinking out loud. "Bruce MacKenzie, Crabtree, Ernie Pope, Jim Oliver!"

"And I know a couple of guys that I just met who would probably be glad to help out." I was stretching the truth a bit, but it was a good bet. If Bob and Dave could get in free and get good seats, it was almost a shoe-in.

So eventually a plan was in place and each member of the band was responsible for getting as many people to the gig as possible, as well as finding volunteers to help get our message out to the people on the strip.

The next item on the agenda was a PA system. We were going to have to rent something on a permanent basis.

Since I had a full-time job I agreed to go with Huard to Long and McQuade's Music on Young Street and get something decent. A job at Simpson's would look really good on a rental application.

We set our sights on getting to Charlie's early on Friday and getting all of the equipment set up and road tested before six o'clock. I was going to get off work early to go to the "dentist" and head straight for The Village. Bill and I made arrangements to meet at McQuade's at 4:30 the next day to rent the PA system.

Long And McQuade's was open late on Thursdays and Fridays to accommodate the growing numbers of local musicians who were gigging all over the city. I got off work at four o'clock right on the dot and headed for the subway. I got on at Queen Street and was at the Bloor Street station within twenty minutes. As I exited the station I was hit by a blast of warm dry air. The damp cool of the subway gave way to the sweet heat of summer.

I headed up the east side of Yonge Street and ducked in the front door at four twenty-five. Huard wasn't there yet so I headed for the rental desk and asked about the PA situation. An older guy was standing at the counter reading some paperwork and glanced up at me.

"Can I help you, young man?" His eyes looked up over the edge of the paper in his hands.

"Yeah, I guess so," I responded. "I'm here to rent a PA system for my band, we've got a house gig at a new club in The Village."

"Is that so? Well, I'm sure we can accommodate you. I'm Jack Long." He extended his hand.

"Dave Bingham, from The Ugly Ducklings."

As he shook my hand he turned slightly and called to someone in the back room.

"Bob, I've got a customer here for you."

A skinny looking dude came around the corner with a smile on his face. He was about five-nine and was wearing expensive looking glen-checked pants and a medium blue buttoned-down collar shirt. His hair was jet black and reminded me of Gene Pitney. He exuded self-confidence.

We shook hands. "Bob Abbot's the name," he grinned again, "What can I do for you?"

I told him all about Charlie Brown's and our need for a PA that would work just as well at an arena gig as it would in a small club. He raised an eyebrow and asked tentatively, "How loud does the band play?"

"As loud as we possibly can!"

He smiled. He turned to Jack who was still perusing his paperwork at the other end of the counter. "Maybe these boys could try out those two new columns of Pete's and see how they work in a club setting."

Jack looked up and bit the end of his pencil. "Don't see why not."

"Tell you what we'll do. We'll let you have these new columns with the five ten inch speakers in each, and give you a sixty watt Bogen mixer to go with 'em. And we'll charge you the same as for the regular columns with the eight-inch speakers."

"Sounds O.K. to me. How about microphones?"

Bob was way ahead of me. "Excuse me Dave, I'll be right back." As he turned to go and get the mikes I noticed a shadow at the front of the store. The sun was moving slowly downward in the west and streaming in the display windows. It back-lighted Huard as he entered the front door and sauntered up to the counter. I introduced him to Jack just as Bob Abbott emerged from the rear with a case of mikes and chords.

"Take your pick, Dave."

"I don't know what's what, Bob. You tell me. I want something that's going to be loud and clear and have good treble response without feeding back too much."

"O.K. how about a couple of Shure 57s?"

I said, "Fine, but I want to hear them. Can we set this whole thing up and see what it sounds like? It's pretty important for our debut that everything is just right."

Bob responded, "Don't you boys worry about a thing. We'll get you all set up and you just won't believe the sound of these speakers. This kid Pete Traynor is a genius when it comes to PA stuff."

He disappeared in the back and came out with a helper, carrying what looked like a seven foot high column speaker, which they stood up on the floor in front of Huard.

Bill's reaction was typical. "Holy shit, what is that? It's gigantic."

"It's a prototype of a new design that Pete just finished a week ago. It should take up to one hundred watts RMS without a problem. And, you should be able to run them all night long at peak power."

Bob quickly went back to the rear of the store and reappeared with a big black Bogen PA amplifier-mixer and set it on the counter. It was all silver and black up front and laced with serrated heat vents, top and bottom. He reached out and patted the amp like a baby. "This should make sure that everyone can hear you, Dave. And it's virtually indestructible."

All the time he was talking he was plugging in speaker wires and mike chords. He reached down under the counter and plugged the Bogen into an AC outlet and then hit the switch and started twisting knobs on the front panel.

"Try that Dave." He handed me one of the fifty-sevens.

"Testing, testing, test*ING*!"

"Holy shit!" exclaimed Huard. He stuck his fingers in his ears.

Bob had cranked it right up to ten on my third cue. The result was pure sweet unadulterated power, clarity and volume. Huard had been standing right in front of the cabinet and had taken the blast full force.

"And that's only with one bank of speakers! What do you think boys?" Bob was all confidence. His grin showed a set of pearly white teeth. Huard was all smiles as well. I was thinking to myself how great it was going to be to have the audience hear me, for a change.

I turned to Bob, "You've got a deal!" This was exactly what we needed. Everyone shook hands.

After fifteen minutes of paperwork and an appropriate down payment we loaded the gear into Huard's car. When the guys arrived at the club tomorrow they were going to get a real surprise. By the looks of things there was no doubt that Charlie Brown's was really gonna be rockin' this weekend!

When we got into the car Bill placed a four by six flyer in my hands and we pulled out onto Princess St. and headed for Yorkville Avenue.

"Go ahead read it, Dave."

The headline read, GRAND OPENING - CHARLIE BROWN'S, 26 Cumberland Avenue, Introducing The UGLY DUCKLINGS. Friday June 12 - Sunday the 14th. Cover Charge $1, First 20 people get in FREE! Door Opens at. 8 p.m., music 9 – 12 p.m.

It was printed on orange paper with black lettering; something to definitely get people's attention. I was filled with optimism. Things were going so right, I just couldn't see how there could be any major screw-ups at this point. Huard dropped me off at 16 Admiral and then headed back to Scarborough. As I walked in the front door I could smell herbs and garlic wafting into the hall from the kitchen. The door to Woody's room was open and I glanced in to see Woody standing in front of a full length mirror in nothing but his black bikini underwear. He was turning at various angles to the mirror, flexing his muscles and assuming traditional dancing poses. He noticed me and rotated slightly, gazing at me over his shoulder.

"What do you think Dave, am I too skinny? I've got to have just the right balance of muscle and suppleness if I'm going to have any success as a dancer."

"You're just fine Woody, if your muscles get any bigger you'll look like a body builder or something."

"Yeah, I guess Hercules isn't really the right image to project." His lisp was almost comical sometimes, but I resisted the temptation to laugh.

"Are you going to go to our opening at Charlie Brown's tomorrow night?"

"Oh, I wouldn't miss that for the world! I'm going to bring my friend Jack, who works at the CBC. Is there going to be any alcohol served there?"

"Uh, no Woody, you'll have to bring your own. But just keep it out of sight, O.K? We don't want to have any trouble with the cops." He smiled and licked his lips. I was feeling a little uncomfortable and headed for my room, unable to restrain a muffled laugh. My plan was to eat some good food and get a lot of sleep to prepare myself for the big night.

I called Bob Melbourne and told him about our plans for distributing the flyers around Yorkville. He was gung-ho. "Are you going to get all the flyer people there a bit early and organise a sort of plan of attack?"

"Yeah, the band will all be there by seven, so you and Dave can come over whenever."

"O.K. sounds great. By the way, do you want a ride to work tomorrow? I'm taking my scooter in so that I can avoid the rush hour."

"Bonus! Sure, do you want me to meet you somewhere?"

We made arrangements to meet at Avenue Road and Davenport at 8 a.m. From there it was a simple matter to head straight down Bay Street to Adelaide, where Bob worked. It looked like my special day was turning out to be even more than I expected.

Like a friend had once said, tomorrow never knows!

I woke up on Friday at seven a.m. with sunlight streaming into the room through my monstrous bay windows. No need for an alarm clock. At this time in the morning it was even more obvious that curtains were an absolute necessity if I was ever going to enjoy a Saturday morning sleep-in.

The long sleep had had the desired effect. I felt refreshed and hopped out of bed with a spring in my step. I made some instant coffee on my grubby little hot plate, gulped it down and then went upstairs to wash up and shave. I'd decided to head out a bit early so that I could make it a casual walk to meet Bob.

When I walked out into the hall and closed the door I noticed the silence. Everyone else was still sound asleep. I wondered what Woody did for a living and what time they would all come to life.

The morning was windy and warm. A slight breeze pushed me along as I made my way across Lowther Avenue to Avenue Road. I turned left and headed north reaching Davenport Road a few minutes before eight. The streets were already full of traffic and alive with people. I gazed off towards Belmont Street where Davenport Road started to curve upwards to Dupont Street and saw a silver grey Vespa just emerge from the stream of cars. It made a buzzing-whirring sound as it sped up on the curve and passed a black Pontiac. The driver wore a light grey suit with a buttoned-up vest and thick black sunglasses. His jet-black hair flew backwards in the breeze as he rounded the corner. In another minute the scooter pulled up in front of me.

"Hop on Dave, we might be able to make the light!"

I was on in a flash and we booted it across the intersection and merged into the main lane of traffic headed towards downtown. It was a glorious way to start the day.

My experience with bikes was minimal but the joy of discovering the city this way was really a treat.

Bob dropped me off at Adelaide Street and Bay Street and I walked over to Simpson's, arriving ahead of the rest of the crowd at the office. I knew it was going to be a long and anxious day, so I made it a point to get right down to business in the hopes that time would pass more quickly. By lunch time I could feel little fluttering waves of anticipation moving through my guts; a prelude to the feelings that I would feel just before we went on stage to play.

As the afternoon wore on my anxiety increased and time seemed to slow down to an unbearable crawl. I looked up at the clock once again and swore that the minute hand hadn't budged since my last furtive glance. Eventually three thirty came and I rose and exited, passing my boss Jack Moll on the way out the door.

"Hey everybody, have a nice weekend." I waved; I was on my way.

Woody was waiting on the porch to greet me as I arrived back at 16 Admiral Road. He was wearing black dancer's tights and a navy blue and yellow striped soccer shirt. As he placed a leg up on the banister of the porch and started to stretch he ran his fingers through the curly lock of hair that dangled in front of his face.

"John Read called you and said he's going to bring his girlfriend Chris and her sister Sylvia to the gig. And Bruce is bringing some other friends from Cedarbrae." He spoke in a sort of flat monotone, as if he was some kind of robot delivering a message. Sweat was running down onto his cheek from his forehead.

I suddenly felt hot and took my sports jacket off and flung it over my shoulder. "Thanks Woody, is Tannis home?"

"Nah, she had to go for the early shift at the Mousehole for one of the other girls. But she's not pissed 'cause she'll be able to get off earlier to see you guys."

Once inside I grabbed everything I would need for the night and laid it all out on the bed, including my harps and a couple of old tea towels. I figured a few extra t-shirts would be in order, and my brocaded vest.

Then I quickly had a bath and got the hell out of there. Sometimes when I was un-nerved I'd just get antsy and have to move.

When I got to Avenue Road it was a bit early, so I stopped in at The Record Villa to see what kind of new releases they had. There wasn't much, just some new Album of tracks that The Beatles had recorded in Germany before they made it big. It was actually some dude named Tony Sheridan, backed by the Beatles. I passed. I didn't like that kind of shit. It was either The Beatles or it wasn't. Simple.

Pretty soon I was bored and out the door. I was at Charlie's at quarter to five. Huard had just arrived. We got down to it and got all the new PA gear into the club before anyone else got there.

The next arrival was Roger with Rob and the drums. The timing was impeccable. As soon as Huard had moved the car around back to the parking lot, Roger pulled in, in his big black '63 Pontiac Laurentian. He came to the door straining to manoeuvre his Fender Concert inside without doing any major damage to it or the door. When he saw the PA cabinets he did a double take.

Five "Ugly Ducklings" @ Scarborough Bluffs, May 1965

"Wow, where'd they come from?" He looked at me and Huard.

"They're a new prototype, Roge'. Bob Abbott got Jack Long to agree to let us try them out in a small club setting." A slow whistle came from Rogers lips. "Not bad, eh?"

I was guessing he was impressed. I went on to explain that we were getting them for the same price as the regular cabinets that had the eight-inch speakers.

Just then Rob entered with a big black vinyl bag, full of cymbals. His reaction was almost the same.

He looked directly at me. "They're not gonna be too loud are they, Dave?"

I reassured him that it was clarity we wanted, and that the amp really wasn't heavy duty enough to overpower the band. He went back to unloading his drums.

Within half an hour everything had been arranged and was ready to be primed and checked for the big night. The stage that we had created was located in the bay window area as it had been when the club was the Inn On The Parking Lot. It was raised about eight inches above the floor level of the rest of the room. To accommodate both John's and Glynn's amplifiers we had added a two foot extension on the right side where the stage met the living room wall across from the entrance.

We were still waiting for Glynn and John, but it was evident to me that they might be a bit late because they had to pick up John's girlfriend Chris and her sister Sylvia in Scarborough and drop them off somewhere before they made it to Charlie's.

John had been going out with Chris for a few months and I had met her sister Sylvia on the Eglinton bus sometime in March, while on my way home from work. In fact I had seen her many times while waiting to transfer on to the bus from the subway at Warden Station. It had become a highlight of my day to arrive simultaneously with her at the station and eventually I had overcome my shyness and introduced myself as a friend of John's, and we had struck up a conversation. Soon, our daily conversations became something I looked forward to. In the last couple of weeks since I'd moved to Admiral Rd. I had missed our daily meetings. I was glad she was going to be here for the big debut!

Roger had just changed strings on his Les Paul Jr. the night before and was busy tuning and trimming them, when John and Glynn arrived.

Glynn made his way through the door first and got a glimpse of our silver-clad cabinets and the flashy Shure 57s on stands across the front of the stage. He smiled, "What's all this, then?"

I reiterated my previous explanation, as John came through the front door, his

Porta-Flex amp rolling on smooth casters across the linoleum floor. Why couldn't all amps come with such obviously practical equipment? He rolled his amp out in front of the cramped stage and then sat on it, facing the drums.

"Not much room to move around, is there?" He pursed his lips and made a strange sucking sound as he drew a quick breath.

Roger turned, "I'm O.K., I'll just have to watch that nobody gets a shot in the head from my tuning pegs." He was going to be standing right at the entrance to the club, next to where the doorway entered the living room space at an angle. "It's you guys that are going to have a problem. You'll have to space your stuff out so that you'll all have a bit of room."

Glynn and John got to work and managed to set their amps right against the wall with Glynn's in tight beside Rob's drums. The main criteria was that everything still had to be accessible. When everyone was satisfied with the setup it was time to do a run-through to get the PA adjusted for the band's volume. We cranked up and started in to "Everybody Needs Somebody". We just kept playing verses continuously while Huard made himself busy running back and forth setting the PA controls and checking out the sound level at various points in the room.

When everything was pretty well set we ran through the three new tunes. Huard smiled and clapped his hands rapidly after each song, muttering a quiet "Wow" and sighing as we finished each one. Just as we were nearing the end of "Spider and the Fly" there was a knock at the front door. It was Bruce McKenzie and Jim Oliver and some friends from Cedarbrae that they had brought along with them. I kept singing and walked over to the door to let them in. Bruce walked into the middle of the room, stood beside the tables and made a bow to the band. "Hail, hail the Ugly Ducklings!" He made a motion like he was tipping his hat. He was already putting us in a mood. Glynn smiled garrulously and turned to Jim and Bruce.

"Are we ready?"

"Are we?" Jim looked at Bruce. Bruce looked at Jim, "Ready?"

"Yeah, let's do it!" they spoke in unison.

Huard retreated to his car to get the flyers for the boys to hand out on Yorkville. He had only been gone for a minute or two when Bob Melbourne and Dave Tygeson stepped through the doorway. They had also brought a friend.

Bob was the spokesman, "Hi Dave, this is our friend Danny Carney." I reached out and shook Danny's hand and then turned and introduced everyone to the band and then to Bruce and Jim and their buddies from Cedarbrae.

"So it looks like we've got quite a team to give out these flyers! Is everybody ready to do a real sales job on the band?" I was trying to be inspirational.

Bob was the first to reply, "Yeah, but it would be nice to hear what we're going to be selling."

John had been leaning up against the wall beside his amp observing all the goings on and was about to say something when Huard came back in the front door, his arms full of orange flyers.

"These guys want to hear something, Bill, what do you think?"

Bill looked back at John, "How about going through 'Heart Of Stone'."

Glynn smiled and glanced over at Rob and Roger. It was automatic. Rob shouted the count and we were off. It was very loud in the confined empty space of the club, but no one seemed to care. Heads were nodding along with the beat, smiles were plastered on everyone's faces as they got the message. After three and a half minutes the last cymbal crash came down and Glynn let the last chord hang until it dissipated on its own.

The assembled flyer distributors all gathered in the centre of the room near the back of the club where the original dining room had been. Bill and Charlie installed a modest bar there, behind which they had set up a small kitchen with a fridge and cupboard.

Bill piled the flyers on the bar and then held court with the guys in order to get some kind of a system organized to achieve maximum coverage with the flyers around The Village. There was a total of seven guys and they were all keen on doing the best they could do. Together they quickly worked out a strategy, grabbed their share of the flyers and headed out the door to do their "thing".

The band shut down all the amps, placed the guitars on their appropriate stands and retired to the dressing room, upstairs. There was a little over an hour and a half 'til we were due to go on. Time to plan out the sets, get changed and psych ourselves into the kind of headspace that suited the venue. This was going to be something different. The club was an exercise in claustrophobia. The audience were barely six feet away from us. The tiny little tables that lined the walls placed many in the audience in a position where they could reach out and touch us.

As we were changing into our stage gear and preening ourselves, Roger mockingly suggested, "Don't turn up 'til you see the whites of their eyes!"

Glynn replied, "Aye captain, and no fartin' or scratchin' your nuts on stage!"

It was a pattern that all of us would use repeatedly over the next few years. Through everything that was about to happen to us our defence against anxiety was to be as irreverent and mockingly irascible as possible. And to never, ever take things too seriously.

Time passed too slowly. We sat and stared at the rattan rug on the floor of our private little domain. We could hear the sounds of activity beneath us; muffled voices, doors closing, the sound of music blasting from a transistor radio. We had no way of knowing what was going on and waited patiently for Huard to come up and make an appearance and fill us in on the scene down below.

We went over the sets one more time, trying to evaluate the impact of various songs and get a feel for the flow. We wrote out three copies of each set. One for Roger's side of the stage, one for Rob and one for Glynn and John's side. I could easily keep track of the tunes from either Roger's or John's copy.

At 8:40 Huard clamoured up the stairs to give us the goods. Everything was going according to plan.

"It's packed down there. I don't know where they're all coming from. Bob and Dave and Danny came back with, like, twenty people right off the bat!" Huard was showing excitement in his voice. "I just got Jim Oliver to go out and get some more lemonade and coke, 'cause we're almost out. I think it's probably eighty degrees down there already."

The windows downstairs didn't open. The only way we could get ventilation in the place was to leave the front and rear doors open and hope for the best. I wasn't too worried, I liked it steamy. The heat made everything more vivid and added sexual energy. Sweat was an animal thing; it was hard to stay really snooty and refined when you were sweating your balls off.

Bill headed downstairs, turning to give us one last glance before he disappeared.

"Ten minutes to go! And give them something they'll remember!" It was Rogers's credo. We all looked at each other. Nobody was gonna fuck up now! We were ready. We grabbed our drinks and set lists and set the night in motion. It was up to us!

We were somewhere in the middle of "Not Fade Away" when I came out of my reverie and regained consciousness. I was suffering from acute tunnel vision; every-thing looked fuzzy and yellow and my eardrums seemed to be overly sensitive, exploding with every thumping beat. I looked out at the audience and saw a sea of faces. They all looked back through the haze very intently, smiling and urging us on. They were hot and humid and they had been waiting for us for such a very long time that they didn't care about the sweat that was running down their foreheads or crawling down the small of their backs. They were moving to the rhythm, swaying from side to side. It was like being in a dream.

I felt my harmonica in my right hand and immediately brought it up to my lips and started to play.

In that very instant I suddenly became part of reality again and the magic of that very moment burned a lasting impression in my memory. I would never forget this night.

I wailed away on my harp forgetting all the anxieties of the day, oblivious to all earthly concerns. I looked around at the rest of the band and saw smiles of joy as arms flailed and bodies moved to the music. John was pumping it out emphatically, riding the wave of rhythm that emanated from Robs drums; punching up the beat to a frenzied pulse. Roger and Glynn strummed away, gleefully playing off each other's accents and anticipations.

When the tune ended the audience were just as relieved as we were. There was an odd silence, and then a kind of relief. Finally a smattering of applause started at the back of the room and worked its way forward.

Glynn immediately began the intro to "Well Respected Man" and we were off into another world. It only took a verse or so and the audience were singing along, even harmonizing, with the band. After that we quickly moved through "Kicks" by The Raiders and into some Jimmy Reed, with "Goin' To New York" and "Peepin' and Hidin".

By now the temperature in the club was moving upwards towards 90 degrees and we were feeling the heat. I grabbed one of my towels from behind Rogers's amp and dried my hair just in time for the beginning of "The Last Time".

"The Last Time" was one of the first Stones hits that they had written themselves. We had read an interview with Mick and Andrew Loog Oldham in "Melody Maker" about the importance that The Stones placed on writing their own material. Mick had stated rather prophetically that in the future all bands would have to write their own tunes to survive.

As Glynn punched out that glorious, hooky intro to the tune, I looked out at the audience and saw guys playing air guitar along with him. When I started to sing the tune they sang along with me. I could hear a chorus of voices singing along; *Well I told you once and I told you twice, but you never listen to my advice!* They were almost drowning me out! I felt a wave of energy rush up my spine and down my arms to the tips of my fingers. Goosebumps! I was loving every minute of it.

The remains of the evening took on an ethereal quality. Every song was a journey that the audience shared with the band. It was strange and invigorating to be so close to them. At times when they were on their feet, swaying to the music, it felt to me like their bodies produced a huge charge of static electricity that jumped across the gap between them and the band and energized us even more, enabling us to continue playing without a break for up to an hour and a half.

Just after we started the last set, I was looking at the back door of the club and saw two familiar faces as they entered and walked up to the standing room only crowd. It was Mike and Peter from Luke and The Apostles.

We had just started into "The Spider and The Fly" which was a real favourite of Roger and Glynn. The two of them loved the interaction that they were able to work out for our version of the tune, using totally excessive hammer-ons and greasy slides and trills, in an obvious Jimmy Reed homage. I just liked the opportunity to wail on the harp in a more refined and obsequious tone. The lyrics to the tune were as sensual as you could get. There was no hidden meaning. As I sang the tune I put some real attitude into a few of the lines, accentuating the obvious sexual double entendres and a few voices in the crowd whooped and hollered encouragement. The tune ended with loud clapping and whistles.

I picked up my brand new maracas as Glynn launched into the intro to "I'm Alright"; our new Stones number that we had learned for the Club Trocadero gig. Once the song was underway Glynn started doing his patented windmills and slides as I wailed on the harp in one hand while keeping the maracas going in the other.

I was watching Mike and Peter's reaction at the back of the club when I noticed a couple of other familiar characters come in the back door. One was the skinny bass player Bruce Palmer from Just-Us and the other was their gangly "sometimes" singer Ricky James Matthews from the Myna Birds. They stood at the back beside Mike and Peter.

Eventually the audience started singing along to the choruses of "I'm Alright". By that point in the song the same phrase just repeated time after time until the end when the whole thing came to a crashing halt in a cacophony of percussive splendour, with Rob rolling around his tom-toms and the guitars screaming out with crunching chordal insanity. The audience loved it.

We said our goodnights to the crowd and thanked them for such a great reception. As we did so, they bemoaned the end and started calling out encore! encore! We all looked at each other with blank stares. We had done every tune we knew and we were spent. We needed a number that we could sort of ease into. An awkward pause gripped us on stage and then John called out my name in a half-whisper and started playing the bass riff to "2120 South Michigan Avenue", from the first Stones album. Glynn jumped right in and then Rob tumbled in on the drums and we were off. Roger cranked up the volume and wailed on his mighty Les Paul Junior to whoops and hollers. Everyone took a turn; and then another and another. After at least ten minutes we came to the end.

There was nothing left to give and the night ended with the crowd feeling as spent and exhilarated as the band. We made our way off the tiny stage and mingled with the audience. For the next half hour we met and introduced ourselves to our future fans and friends. The word would soon be out on the street. Glynn's plan had worked flawlessly and packed the place for the whole night. Hardly a soul had left the club once they had come in and experienced the music. From this point on our confidence could only grow. There was so much we wanted to do.

CHAPTER 5
JUBILATION

After that first night at Charlie's our reputation spread around The Village like wildfire and made its way to the suburbs via word of mouth. Huard was finding it easier and easier to get us gigs as the summer progressed and once the school year started we managed to do a few high school gigs around Toronto and Scarborough. Within a month we were making 50 bucks a week each, after expenses, which was 8 bucks more than I had pulled in at Simpsons as a Customs Clerk. We lived as we pleased, staying up until the wee hours of the morning after which we would finally hit the sack at 8 am.

As we started to play other gigs out in the suburbs Charlie had to bring in other bands to play at the club. He struck it rich with the first band he brought in, Mild and Bitter. They were another bunch of Scarbarians with a massive dedication to music. Led by front-man and lead guitarist Kenny Brown and bassist Ross Stevenson, they laid down a totally original country folk-rock vibe, with a little bit of blues thrown in to make it less jangly and more soulful.

The third weekend in October we played at a Sadie Hawkins Dance at Woburn Collegiate in Scarborough and made some good money, so we had the Saturday night off. I booted it over to Charlie's in time to catch the last half of their first set and was surprised by their tight harmonies and over-all musicianship. At first break I introduced myself and Kenny and I hit it off right from the start. He was a lifer too. He had a wicked glint in his eyes. You could tell that he loved what he was doing. The audience picked up the vibes too, and over that summer they became the second resident band at Charlie Brown's. The Sunday night of that same weekend we played Stanford United Church and established ourselves as the premiere Band from Scarbaria!

At Woburn Collegiate: Roger & Rob

Right after our first success at Charlie's we were approached by a really slick dude in a pin-striped suit who was putting on a "Battle Of The Bands" at The Birchmount Arena out in Scarborough. Bill and I were at Charlie's picking up some gear when he walked up to Bill and introduced himself.

"Hi there, I'm Mark Royal. I'm a promoter from Scarborough. I heard about the recent opening of your club and the 'Ducklings' gig last weekend. I wondered if you might be interested in appearing at my 'Battle Of The Bands' show in ten days' time."

Huard was curious. "What's the take, then? How do the bands get paid?"

Mark explained the set-up as being a typical contest. Winner gets $300, two runner ups get $150 each, and each band gets $75 for a half hour set. It sounded like an opportunity to make some quick bucks. Eleven bands and $5 tickets.

He showed us some promo material that was going to go in the newspapers and in the end we decided to go for it. Couldn't lose much for doing a half hour set!

It was our first bad decision. Not that there was very much that was obviously wrong with the whole set-up. Everything went exactly as according to plan as much as was possible. We did a spectacular show and brought the house down, but the fix was in. Another band who went on just after us, called The Lovells were judged the winners. But by the time the three top winners lined up to receive their prize money, Mr. Royal had departed for parts unknown and taken the spoils with him, never to be seen again.

It was a hard lesson to learn, but one that would never be forgotten. From then on we didn't do anything without a contract. And maybe we would do a little bit of prior research as well. There were some club owners who had pretty despicable reputations and would try to find ways to *not pay* bands, or to dock you a certain amount for petty, perceived transgressions. It was our responsibility to stay on top of the game and know who and what we were dealing with!

Winding it up at the "Stanford United Church", fall 1965.
Roger had just got his new GIBSON ES-335!

The summer of '65 was a special time in Yorkville. Clubs were opening up all over the village. The place had become a powerful magnet, attracting kids from the suburbs and from all over southern Ontario as well. Every night was a happening and on the weekends the place became almost a carnival of hippie excess. Local television stations sent crews downtown to report on the awakening of Canada's baby boomers. Much was made of the anti-establishment opinions of the students and hangers-on and a lot of reporters speculated about the proliferation of drugs and free sex. The more press the place got, the more the people came.

One night at about six o'clock Huard and I were cruising west on Yorkville in a rented Thunderbird checking out the scene on the way to Admiral Rd. We had the radio tuned in to 1050 CHUM.

The announcer came on and introduced the new single by Bob Dylan. He was telling us that this record was going to change the face of rock music. He said it was called "Like A Rolling Stone", but that it didn't have anything to do with the Stones whatsoever, and that we would never forget this day. He was right.

Snap! - A snare shot pierced the humid air and then the most glorious guitar and organ riff in history permeated the summer stillness. I cranked the volume up and we listened intently, nodding heads like stoned out jazz cats in a New Orleans dream.

Once upon a time you dressed so fine, threw the bums a dime, in your prime, then you. It hit us! It was all so appropriate. It fit the time and the place. Right here, right now. As we watched the cavalcade of misfits, hippies and straights walking bliss-fully along Yorkville, it seemed to be telling us their stories. And ours, too. It was an anthem, a poem of the age. It was really quite long too. It seemed like it went on for ever and ever, compared to the two and a half minute pop ditties that we were so accustomed to hearing on the top forty.

After it was over the DJ just blurted out, "man!' in an elongated and wistful exclamation. I was trying to make sense of what it was all about and I asked Huard what he thought. He just looked at me dumbfounded and replied, "I don't know, Dave, but I don't think I care". That was sort of the way I felt too. It was a song for everybody. You could make it your own; interpret it any way you wanted. It was supposed to make you feel something; anything. And it hit the mark, right in your heart and your gut; there was no denying it. The D.J. was right, it was a turning point. I went to sleep that night with the chorus, *How does it feel: To be on your own, like a rollin' stone!* echoing in my mind.

A week or so later, John Hammond Jr. came to town to play the Riverboat in The Village. I had bought his first album on Vanguard when I started working at Simpson's Sears in January, and then the second one, "Big City Blues" in April. By this time I was a total fan. He was a consummate bluesman at the tender age of 23. I was really pumped to see him "live" and managed to grab a balcony seat right across from the stage in the tiny club. I was six feet away from the bar-stool and mike that waited under the lights. He came to the stage in denims and boots and was careful to get his harp-rack set up just right, while at the same time introducing himself and thanking the audience for coming out.

First up was "No Money Down" a Chuck Berry opus that John took to another level. The sound of his guitar and harp were so complimentary to his voice I was awed. His rhythm thing was a treat too. Between the strumming, the harp chucking and vibrato and his deep punctuating vocals, he just lifted the audience up and took them along on a barrelhouse ride with the blues.

After twenty minutes of strident grooves he got down to the nitty-gritty and stepped into "Louise". It was the tune that had given me goose-bumps the first time I heard it on my little "Sea-Breeze" record player at 16 Admiral, and tonight "live" on stage in Toronto was no exception. The hair on the back of my neck raised up and I felt a rush of energy. When John played the middle eight on the harmonica I was in seventh heaven. His vibrato on the harp was so nascent and sensual it enthralled me. I had to learn how to do that!

I left the Riverboat more determined than ever to get my harp playing together. John was only four years older than me. If he could do it then my prospects were good. The next day I went out and bought a bunch of Little Walter and Sonny Terry and Brownie McGee records, and a Muddy Waters Greatest Hits Package. Every night I sat in my room and played along. It wasn't easy, but every time that I stumbled into discovering how one of those cats played a certain riff I felt so elated I would keep at it until I was too tired to move, or my mouth was so dry that I couldn't slide it across the harp anymore.

Around the end of August I heard about a new album that was coming out on a label called Elektra, out of New York. It was a genuine blues band from Chicago made up of both white and black players. The harp player was white and the news was that he was probably the best to ever come out of that city. His name was Paul Butterfield.

The band was The Paul Butterfield Blues Band and they changed the way that I thought about music. They were groove monsters. They really listened to each other and played as one entity, complementing each other's playing with unlimited intuition and finesse. Some of the members had backed up Dylan at The Newport Folk Festival and Mike Bloomfield, the lead guitarist, had played on "Like A Rolling Stone". I got the album and wore out the grooves playing along with it at every opportunity.

Butterfield was really a piece of work, though. Not easy to figure out. He was very percussive and dynamic. His sound and amplifier set-up was so much more modern, in a way, than the older established cats. He wailed with a lot of energy in a fashion that was more in kinship with the lead guitarists of the day than with other harp players. James Cotton was obviously one of his major influences, but once again he had taken James's thing to another level. He rocked!

The first few weeks I had that album I stayed up 'til three and four in the morning wailing along. It was a tough nut to crack but eventually I started to get the feel of it. The next time we gigged I started cupping the microphone in my hands and manipulating the harp to get various tones and more sustain. Up until then I had just been playing it acoustically into the mike and cupping the harp in my hands to get that vibrato and quavering tone. The guys in the band dug the new electric sound and started working more and more percussive rhythms into the arrangements for our tunes. Rehearsals became a joy as we got tighter and tighter and learned how to emphasize our dynamics.

By mid-August the word was really out on the street about the band. Whenever we played at Charlie Brown's the place was always jam-packed with dozens of hot, sweating, smiling and dancing fans. We had learned how to do the turn-over thing, playing longer sets and taking longer breaks in the hope that some folks would leave during intermission, thus giving us a higher gross for the night. Also, Bill had opened up the backyard of the club and Charlie had had some gravel brought in and spread it all around so that people could go outside for a walk and some fresh air and get a break from the steam-bath that would overcome the audience by mid-evening.

On August 17th the Beatles came to Toronto. It was a given that we would go to see them. Everyone at 16 Admiral Rd. was on cloud nine in anticipation of the event. Tannis and Jeannine and their good friend Bev Davies scooped up tickets for everybody. Once the tickets were in hand the whole household sat around the kitchen table, trying to think of a way of getting to meet them in person. On the day of the concert we knew from radio reports that they had arrived and that they were staying at The King Edward Hotel on King Street.

After a lot of discussion and speculation it was decided that the only way to get to see them would be if we could get a message to them that would get us clearance right through to their rooms. We knew that security would be impossible to crack, as we had seen all the media reports about the other stops on their tour.

Tannis and Jeannine were absolutely convinced that John, Paul, George and Ringo were all certainly potheads. To them there was no other explanation for the contexts of some of their music. Of course this was because they and all of their friends constantly listened to the Beatles' music while under the influence of the weed. At the time The Ducklings had not yet tasted the herb but we speculated along with the rest of them, especially after Glynn and I had read "In His Own Write" by John Lennon.

So, Tannis and Jeannine sat down and contrived to write a Telegram to The Beatles that would infer, oh so innocently, that they had some special treats that the Beatles would appreciate. They sat around the kitchen table and wrote and re-wrote and refined their surreptitious telegram until they felt that it was innocuous enough but still conveyed their secret intent. Then they phoned the telegraph office and happily sent it off to the Beatles at the King Eddy. They had included the telephone number for the pay phone that was on the second floor landing of the house. So afterwards everyone sat around the house and waited. And waited. And then waited some more.

An hour went by and then another. Everyone got discouraged. No phone call.

Any other day would be interspersed with phone calls for any number of people that lived in the house, but today, nothing! Eventually Tannis and Jeannine left to do some shopping and Glynn split to go downtown to meet his girlfriend, Helen. Woody and I were the only ones left. I retired to my room and put "Beatles '65" on my little "Sea-Breeze" player. My favorites were "No Reply" and "Mr. Moonlight". After I listened to the album I decided to have a bath to get ready for the concert that night. I gathered all my shampoo, shaving kit, towels and clean clothes and headed upstairs to the bathroom.

I had just entered and got all my stuff laid out when the phone rang. We had all given up the prospect of the Beatles answering the telegram but I decided to answer the damn phone anyway, so that I could have my bath in peace. I pulled the bathroom door closed behind myself and walked down the hallway to the phone in my bare feet.

I picked up the receiver and put it to my ear.

"Hello, 16 Admiral," I said.

"Oh, hello. Is Tannis or Jeannine there?" This voice had a thick Liverpudlian accent!

I said, "No they've gone out shopping for groceries."

"Oh. Well who's this, then?"

I answered my name.

"Oh, well hello then Dave, its John Lennon here."

I panicked and thought to myself it had to be someone putting me on. Most likely, Glynn. He was very good at doing that Liverpudlian accent.

"Oh it is, is it?" I countered. "You're sure it's not you Glynn?"

"Glynn? Glynn who? No this is John Lennon here, mate; really. It's really me. I'm calling about this telegram we got this morning. It sounds quite interesting actually. But there's just no way that we can 'ave anyone up to our rooms, or get away from them a'tall. There's all the press here and there'll be no time."

"Oh, well thanks for calling, John," I replied with a hint of sarcasm in my voice. "The girls will be very disappointed." I wanted to believe that it was really him, but there was still a lingering doubt in my mind.

"Well, right then. Tell everyone we would've loved to accept the invitation, but we're in a right bind here and it's a busy, busy day! Oh, and tell 'em that we love Toronto and we would've loved to have seen The Village!"

"O.K. John." I let up on the sarcastic tone.

"Right, then. G 'bye."

The line went dead. I stood there silently mulling over in my mind what had just taken place. Sometimes reality is more like a dream than a conscious experience.

This was one of those moments.

Everyone was going to meet at 16 Admiral Rd. at six o'clock and then take off to Maple Leaf Gardens for the concert. We all wanted to check out what was happening down on College Street around Maple Leaf Gardens. There was usually quite a lot of action surrounding a Beatles concert.

Just before six Glynn arrived with Helen and I gave him the third degree about the phone call that afternoon. I had told everyone else about it, assuming it had been a practical joke on his part.

Glynn looked at me incredulously.

"Well, I hate to say it, but it wasn't me Dave. No way. I just went down and met Helen at work and we went up to Sam's and then had a bite to eat at Webster's." He was dead serious.

"Well who was it then? No one else knew about the telegram!"

We looked around at each other and started to laugh. What a dolt I had been; I could have had a conversation with John Lennon! Well, I had. Sort of.

But we had made the connection. We had actually gotten through.

We headed for the subway, very pleased with ourselves, on our way to see the boys!

When we got there, there were hundreds of people standing around on the streets and milling about in the parking lot across from the Gardens. Scalpers would recite seat numbers in muted voices as we walked by. There was a CBC van in the parking lot but we couldn't see any crew or cameras. We guessed that they would be inside by now.

We walked over to Church Street and looked down towards Gerrard Street and then north towards Bloor. People were streaming our way from every direction.

Off in the distance walking south on Church Street we spotted Brian Fleming, along with Danny Carney, Bob Melbourne and Max and Kevin Brown. All regulars from Charlie Brown's. We waved and they joined us on the corner.

Bob lit up a cigarette. "When do you guys think we should go in?"

Tannis was smiling. She had a smile that could light up a room.

"It's a lot easier to wait out here; you can smoke. There's still forty five minutes 'til they go on, so we might as well take it easy."

Bev pulled out the tickets and handed them out. We all examined them, trying to determine where we would be in relation to the stage. We were about twenty rows up in the "blues", at almost centre-ice on the east side. I'd only ever been to the Gardens once before, so I couldn't really place where we would be. Glynn figured we would be two hundred feet from the stage.

Another fifteen minutes went by and there was basically no action where we were so we decided to go in and get our seats. Ten minutes later we were staring down at the tiny little stage at the north end of the Gardens. It looked so far away. It was the height that did it. If we had been on the floor I was sure it wouldn't have felt so distant.

The anticipation in the place was palpable. There was so much nervous energy in the air it was stifling. Voices carried in this gigantic concrete cavern like we were sitting on the edge of the Grand Canyon. It was difficult to hear each other speak, for all of the jabbering going on.

Finally the Beatles made their way to the stage and the immediate result was pure unadulterated hysteria. So many flash-bulbs were going off simultaneously that the place was lit up like a Christmas tree. The stage lights had no effect. They started with "I Want To Hold Your Hand" but it was almost impossible to hear them through all of the screams. Every now and then the audience would collectively have to pause and take a breath, and when that happened we actually got a chance to hear what they were singing and playing.

Not once did I hear Paul's bass. It was as if it wasn't there. The guitars cut through now and then, but their voices seemed to slosh about the gardens like water in a fishbowl. Waves of gorgeous harmonies would slide by us as they passed over our heads in a circular pattern around the saucer-shaped gardens. It was like listening to some far off radio station as the distant frequency modulated in and out of existence, bouncing off unknown bodies and obstructions. Sort of a disappointment, but not totally unexpected.

We all went along on the ride with everyone else and after an hour and a half we were absolutely exhausted, our heads ringing from all the noise and screaming. It was magical to have heard those songs being played "Live" by the Beatles, but it would have been so much better to have really *heard* them. It was hard to believe they were only two hundred feet away. And right in our own backyard!

CHAPTER 6
AUDITION

The week after the Beatles concert Huard got a phone call from The Bigland Agency. They were the largest booking agency in Canada and they had obviously been informed of our presence on the Yorkville scene. They were curious as to what our niche was and how we might fit in to their roster of talent. It seemed to Bill that they were anxious to sign bands that were perceived to fit in as part of the British Invasion. He arranged an audition for their top brass at our next Thursday evening rehearsal. After talking it over amongst ourselves we decided to be nonchalant about it and to not make any special concessions or change any aspects of our repertoire or our presentation. We wanted to start off on the right foot. These guys were going to get to know the "real" Ugly Ducklings and then make a decision based on their first impressions.

When the big night came we all showed up early at rehearsal and rolled through most of our favourite tunes. We picked a list of songs to play for our little audition and then started working our way through a new tune that we had picked at last week's rehearsal. It was "Crawlin' Up

A Hill" by John Mayall and The Bluesbreakers. It was a perfect fit for us. It had a great descending chord progression similar to "Walk Don't Run" by The Ventures, but it was anchored by very strong lyrics that very clearly stated our own feelings about life and love and playin' the blues, and it had a great framework for some hot guitar and harmonica solos.

I had ordered "John Mayall - Live at Klooks Kleek", and the first Pretty Things album from Rendezvous Records, a really special record shop on Yonge St., North. The owner Walter Hornsberger went out of his way to order direct from England any discs we needed to stay ahead of British Music trends. The result was that we usually had the latest U.K. releases at least a month before they were released in Canada.

By the time the guys from The Bigland Agency showed up we pretty well had the John Mayall tune down pat. They had parked out back in the parking lot of the adjacent apartment complex on Yorkville Ave. Huard went out to greet them and then brought them inside. They stood in front of the stage and introduced themselves. The owner of the agency, Ron Scribner, introduced himself last. He didn't look more than eighteen years old! His blond curly locks were cropped short and added to his cherub-like look. He had a permanent grin etched into his cherub-cheeks and spoke like some kind of mild mannered reporter for the "Gotham City News". However, Jimmy Olson he wasn't. He stepped forward and shook each of our hands as we introduced ourselves one by one.

After all the formalities were done it was time to get down to it. I spoke up and introduced the first number as the tune we had just learned tonight. We tore into it with unbridled enthusiasm and laid out some pretty over-the-top solos. Huard stood beside the agency guys grinning. He was always grinning while he listened to new tunes. They were the tools that we were going to use to crush our future audiences with and he loved anticipating the crowd's reactions to them.

Once we got through the first tune we announced that we were going to do a medley of our first set. By this time we had that first set down extraordinarily tight and we played through it with measured precision and confidence.

As we played I watched Ron Scribner's face for clues. When we did "All Day and All of The Night" he smiled. When we aced "Gloria" his toes were tapping and he reached up and scratched an invisible itch on the back of his head.

Finally we reached the end and finished with "The Last Time" by the Stones.

His grin got even bigger and as the last chord faded out he broke into spontaneous applause, after which the others joined in enthusiastically. I sensed that things had gone rather well and walked over and sat in a chair directly across from Roger.

The guys all started packing their axes away and then pulled up chairs facing our new acquaintances. Glynn shrugged his shoulders and shook his long golden locks, staring directly at the line of critics in front of us. Rob slid out from behind his kit and placed his cymbals in a vinyl case and propped it against the wall.

Huard moved to the front.

"Well, Ron, what do you think? We're not interested in any of that 'don't call us, we'll call you', stuff. Just give us a straight answer, O.K?"

Ron smiled, "Of course, Bill." He looked at everyone. "We can have you guys playing at whatever level you want, right away. What I see here is something that is going to grow. You guys have got something special. I can't put my finger right on it, whatever it is, but that doesn't matter. I know that you've got what people want and that your reputation will only grow." He looked around at the rest of us. "I know that Bill has been booking you quite well and the word on the band has really gotten around. But we can get you known outside of the city. Let's get together and work something out." He looked at Bill.

Huard stood and looked around at us. We were all pumped. Heads nodded in agreement, a few muttered "yeahs" broke the silence.

Everyone stood and shook hands again as the "Bigland" delegation prepared to leave. After they walked out the back door we all looked at each other.

"What do you think, guys?"

Glynn answered first. "That was pretty straight. No bullshit."

"Yeah," I said, "I'm impressed. Sounds to me like we can work with them, Bill."

Roger and John picked up their guitar cases and headed out the front door. "We'll see you guys tomorrow. Call him, Bill, set up an appointment. There's no hurry, we're booked for the next month anyway. See you at eight o'clock tomorrow, O.K?"

"Yeah, yeah."

Rob and Glynn split too and Bill and I locked up and headed for Webster's Restaurant and a bite to eat.

"Good work, Dave."

"Not too bad yourself, Bill."

We headed west on Cumberland Avenue.

That Friday and Saturday at Charlie Brown's was the busiest that it had ever been since those first few gigs. The place was absolutely jammed. People were starting to show up an hour before we went on stage, just to get a seat. By nine o'clock it was so jam-packed that people could barely move. There was no possibility of dancing, but no one seemed to care. By this time we had started advertising two shows a night, so that we could clear the place out at eleven and get a fresh audience. With the heat that was generated in that stuffy little room, no one ever complained. Once the temperature reached ninety degrees they were perfectly willing to leave. We scored big for the two days and then Mild and Bitter came in on Sunday to fill in for us while we did a Church gig out in Etobicoke.

Bill had booked this Church gig almost a month in advance to allow them time to advertise and bring in a sizable audience. It was a fundraiser for various organizations within the church community and looked promising.

Roger had picked up Rob and his drums and then come over to my place and grabbed me and Glynn. We were to meet Bill and John at the church.

Once we reached the west end we proceeded to get lost. We were driving around in circles it seemed, trying to figure out the directions that we had been given to find the church. Roger never bothered with silly things like maps. He was convinced that he had a sixth sense that would always kick in just in time to guide us to the gig. The gig was due to start at eight o'clock and we managed to pull into the parking lot at about six thirty. The old '63 Parisienne was riding pretty low with the weight of the four of us, plus all of the equipment that we had managed to squeeze into the trunk and between our asses on the seats. As we wheeled around a ninety degree turn into the lot and slid a bit too-quickly into a marked space, there was a strange crunching and grinding sound that echoed up from beneath the front of the car. It sounded as if something had torn through the oil pan or radiator.

Roger swore under his breath, "Shit! What the fuck was that? Jesus, we better check it out. I can't afford to put any more money into this damned car."

We all piled out to check out the damage and got down on our hands and knees to look under the front end of the car. I was directly in front and spotted the problem right away. Roger had driven up to the concrete parking curb very quickly and not noticed that the steel rebar that held the curb in place at the edge of the pavement was sticking out of the cement by a good six inches!

The front bumper of the car was too low and had scraped over the rebar which was hooked into the gap between the bumper and the radiator cradle. It was still sticking up at least two inches into that same gap.

Roger breathed a sigh of relief as I explained the situation. There was no permanent damage, we just had to get the car off of the stupid rebar! He reached into his left pants-pocket for his keys and then tossed them in the air with complete and utter confidence, catching them in his right hand. He got into the car and put it in reverse, and feathered the gas pedal lightly. Immediately, crunching and scraping sounds threatened unknown consequences. It sounded like it was going to do some real damage if he went any further. I had a flash.

"Hey, Glynn you get on the back bumper and put all your weight on it and Rob and I can lift up on the front. That might just get enough height to clear it."

We worked as a team and almost made it on that first try. Almost.

We decided to try one more time, with Roger rocking the car ever-so-gently with the accelerator. What we didn't realize was that the parking curb was actually *tilting* as Roger rocked the car and tugged at the rebar. After some more rocking and some heavy lifting the car suddenly jolted backwards as it was released from the rebar, and the tilted concrete parking curb slammed back to the ground at the speed of light, just catching the end of the big-toe on my left foot!

I jumped back instinctively. There wasn't any pain, initially, but after a few seconds a deep throbbing wave of it pulsed into the tip of my shoe. It started to feel warm and numb at the same time. I looked down at my shoe and saw a deep line embedded across the tip of my toe about an inch from the end of it. I started to feel a little woozy and sat down on a small patch of grass between the curb and a flower bed. I touched the toe through my shoe. The result was searing hot pain!

"Shit, man!" I blurted out, "It feels like the end of my toe is gone!"

Just as I said it, the tip of my shoe darkened and turned blood red. I wasn't feeling too good at this point.

"Oh man, we're going to have to go to a hospital or something, you guys! The end of my toe's been chopped off! I won't be able to go on stage like this."

Rob took the initiative and headed inside the church to see if Huard and John had arrived. "I'll be right back, Dave. Just keep your shirt on, and try not to faint."

So we sat and waited, with me massaging my lower leg and ankle and Roger and Glynn telling me to keep my head screwed on straight, 'cause "everything was going to be alright."

Then blood started to drip from the end of my shoe. I was feeling kind of woozy.

And then all of a sudden Rob was back with Huard and John in tow. They had everything figured out. Huard had found out where the nearest hospital was and was going to drive me over. John and the rest of the guys were going to set up the gear and of course every little thing was going to turn out just fine! I was so glad they all had such positive attitudes.

Now, if I could just keep from fainting.

I resolved to not look down at my toe anymore.

As it turned out, once we got to the hospital, there was nothing they could do for me. After removing my shoe and sock and looking at my toe, the doctor said quite matter-of-factly, "There's a fifty-fifty chance you might lose the toe-nail. But there's certainly nothing we can do for you, other than clean it up and give you a tetanus shot.

You'll have to stay off your foot for a few days and give it a chance to heal."

I told him about the gig, the one that was supposed to start in about half an hour. "Well, if you have to do it, I'd suggest sitting down and not doing any strenuous exercise. Don't move around too much. You'll want to get the bleeding stopped." He had a hand on my shoulder. He put out his other hand, shook mine and then disappeared down the hallway.

Once back at the church we found a wooden barstool that I could use to sort of half-stand, half-sit through the evening. We were a bit late getting started, but the guys had already told the audience the whole pathetic story, and as I made my way to the stage, my left foot swathed in bandages, the crowd erupted in spontaneous applause.

We were off to the races. Nothin' was going to keep us down. There was no sacrifice that we wouldn't or couldn't make for the music!

CHAPTER 7

HIBERNATION

For the rest of the summer the band stayed on course and rehearsed regularly, learning more and more material, determined to challenge our limitations. As we bought and listened to more R&B and blues records, and imported more British vinyl through our friends at Rendezvous Records we evolved into a relatively consistent act. We dropped the shiny pop tunes and got a harder and grittier edge.

Roger was still working at the CBC, and had set out to find his perfect guitar and his own sound. Just before Labour Day he had scored big. He bought a 1964 Gibson ES-335 TDC. Cherry red. Absolutely beautiful. At the same time he purchased a brand new "Zonk" machine, which was the raunchiest "Fuzztone" sound effects pedal that had yet been invented. Around the same time Glynn had purchased a sweet orange coloured Gretsch Tennessean. Long & McQuade's were really getting their hooks in deep. They had done everything and more to accommodate us and to help us achieve whatever our eventual objective was going to be.

John had traded in his Ampeg Porta-Flex and copped a much larger 100 watt Traynor Bass Amp, and a brand new Gibson Bass with the new revolutionary black flat-wound strings in order to compete with our ever-louder back line. Now, when we played at Charlie Brown's we literally shook the foundations of the building!

Rob had accumulated the beginnings of a fabulous set of Gretsch Drums and had started collecting an impressive array of Zildjian Cymbals. The sound that came from that little stage in Charlie's was getting tighter, edgier and louder, and the audience was loving it. Every weekend was organized chaos and even the week-nights occasionally drew two completely packed audiences. We were gradually working our way up to the incredible salary of sixty bucks a week each!

Every now and then The Bigland Agency would send us out to a high school gig in the suburbs and our reputation would spread farther out. We went to Barrie, Oshawa, Markham, Newmarket and Agincourt. Scribner said they were just testing the waters. They wanted to break us into the big circuit, but it wasn't going to happen overnight. Besides, we had a nice comfortable home base at Charlie's, and, true to their word, the gigs were getting better and better and the pay was going up slowly but surely.

We took advantage of the situation and rehearsed our butts off.

One Saturday in September Huard went to see Duke Edwards, the manager at The Devil's Den at The Avenue Road Club. John & Lee and The Checkmates played a Saturday matinee there every week. On the strength of our success at Charlie's and the fact that we had been picked up by The Bigland Agency, he asked Duke if we could do a guest set at one of their shows. To his surprise Duke was agreeable and it was all set and arranged for the next weekend.

The Devil's Den was a major R&B greaser hang-out and normally not the place that a grubby Village band would play. But we were gaining more confidence and since we had succeeded, albeit modestly at The Club Trocadero, we decided to give it a shot.

When the Saturday arrived and we arrived at the club, we were greeted by singer John Finley, who was a perfect gentleman. He escorted us into the club and backstage to the dressing room. I had always been in awe of his singing, starting from the very first time I saw him perform at Cedarbrae Collegiate, in my last year of school. In my mind he was as wickedly soulful as James Brown. I felt that we were in good company.

Our set was greeted with enthusiastic applause, but we noticed that only a couple of dancers got out on the floor. We felt slightly out of place. Nobody else was wearing jeans or running shoes and there was hardly any long-haired guys in the place.

So we not only sounded different, but we looked much different, too.

John reassured us that we had been appreciated and thanked us for dropping in.

As we left we felt a strange disconnect from that whole scene. It was peculiar that we had the music in common with all of those people, and yet in some way we were still spiritually separated from them by some sort of supernatural wall of intolerance.

At our next rehearsal Huard brought up the state of our lack-lustre stage appeal.

We didn't stand out. After a short discussion we decided that we needed some far-out stage clothes in order to ratchet up our status with The Bigland Agency, and with our fans. In the end we found we couldn't buy anything satisfactory. So, I went out and bought a used sewing machine and set out to make my own stuff.

The "DUCKS" @ the "Elane Plaza in Scarboro, Early summer '65

Glynn had finally moved into 16 Admiral and one Saturday morning we went out and bought some really funky striped pants, and patterned shirts at a used clothing store on Queen Street West. Then I altered them to make them look like they were imported directly from Carnaby Street in London. After doing my second or third outfit

I started getting good at it and I made a pair of pants for Glynn as well. I wasn't very good at pockets, though. So in actual fact my fancy-pants had flaps that designated the presence of side-pockets that really didn't exist. But man were they cool. I always picked tweedy herringbones and burgundy and charcoal pinstriped materials. Nobody on the street had anything like them!

Around the end of September everyone at 16 Admiral got notices of eviction. The house had been sold and we were being given the heave-ho! What a drag. I wasn't looking forward to finding a place, but there was no way out.

Glynn managed to find a place on Madison Avenue and I decided to look up and down Admiral Road itself. Number one Apostle, Luke Gibson lived just up the street at number 56 or so. The street was lined with rooming houses. There had to be something close by. After a couple of days with no success I was walking home after shopping and noticed a guy across the road from sixteen, moving some cardboard boxes out of the front hall of the house and on to the front porch. I zoomed over and asked him if he was moving out. He answered in the affirmative and told me I'd have to come back and see the owner after six o'clock, as that was when he usually arrived home. I went home, cooked a typical musician's supper of Kraft dinner and hot dogs, downed it and cleaned up the mess and was back across the street knocking on the owner's door at six-fifteen.

An older gentleman of fifty or sixty answered the door and spoke with a thick German accent. "Good day, young man, my name is Hans, what can I do for you?

I inquired about the room and he led me upstairs to the third floor. The place was an absolute shambles. Wallpaper peeled in layers from the walls and dust-covered bare light bulbs hung starkly from ancient cloth covered wires. A dry pungent odour that smelled like fifty year old newspaper, hung over the whole house. At the top of the second flight of stairs he showed me into the room. It was pitiful. It hadn't been cleaned or painted in twenty years. There was a small dormer jutting out on the far wall where the ceiling angled inward. The window in it was so dirty that almost no light penetrated into the room.

I asked him, "How much is it a week?"

"Five dollars."

"I'll take it," I said. I was sort of jumping the gun, but hey, it was three bucks less than I'd been paying across the road. A little paint and some elbow-grease could make it a cozy little hideaway, and I'd only have to change one digit on my address. I was now a proud resident of number 15 Admiral Road.

Later in the fall I went to see Jesse Colin Young & The Young-bloods at The Riverboat. It was prescient. They were so clearly "of-the-time". Jessie's voice was a clear and sweet beacon for the sixties, and their big hit, "Get Together", was really an anthem for a whole generation. I walked out of the club inspired and feeling so alive. They made me feel like anything was possible.

The next week I was visited by Ken Porter who worked occasionally with Luke and The Apostles. I had just finished a very psychedelic paint job on my brand new room and had invited him over to check it out. I had painted one wall bright yellow, one orange, one lime green and one red; and then I washed the ceiling with sky-blue and added some smudgy white clouds to it.

I heard him trudging up the stairs. When I opened the door he looked at me with a puzzled look on his face.

"I just saw a guy with a Nazi uniform on, go into the landlord's place downstairs!"

"Yeah", I said, "and I just had breakfast this morning with Winston Churchill!"

He looked insulted. "No shit Dave, they were all talking in there like it was World War Two all over again. 'Sieg-Heils' and the whole bit!"

"Really? Should we go down and check it out?" This was something I had to see.

Ken wasn't the kind of person who would put you on over something so serious. He liked a laugh now and then, but at the moment there was absolutely no humour in his face. He had really piqued my interest.

So, downstairs we went. Quietly and surreptitiously. We took off our shoes and slowly negotiated the stairs in our sock feet. When we got to the main floor landing we could hear the sounds of serious impassioned voices in the dining room. Someone was denigrating the Jews and espousing the purity of the Aryan race. We approached the French doors without making a sound. They had heavy lined grey drapery material over the inside of the windows, but there were little slices of a view visible where the curtains were drawn too tightly against the sash.

There were brown shirts, and red armbands with black Swastikas.

We took turns looking through the key-hole of the door lock to get a view of the speaker. He looked like a young version of Adolf Hitler. His hair was slicked back across his forehead and his face was adorned with a puny attempt at the putrid little moustache that Hitler had made so famous. He looked angry and full of hate. He made me want to vomit.

I gave Ken's sleeve a tug. "Let's get the hell out of here."

Once back upstairs we were almost speechless.

"What the fuck was that all about, Ken? What country are we living in?"

"Hey, we're living in Canada, Dave. But it looks like those guys just went through the 'Time Tunnel' or something. They're fucked-up in a major way. I wouldn't be surprised if some kind of shit hit's the fan around this. It's pretty sick."

Sure enough, a couple of weeks later our Nazi friends had a huge confrontation with the Canadian Jewish Congress in Allan Gardens, downtown. It was all over the papers, and as it turned out the right hand man for the fearless leader was none other than a former student of Cedarbrae Collegiate named David Stanley. His boss John Beattie was a genuine freak of nature with shit-for-brains. For the next three months they and their cronies in The Canadian Nazi Party got all kinds of free publicity, until the Toronto media realized that they were playing right into the hands of the stupid and vile hate-mongers, and then made the decision to cut the cord and shut them out.

It was so simple. Turn off the tap and the story dries up. And mercifully, it did.

On the 31st of October The Rolling Stones finally came to town. The Ducklings bought tickets immediately, along with almost all of the Charlie Brown's crowd. Luba Klachock, who was by this time a regular at Charlie's and the president of the Rolling Stones Fan Club in Toronto, came along with us to the Gardens.

Toronto's own John & Lee & The Checkmates opened the show in fine form, warming up the crowd for the heat of Patti LaBelle & The Blue-belles. I hadn't heard much of Patti LaBelle at that time but was astounded by her vocal range and the power in her performance. Both bands did a fine job of building the tension for the inevitable entrance of The Stones.

When the Stones finally did emerge from the rear of the gardens stage, led by Brian Jones and Bill Wyman, the noise that accompanied their entrance was deafening. The arrival of Mick and Keith, with Charlie following at the rear encouraged more and more screaming. When they were all plugged in and set to go Brian led with the intro to "Not Fade Away" and the noise level increased to the point where it was almost impossible to make out Mick's voice on the house P.A. system.

Looking down from half way up the east bank of seats at the Gardens it struck me that The Stones looked almost the spitting image of their performance on The T.A.M.I. show. We were all enthralled. They moved through "Little By Little" and "Surprise, Surprise" and then launched into "Time Is On My Side".

The din was almost too much to take. As they went through a repertoire of tunes from their first three albums, time became compressed the way it always does during states of longing. Before we knew it, the show was over.

As we made our way to the exits various discussions developed about the possibility of hanging around at The King Eddy to see if we might get in to meet them. As the president of the local chapter of The Rolling Stones Fan Club, Luba was game to try. I was too drained and wasted and decided not to bother, but Glynn and Rob set off with Luba and some of the others to give it a shot.

I headed back to Admiral Road to grab some much needed sleep.

Lately, at rehearsals we were having trouble coming up with new tunes that fit with our repertoire. We wanted things that we might be able to record in the future. The problem was that most of the great Chuck Berry tunes had been done. We decided to dig a little deeper and look for tunes that were more obscure. I started paying regular visits to Happy Harold's Discount Records and spent many an enjoyable afternoon at Sam The Record Man and A&A Records on Yonge Street, combing through the blues and R&B sections for little gems.

One afternoon in early November I had been out mining the record stores and had stopped for groceries on the way home. I had found a couple of real bargains at Happy Harold's. Namely; a James Brown & His Famous Flames and an Otis Redding; both, greatest hits packages. I was looking forward to checking them out when I got back, but as I made my way up Admiral Road after turning north from Lowther Avenue, all the lights went out in the windows on both sides of the street. It wasn't really dark yet, but it was overcast and early evening.

Once I got home I lit a couple of candles and figured I'd wait out the power outage. Turned out, it was a long, long wait.

I had one of those tiny little pocket-sized transistor radios, with one rectangular nine-volt battery, that I kept tuned to 1050 CHUM. I pulled open the bookcase drawer, took it out and turned it on. The news was heavy duty. It seemed the lights were out all across the east coast of the U.S and Canada. Kind of a drag. It was one of those peanut butter and honey-sandwich days. Not a real hardship, just a minor inconvenience. I guessed I was going to have to wait a while to check out James and Otis.

The next week I went to see Sonny Terry & Brownie McGee at The Riverboat. I was becoming a regular. I was now recognized at the door and because I had arrived so early, I was shown to my preferred seat across from centre stage.

On this night I sat spellbound, directly in front of Sonny.

Near the end of the second set he did one of his patented harmonica solos, incorporating whoops and hollers, and generally bringing down the house. The reaction of the crowd was entirely predictable. They were ecstatic. I just sat there transfixed through the whole thing wondering where it all came from. It was obvious to me that it was all improvised, because at certain points Sonny seemed to have surprised himself; breaking into a huge grin when he pulled off a particularly funky and delicious lick. His playing was so fluid and instinctual and punctuated by a joyousness that I had never heard in other players. It felt like a spiritual thing, a special place, and a surrender to some inner musical being. I went home determined to find that special place myself.

@ "The Balmy Beach Canoe Club" in Scarborough, Winter of '65 – '66

The winter of sixty five was short and sweet. For all of us, it was our first winter away from home and it literally seemed to fly by. The band drifted along on cloud nine, rehearsing our asses off and learning as much as we could about the music we were playing. We played at Charlie Brown's on a regular basis and at The Balmy Beach Canoe Club in Scarborough. Now and then we would get a higher paying booking through The Bigland Agency. Occasionally they would send us out as far as Port Hope or Guelph.

On one of our trips to the agency to pay our commissions, Ron Scribner offered to get us some much better bookings for the spring, on the condition that we would get a proper van for transporting the band and equipment, and that we would be willing to tour as far west as Fort William and as far east as Montreal. He also suggested that it was time for us to get some professional photos taken that could be used to promote the band. We started saving the money for a down payment on a van and then looked around for a photographer to do our promo shots.

By the end of March we had saved a down payment and managed to find a 1962 Chevy panel truck for four hundred and fifty dollars. The first time we used it to do a gig, we felt like we had really arrived. All of our gear fit neatly in the back and we used old quilts to soften up the amplifiers, arranging a nice semi-circular bench just behind the two front seats. We would drive along on the way to gigs with the radio blasting the top forty; the speaker buzzing incessantly whenever the bass response got too heavy for the cheap paper-coned six-by-nine speaker mounted in the front dash.

At the beginning of April we finally got our photos done. An older gentleman from Etobicoke came to Charlie Brown's in the early evening just before rehearsal and took us through the motions. He was quite good, actually, and we came up with a couple of great shots that really showed the character of the band. Scribner was ecstatic when he saw them. He chose the straight-on shot that had been taken of us spread across the upstairs hallway at Charlie's. He was sure that he would get all kinds of extra gigs for us, just on the strength of that shot.

First Professional Promo Shot

He stared at the eight by ten that Huard had just handed him. "You guys look like you're goin' somewhere in this shot, you know what I mean? Leave it with me and we'll have a thousand printed up by next Thursday." I loved the way he talked. "Sure would be nice if you had a record out, though. That's a one-two punch, when it comes to promo packages. You been thinking about recording? You know that's your ticket to another hundred a night, eh? At least that much, maybe more! Think about it boys, think about it!"

Bill and I talked about the prospect as we drove home. Scribner was right.

All we had to do was look at Jack London and The Sparrows' itinerary. They were heavily booked all over southern Ontario, and they weren't even that great a band. But the difference was that they had records on the charts!

At the next rehearsal I started bugging Roger about writing. We still hadn't written a song at this point, but I figured that it was time we gave it a try. Roger was always screwing around at rehearsals; playing a lot of spontaneous chord progressions and flying off on weird tangents when we were doing rave-up solos. All we had to do was organize the chaos and we could put some lyrics to it and we'd have a song. At least that's what I figured. It turned out that it wasn't quite that easy. One thing we did eventually discover though, was that if you tried often enough, then eventually things would happen.

In less than two weeks Scribner was back at us with a proposal for a little mini-tour of northern Ontario. The money was quite good and we would only be gone for nine days. We'd start with North Bay and Sudbury the first Friday and Saturday and then finish with Sault St. Marie and Kapuskasing the following weekend. After agents fees we'd walk away with just over eleven hundred dollars.

This was big time; it was time to shit or get off the pot, as my mother would say.

Bill gave him a thumbs-up and said we'd call him back to confirm the next morning.

We held a band meeting after rehearsing and decided that we would do it, providing that we hired a road manager to drive the truck and carry the gear. We were all getting tired of that aspect of playing. If we were going to be doing this professionally, we figured it was time to get professional. Bill called Ron the next morning to confirm and then the search was on for a decent Roadie.

That weekend we checked out all the regulars who came into Charlie's to see if one of them would make a good candidate for the job. Most of the guys who hung around the band already had jobs, or just weren't into that real physical thing. Anyway, on Saturday night we made announcements between sets. Who knew? Maybe there was someone out there, we just had to put things in motion.

At the end of the night as we were packing up our stuff a small diminutive man in faded denims approached Huard and introduced himself.

"Hi, my name's Charlie King, I heard your announcement and I'm interested in doing the job."

I checked him out. He was a bit older than us, maybe five-eight or five-nine; and couldn't have been more than a hundred and ten pounds soaking wet. He looked real wiry though, and slightly rough.

Huard asked, "You working right now?"

"Yeah, but it's a shit job man, nothin' special. I'm into having a good time this summer. You know what I mean?"

By now, everybody was watching, and checking him out. He noticed and sort of spun around looking right at each of us, in turn.

"Hey, I can do the job man, and I'm not afraid to work. Right now I'm doing construction shit, but it's not very inspiring, you know?"

John looked up from putting his Gibson in the case and asked, "You want to show your stuff and help me get this monster amp out to my car?"

Charlie walked right over, grabbed John's Traynor by the top strap-handle, pulled it up against his side and said, "Which way?"

"Out the back, man. You sure that's not too heavy?" John was perturbed. His amp weighed about eighty-five pounds and this little guy was walking around with it glued to his left hip, like it was a case of beer.

Charlie returned, all smiles, and spoke right up, unself-consciously, "Give me a shot guys? I won't let you down."

We all looked at each other, nodding.

"I'm in - Me too - Yeah - O.K - Yeah."

Looked like it was a done deal.

Only thing was, no-one had thought to ask him if he had a driver's license. Oh well, you live and you learn.

So, Charlie was true to his word. He was eager and on time, and he was surprisingly strong and independent. He never asked for help unless there was no other possible way to do a particular job. When we met at Charlie Brown's to load the truck he was all work and no play, and when we hit the road he was prepared with the latest road-maps and weather reports.

On shorter trips we might have taken Roger's Pontiac, but for this long a haul it didn't make any sense. So, at eleven in the morning on the Friday of our first gig we were heading to North Bay. We were mostly quite comfortable sitting around on our little circular bench seat. Roger was probably the least comfortable because of his immensely long legs, but he didn't complain. Charlie drove and Huard sat in the right front. We listened to 1050 CHUM all the way up Highway 11 until it started to fade out, and then tuned in to one of the Barrie stations.

When we got tired of the radio, we played cards or told jokes and took turns catching a few winks. As we drove further and further north we could see the remnants of winter beside the highway. Wherever there were stands of evergreens we could see patches of snow that still lingered in the darkest sun-starved spots. But winter was now history. The temperature was a balmy forty-five and climbing and we could feel the summer coming.

We stopped a few times for snack breaks and gas and pulled into North Bay at around six o'clock in the evening.

First stop was a Harvey's and some dinner. Then off to the Community Hall where the gig was happening. We tuned in to the local Radio station and heard the ad for the dance, where they announced us as "The Coolest New Band from Toronto". We were happy to be "cool"; it was better than being hip, or "up-and-coming", or any of the other standard Radio-hype-of-the-day descriptions.

The audience in North Bay just blew us away. Right from the start it was a mutual admiration society. As the opening chords of "2120 South Michigan Avenue" filled the room, they showed their appreciation with as much noise as could possibly be generated by a crowd of two hundred people. We moved on from The Stones and worked our way through The Kinks, James Brown, Chuck Berry and Wilson Pickett. Then more Stones, some Jimmy Reed and Bo Diddley. We were cranking it out with unbridled enthusiasm and reckless abandon, revelling in the heat and the volume. We couldn't have asked for a better crowd.

Putting on a Show

What a great start to our little tour.

Right after the gig ended we packed up and headed for Sudbury. Huard had phoned ahead and made reservations at a small motel just outside of town. The drive took a little over two hours.

As we drove into the outskirts of Sudbury under a bright and full moon we noticed how much the geography around Sudbury looked like a lunar landscape.

Ripping It up

We parked in front of our motel rooms and got out of the truck to off-load our luggage. About five hundred yards behind the motel was a huge slag-heap approximately two hundred feet high. It was glistening in the dark, radiating pixels of crystallized nickel-waste through the blue-white moonlight. It looked like an extinct volcano.

Now, what kind of crowd were we going to get in this town? We would have to wait until tomorrow to discover the true vibes of a Sudbury Saturday Night!

We got up at about nine in the morning and headed downtown for some breakfast. Everywhere we went we got the usual stares. As we walked down the main street we noticed that we were being followed by a couple of young kids on their bikes. They were giggling and chattering back and forth in hushed tones. Long hair was a big deal up here. We had sort of forgotten how far we were from Toronto.

After an uneventful breakfast we set out to find the local music store so that Rob could grab some drumsticks. When we pulled up to the front door our brand new "Bigland" promo shot was plastered all over the front window of the shop along with a poster announcing the gig. The staff were glad to see us and asked everyone for autographs.

Rob purchased his extra sticks and I grabbed a brand new Hohner "A" harp, having blown out one of the reeds on my trusty Marine Band at the North Bay gig. We headed back to the motel to clean up and pack the truck for the gig.

That night was a special treat. There was a local band opening for us, and they were quite good. Good enough to inspire us and get us excited about getting up on stage. They were obviously well liked by the local kids and really cranked up the volume and got the crowd hot and sweaty. That was the way we liked it. The fact that they were so good really spurred us on and when we finally hit the stage we raved-up with utter confidence and a certain amount of bravado. The audience loved it. Late in the last set when we did "That's How Strong My Love Is", I could feel the goose-bumps start to rise on my arms as a slow chill worked its way down my spine. It was heaven.

Glynn was grinning profusely and pursed his lips in concentration as we hit the accent chords to the bridge of the song. To my left Roger was demonic in his robot-like movements as if he was in some kind of religious trance. The song ended to incredibly enthusiastic applause and whistles and Roger looked over at me, indicating that he needed a little time.

So I introduced the band one by one, starting with John over on the right side. The crowd roared. Then it was Rob's turn at the drums. He stood up behind his kit and did a roll around the toms and ended with a crash on his ride cymbal. People stomped their feet and hollered. Meanwhile Roger was taking his guitar off and setting it against his amp while he quickly removed his leather vest.

I introduced Glynn. He stepped forward on the stage and then wound up and punched out one massive heavy duty chord with a perfect windmill stroke. The crowd went nuts. When things calmed down a little bit he stepped up to his mike and introduced me, and then Roger, who had just managed to get his guitar strap back over his shoulder. Suddenly we were all set to go.

Rob called out the count and we set off into "I'm A Man" by The Yardbirds.

Over the next ten or twelve minutes the temperature in the joint rose by at least ten degrees. When I went to blow my harp I could taste the salt from my sweat as it ran into the reed holes off the ridge of my upper lip. My eyes burned with sweat as I struggled to keep them open; watching the audience reaction as Rob went into his mini-solo in the middle of the tune. For five minutes he held the audience's attention with a blistering rhythmic assault that left them breathless and dumbstruck. It was oddly hypnotic. Whenever he laid back in his solo to get a little rest, the crowd continued on dancing, frantically shaking and spinning as if involved in some kind of tribal ritual. When the toms started pumping again they would go ballistic.

At a certain point that we had pinpointed at rehearsals, Rob played a special cue that brought us back to the verse and we all came in together to thunderous applause.

At the end of the verse Glynn did his patented windmill slide up the neck of his guitar and we ended the night pumping out that last "G" chord as if our lives depended on it.

One more flourish around the toms and the last crash died and was followed by a piercing feedback wail from Glynn's Fender Showman as he reached around to try and hit the on-off switch.

The crowd roared. They were diggin' it.

It had been another night in paradise.

Dave & Roger Wailin'

Glynn & Dave (ghosts)

CHAPTER 8

INDISCRETIONS

After our successes in North Bay and Sudbury we were in a magic space. Elation was only the outward manifestation of our inner bliss. Inside, everything was beautiful. Everything we were doing, everything we played; all of our experiences on the road and even the road itself, was beautiful. Our confidence level hit a new high and we were filled with optimism.

The morning after the Sudbury gig we were up early. We cleaned ourselves up, packed the truck and headed for a good restaurant for a premiere breakfast. Everyone was famished and eager to get on the road to Sault Ste. Marie.

After filling up with gas and making a few inquiries, we ended up at a mom-and-pop style eatery sporting a sign that read, All-You-Can-Eat Breakfast: $2.50.

We shuffled into a large corner booth at the rear that was just big enough for all seven of us. Glynn smiled broadly as the waitress approached. She looked about seventeen or eighteen, with long blond hair and enormous dimples in her cheeks.

As she handed us our menus I noticed a slight blush.

"Would you guys like some coffee or juice to start off?" she asked.

Glynn cleared his throat rather loudly and ordered a pot of tea and some toast.

"Have you got any fresh tomatoes?" he asked.

"I'll check on that," was the reply. She grinned and turned to Huard.

The rest of us ordered typically Canadian fare, stuffing ourselves with much-too-much bacon, too many eggs and lots of melted cheese and ketchup. Glynn enjoyed his eggs with fried tomatoes.

Midway through breakfast Charlie retired to the truck and returned with his Ontario Motor League map of Ontario.

"Hey you guys, check this out!" He held the map out at arm's length over the table, while we munched away. He had folded it so that Sudbury and Sault Ste, Marie were tucked into the bottom left corner and the rest of mid-northern Ontario was spread out to the right.

"See, we're down here (he pointed to the speck in the corner), and Sault Ste. Marie and Kapuskasing are over here to the west, and then way up here to the north." He slid his finger slowly along the map, emphasising the great distance between the three points.

"Okay." Roger chimed, "So what's the big deal?"

Charlie reiterated, "Well, it's a hundred and ninety miles from here to the Sault, but then it's a huge distance to Kapuskasing if we go back through North Bay; it's something like five hundred and thirty miles!"

Roger came back, "So? Let's just get to the Sault first and then we'll deal with Kapuskasing later."

Charlie was pumped. "I've already got it figured, Roge'. After we finish in the Sault, we backtrack a bit towards North Bay and then take Highway 129 through Chapleau! We can cut across 101 to Timmins and eliminate about a hundred and fifty miles from the trip to Kapuskasing!" We had no way of knowing if he was exaggerating.

Charlie folded his arms over his chest and awaited our response.

John mumbled through half chewed toast, "Hey man, that's like three hours of driving and a whole lotta gas money that we'll save!"

Charlie smiled. He retrieved his map and folded it carefully, then took a sip of coffee.

"We should get moving, guys. If we split soon we'll have some extra time to stop and check things out along the way." Huard called for the check and the waitress returned promptly.

"Are you guys the band that was at the community centre last night?"

Bill answered cheekily, "I guess we sort of stand out, eh?"

"Could I get your autographs?"

Bill grinned and opened his briefcase, removing one of the Bigland glossy promo shots. He took a pen and started to write: "To? - Who should I make it out to?"

"Oh, to Sandi, with an 'I'," she said.

There was that blush again.

He passed it around and we signed one by one. It was getting to be a normal thing - this, signing. Maybe our heads were starting to get a little bit big. But it was still nice to be recognized.

As we left Sudbury we were shocked by the extent of deforestation around the city. All around us the landscape was grey and lifeless. As we got further from town little patches of green began to appear here and there and dwarfed evergreens tentatively clung to craggy rock faces. It wasn't until we were twenty miles out that we started to see normal stands of large trees. It was a revelation to us; not something that we ever could have imagined.

The highway was a glorious inspiration.

I had been on this route once before with my folks, when the whole family had packed into our prized '57 Chevy and headed west to visit my cousins and grandma in 1960. But that was a distant memory. I had few, if any, recollections of that trip that had stayed in my mind.

We were astounded by the size of the rock faces and the proliferation of huge white pines that framed the highway as we rolled westward towards the Sault.

Huard turned on our crappy little radio with the fuzzy speaker.

Right away the truck was filled with the sound of the Rolling Stones' "It's All Over Now". Glynn started singing along and Roger played air guitar.

Charlie lit a smoke and rolled down the drivers' side window and an unusually warm April breeze spilled inward. Everyone joined in the singing enthusiastically, and soon an off-key choral version of the chorus reverberated off the steel walls of our cramped little blue truck.

Because I used to love her, but it's all over now! and then a second time, *Because I used to love her, but it's all over now!*

Then suddenly Keith Richards' blistering "Chuck Berry-like" solo filled our ears with pure unadulterated mayhem. What more could we ask for? It couldn't get any better than this!

The highway became a river of asphalt with us floating downstream to our destination, singing in ragged unison and marvelling at the backdrop of Canadiana that flashed by outside, like a never-ending newsreel.

The ride to Sault Ste. Marie was casual and slow. We weren't in any real hurry because there was no gig until Thursday night. We hadn't made any hotel reservations either, as we were arriving on a Monday and we wanted to find a place that was private as well as convenient. We stopped in Blind River to stretch our legs and then later had burgers at a truck stop in Thessalon, taking the time while we were there to check out the exit to Highway 129 north, which we would be taking on our return journey, on the way to Kapuskasing.

Everywhere we stopped we got a lot of stares.

It was something we were getting used to. It was obvious that the kids up here didn't have the same freedoms as we had down in T.O., and evidently it was true that these small towns lagged behind in their ability to adapt to cultural change. One thing we did notice though, was that we didn't get the same reaction from Native Canadians. They seemed much more open and tolerant and more often than not they gave us big smiles, or a thumbs-up sign.

We found a nice motel on the west side of town on the river and settled in for some much needed rest and relaxation.

After dinner the guitars came out and we worked on arrangements for some of the newer tunes and then jammed into the wee hours of the night. Roger showed me a couple of chord progressions that he was working on, toward our goal of writing some songs. One of them was really intriguing to me and I started writing lyrics to it right away. We called it "A Time and A Place" as it was about how we, as a band, fit into the world. *There's a time and a place for everything – There's a truth that reveals the love we bring.* Roger thought the idea was too intellectual and schmaltzy. I was neutral. At least it was a start.

We filed that one away in our collective memory.

Of the others, I was really struck by this one three-chord riff that he kept playing over and over every time we took a break from trying to write. It was straight-ahead and pretty aggressive and it stuck like glue in my memory bank. I told him in no uncertain terms, "Roger, DO NOT FORGET THAT ONE!"

He replied, "Don't worry Dave, it's my own personal musical signature!"

The next couple of days we split up and checked out the town. Glynn and I went down to the river to watch the huge great lakes freighters make their way through the channel on their way to lakes Superior or Michigan. They were stupefyingly enormous. We walked down to the edge of this one jetty and stood behind a chain link fence, within five feet of a gigantic five story high ship as it glided by at about five miles an hour. We listened to the ominous sounds of the engines chugging away mercilessly in the bowels of the immense steel hull. There were ghostly moans and metallic scraping sounds mixed in with the relentless pounding rhythm of the engines. I was sure that our ears were incapable of hearing the total depth of those sounds. As we walked toward downtown we could feel deep vibrations pulsing through the concrete beneath our feet.

Later we tried shopping for clothes on the main drag, but we were mostly disappointed at the lack of anything fashionable. I found a nice brocaded vest for a buck in a small used-clothing store and added it to my stage wardrobe.

John, Roger and Bill had hit the local liquor store on Tuesday afternoon and each returned with a few bottles of their precious favourites to get them through 'til Thursday. As a consequence there was much laughter and merriment in our rooms for the next couple of days. Rob was content to practise his drum rolls on an arrangement of books and empty take-out boxes placed in a corner of his room. Charlie read comics and worked on crossword puzzles from the local newspaper.

On Wednesday night we all got into the booze a little heavy and around eleven the desk clerk knocked on our door and politely asked us to "Please stop having such a good time!"

By Thursday we were itching to play and well rested.

We had already cased out the Community Centre where we were going to play, so in the afternoon we arrived to set up the gear and do a sound check. It was great that there wasn't a cadre of people hanging around. We managed to get set up and out of there by six o'clock and headed off to our favourite restaurant in town for some major protein for the night. At five to eight we strode into the building with devilish intent and much anticipation.

The night turned out to be spectacular from both sides of the stage; with us giving our all and the audience responding appreciably with manic devotion and unrestrained vocal support. It was as we always dreamed it would be. After two hours of music and two sweaty encores everyone was spent and the evening finally came to an end.

As we dismounted the stage there were five or six beautiful girls standing around waiting for us to sign autographs. They asked if we could go over to their place to party, but alas there was no possible way, as we had a four hundred mile drive ahead of us, starting in the early morning. The rest of the evening would be spent packing our gear and grabbing as much sleep as possible.

The realities of life on the road were beginning to sink in.

So, with four hundred miles ahead of us we left Sault St. Marie at 7 a.m. ready for whatever the world could possibly throw at us. We stocked up on water and snacks at a gas station and headed back to Thessalon. We figured we would have a good breakfast there that would last us until we got to Chapleau. Everything went according to plan until just after we left Thessalon.

The highway was very old. Old old! Pavement was much too pretty a word to describe what we were driving on. At some point Rob asked to sit up front with Charlie and after half an hour or so he declared that we hadn't yet been on a straight-of-way.

"Hey guys, I think we just finished five miles of double-white-line!"

Charlie piped up, "When was this fuckin' road built, anyway?"

So far we hadn't been able to manage more than fifty miles an hour.

John sat at the back of our little circle of amps with Roger to his left, just behind Charlie. Glynn and Bill and I were behind Rob in a sort of staggered line, sitting on the P.A. columns.

John reached into his duffle bag and removed a bottle of vodka. He offered it around.

"Somethin' to pass the time guys, looks like it's gonna be a shitty ride."

"No thanks, John," was the almost unanimous answer. Except for Roger, everyone passed.

Roger however was quite enthusiastic as he was severely allergic to boredom. He and John carried on oblivious to the road and our circumstances.

Presently the road straightened out ahead and Charlie whooped as he pushed the truck to sixty miles an hour. Off to the left through the trees we noticed a big beautiful river; a sign beside the road identified it as the Mississaugi. In places it had to be two or three hundred feet wide.

The road followed the river for quite a while and then turned north-east into a veritable wilderness. At this point it began to career ass over tea-kettle, one mammoth hill after another. It twisted and turned like a circus roller coaster, never revealing which direction it would take next. Charlie cursed as he looked for non-existent signs.

"Jesus, what kind of an ass-hole designed this fuck-up?"

It seemed like there was never going to be any relief from the situation.

And then suddenly we reached some kind of demarcation point. It felt as if we were on a plateau; the road straightened out and proceeded in a straight line through massive deciduous forests. The trees towered over us from both sides of the road and it felt like we were driving in a tunnel.

Rob was hooked, "Hey, this is cool man. It's like the 'Time Tunnel' or something." (The Time Tunnel with James Darren was one of our favourite T.V. shows).

I wasn't impressed. This was no sci-fi experience. It was real.

Up ahead we could see that the canopy of trees started to thin out. More blue sky was slowly becoming visible. In the back of the truck John was in obvious distress.

"Hey guys, I sort of feel queasy!"

Roger was not sympathetic. "Come on John, get it together. What's the matter, can't you hold your liquor?"

John looked ashen. "Uh, I think you guys better stop the truck!"

Charlie looked over at me and Huard.

"Yeah, O.K. pull over. Let's take a little break."

Charlie started to slow down but was having a hard time finding a place to stop. The shoulders of the road were overgrown and crumbling into non-existence at the edge of the spillways on each side of the pavement.

John lurched forward at that moment and moved toward the front of the truck. Just as Charlie applied the brakes to come to a complete stop, John gave the old heave-ho and spewed a huge stream of barf forward, towards Huard. Bill pushed off of my shoulder to avoid the ensuing shower and I went down, my left foot coming up to within six inches of Johns' purple face. I felt a sickening liquid warmth engulf my foot.

The smell was overpowering. Everyone evacuated the truck in a flash, mumbling every profanity known to man. Poor John was the last to stumble out onto the gravel, still retching and heaving with uncontrolled abandon.

I looked down at my foot and almost heaved myself at the sight of it. With steely determination I held my breath and reached down to remove my shoe and my barf-soaked sock. About five yards up the road there was a small culvert and a nice pool of swamp water. I could hear frogs croaking. I hobbled up to the embankment with one bare foot and slid down to the pool on my ass, dipping the offensive shoe and sock into the water; splashing them around for a good couple of minutes.

Charlie and Glynn appeared over my shoulder with an old t-shirt.

"Hey Dave, soak this, will ya? We gotta clean up the mess in the truck, it's disgusting!"

I soaked the shirt and handed it back to them. Meanwhile, back at the truck Roger was hunched over Charlie's seat pulling one of the sleeping bags that served as a cushion for our boney asses out onto the road. He picked it up and carried it over.

"Shit, man. Holy shit, what a stink!"

He lowered the offending corner of the bag into our little washing pool and rinsed off the brackish crud. Flies were descending on us now. Big bug-eyed house flies and huge blue-black, buzzing deer flies hovered over us and dive bombed our heads.

There was no escaping them. They were obviously attracted to such a wonderful smell, thinking they were going to get a scrumptious meal.

Charlie was freaked. He had opened all the windows and the rear doors of the truck in an effort to get rid of the stench. As he stood at the back of the truck he was being attacked by a mass of deer flies. His arms flailed around his head constantly, trying to keep the incessant dive-bombers at bay.

By this time John had sat down at the side of the road and was trying to regain his composure.

I walked back. "You O.K. John?"

"Yeah, my head's still spinning a bit. My stomach feels like it's turned inside-out." He forced a wry smile. "I sort of fucked up, eh Dave?"

"Hey man, it could have happened to anyone. How were we supposed to know that the road was gonna turn into a god-damned roller coaster!"

He looked up, "Thanks man."

After half an hour of clean up and much discussion about the dangers of drinking on the road, we trundled back into the "Blue Goose" and headed down the highway none the worse for wear, with my one tortured sock tied to the radio antenna. John curled up in a ball and went to sleep almost immediately. It was a little over an hour later that we pulled into Chapleau.

The main drag in Chapleau was the highway and it appeared that there wasn't anything else in the way of streets; just one major road that dissected the town, right down the middle. At this spot was the one general store-cum-gas station-cum restaurant and obvious general meeting place for all the town residents.

We were so happy to get out of the "Blue Goose" and smell the unmistakeable odour of hamburgers grilling on an open flame!

As we approached the counter the lady who was flipping the burgers turned to greet us.

"You boys look hungry. What'll it be?"

She was met by a barrage of orders for anything on the menu that spelled grease and comfort. Cheeseburgers, fries and onion rings. Cokes, coffee and cigarettes.

We pulled out of there, gas-tank-full and roundly pleased to be devouring the best burgers north of Toronto. As we had walked out the door the lady's husband had filled us in on the state of the road ahead. It seems that there was going to be sixty miles of gravel in the mix. Not totally new gravel, mind you, but the hard-packed stuff that would play havoc with the paint on a new car.

Charlie was ready for anything, but gravel was a real piss-off. This was going to slow us down for sure and there wasn't much we could do about it. After about two and half hours we finally arrived at Timmins. Everyone breathed a sigh of relief. From here on in it was clear sailing, figuratively speaking.

In the end we took approximately the same time to get to Kapuskasing as we would have if we'd gone through North Bay, but we still saved a lot of money on gas.

The Kapuskasing gig was a Friday-nighter at a high-school gym; a huge cavernous space that would be impossible to get a good sound in. When we arrived at the school there were a bunch of student volunteers carrying risers into the gym for the makeshift stage. When Huard saw the size of the joint he had a flash. He approached the teacher who was monitoring the student volunteers and suggested moving the risers over to one corner. By putting the risers diagonally across the corner we ended up with a wider stage than we otherwise would have, plus we got a nice little storage space in the back corner to store all of our excess baggage. As soon as we set up the gear we were eager to do a sound check to see how the sound would be affected by Huard's brilliant idea.

As it turned out it was fantastic, a vast improvement over the typical gymnasium fiasco of sound produced by such concrete caverns. Somehow being in the corner cancelled out some of the reflected sounds and eliminated the overlapping slap-back that we normally encountered in such situations.

The final test was that night at the show and it was a resounding success. With the gym full of sweaty dancing kids the sound was dispersed even more evenly and the slap-back effect was virtually eliminated. We congratulated Huard and hailed him as our resident genius.

The kids were definitely alright. Every song was met with unrestrained applause and gratitude. Dancers gyrated with remarkable precision and all of the total music freaks (mostly male) crowded the front of the stage for a better view.

They were certainly our crowd and most of the tunes that they called out for seemed to be in our repertoire. When we did "Gloria" and "Here Comes The Night" they went bananas. By the time we finished up with our double whammy of "Get Off Of My Cloud" and "I'm A Man" we had them in our pockets.

We promised them we'd be back soon and the night ended with a ten minute encore of "2120 South Michigan Avenue".

We felt blessed.

After pack-up and a stop-over at a local burger joint for some fries and drinks, we retired to our motel. Huard called a meeting in his room at which we all decided to hit the road early. Everyone was determined to get back home as quickly as possible. We phoned the desk clerk and asked for a 6 a.m. wake-up call.

By seven we were on the road.

As we left town there was a mist over the highway and patches of fog hung in the air like drifting cirrus clouds over the low-lying swampy lands adjacent to the roadway. We settled in for the long ride home.

Charlie was in a great mood and seemed to be in harmony with the road. We tuned in the local station on our little fuzz-box radio and grooved along with the sounds of The Kinks and The Blues Magoos as we sped merrily down Highway 11 towards North Bay. Charlie was managing to keep the speed up over sixty so that we might have a hope of getting back to T.O. by night-fall.

Every now and then we would descend a small hill into a river valley or swamp and become engulfed in a misty swirling fog that danced a few feet off of the pavement, obscuring our vision. As we descended yet another of these small inclines we were rudely shaken about in the little "Blue Goose" by a succession of frost heaves on the road which sent luggage flying about in all directions and caused Charlie to brake hard, cursing under his breath.

"Jesus, they must have had some kinda winter up here! You'd think they would have done something about this situation by now."

Everyone muttered agreement as they picked up duffle bags and clothing from the floor.

Huard spoke up, "Better slow down for a while, Charlie."

Charlie complied.

We carried on with great care for the next sixty or seventy miles and then got back into a nice groove that carried us past Cochrane and Pourquois Junction. Just as we passed Val Gagne we hit the big one. As we came out of a long arcing curve that changed up to a nice even straightaway, we hit three consecutive frost heaves that seemed to each push us in different directions. Charlie braked hard and steered us against the direction that the road pushed us, only to be thrown once more off-line by the next hump. The result of three humps in a row was that after hitting the last one we were thrown into the opposite lane of oncoming traffic. There was a car heading right for us about a hundred feet away. They had obviously seen what was happening and had started to slow down. At the last possible second the driver turned hard right, as did Charlie. We skipped back across our own lane and slid off the right shoulder of the road with the brakes locked solidly. Everything seemed to be in slow motion as we slid out of control and hit a barrier pole at about five miles an hour.

The impact was minimal but it psychically knocked the piss out of everybody, nonetheless.

When the dust settled everyone jumped out of the truck; Huard and I quickly ran around to the back to check the other side of the highway for the other car. They had met with the same fate. Their car had stopped just as they took out the first in a long line of barrier poles. The hood of the car had sprung open and steam was pouring out from under the hood. We crossed the highway and went to see what shape they were in.

There was an older couple in the front seat, both shaken but otherwise O.K. In the back a younger couple were screaming at us in French, holding on to a baby. I couldn't understand anything they were saying, but there was no blood and no broken glass, and everyone was conscious.

"Bill, we gotta call the cops," I barely got the words out.

"Yeah, Dave. Uh, I'll be right back," He started sprinting for a small frame house that was a couple of hundred yards up the road.

In less than ten minutes the OPP were pulling up behind the steaming car in the north-bound lane. Bill had just made it back at this point and spoke to the officer as he got out of the cop-car.

The scene was one of utter confusion and mild disbelief. Just half an hour before we had been confidently cruising along, headed for our triumphant return home.

The officers started taking statements with the people in the other car and then moved over to our side of the road. We were informed that everyone in the other vehicle was O.K. but that their car was in need of some major repairs, which we were going to be responsible for. The officers took Charlie to their cruiser and interviewed him about the circumstances of the event that led us to lose control.

Huard and I decided to check out the truck for damage and found a badly dented front bumper and a hole in the radiator that had been caused by a motor mount breaking, allowing the radiator fan to come forward and pierce a hole in the rad. We weren't going to be resuming our journey for a while.

The officer approached Huard and informed him that, unfortunately Mr. King's licence had expired and that he would not be able to drive the truck home.

Roger had been listening and hit the roof. He was livid. He strode over to Charlie and got right up in his face.

"What the fuck! You ass-hole! How could you be so stupid?" Roger wasn't a pretty sight when he was upset. Huard went up to him and put a hand on his shoulder.

"Save it for later, Roge', it's not the time."

We asked the officers the location of the closest garage where we could get the truck fixed and were directed to a small shop on the highway just north of Matheson. It was only two miles away.

After all of the police reports had been completed and the other car had been towed away, Huard and I approached the family with the baby as they waited by the side of the road to be picked up by friends. We apologized profusely and vowed to take care of their repair bills. They spoke a little bit of English and pointed back at the undulating pavement that had played havoc with the "Blue Goose". They basically said that it could have happened to anyone.

We were so lucky, and it was starting to sink in, just how lucky we had been.

After removing the rad-cap from the radiator and adding some water to the rad we were able to make it into the little shop up the road where an older gruff looking mechanic did us the great favour of soldering the tear in one of our radiator tubes and chaining down our broken motor mount so that we could make it back to Toronto. The road was revealing itself to be a learning experience.

Roger drove us home.

CHAPTER 9

CREATION

It took a while to get back to normal after the mini-northern tour. The success at the gigs was tempered by the looming cost of repairs to the other car that had been involved in the accident. Since we only had minimal insurance on the truck; and since Charlie had been driving with an expired licence, we were totally on the hook for whatever the final bill turned out to be.

Though the scenario was depressing we forged ahead with rehearsals, losing ourselves in the work. There was no better cure for the blues for any of us; we just got lost in playing. Rehearsals were therapy. They were our escape from all things earthly. Sometimes we rehearsed for four or five hours straight, jamming until the wee hours, 'til there wasn't an iota of energy left in our skinny frames.

One night in May, after one of these marathon outings, Roger and I were the only two left in the building and I asked him to reprise the three chord stomper that was his personal calling card. He obliged wholeheartedly, putting everything into it, in an effort to make it seem like a real performance. And that's when it finally clicked.

Something in the way he attacked it that night triggered my subconscious and lyrics just tumbled out of my mouth in a continuous rush.

I'm here baby, I'm sad. You're drivin' me insane. You're drivin' me mad, Yeah, you rattle on my brain. I happened to mention what you said last night. You paid no attention, You just dropped out of sight. Baby, you know I need, Nothin'.

When I got to the point where I sang "Nothin'", we had reached an impasse. I just looked at Roger and said, "That's it Roge'; the turning point, we need some accents or something. That's where there has to be another hook; an instrumental one."

Roger looked at me quite seriously, with a gleam in his eye. "You mean like this?", and he hit two descending chords with great emphasis. He was being facetious but I just got excited and said, "Yeah! Yeah! That's it. Now mix it up - speed it up!" And then he did it, just the way that I asked; and the whole chorus of the tune came together in one fell swoop. We looked at each other in amazement and grinned.

We stayed for another half hour and finished the rest of the lyrics and arrangement for the tune. Tomorrow the rest of the guys were going to get a little surprise.

The next day at rehearsal was the litmus test. If it came together there, we would finally be on that same road that all our heroes walked. We had to have something that identified us. A signature song.

The first time we ran through it we just knew.

Glynn's thumping counterpoint to Rogers' rude and raunchy looseness was magical. John, at this time was just getting used to his new Gibson Bass and utilized it to come up with a rolling cyclical bass line that was a classic from the get go. When it came time for Rogers' solo in the middle eight, he nailed it with a classic patented Roger Mayne solo that cried out to be heard. We couldn't wait to spring this on the crowd at Charlie Brown's.

Sure enough, the reaction at Charlie's that weekend was devastating. When we announced that we were going to do our own tune there was a hush.

People didn't know what to expect. But within a few bars of the opening chords the audience was whistling and clapping as if the Maple Leafs had just won the Stanley Cup! When we finished the tune the din carried on for a good five minutes. When the set ended fans came to the stage asking us when we were going to record it. They sort of caught us off guard. We answered with vague promises and told them to keep coming to the gigs for more new tunes; that more information would be forthcoming.

That evening as we left Charlie's Roger took me aside and said he was going to see his bank manager the following week. He had some money put away, and he was going to look into how much he could borrow; with the idea of recording our first single ourselves. Huard was pumped at the prospect and said he would phone all the major studios in town and get some quotes on recording rates. I went home on cloud nine.

When I got back to my room I dug out a new single that I had bought at Sam The Record Man, that day. It was a version of "I Can Tell" and "I Wish You Would" by John Hammond, on the Red Bird label. It featured Robbie Robertson on lead guitar and Bill Wyman on bass. I threw it on my little "Sea-Breeze" player and sang along for the next half hour, learning the lyrics for the next rehearsal. Maybe one of these tunes could be the flipside.

After Roger got confirmation from the bank the following week, things moved quickly toward a recording date. Huard had phoned all the studios and we decided on Hallmark Sound which was the studio that Jack London and The Sparrows and David Clayton Thomas used. Their rates were reasonable and they said they would give us a slight discount if we were willing to use an apprentice engineer. Sounded good to us: we were novices, too.

The recording date was the afternoon of June 6th, the day after my twentieth birthday. I was convinced that there was something fatalistic in such a coincidence. My first day as a twenty year old. It was a good omen.

We had almost two weeks to get our shit hooked and be prepared. We rehearsed "Nothin'" until we could play it inside out and backwards, and then worked on "I Can Tell" which we had chosen to be the flipside. It was somehow fitting that we were going to be doing a Bo Diddley tune. He was our mentor and our main inspiration.

At Charlie Brown's for the next two week-ends we polished the two songs, playing them both in each set. People loved "Nothin'" so much that they called out for it as an encore every night. My new-found friend Ernie Pope, who helped us on occasion to set up the gear at Charlie's was totally awestruck by the tune and seemed to have memorized all of the lyrics, so that as I sang them, he was lip-synching them directly across from me in the first row of tables!

Roger had to take a half-day off of work to do the session. His work at the CBC was boring and not too inspiring, but paid well and his boss was understanding when it came to the creative side of things. He had given him a one week holiday to do our little mini-tour and now he gave him the afternoon off for the session and wished him well.

The rest of us all met outside the studio on Sumach Street and waited for Roger to show up after he got off work. He arrived right on time and we all strode in through the front doors at one o'clock. We met with the studio manager who introduced us to the young apprentice engineer, Terry Vollum. Terry had been in Glynn's class at Cedarbrae Collegiate along with Carole Pope.

He was a skinny rake in a white permanent-press shirt and black jeans. He told us that he had been working there for about six months and was excited to finally have his very own session.

Roger questioned him right up front. "Have you ever had any Rock 'n Roll experience?"

"Uh, yeah. In fact I've been working on all the audio recording for A-Go-Go'66 for CTV Television and I've done some demo work for a few bands as well."

Roger queried further, "Were they loud?"

Terry looked curious. "Yeah, but they had horns and stuff. I've never done a band with just straight guitars."

"Well we play loud, eh? I mean, like, loud!"

Terry was reassuring, "Hey don't worry, I can handle it."

We unloaded all of our gear and took it into the small studio off to the right of the entrance-way. It was about twenty feet wide and thirty feet long. All the walls were covered with white beaver-board pierced with quarter inch ventilation holes. At one end there was a special cubicle set up for the drums that was surrounded by three foot high baffles. Terry directed Rob to the back and then told John to set up his bass amp on whatever side of the drum kit he was most comfortable with.

Roger and Glynn set their amps on either side of Rob, as if we were playing an actual gig, and then Terry set me up at the opposite end of the room, facing everyone.

Once we were well on the way to being ready, he slipped upstairs to the control booth, telling us to just tune up and ease into playing. We could see him upstairs through a small rectangular window notched into the wall near the ceiling on Rogers' side of the room. It looked to me like he was getting the tape ready.

He came downstairs in a few minutes and started placing mikes on the amps and around and in front of the drums; constantly asking the guys questions about what kind of sound they wanted and what kind of tone they were going to use on their amps for the first tune.

Once Rob was all set up he then proceeded to position the baffles around the kit, so that eventually all that was visible of Rob was his head and shoulders. He gave us each a set of earphones and then headed for the booth. Once he was up there he told us to just jam something until he told us to stop. We did "I Can Tell" a few times around. Next time we heard him was through the phones.

"O.K. guys we're ready!"

We started with "Nothin'". After the first run through everyone requested head-phone adjustments so that they could hear themselves properly in the mix. Then it was a matter of a few more passes.

Terry called us through the phones, "Come on up and have a listen!" There was a slight hint of excitement in his voice. As we listened to the music play back it struck us as odd that there was no vocal.

"That's normal," Terry informed us. "You guys can hear Dave in the phones, but his voice isn't going to tape."

We listened intently. Terry had recorded every run-through of the tune.

"O.K., what do you like and what don't you like?"

Glynn spoke first. "Sounds a bit garbled or something."

Roger agreed. "Yeah, we gotta separate the two guitar sounds more."

Terry reiterated, "Yeah, it's a different thing recording. What makes it in a live situation doesn't always translate to tape. Maybe you guys should go down and work on getting a little more contrast between your two guitar sounds."

Rob was fidgeting in his chair. "The drums sound great, but I don't like what's happening with the third verse when the dynamics come down. It needs some kind of a fill or accent to set it apart from the other verses."

John was happy with his sound. Everyone was pumped by his playing. "Man. that Gibson is so-o-o-o round sounding!"

"Yeah John, just keep it steady like that and don't change a fuckin' thing!" We were all in agreement.

We went back down and plugged in.

Terry came through the phones as soon as we were ready, "O.K. just run through it a few more times. Everybody relax and I'll just record everything." On the third take we thought we had nailed it. Rob had played this little tom-tom flourish just after the third verse came in, and Roger had exceeded even his own expectations and created a signature guitar break that exemplified his own style, to a tee.

We scrambled upstairs to have a listen.

Terry's toes were tapping and the little floating pointers on the V.U. meters were jumping way into the red. Roger noticed the errant needles dancing into the red-zone and seemed satisfied. Glynn sat, arms crossed, concentration etched on his face. Rob smiled when the tom-tom hits flew by. Everyone had big wide grins on their faces.

"That's it! That's a keeper! Yeah man, straight up! Wow!" Heads were nodding in agreement. Huard was beaming.

I looked at Terry. "O.K. what's next?"

"Well we've got one track left for the vocals, so you and Glynn are going to have to do it together."

Glynn reminded Terry that he was just going to shadow me in harmony on the choruses.

"Yeah, well, we'll still give you your own mike. Let's get busy."

I was so hyped by the sound of the track that it only took a few run-throughs and we had a keeper vocal.

The next hour and a half we spent perfecting the mix. Roger was dead set against using too much compression on the tracks. We wanted a natural sound with natural dynamics, and just a touch of reverb. When we reached the point where it sounded like a "live" performance, Roger looked around at everyone for consensus. All smiles.

It was in the can.

"I Can Tell" only took about an hour over-all to record and mix. The sound was in the bag; all we were looking for was a great performance. In the end we went with a "live" vocal, direct to tape. We just weren't able to work ourselves into a great performance mode without it being a "real" performance. The first time we tried it totally "live" it just automatically came together. There was very little mixing necessary, we basically just let the tape run.

Now we had a record.

We thanked Terry profusely and then packed up the gear. As we left we congratulated each other and then we all posed the same question.

Where do we go from here?

That night at about eight o'clock I met Huard and Ken Porter at Webster's Restaurant for dinner. It was a special day, so we celebrated by having a nice meal with all the trimmings. A nice big Turkey plate with veggies and mashed potatoes and a huge helping of rice pudding for desert. About half way through our meal three rough-looking greasers walked in and took the table across the aisle from us. At first we paid them little attention but after a while they started making denigrating remarks about our hair and general appearance. They really were trying to instigate some kind of confrontation, but we kept to ourselves trying to mind our own business. Eventually though, we decided to get up and leave and cut the dessert and coffee short. As we passed their table Huard sarcastically remarked, "Thanks for the entertainment, assholes!"

We paid our bill and then scrambled across Avenue Road to Bernard Avenue and headed to 15 Admiral. We were barely twenty feet down Bernard when a bright-red

Mustang came screeching to a halt beside us and two of our restaurant buddies jumped out of the car and ran up to us on the sidewalk. The first guy creamed me immediately with a solid punch to the left side of my head, knocking me off my feet, sending my glasses flying. As I tried to get up, propped on one elbow, he kicked me in the face. I saw it coming just in time and moved my head back a bit and to one side, thus avoiding losing all my teeth.

Ken Porter ran straight out to Avenue Road and tried to wave down a taxi to call the cops. Huard stood like a statue and told the two thugs that they better get the fuck out of there right now, 'cause the cops would soon be arriving. They took his advice and hopped in the Mustang and sped away.

Huard dutifully wrote down their license number in his little black notebook and then helped me get up on my feet. Everything was woozy at first. It seemed like I was looking through a gauze curtain.

Porter returned to aid Bill in helping me get back across the street to Webster's. When the owner saw us come through the front door he quickly brought over some clean towels to help stop the bleeding. Huard handed me my glasses, which were still in one piece, but severely bent at the nose-bridge. I sat at the first table inside the door. Patrons in the place were very concerned and helpful.

Huard called the cops and they were there in ten minutes. He gave them the plate number and I gave them a detailed description of the brave warrior who had nailed me. They said I should go and get my mouth checked out, so Bill called a cab and we headed for Wellesley Hospital. After a half hour wait a nice young internist came in to my little cubicle and gave me three stitches to close the wound inside my mouth. My upper lip looked like a bratwurst sausage and my left cheek was stained with a yellow and blue bruise from my ear to the crease of my nose. Talk about suffering for your art!

Later that night as I was just beginning to get comfortable I got a phone call from the cops, saying that they had my tormentor in custody up at 53 Division at 75 Eglinton Ave. West. I went in to identify him, taking the subway at my own expense.

When I walked into the station I was met by a big burly cop with his sleeves rolled up as he typed reports at a desk behind the counter. He saw my face.

"Holy shit, he really popped you one, didn't he?"

"Yeah, it was a sucker punch and a kick in the head."

"Yeah, this guy's got a bit of a reputation. We've seen him before."

He gave me the prep-talk and then led me into the back where the holding cells were. When we reached the appropriate cell we stopped and he asked formally, "Mr. Bingham, do you see the man who assaulted you earlier this evening?" I looked at the

Creep-O sitting on the bunk in the cell and said, "Yeah, the one over there who thinks he's James Dean."

"O.K. Mr. Bingham, please come with me."

We went back out front and he informed me of court procedures and prospective court dates. At this point I balked and told him that because of the nature of my business I couldn't guarantee that I'd be available for testifying in court. I knew that our schedule was going to be heavy in July and August.

"So then you choose not to press charges?"

I hesitated for a second or two and then confirmed.

"O.K. then, we'll just have to impart to Mr. Savage (believe it or not, his name was Rod, or Rob Savage!); that we really don't appreciate him behaving in such a crass manner in our jurisdiction." He stood up behind his desk and motioned to two other officers who had just come in the rear door and they all disappeared into the area of the holding cells. Almost immediately there was the sound of cursing and then the sound of a metal door clanging. A raucous commotion ensued with much shouting and grunting and the sound of squeaking boots on cold marble floors.

Momentarily, the Sergeant reappeared in the rear hallway none the worse for wear, and came back over to his desk.

"O.K. Mr. Bingham, we've reached an agreement with Mr. Savage on how he should conduct himself in the future when he is in our area. Especially when he is in the area of The Village. I don't think we'll be seeing him around here in the near future. I think maybe you should get back home and get some ice on that lip of yours!"

I had just gained a new respect for the police. I thanked him profusely and reached out and shook his hand.

The grand total for the session came in at $330.50. Roger paid for it directly from his bank account. We had expected it to be a lot more, but they had given us a 10% discount because we had used an apprentice engineer. Fate had intervened to provide us with the perfect guy for the job. He was just as unschooled as we were, and willing to take a chance by going along with every request that we made in the studio, including disregarding the dreaded V.U. meters as they jumped repeatedly into the red-zone, signalling unwanted distortion.

Sound engineers around the world were learning to deal with recording at louder levels by disregarding the occasional spike on the stupid little red and black gauges. The result was that recordings, especially rock 'n roll recordings were becoming more realistic representations of the actual sound that the bands produced. Terry made that critical concession and in so doing, captured the true essence of The Ducklings' sound. And he had done the job in half of the time we had anticipated.

Now Huard was armed with some real ammunition for promoting the band. His first stop was The Bigland Agency and Ron Scribner. When Scribby heard the tape he flipped. He was ecstatic.

"Bill, you guys have got to get this out as soon as possible. I just got confirmation that The Stones are coming back to Maple Leaf Gardens at the end of June! We can get you on the bill on the strength of this record."

He sent Bill to meet with Tommy Graham from The Bigtown Boys who had just formed a partnership with a gentleman named Fred White. Together they were planning to start up an independent record label. Ron was sure that they would be interested in "Nothin'" as their premiere release and he arranged for Bill to meet with them the next day.

The following Wednesday at rehearsal the guys were totally shocked at the size of my lower lip and the jaundiced hue of my left cheek. Bill and I told the whole juicy story and everyone felt that justice had been served. My consolation came as Bill told everyone the good news. "Nothin'" was to be released in two weeks as the first single on the new Yorktown label. Tommy's partner Fred White had worked out a distribution deal with Capitol Records of Canada.

Huard announced that as we spoke the single was being prepared and mastered so that the first pressing would be finished in advance of The Rolling Stone concert on June 29th. Tommy and Fred White had agreed to release the record on the strength of a handshake, as everyone in the band was dead set against signing any kind of a contract. We had all heard stories of how bands had been screwed out of everything by signing contracts with unscrupulous managers and promoters. So we had forged a gentleman's agreement.

That afternoon Huard was off to Capitol Records to get a couple of acetates cut, so that we would have something to play for the promoters of The Stones concert and also for the guys at 1050 CHUM.

The acetate went to the promoters on the Friday after we recorded the song and the opening spot on the Stones Concert was confirmed by Scribner the morning of the following Monday.

It was hard to believe how fast things were moving.

All of a sudden our Wednesday night rehearsals became pep-rallies. Kids from the Village were camping outside of Charlie Brown's making it difficult for us to get any work done. They were hoping to hear any new tunes that we were learning and in the case of some of the girls, they were intent on meeting the guys. It was becoming clear that we were going to have to find a more private rehearsal space. Roger, Rob and Glynn suggested that it would be nice if it was in Scarborough, since everyone but me lived there. Besides, we were making enough money now that we could afford to get something a little bigger and less cramped. Huard got on it right away and started checking out places.

After the announcement on 1050 CHUM that we were going to be opening for The Stones, we decided to have a special night at Charlie Brown's to celebrate. The Saturday of the following week we invited musicians from all over the Village to drop by for the gig. All the treats and drinks would be on us, everyone just had to pay the regular admission.

We all brought our girlfriends and brothers and sisters. I invited Sylvia Ruffle, whom I had met all those months ago on the Eglinton bus to Scarborough. I was totally infatuated with her and thought she was the spitting image of Audrey Hepburn. It was only our third official date, although we had seen each other in the Village numerous times over the previous winter.

The party gig on the Saturday was an absolute smash. Members of Luke & The Apostles, Just Us, The Paupers, The Myna Birds and Mild and Bitter, all popped in at various times to wish us well. We told them about the single and that it would definitely be out before The Stones gig. The audience were pumped to get it, but we told them to just phone Sam The Record Man to see when it would be available.

After another sweaty, loud and intense night crammed onto the tiny stage at Charlie Brown's we all said good-night and I walked Sylvia to the Bay St. subway station. We kissed good-bye and then she disappeared behind the sliding doors of the train that would take her home.

I headed for the Village and sat at an outdoor table outside The Penny Farthing. I ordered a coffee and sat there watching the parade of revellers walking by on "Yorkville". It was just after 1 a.m. and the scene was still in full swing. Presently I heard a band start to play inside. They were playing free and loose. It was a loping blues jam, punctuated with chunky Jimmy Smith styled organ jabs and slippery Fender electric guitar fills. All of a sudden the night air warmed as a smooth velvety clear jazzy voice entered the fray with the most uninhibited scat singing that I had ever heard. It wasn't a real traditional scat like the stuff I'd heard on my mom's Ella Fitzgerald records, but a little more blues influenced and even more free-form than that. And then all of a sudden a harmonica fell into the mix.

It was hauntingly sweet and pleading, seamlessly fitting between the spaces and pauses of the other players; like another voice. I got up and moved. At this point I was hooked and just had to follow the music.

I slid in the side door of the "Farthing" and came out into the main room from the hallway where the wash-rooms were by the entrance to the kitchen. On stage was Hughie Sullivan, a master of the Hammond Organ, laying down a delicious groove for the other players with his feet moving unconsciously over the bass pedals. Off to one side Domenic Troiano added the fender Telecaster magic. Standing by the Hammond, Don Franks lent his mellifluous voice to the mix, and seated to one side of the stage was John Hammond Jr. playing the Harmonica.

I stood there transfixed for an indeterminate time. It was the bands goodnight jam session for the benefit of a lucky audience, who were no-doubt in a very appreciative mood.

I stood motionless until the jam ended and the musicians said their good-byes and then I headed back to my table and my cold coffee. I ordered another and then removed a harp from my jacket pocket and pulled a few notes in muffled silence.

I was still sitting there fifteen minutes later, practising licks, when John Hammond slid out the side door with his guitar case. He must have seen me or heard me moaning away quietly, because he walked right over to my table and set his guitar case down on the patio.

"It's a warm night. Were you there for the show?"

"Nah, I just made it in for the encore. I was playing down on Cumberland Street at Charlie Brown's for the night."

"Blues Band"?

"Sort of; R&B mostly. Stones, Chuck Berry, Otis, James Brown stuff, you know."

"And you're the harp guy, right?"

"Yeah, and the singer."

He pulled up a chair, turned it around and straddled it and motioned for one of the waitresses walking by to bring him a coffee.

"How long have you been playin'?"

"About four years," I was stretching it a little bit.

We carried on this sort of clipped conversation until the waitress brought his coffee, and then he came right out and asked me to give him a few riffs. I was pretty nervous but obliged. I pulled out my B-flat marine band and did a few Sonny Terry licks, (minus the hollers).

"Hey, for four years it sounds like you've been workin' at it, man."

I was feeling a bit more relaxed. "Yeah, I've got all your albums. My favourite is "Big City Blues". And the Redbird single, too. We just recorded a version of "I Can Tell" last week for the flip-side of our first single."

He sipped some coffee and looked at me inquisitively. "What's the name of your band?"

"The Ugly Ducklings."

He smiled, "Oh yeah, you guys are opening for The Stones in a couple of weeks."

"Yeah, it's a pretty big deal. Like we were in the right place at the right time."

He reached in his pocket and pulled out a few harps. "What key have you got, B-flat?"

"Yeah," I was wondering what he was up to.

He asked, "Do that Sonny Terry thing again?"

I wailed enthusiastically, although not as loudly as I would have on stage.

He copped the same licks almost to a tee, except with a depth of vibrato that was simply beyond my reach at that time. "You diggin' the difference?"

"Yeah man, how are you doin' that?"

He held the harp at one end by the tips of the index finger and thumb of his right hand. And then he pulled just one note. It was so sweet and had such a sensuous quaver in it, it blew me away.

"It's all in the mouth action, man. Just watch my neck and jaw."

He did it again and then motioned for me to give it a try.

I tried, but inadvertently copped a few adjacent notes.

John smiled and put his harp down on the table.

"You've got the feel man, just relax and get the action going by moving your tongue up towards the roof of your mouth, and then down again. And practise staying on the one note."

The next time I did it his smile broadened. "See? That's it. Can you hear it? It feels different too, when you're playing."

I was flabbergasted. It was such a simple thing, but I had never imagined that I should have to move my whole neck and jaw in such a convoluted way to achieve that sound. I had never been able to get that close to a real powerful vibrato before.

"Hey, thanks man!" I reached over and shook his hand.

He finished his coffee and then stood to leave. "Gotta get up to Rosedale where I'm stayin' tonight. Pleasure to meet you, man; and good luck at The Stones gig!"

We shook hands again, and then he was gone.

I pinched myself and then walked home on cloud ten, pulling just one note on my B-flat, all the way across Lowther Ave. and back up to 15 Admiral Rd.

CHAPTER 10

ASCENSION

Time passed very slowly over the next week and a half. The closer The Stones gig got, the farther away it felt. The excitement for Stones fans was palpable, but for us it was debilitating.

We rehearsed our asses off, never being satisfied that we were getting it right. Huard was always there to build us up and convince us of our invincibility.

The week before the show we learned that we would have twenty five minutes of stage-time and so we began to work on a set list of our best material.

The problem was that we only had one original song at this point, and we surely couldn't do any Stones' material. Glynn came up with the final plan.

"Why can't we do some of the covers that the Stones do? It's not like they own them!"

Roger added his two cents worth, "Yeah, I think we should start with 'Everybody Needs Somebody', just like we're doing a regular gig. Then we can do some Chuck Berry or Bo Diddely."

Then Rob added, "Yeah, and we've gotta end with 'I'm A Man', it's a killer finisher!"

After an hour or so we had the songs picked, and then it was just a matter of sequencing them to best effect. We decided to do 'Nothin'' just before "I'm A Man", and announce that it was finally in the stores.

Ad for The "STONES" Concert

The weekend before the show all of the regulars at Charlie Brown's came out for both nights and shouted out encouragement from the crowd. They were all going to be at The Gardens and make their presence felt. On Saturday night we got visits from a bunch of other musicians who were playing in Yorkville in the clubs. They slipped in to catch a few tunes when they were on break, and wished us well on their way out the door. It was strange, but a sense of community was starting to emerge among the musicians and fans who lived and played in our little musical nation-state of Yorkville. We were starting to feel that we belonged.

Eventually June 29th arrived and I awoke with a feeling of relief. Everything was in place. We had all gone out and bought great outfits to wear for the show and the guys had cleaned and polished their instruments to perfection. I had really binged in the clothing stores on Yonge Street and came home with a pair of madras seersucker pants and a dark floral shirt with epaulets. My biggest purchase however was a pair of white Clarke's slip-on brogues. My brother Dale joked that I looked like I was on the way to the golf course as soon as I put them on.

We all met at the rear doors of Maple Leaf Gardens on Wood Street at 6 p.m. Our new interim road manager Ken Porter had spiffed-up and showed up in brand new jeans and jeans-jacket. Huard was late. As we stood around waiting, Roger and Glynn were getting more and more pissed at Huard and grumbling incessantly under their breath. I was optimistic.

"Hey guys, there's probably a good reason, you know. This is, like, the most important gig we've ever played, right?"

They agreed half-heartedly.

Glynn asked tentatively, "Should we go inside? Who knows how long he's going to be?"

Just as John mouthed the words, "Don't worry," Bill slid around the corner from Church Street.

"Sorry guys, I just came from the 1050 CHUM building. They're going to play 'Nothin'' on The Battle Of The New Sounds - Tonight!"

Everyone was impressed. In a little less than an hour, at seven o'clock, "Nothin'" would be up against another new release on the famous 1050 CHUM. There was no way to be more democratic. Listeners would phone in their choice between the two contenders of the day and the winner would go on to the next night against another new release. And of course the irony of this happening on this night, right before we opened for the Stones, was inescapable.

Huard pushed open the rear entrance door beside the vehicle entrance and was immediately met by security. A big burly dude with a ducktail haircut stuck his head around the corner, checked us out and motioned for us to come on in. The place was a hive of activity. A wide concrete ramp led down to the stage area at the north end of the building. At the bottom of this ramp directly behind the stage risers was a cluster of amps and equipment that obviously belonged to The Stones. A large upright Vox amp stood right in the middle of the circle. In an odd way the configuration looked like a modern day rock 'n roll Stonehenge. The Vox amps were enormous and looked like huge monoliths spread out on the floor.

After a few consultations with the Gardens' staff Huard and Porter managed to bring the "Blue Goose" through the large rear doors and started unloading our gear. Glynn had rented a Fender Showman amp for the occasion and Roger was going to use a brand new Traynor prototype that rivalled the Vox amps in size and height. Rob by this time had acquired an almost complete set of beautiful Gretsch drums.

After off-loading our gear, Ken moved the "Blue Goose" outside to the parking lot and we proceeded to sit and stand around doing nothing. We couldn't place any of our stuff on stage until the Stones' roadies had all of their equipment set up. After a wait of about twenty minutes we got the go-ahead and set everything up a.s.a.p.

Now it was a matter of waiting for The Stones to show up.

There were quite a few press people hanging around, no doubt hoping to get a chance to talk to Mick and the boys. We were wondering what the chances were as well. We noticed that the security people had roped off an area over to the east of the main cargo doors. There were large black crates stacked there that we speculated, held all of the Stones guitars and stage accessories.

There were three other bands on the bill with The Stones who would be working their way to the west coast with them on the tour. Among these were The McCoys who had had a great hit with "Hang On Sloopy". Their guitarist Rick Derringer was hanging around backstage in a state of expectation, just as we were. When he saw us clustered in a circle in conversation he approached and asked with genuine interest, "Are you guys the Band from The Village?"

I answered, "Yeah, we just got this gig a couple of weeks ago. We lucked out! How many shows have you guys done with them?"

"This is the fifth. Montreal was really cool. French people have no inhibitions!"

He checked out Glynn who was wearing some nice maroon corduroy pants and a cream-coloured turtle neck. "You must get a lot of comments on how much you look like Brian Jones."

Glynn was nonchalant. "Yeah, I can't help it, it's just the way I was born."

"I heard about you guys from someone in New York City, some guy backstage said he saw you in Yorkville and was really impressed."

Glynn smiled, "Wow, word really gets around. Thanks man."

At this point a crunching and grinding sound filled the backstage area as the main cargo doors opened and a dirty, beige coloured paddy-wagon entered from Wood Street. The driver pulled the truck up to the backstage area and then got out of the truck and went to the back and opened the rear doors. Charlie and Bill were the first to jump out onto the grey concrete floor. They were all smiles and waved to the admiring fans and fellow musicians.

Next came Brian and Mick. Brian was decked out in rust coloured chords and a turtle necked polo shirt. He glanced our way and did a double-take when he saw Glynn standing outside of our little circle. He must have said something to Mick, as Mick turned and had a quick look at our little crowd as well.

Momentarily, Mick walked over to the back of the paddy wagon and peered inside. He then motioned to one of the drivers, to come to the rear of the truck. At this point a somewhat impaired Keith Richards appeared at the door. As he stepped from the truck to the floor he dragged the toe of one boot across the lip of the bumper and lurched forward ready to take flight. The driver who was just approaching, reached out and grabbed him staunchly by the left arm and steadied him on his feet.

Keith blurted out, "Thanks mate," and walked over to The Stones enclave.

I looked at Derringer and he confided, "He had a few on the flight; should be alright for the show, though."

We noticed two heavy looking dudes hanging around the Stone gathering, talking to a large heavy-set guy with dark hair who we believed was Ian Stewart. Derringer volunteered, "Nobody gets near the Stones unless they're invited. Those guys are brutal, and they do a good job."

Finally, the Stones and their entourage were whisked away to a dressing room somewhere in the bowels of The Gardens. Their equipment was set up within the hour and then the other bands were allowed to bring their gear to the stage. Ken and Huard managed to get the stuff all out there and plugged in, while Rob assembled his kit so that it could easily be moved forward between sets.

The stage was set, now came the pain of waiting. The anticipation was tangible. I was glad I was wearing a dark shirt, because I started to sweat like a pig. We all paced and sweated together as the time drew near for us to hit the stage. When it finally came we were pumped. We literally glided up onto the stage. There was an eagerness in our step and anxiety in our hearts, and we wouldn't have had it any other way.

As soon as Glynn plugged in he started the opening riff to "Everybody Needs Somebody To Love" and the crowd went nuts. The first twenty rows were salted with Ducks fans from The Village and beyond, and they roared their approval. I looked out into the crowd and spotted Bob Melbourne and Kevin Brown. I scanned the sea of faces and tried to connect with everyone that I recognised.

As each of the guys joined in with Glynn on the riff; they got a round of applause from the audience. It was just what we all needed. I could feel a wave of energy rush up from the base of my spine.

I yelled out, "Good evening Toronto!" *We're so glad to be here, and it's so good to be home! And we've got a message tonight for everybody that ever needed somebody to love! Someone to be with them all the time. Someone to hold them when they're up and to soothe them when they're down! You know if you've got someone like this you should be glad; 'cause sometimes you might get what you want, but you lose what you had!*

When I went into the lyrics of the song the audience joined in and sang along. *Everybody needs somebody, everybody needs somebody to love; Someone to hold, someone to kiss, someone to love at a moment like. this.* It pumped us up to hear them sing it. Glynn slid forward to the edge of the stage and punctuated the choruses with some grand windmill strumming on his beautiful Sunburst Gretsch. I was running back and forth between Roger and Glynn, exhorting the two of them on and turning to the audience to get them to join in on the choruses. Rob and John just sat back in the pocket and thumped out a delicious groove that held everything together seamlessly.

As that first tune ended we drifted through a haze of popping flash bulbs and raucous cheering and whistles into the opening bars of "Smokestack Lightning". I pulled my trusty Marine Band out of my right front pants-pocket and wailed plaintively into the massive Electro-Voice microphone from the Garden's P.A.

Whoops and whistles!

Roger joined in on my riffing and away we went. We were sailing along blissfully responding to the urgency of the crowd's energy. Somehow we became one solid instrument conjoined impeccably by the unreality of the moment. As I gazed around the stage, the Gardens' spotlights bathed everything and everyone in a misty soft-focused glow. We rolled through "Ain't Gonna Eat Out My Heart Anymore" and "Hey Mama Keep Your Big Mouth Shut" with daring and total precision. Roger wailed mercilessly on his cherry-red ES335 and Glynn pulled out all the stops, accenting every anticipation and punctuating every pause and push from John and Rob. The audience was ecstatic and so were we.

As soon as "Hey Mama" ended I announced that we were going to perform our own song. "It's our first record", I announced proudly, "and it just won the Battle Of The New Sounds on CHUM. It's called 'Nothin' folks!"

And away we went.

Right from the opening chords the audience was into it, and once they cottoned on to the lyrics of the chorus they started to sing along. When it ended and the crowd reacted I looked over to Roger and gave him a nod. Before the applause had died down we were already into the intro to "I'm A Man". I looked out into the crowd and saw one of our biggest fans, Earl "Scamp" Cunningham standing and screaming at the top of his lungs, "Ducks, Ducks, Ducks, Ducks, Ducks!" He knew precisely what was coming.

This was where we took it to the limit. Scamp and our fans knew what we were up to, but the rest of the Gardens' patrons were in for a treat. We had been listening to The Who and The Yardbirds for almost a year now, and we felt an obligation to go beyond what they had done. When we performed "I'm A Man" it was really like a "Performance Art" set-piece. It was never the same. We each had the freedom to go where we wanted to go and each member in turn, was supported by the rest of the band. The idea was to make what happened sound as if it were one voice – one mind. After the second turn-around Robin would set off into a solo that would easily satisfy the most drum-thirsty ears and also take the breath away from the most die-hard music freaks. It was the penultimate closer and it seemed that it never failed. We dusted it off one more time and sure enough the crowd responded. They were suitably impressed.

We had accomplished our goal!

For the next hour we watched as the other bands on the show, including "The Rogues" did their thing to mixed reactions from the crowd.

Of all the other back-up bands, the one that got the biggest reaction was, of course, The McCoys. As soon as they hit the intro to "Hang On Sloopy" the crowd roared its approval and immediately began to sing along. Their "live" sound was so much ballsier than their sound on record and they came across much heavier sounding than we expected. Rick Derringer was simply light years ahead of the sound that he had put down on wax.

On Stage At Maple Leaf Gardens June 29, 1966

The Standells got a rambunctious reaction to "Dirty Water" & The Syndicate Of Sound managed an admirable stab at some alternative R&B.

But what people really wanted was The Stones. And when the last backing band finished up a hush fell over the crowd. It was party time! The next few minutes couldn't pass fast enough.

After a wait of only ten or fifteen of those precious minutes The Stones took the stage to an unbelievable cacophony of human noise-making and vocal admiration. When they started playing we couldn't hear the vocals backstage. The sound of the band was remarkably tight and clear, although it sounded to me like they were having problems hearing each other through the wall of noise created by the thousands of screaming girls. The tempo of the tunes sped up and slowed down as Bill and Charlie struggled to hear each other. Brian's rhythm guitar came out loud and clear backstage and served to impress all the guitarists huddled directly behind, especially when they did "Little Red Rooster".

We couldn't see Mick very well. We saw only scattered glimpses of him between the amps and drums, as he dashed from one side of the stage to the other.

Keith was definitely the centre. The core. He set the pace and tone of every tune and seemed to lead the others on stage with his indomitable spirit. And all of them were constantly smiling. Smiling at the audience out front, at each other and also at the small cluster of musicians hanging backstage, observing from their privileged vantage-point.

It was all over so quickly that time seemed to have been compressed. We emerged reluctantly from an almost dream state, our ears buzzing with the echoes of ripping riffs and crashing cymbals. After the audience had left and the gardens' lights came on we all headed up onto the stage to retrieve our equipment. As Bill and Ken handed Rob's drums down from the platform to the backstage floor, I spied a small piece of cardboard taped to the head of Bill Wyman's huge Vox bass amp. I went over for a closer look. It turned out to be a complete set list for the Stones' show, with all of the keys for the tunes itemized neatly beside each title. I carefully removed the scotch tape and pocketed my own special souvenir of the show!

The next day we bought the Toronto newspapers to read the reviews of the show. Arthur Zeldin of The Toronto Star called us "seedy looking" and never said one word about our music, while John MacFarlane of The Globe and Mail grudgingly endorsed The Stones' performance, while glibly referring to our set as "Noise From The North End" (of the Gardens). His phoney intellectualizing and dismissive tone was an embarrassment to all of the musicians in the show and served to totally reinforce my disdain for critics.

I thought back to the previous night and wondered; was he really there? Or had he actually been sitting at home watching Andy Williams on TV, while receiving a report from some friendly accomplice who didn't mind enduring a two and a half hour Rock 'n Roll show at 120 decibels, in 95 degree heat?

"Nothin'" moved onto the CHUM Chart the very next week, starting off at number 39. Glynn and Rob and I went out to get some charts at Sam the Record Man and got cornered and had to sign autographs to get out of the store. It was a strange feeling, seeing our song right there on the Charts, along with The Beatles and The Stones, and Simon & Garfunkel, Wilson Pickett and Aretha Franklin. It was humbling and scary at the same time. For sure we were going to be getting some better gigs, just like Ron Scribner had said, but there was also the prospect of coming up with more original songs. The first time we saw Ron Scribner after the Stones Show he told us it was essential that we get another single out in the fall, right after the school year started.

To quote, he said, "You've got to throw another log on the fire, boys. You're hot now, and you're going to have to keep it that way!" We took it to heart and set out to materialize some new tunes as quickly as possible.

SHOW REVIEW by David Foley

Toronto: The Rolling Stones' Show at The Maple Leaf Gardens (June 29) was, to say the least, a wild one. Preceding the Stones, Canadian and American acts warmed up the audience. The show began with the Canadian group, The Ugly Ducklings. Within minutes after their entry the entire audience was raving (those who knew how). While I heard comments that the Ducklings could have been better, I think their act was really good. Their version of "I'm A Man", that old Yardbirds hit, was nothing short of fantastic. It was obvious that Torontonians supported this group. If the Ugly Ducklings represent Canadian talent, then we, as Canadians, really have something to shout about.

Of the American acts, I thought the Standells were the best. To their act, they added their own brand of humour, especially to that too well known tune "Gloria", already recorded by Them, Shadows of Knight, and the King Beezz. The McCoys sounded too much like the records they release.

As the temperature and the screaming rose astronomically, the minutes ticked by, bringing the Stones' fans (about 11,000 of them) closer to seeing their idols. After a few words from Bob McAdorey, and a speech by the police department, the great moment arrived. The Stones could be described as floating in a sea of screams. Surprisingly enough, one could hear The Stones, as they went through their act. For close to 45 minutes they entertained all, and well.

RPM Magazine Review

Stone's Ticket Stub

Upstairs @ "Charlie Brown's" Summer of '66

By the second week of July "Nothin'" had moved into the top thirty and Scribner got us a gig opening for "Gary Lewis And The Playboys" in Kitchener. Gary's style definitely wasn't our thing, but I had always been impressed by his songs. His number 1 tune, "This Diamond Ring" was pure pop magic. It sort of proved the point that a great song could transcend a mediocre singer and still break through.

We had done high school gigs in Kitchener before, so we had a small fan base there and we were expecting to do well. It was a Saturday night show, the prospects were quite good, and we were getting paid more money than ever before. We felt like we had arrived.

The drive down The King's Highway 401 to Kitchener was relaxed and leisurely. The sun shone and the band basked in a new glow of contentment. We sang and joked all the way there and picked each other's brains for song ideas for our next record. Robin and I had met at his apartment on St. George Street and started working on the lyrics to a brand new song while we waited to be picked up. The riff and the inspiration for the tune had come from Jimmy Reed who had been a major musical influence on us in high school.

I would hum the riff and then casually drop a line in a stream of consciousness fashion and then Rob would fill in the next line with whatever he could think up that would rhyme. Then we would evaluate whether the lines were cool enough or not. By the time the band pulled up out front in the "Blue Goose" we had two verses and we were well on the way to the third. It was called "10:30 Train" and was intended to be our most laid-back and lackadaisical tune. Rob said he could feel the drums splashing around in-between all of the spacey riffs. When we hummed it and sang the words for everybody they all got hyped.

As we pulled into Kitchener the third verse was finished and the song was safely in all of our memory banks, ready for next week's rehearsal.

We were to play at a community auditorium downtown so we stopped on the outskirts at a Harvey's and got some lunch before we headed to the auditorium to set up. When we pulled into the parking lot we saw a great big Bluebird bus with Gary Lewis and The Playboys written on the sides in gigantic letters. It was impressive.

Once inside we were introduced to the guys in the Playboys who were busy setting up their individual gear. Their roadies were also busy arranging the big P.A. speakers on each side of the stage.

The keyboard player rose from the floor where he was setting out some pedals and cords and reached out his hand to me.

"Hi, man. I'm Leon Russell. I'm sort of the musical director for Gary. What's your name?"

"Dave Bingham. Nice to meet you. I'm the singer for the Ducks."

"Hey man, we heard your tune on the radio comin' up from Detroit. It was on the Windsor station, man. Nice! And then when we switched over to the Kitchener station just west of town, it was on again. Lots of energy there, man! Who wrote it?"

"Oh, I wrote it with our lead guitarist, Roger. It's our first effort, we wanted something that would sort of be our signature song."

Leon looked me right in the eye and said, "Well, you got it then, man. Nobody's ever going to forget that riff.

Nice raw production too. Real rough and ready. Must'a busted a few VU meters recording it, I'd bet!"

"Yeah, we did. Thanks man. You wrote 'This Diamond Ring' didn't you?"

"Well no, but I did a hell of a lot of work on arranging it. It's not just the song but how you put it together, you know?" His voice had a really smooth southern drawl to it. "What you gotta do is just keep on writin' them, put'em on tape and then don't worry too much about it. Leastways that's how I figure it."

I thanked him for the encouragement and we both went back to setting up our gear. Both bands were set to go and had run through sound checks by six thirty. After that it was time for dinner and a rest.

Kitchener Show: Dave

Roger in black vest

We were back at the show by eight and hit the stage by eight thirty in front of a packed house. Glynn was decked out in his chords and polo shirt and I had on a nice white shirt with the sleeves rolled up and my brocaded vest that I'd found in Sault Ste. Marie. Roger stood tall in his grey mohair pants with a black leather vest over a red dress shirt. His cherry-red Gibson 335 reflected red and blue light back out into the audience. Might as well make them sweat! Rob and John wore sleeveless T-shirts in anticipation of the heat that no doubt would soon envelope the stage. It was eighty degrees Fahrenheit outside and bound to get hotter inside as the night progressed.

We rumbled through a fifty minute set with typical Ducks aplomb and whipped the crowd into a minor frenzy by the time we finished up with "I'm a Man". When we played "Nothin'" it almost shocked us to hear people singing along with the chorus.

We couldn't have asked for anything more.

OFFICIAL RADIO

	THIS WEEK	LAST WEEK	
1.	Cherry, Cherry	Neil Diamond—Bang	4
2.	Yellow Submarine/ Eleanor Rigby	The Beatles—Capitol	18
3.	Say I Am	Tommy James—Roulette	9
4.	You Gotta Have Love†	Robbie Lane—Capitol	13
5.	Sunshine Superman	Donovan—Epic	25
6.	How Sweet It Is	Jr. Walker & The All Stars—Tamla	12
7.	Nothin'†	The Ugly Ducklings—Yorktown	1
8.	Sunny Afternoon	The Kinks—Pye	18
9.	Bus Stop	The Hollies—Capitol	2
10.	Sugar And Spice	The Cryan Shames—Barry	19

*Chart for **CHSJ**, St. John's, New Brunswick. "Nothin'"*

is #7 & the previous week it had been #1

As we left the stage, Leon approached me and reached out his hand once again. "That was killer, man! You guys are somethin' else. Great show, great show!" He smiled a huge smile and then turned and headed to the opposite corner of the backstage area. The rest of the Playboys were waiting for Gary Lewis to come out of his dressing room. The roadies were all on stage busily rearranging the equipment and switching drum kits. Within ten minutes Gary and rest of the band were onstage and into the first song, which was of course "This Diamond Ring". They were tight and well-rehearsed and I was totally impressed with their professionalism. Leon sang harmonies and mesmerised me with his impeccable keyboards. It was strange, but all the way home that night, as we drove east on the 401, the melody of "This Diamond Ring" worm-holed its way end-lessly through my mind. Even when I tried to force it out by singing something else to myself, it would creep back in and start bouncing around once again, no matter what other tune I tried to substitute. It was something that had plagued me all of my life. I was a sucker for a great melody. Plain and simple.

The first week of August Huard informed us that "Nothin'" had reached #1 in The Maritimes. It was surreal, in a way. We never got to see an actual Chart or hear it announced on the station, but, Bill assured us, it really was for real! Years later I obtained a copy of a chart from the week that followed our Number 1 appearance.

Next up, was a gig at "The Club Kingsway" in the west end of Toronto with Sam The Sham and The Pharaohs. Scribner was totally confident in our abilities by this point and was determined to build our fan base within every musical community in Southern Ontario. "Sam" was one of our early heroes during high school. We had all heard the story of how he had first been a DJ and then decided he could make records as good as any of the artists he had played on the air. After the success of "Woolly Bully" he had arrived. "Little Red Riding Hood" was a great second effort and ultimately proved his point. He certainly wasn't a one-hit-wonder!

We had never seen him on T.V. so we had no idea of what to expect for a stage show. All we knew was that there was a lot of energy in his music, and we were pumped to see him perform "live".

We arrived a little late at The Club Kingsway and when we dragged our sorry asses in there, the Pharaohs were almost set up and about to do a run-through to check out the sound. Sam was really different looking. With his dark hair and Omar Sharif beard he played on his Arab look, but he was really more Spanish-Italian looking to me. He was gregarious and friendly.

His band was set up more like a large R&B outfit than a rock band. He had a sax player and two girl back-up singers, as well as the basic rhythm section, a guitar and his Hammond organ. When they ran through the sound check it was a very rich and full sound, with a tight R&B feel. It would be a good contrast for us.

When they were happy with their set-up they left the stage and motioned for us to do our thing. They were off to The Holiday Inn to have some food and get changed. Their drummer set his drums off to one side so that Rob could set up. The rest of us set up our amps in front of theirs and soon we were done.

Roger was always theorizing about how we were going to go over compared to whatever band we were playing with. As we set the guitars on stands and got ready to leave for dinner he asked, "Well, what do you think Dave? These guys are really different. I wonder how many fans we're gonna get out of this gig."

"Doesn't matter Roge'. We can move them just as well as "Sam". All we have to do is stick by our guns. It's just like any other gig."

Glynn added, "Yeah, they look a bit greasy, but I've got a feeling that they can really cook. I'll bet we're in for a real treat."

John was even more positive. "I'll bet that "Woolly Bully" sounds 10 times better than the record. This is definitely not the band that recorded it. These guys are hot."

Rob hit his bass drum hard, then crunched the bell on his ride cymbal and grabbed it with his left hand, cutting the ringing short. "Yeah, well no use worrying about it. We'll find out in a few hours."

We left the stage and headed for the local Harvey's.

When we came back at eight-thirty the place was jammed. We were a bit shocked. This was a new scene for us. The only other true R&B club we had played was the Trocadero, and that had been almost a year before. The crowd here was a mixture of R&B greaser types and all-out hippie stoners. We noticed a few fans from The Village as well as some old friends from Scarborough. Scotty Kessler and Dave Ellis walked over to our party as we headed for the dressing rooms at the left of the stage. We shook hands, all smiles and surprise. It was just what we needed to relax and get in the mood.

The owner of the club acted as MC and brought us to the stage with a big introduction about the success of our new record "Nothin'". The audience were already hot and sweaty and cheered as we came up to the stage. The lights at this place were great. We hadn't seen anything of them in the afternoon, but now they were shining on us with deep purple and emerald green focused-columns. We started off with "Everybody Needs Somebody" and the crowd immediately got into the spirit of things. And right then as we felt the positive vibes from the audience, we mysteriously moved into another one of the dream-states that had lately driven our playing. These were the times that we floated on a cloud and playing felt almost as good as having sex!

The night went by in a flash of heat and light and sound. At times the audience got really vocal and shouted out their approval. I looked over to stage left at one point and saw "Sam" and his sax player hanging in the dressing room doorway, taking in our show. He noticed me as I walked to the left of the stage, and smiled. I wailed a few more licks on the harp and then turned to Roger and Glynn and we started the climax that would end "I'm A Man" and bring our segment of the show to a close.

We left the stage in a state of total exhaustion and slipped into the dressing room where we peeled off our soaking wet shirts and dried ourselves off with cotton towels. Huard was positive as always. "Wow, man. You guys had so much energy. Scotty and Dave were boppin' like a couple of mad-cats. They couldn't believe it. They hadn't seen you play since the gig at Club Cedar!"

Everyone packed their guitars away and changed into dry shirts. Ken Porter had quickly packed Robs drums up and brought them into the dressing room, along with our two Shure 57s and the guitar amps. When everything was stacked in a corner of the dressing room we went out and joined Scotty and Dave to watch the Pharaohs' show.

It was just as we had surmised; and more than anyone would have imagined considering the tunes that "Sam" had made famous. This band was all heart and steeped in R&B, as was Sam. The show was more like an Otis

Redding performance than what one would have expected from him, given the novelty nature of his hits. It was very clear where his musical allegiances lay.

When the night was done the crowd went wild and gave him a very deserving encore.

We packed up the "Blue Goose" in short order and headed home to The Village, but just as we got to the foot of Spadina Rd. Huard realized that he had left his priceless black corduroy Beatle jacket in the dressing room. We turned around and booted it back to the Kingsway. When we arrived, the staff were just about to lock up and Huard just made it through the doors in time.

When he came back he had a surprise for us. Along with his jacket, which was draped over his left arm, he carried a large road case that was very worn and plastered with decals from dozens of cities across the U.S. and Canada. He heaved it up onto the right front seat and opened it up, revealing a beautiful "King" alto saxophone. It looked to me like it was an older model, maybe from the thirties or forties and probably worth a lot of money. It had obviously been left by accident.

So, suddenly we were faced with the question; what were we going to do?

Huard piped up, "Hey, they said they were staying at The Holiday Inn, right?"

Glynn grimaced, "Oh man, are we going to go all the way out there? That's going to make it a really late night."

"Well shit Glynn, what if it was you that accidentally left your Gretsch at a gig, wouldn't you want the finder to return it if they could?" I was being diplomatic and practical. "It's only going to be an extra hour or so, and we'll be back at Admiral Road."

Glynn conceded, "Yeah, what the hell."

Porter looked at Bill and popped the obvious question. "You think they might give us a reward or something? You know it is a beautiful instrument and it's probably worth a bundle. If it was mine I'd be shittin' bricks right now."

Bill added, "They might not even be aware that it's missing, yet. They might be just crashed out in their rooms, totally oblivious."

Ken turned west after we pulled out of the Kingsway parking lot and headed to The Holiday Inn. There was nothing else to do but try.

Twenty five minutes later we arrived at the hotel and Ken pulled up at the front entrance and parked in a little spot that was obviously reserved for taxis. Bill and I grabbed the sax and walked up to the front desk. We explained to the night clerk what the situation was and got the room numbers for "Sam's" party. When we finally approached the first door we heard the sounds of a TV blaring and lots of animated conversation.

Huard knocked on the door, quite loudly.

"Give them a bit of a scare," he grinned wickedly.

One of the band members approached the door and without opening it inquired, "Who's there?"

"It's a couple of the guy's from The Ducklings we've got something for you that you left behind at the club!"

The door opened slowly and a face peered around it and into the hallway. Immediately the eyes on the face opened wide and the door followed.

"Holy shit, that's my sax!"

Huard responded, "Yeah, it was shoved in the corner of the dressing room, with my black jacket laid on top of it. I guess someone missed it on their way out. We wouldn't have noticed it either, except that we forgot my jacket as well and had to go back for it!" He passed the sax through the door and waited for some kind of response.

What he got was a shock.

We heard a mumbled "Thanks, man" in a very low, diminutive voice as the door slowly closed and clicked shut. We stood there and looked at the door, and then at each other. Geez, that's it? What kind of freaks are these guys?

I was tired and stumped, "Let's go Bill, I'm beat."

"Yeah, me too."

When we got back to the truck, Ken and Rob and Glynn were rightfully pissed off at the sax player for not being a little bit more appreciative. He was probably just too tired. Or maybe too stoned. Or maybe just ignorant.

We would never know.

Our next big gig was at the Canadian National Exhibition grounds, in the "Food Building", on the CHUM Stage, opening for The Grassroots. This was going to be special, because Jungle Jay Nelson was going to be the MC for the show, and he was *thee* major radio personality in Toronto. We had spent our high school years listening to his show and we were really excited at the prospect of meeting him.

CHUM radio had a little pavilion set up on the exhibition grounds just as you entered at The Princess Gates off of Strachan Ave. They would broadcast "live" from this tiny little booth during the duration of the EX. On the day of our concert at the Food Building, Glynn and Rob and I slipped into the little cubicle for an interview with CHUM DJ Bob MacAdory, to promote the show. We told the story of our emergence in The Village and the recording of "Nothin'" and then Bob spun the disc and we left the booth to sign autographs and headed off to the Food Building.

The show with the Grassroots was memorable for the fun we had with Jungle Jay. Being around Jay was a laugh a minute and it made the gig something more than it otherwise would have been. The guys in The Grassroots were super friendly and really interested in learning about the Toronto scene. They peppered me with questions about David Clayton Thomas and The Shays and Ronnie Hawkins and The Hawks. They were impressed with the Canadian connections to The Buffalo Springfield and The Lovin' Spoonful and wanted to know more about the other Village bands like Luke & The Apostles and The Sparrows. I joked with their singer, Rob Grill that Canadian musicians were going to take over L.A. and he said that that wasn't really very likely, but it certainly looked to him like Canada was a hot-bed of musical talent.

Our set for the concert was only thirty-five minutes and it was completely different than the shows we had experienced up to that point. Since it took place in the Food Building, our audience was comprised of more than just the fans who had come to see the bands. Older ladies and gents and young kids were strolling around too, and stopped by to watch our set. The reactions were mixed. Little girls danced and pranced and pirouetted like whirling dervishes, while some of the older folks covered their ears with their hands, grimacing at the decibel level.

We endured and enjoyed.

As always we upped the ante when we ended with "I'm A Man", and over-all we judged that most folks enjoyed the show. We certainly did, and that was all that really mattered. And Jay was suitably impressed as well.

The next week "Nothin'" peaked at its highest position on the CHUM Chart at number 18. Life was oh-so-good!

CHAPTER 11
CELEBRATION

At the beginning of July, Huard was approached by a group of promoters who wanted to put on a big concert at Maple Leaf Gardens showcasing all of the best bands from Toronto. It was to be called The Toronto Sound Show and run all day and night in one orgasmic eleven-hour marathon. As soon as they approached us about it we said yes. The excitement created by the prospect of such a high profile show absolutely lifted everybody's spirits through-out the Toronto musical community.

Every Saturday night after gigs in The Village and on the Yonge Street Strip a small community of local musicians gathered at the Colonade Restaurant on Bloor Street West or at Webster's or The Mont Blanc on Avenue Road. And all through the summer the topic of conversation at the various tables would revolve around this one impending gig. Nothing like it had ever been attempted before and it was a huge risk for the promoters.

One Saturday after a hot and sweaty night at Boris's in The Village, Bill, Rob and Glynn and I met up with some of the guys from Luke & The Apostles and The Rogues at the Colonnade Restaurant. The discussion centered on how the media would react to The Toronto Sound Show. Our experience with John MacFarlane and his glib dismissal of the Ducks' performance at The Stones Concert in June had pissed off a lot of people in The Village. He hadn't even mentioned The Rogues. Ricky James of The Myna Birds overheard our conversation while sitting with a group of people directly behind us. He promptly stood up, walked over to our table, got everybody's attention and then loudly declared to everyone within earshot, that Mr. MacFarlane was a, quote, total asshole.

Most of us agreed, but Mike McKenna felt obliged to defend MacFarlane's verbose transgressions as a "jerk response".

He explained, "Not a knee-jerk response, eh Dave? But a response that's sort of what you would expect from a *real* jerk. And a real jerk in this case is someone who's in way over his head and has no knowledge or understanding of what's really going on with the music!"

Luke Gibson added, "Yeah, I hope they don't send him to write about this show, he's got such a negative attitude."

Huard looked around at everybody and countered, ""Doesn't really make any difference, does it? What matters is what gets out on the street. Word of mouth is way more powerful than a bunch of insincere crap from some twit-critic who's never even played a lick or wrote a tune in his life."

I responded, "I wonder if critics have a deep-down hidden desire to be disliked. They must be closet masochists or something."

Dom Troiano looked up from his plate of spaghetti, "Naw, they're just tryin' to get attention. An inferiority complex is a lot more likely. We should feel sorry for the guy!"

Eventually The Toronto Sound Show was announced on CHUM and ads promoting the show started appearing in The Toronto Star and The Telegram. The line-up was a who's who of the Toronto music scene. The ads presented the band-list in aquasi- alphabetical order;

Bobby Kris & The Imperials
The Bigtown Boys
Luke & The Apostles
The Tripp
The Secrets
Susan Taylor & The Paytons
The Rising Suns
The Ugly Ducklings
The Last Words
The Spastiks
The Paupers
Roy Kenner & The Associates
The Stitch In Tyme
Little Caesar and The Consuls

The show was set for September 24th, starting at noon and running until 11 o'clock. No one would know the order of the bands until the week before the show. Each band would have 40 minutes to do their thing, allowing for a ten to fifteen minute transition period to re-set the stage. We were told that the set positions were to be drawn by lottery, to make it fair. Nobody really believed that. It just didn't make sense from a logistics point of view, let alone a musical one. The show was going to have to have a flow. It wouldn't do to have really similar bands lumped together, playing one right after the other. We all took a wait and see attitude. In the end The Ducks got a prime slot in the evening at around eight. Lady Luck just seemed to be forever smiling down on us.

Before we could seriously start to prepare for the big show, we had some more important work to do. Huard showed up on a Wednesday night at Charlie's and announced that Fred White and Tommy Graham had secured us recording time in New York City at Stea-Phillips Studios, which was a primo four-track in Manhattan.

We were "Goin' To New York" to record our second single! Another dream come true, foreshadowed in the Jimmy Reed song that we had performed since we first arrived in The Village. We almost panicked at the thought. By this time we had learned our newest original tune, "10:30 Train"; but it was definitely a "B" side. We needed an "A" side; something fast. Something high energy.

Rob had been screwing around, lately, with a strange variation on the Bo Diddley beat and at the next rehearsal Roger and I got him to play it over and over again while the rest of the band flailed away in the back-ground, trying to come up with some semblance of an original chord progression to match the energy of Rob's playing. We had four days until we left for the recording session. There was no giving up, or turning back. One way or another we were going to come up with a song.

After about two hours of mindless jamming we got the groove for the verses happening and we were satisfied. We ended up doing a progression that Roger and I had written months before but never finished. Now we needed a chorus. We took part of something else we had been working on and sped it up. It fit beautifully. Over the next couple of hours I worked on getting the lyrics into a workable state. Once the idea of "She Ain't No Use To Me" slipped out of my subconscious, the rest of the words flowed magically. By four in the afternoon we were almost finished, but stymied by writers block.

Frustrated at coming up against a brick wall, we called a time out and took a break outside in the backyard of Charlie's. A bunch of our Village fans who had been hanging around outside listening to the rehearsal had heard our predicament and started yelling out lines that they thought would fill the void.

We were stuck on the lead-in to the choruses. At this point we had *She's like a door without the key, yeah she ain't no use to me!* and *She's like a sting without the bee.* We needed one more hook to link up to the title-line.

Suddenly, one of the guys leaning against the back fence shouted out "She's like a dog without the fleas!"

We all looked around at each other. That was it. A perfect fit.

It was Jerry, a huge Rolling Stones fan, a dedicated Ducks fan and a Charlie Brown's regular. I didn't know his last name, but I went over and thanked him profusely and then we all headed inside for a final run-through of the tune. (Later on in the eighties, Jerry opened "Stone's Place" on Queen Street West in Toronto. The Rolling

Stones ended up using it as their private hang-out while they rehearsed in Toronto for their tours, during the eighties and nineties).

We practised for another full day before we packed up the truck and headed for New York. Crossing the border was exciting, but driving to New York seemed to take an excruciatingly long time and was extremely boring until we got to Lake Champlain country. But even the beautiful landscapes around Lake Champlain paled when compared to Ontario.

The only truly interesting thing we noticed about New York was the radio. When I tried to dial up some music, a new station popped up every thirty-second of an inch as I slid across the radio dial. There were hundreds of stations. R&B, pop, top-forty, jazz, country, just about any kind of music you could think of, you could find it somewhere on the dial.

Huard was our navigator. He had the big "New York State" map spread out on the amplifiers and called out directions for Roger to follow. The real test came once we got into the city. After a few screw ups due to one-way streets we managed to find the right street and negotiate our way to Stea-Phillips Studios. We were an hour early, so we off-loaded our gear and took it up in the elevator to the studio. We left it there and went to grab a bite to eat. We came back invigorated and ready to go.

Huard went into the studio offices and came out with a cool lookin' dude who introduced himself as Eddie Youngblood. He was about twenty five or so, and had slightly longish hair and a very straight ahead manner. He gave instructions to everybody as to where to set up and within half an hour we were ready to roll.

As always we jammed a little bit on "2120 South Michigan Ave" by The Stones to loosen up and get in the mood. While we were thumpin' and twangin' Eddie was getting all the levels set for the drums and amps.

This time Huard was conscious of the clock, as this was going to be a little bit more expensive than the Hallmark session. After five or ten minutes of screwing around with 2120 we were pretty relaxed and Bill called the session to order.

He came on in our headsets, "O.K. guys let's get down to it. Which tune do you want to do first?"

Rob answered first, "I'd really like to do 'Ain't No Use' first; it's more straight ahead, I've gotta get rid of some of this tension."

Glynn was up for it, too. "Yeah, I'm sorta pumped, let's get the lead out."

Roger took charge. "O.K. let's do the intro a couple of times." He turned toward the glass partition and spoke to Eddie, "We've gotta get this really clean, eh, Eddie?"

Eddie came back, "Roger that, Roger."

Everyone got a chuckle out of that, and then Roge' started the count. "One, two three four, one two!" Everybody hit the first chord together and then everything promptly fell apart on the next downbeat. John was half a beat late.

"Well, that's gonna have to change!" Roger's voice jumped by an octave in one breath.

He called it again. Same result.

"Aw, shit! Come on, John."

Eddie cut through on the earphones, "Hey, if this is gonna be a problem, let's go for it once we get a good opening intro, O.K.?"

Everyone agreed and we started the process again. At the third or fourth try we got pretty close and everyone kept going. This time we got to the break in the middle and then folded. Eddie came on the phones, "Hey guys, everyone take a deep breath and we'll nail it on the next run-through, O.K.?"

"Yeah, uh-huh, you got it, sure, no problem," we were all in a positive mood.

I leaned into my mike, "Give 'er!"

Next try we nailed it. John muffed one grace note, but it wasn't anything to worry about and we just went for it. Roger and Glynn nailed the middle eight and we had the bed tracks in the can. The vocals followed in short order. I sailed right through all the verses, feeling really inspired and then Glynn and I did the harmony for the choruses. After that the two of us winged it on the end twelve by calling out some heys and yeahs. We headed into the control room to check out what we had.

Eddie was sure this was it and it was pretty easy to convince us. Other than the slight hesitation by John on that one grace note during the intro, there was no other obvious fault. It was in the can.

We decided to take a break and then come back for "10:30 Train". It was such a laid back vibe that we just had to slow down and get all those anticipated accents out of our heads. Glynn stayed behind in the studio and worked on getting a nice fuzz-tone sound on his amp. It was a super-important component of the tune. Roger got out his acoustic guitar and started tuning it up. I had brought a brand new Hohner Marine Band harmonica and I got it out and blew a few phrases.

Eddie, Bill and I planned out the track designations for the tune. Because we were going to add the acoustic guitar later, that meant that drums and bass would have to be on one track. And the two electric guitars would be on one track as well, leaving the third track for acoustic guitars and effects and the fourth for vocals and harp.

When we started the session Eddie's main thing was to get the balance between the bass and drums. Once we had that, we just moved right along. The rhythm of the track was infectious and put everybody in a great mood. Laying it down was pure joy. The simplicity of it let us relax and get into a delicious groove and we were so confident that we decided that Roger could add the acoustic guitar at the same time that I did the final vocal and harp. We only needed two tries to get it.

This was exactly what Eddie wanted. We were an hour and a half into the session and the tracks were minted. Now we could get into the mixing, which was always the most crucial part of any session.

Eddie played each of the tracks back for us a couple of times and told us to try and envision what we wanted them to sound like when they were coming through on a car radio system.

"That's where you really have to sound great, guys. If it sounds great on some puny little six inch car speaker, it's gonna sound way better on a big stereo set. And chances are that a lot of people are going to hear it first in their car!"

Huard's request was for a touch of reverb on Roger's guitar and on the drums as well.

We told Eddie to just go for it and we would feel our way through it. In the end we used much more reverb than we had at Hallmark when we did "Nothin'", and we got a much cleaner and clearer sound on all of the guitar tracks. "She Ain't No Use To Me" took about two hours to mix and "10:30 Train" zoomed by in an hour. We tested both of them out on a six inch oval speaker that Eddie had mounted on top of his mixing board. They both sounded great!

By eight thirty at night we were on the road again, heading out of the city with our next single in the can, feeling like we were sitting on top of the world. There was no way we were going to blow another hundred dollars, just to get a half decent night's sleep. We could sleep in the truck and take turns driving.

We waited until we were an hour north of the city and then stopped and had a rather large dinner, in celebration. Roger drove afterwards to give Huard a chance to catch some shut-eye. The plan was simple; we drive all night and go straight to Tommy Graham's place to drop off the tapes before we head home. Around 2 a.m. Huard took over from Roger, while everyone else snored and shifted aimlessly on the sleeping bags that were draped over all of our equipment. It wasn't a pleasant way to sleep but we could endure it. The pay-off was worth all the aggravation.

Just before 6 a.m. we were bypassing Buffalo, NY when the disk jockey on WKBW announced that they were going to play the brand new Beatles single right after the six o'clock news. I was awake keeping an eye on Bill who at this point was starting to bliss-out. I woke everyone up and clued them in.

The sun was just about to crawl over the long skinny cumulus clouds off to the east when the weather report ended and the opening bars to "Good Day Sunshine" blasted through the grill-cloth of our crummy little car radio. It was the perfect finishing touch to a remarkable journey. A summer anthem. We grooved with the song and sang along tentatively on the choruses as we pulled into the lineup at the Rainbow Bridge ready to cross back over the river to Ontario, and home. We wondered aloud how long it would be before we would get to hear our next little audio-gem come over the airwaves in much the same fashion.

We had the new single and it would come out right in the middle of summer, in time for the beginning of the school year. Perfect. Huard planned a rendezvous with Scribner for early the next week. It was time to up the ante.

The very next weekend we headed up north to Peterborough, Ontario. The Kawartha Lakes were quickly becoming an enclave for Ugly Ducklings fans, and Scribner would put us on just about any show that made its way there. The particular show that we headed to that weekend was at the Memorial Arena and featured one of the hottest Soul Singers of the day, Wilson Pickett. There were lots of cottagers up in lake country and no other big shows were planned for the civic weekend, so chances were good that this would be a sold-out gig!

The prospects of opening for Wilson were mind-altering. He had been one of our major inspirations since day one and he had been all over the charts for the last couple of years with one hit after another.

I asked Scribner why he picked us instead of Mandala or Roy Kenner and The Associates and he said, "Contrast, my friend. Contrast! You guys will simply make him shine and he will add so much authority to your reputation that your price will inevitably go up on the circuit. It's all a matter of integrity and perception."

He was a very clever businessman and I knew he was right, but I was into the gig for much more esoteric reasons. It would be an experience and an education; something that would inform us and stay with us. Just like opening for the Stones. Those kinds of experiences permeated your very being and made the pursuit of music more than a game. Connecting with other musicians was the ultimate goal and in my mind it justified my own musical existence. This was going to be a pleasure.

Since it was such a short distance to drive, we had decided to take two vehicles to the gig. So, Ken Porter and Bill and I set off in the van early on Saturday afternoon, to be followed later on by Roger and the rest of the guys in the Pontiac.

After an uneventful drive along the 401, and the tedious unloading of gear, plus the usual monotony of set-up, we were treated to the arrival of the headliners in a large Chevy panel truck and a forest green Buick station-wagon. It seemed like we were always the first ones on the scene as the opening act, and the headliners were usually more relaxed and casual about showing up. But evidently not in this case.

Two guys got out of the truck and walked up to the loading dock. The musicians, including Wilson got out of the station-wagon and stretched their legs as they walked around the parking lot checking out the venue. Huard and Ken introduced themselves to the two guys from the truck and told them that we were finished set-up and that the stage was all theirs. We intended to go get something to eat and then return. We asked if they would like us to get them some take-out but they declined with thanks and set about backing the truck up to the doors.

As we left we noticed a skinny, cool lookin` dude and a stocky, cherub lookin` dude leaning against the front fender of the Buick wagon having a really good laugh. Whatever it was that had them in stitches was totally unknown to the others and drew attention from their fellow musicians as well as us.

We wondered what instruments the two of them played and how they fit in with the band. They seemed to be off in their own little world having a really good time, oblivious to whatever else was going on around them.

Intrigued, we headed out on to Lansdowne Ave. looking for a burger joint. We were in need of heavy protein and calories. Nothing fancy. Just fuel.

We were sitting in Harvey's on Lansdowne, finishing our dinner when Roger and the rest of the guys pulled up in the Pontiac and walked into the restaurant.

Glynn approached first, "Hey, have you guys finished setting up already?"

"Yeah man, it's all ready to go. Wilson Pickett and his crew got there about forty minutes after we did." Huard wiped his lips and chin with a napkin and took a sip of coke.

John ran his hand through his hair, "Man, I'm so hungry I could eat a horse. Let's order. The sooner we're done, the sooner we can get there and relax. I want to be in a good mood for this show".

Rob agreed. "Yeah".

Roger asked bluntly, "Did you guys get any booze yet?"

John spoke up, "Hey Roge' we've still got the rest of that Black Label from last week. It's in the mike-cord box".

"Oh, O.K. Just wanted to make sure that we have somethin' to cut the tension with, eh?"

By now everyone was crowded into two cubicles across from each other and the new arrivals got busy placing their orders. For the next half hour the rest of our entourage consumed the standard Ugly Ducklings dinner of burgers and fries and then cleaned up and dutifully headed back to the Arena.

There were already fans hanging around outside by the time we arrived. As always, that was a good sign.

By show-time the joint was packed and the humidity was getting near ninety percent. It seemed that every time we played Peterborough we were subjected to a steam bath on stage.

In the dressing room we stripped down to bare essentials in order to endure the next hour or two in comfort. All summer long I had taken to wearing colorful T-shirts with the sleeves cut off. Tonight I accented an orange T-shirt with grey and white sear-sucker pants and white running shoes. Roger had given up on his black leather vest for the time being, and was into wearing plaid short-sleeves. Glynn, Rob and John liked the sleeveless look as well, so we appeared to have a unified sense of fashion as we hit the stage.

We started off with "Everybody Needs Somebody" to get everyone in the mood and then worked our way through a very complete Ducklings' repertoire; ending of course with our version of "I'm A Man", complete with Rob's killer drum solo.

As we worked our way through all the tunes we kept noticing members of Wilson's band, and occasionally Wilson himself, peering from behind the curtain of their dressing room, watching and listening with great interest. Especially the two guys that Ken and Bill and I had seen laughing hysterically in the parking lot. They seemed to find something interesting in almost every tune.

Once we had finished, the local DJ from CHEX Radio walked back out to centre stage to introduce Wilson Pickett. There was only a very short break between acts because of the fact that the two bands had set up side by side on the very large stage. As we arrived in the wings Huard came over and told us that Wilson's band wanted us to join them on-stage for an encore at the end of their set. We were stunned. We had hardly spoken to them.

They surely must have liked what they had heard in our set.

Wilson came running out onto the stage in typical "Soul Brother" fashion as his band extended the intro to "In The Midnight Hour", and then he tore through an incredible set, featuring all of his hits, including, to my delight, his newest one, "Ninety Nine And A Half". He was constantly moving around the stage and directing the band via hand signals, in order to control the dynamics of the show.

We were watching the guitarist and the drummer, as they were the two that we had noticed having such a great time in the parking lot. The cherub looking guy was the shorter of the two and was having a ball behind the drum kit. The sound of his drums was phenomenal and resonated through-out the arena. And the guitarist was a perfect foil for everything that the drummer did. He played his Stratocaster upside down and backwards and never stopped moving with the music. The two of them complimented each other's playing precisely and along with the bass player they created an incredible rhythm for Wilson's ragged R&B style. At one point in a slow ballad the guitarist inexplicably played his guitar solo over his head and behind his back and then pulled the guitar back down in front of his face, and played it with his teeth.

Pickett was furious and pointed his finger menacingly as he watched from centre stage. The drummer and guitarist looked at each other and smiled impish smiles as Wilson glared at them. It looked to us like some strange politics were going on.

Meanwhile we stood in awe of their showmanship, amazed by what we had just seen. It was one thing to pull off such a show-stopping feat; but to do it seamlessly without missing a note was astounding.

At the end of his set Wilson introduced his new single called "Land Of A Thousand Dances" and then to resounding applause he gracefully left the stage.

The audience started the old familiar stomp, stomp, stomp, and demanded an encore. Momentarily Wilson bounded back on stage, quickly grabbed the mike and shouted to the audience, "What do you all say we get the Ugly Ducklings back up here on stage to do the encore with us?"

The crowd went berserk as we all strode onto the stage.

Wilson shouted out, "Night Train, boys!", and away we went. Their bass player called out, "Key of B-flat", to us over the din, but Roger didn't hear it. He was just too far away. I grabbed my E-sharp harp and we tore it up for a good ten minutes with everyone getting a chance to solo, including the left-handed guitarist with the penchant for playing with his teeth, and our own fuzz drenched Roger-Ramjet on his big ES 335.

The sound of two drummers was really the knock-out punch, though. There was just no way to describe it. I swear you could feel the sound hit you in your chest and then just pick you up and carry you along with the beat. We were all in a dream.

But like all good dreams it came to an end and eventually the audience drifted off in a haze as we gathered our composure and set about tearing down the equipment.

This night was different, though. There was a feeling of total satisfaction. We had made a connection. We weren't up there tearing down the stuff with the same old mind set. We were contemplating. Slowly but surely we drifted over to the other side of the stage and introduced ourselves.

It turned out that the two jovial guys who were having so much fun all night were Buddy Miles, (the drummer) and Jimmy James, (the guitarist). Buddy and Rob got into a technical discussion on drum skins and gear and Rob asked him point blank how he got such a punchy sound out of his snare. Buddy grabbed his snare and turned it over to reveal four small holes burned through the bottom skin. There was one on each side of the snare about two inches in from the rim.

"I burned them with a cigarette. Let's the air out and helps to stop snare-rattle. It's really good for big rooms where the sound really reverberates because it shortens the decay". Rob made a mental note.

Jimmy James went over to Roger as he was stuffing his beautiful Cherry ES 335 into its case.

"Hey man, what was that stuff you were doin' in your solo? It was like, some kind of a modal thing, right?"

Roger was startled, he didn't know what a *mode* was.

"Don't know man, I just played whatever came into my head".

Jimmy smiled, put his right hand on Roger's shoulder, shook Roger's left hand with his left, and said in a soft and wispy voice, "Well it was good stuff, man. Nice. Sort of like a Middle Eastern thing mixed in with a blues kinda thing goin' on at the same time. Nice stuff, nice." He drifted away and went back to packing up his own gear.

Later on as we drove home it came out in conversation that Roger hadn't even been playing in B-flat. He'd never heard the key called out. He was playing in E-flat, and somehow with his temperament and his own style of fretting he had come up with something utterly original that fit into the music in a totally unique fashion and Jimmy had been suitably impressed. Joy will find a way!

It wasn't until almost a year later that we found out that Jimmy James was actually Jimi Hendrix. Roger never said a thing, but I'm sure he felt a sense of accomplishment.

The month of August was all about promoting the release of "She Ain't No Use To Me" as our second single. Scribner had us playing in all of the dance halls around the city and in the resort clubs up near Lake Simcoe and Muskoka. We especially loved playing The KEE To Bala. It had a great stage and an incredible "Live" sound due to the abundance of wood panelling in the hall. After a hectic month of gigs we took a day off on Labour Day to rest up for the big show at The Gardens.

Finally, the day of The Toronto Sound Show arrived, but because we had all seen the various bands that made up the show, none of us felt any need to be there for the whole she-bang.

The promoters had sent out show packages to each of the bands, with passes for each musician, roadie and manager to get into the backstage area. With these we could come and go as we pleased. Glynn and I met our girlfriends, Sylvia and Helen at about three in the afternoon; went shopping downtown for a bit, had some lunch and then walked over to the Gardens in time to catch Luke & The Apostles. The girls had tickets for the concert, as the promoters had decided not to allow band members to bring guests backstage. It was a concession that had to be made, just out of respect for (or fear of) the sheer numbers of musicians and related personnel that might end up backstage. So Sylvia and Helen entered off of

Carlton Street and Glynn and I went around to the Wood Street entrance.

Once inside we were blown away by the amount of equipment and people hanging around the backstage area. There were employees of the promoters organising the constant movement of band gear toward the stage. The show was being MC'd by Jungle Jay Nelson & Bob MacAdorey from CHUM, who were at this moment, both hanging around directly behind centre stage. We walked in and said hello in passing.

CHUM Chart, August '66

The Stitch In Tyme were onstage and just finishing up their set. Luke and The Apostles were up next and stood slightly off to one side of centre-stage. Their stage gear, at this point, was already on the stage directly behind The Stitch In Tyme's equipment. When The Stitch's set finished and they dismounted the stage, we all watched as the roadies did their thing. I timed the transition at twelve minutes, which included switching all of the normal gear, as well as moving Peter Jermyn's Hammond organ up to stage-right.

Immediately Bob MacAdorey was onstage for the introduction and brought The Apostles onstage to loud and intense applause. They started off with "Been Burnt" and had a third of the audience singing along, without having to encourage them in any way.

Watching Luke's moves was mesmerising. He was like a James Brown clone moving to a perfect soul beat. The degree of professionalism that the guys brought to their show was inspirational. The whole band worked as a unit and they were so tight that it almost sounded like you were listening to a recording. When Luke slowed things down and sang "Good Mornin' Little Schoolgirl" there were more than a few screams from over-emotional girls out front. I regarded Luke Gibson as one of the most soulful singers I had ever seen and at times when he sang, I literally felt the hair stand up on the back of my neck. Tonight was no exception. The whole band was on the mark and turned in an extraordinary performance.

In fact, it was a given that every band in the show was going to be in the pocket tonight and striving to out-shine everyone else. But it was still a friendly competition. The vibes were all harmony and light and we all knew that the night was just beginning.

After another short break a very special band graced the stage.

The Tripp really lived up to the image implied by their name; both musically and appearance-wise. We had seen them on a few occasions but never been able to peg them, musically or personally. Their front-man Jimmy Livingston was an enigma. His persona was totally unpretentious and comprised of the most startling and original personality.

His music came from some deep inner place and seemed to just flow through him like a river. Tonight he sang the most soulful and funky version of "Ninety Nine and A Half" that I had ever heard, and then turned around and sang the sweetest original song of the night, "Bird On A Wire".

The contrast through-out a Tripp performance was always like this and it all stemmed from the two sides of Jimmy. Demonic maniacal funk-master and sensitive shy unassuming troubadour. And the audience always ate it up. Because Jimmy was compelling; you couldn't take your eyes off of him. Onstage he was the most fascinating character you would ever see, and off-stage he was so humble and shy that his voice would barely be perceptible.

Their guitarist Stan Endersby was super funky and he and the other members of the band were really clued in to Jimmy's eccentricities. Somehow they managed to back him up with a rich musical tapestry that fit magically with Jimmy's strange brew.

Their forty minutes just flew by.

Before their set was finished Glynn and Rob and I joined Roger and John in the dressing room to the left of backstage and changed into our stage clothes. The two of them had arrived just before The Tripp hit the stage, but we had been too enthralled with Jimmy and Stan's performance to notice. Roger had bought some new grey glen-checked pants and a fluorescent orange shirt to wear with his black leather vest. I was wearing almost the same outfit that I'd worn for The Stones Concert, as were Glynn and Rob. But we had a special surprise up our sleeve for the crowd tonight. Glynn had brought two guitar cases along that were almost identical. When he opened the cases the two guitars looked remarkably similar. One of them was his favourite sunburst Gretsch Tennessean and the other was a Harmony Sunburst that was almost a clone of the Gretsch. The difference between the two was the cost. The harmony was only $75.00, one tenth the price of the Gretsch. Glynn smiled as he moved the Harmony in its case to the rear of stage-right, where his Fender Showman amp was waiting to be moved forward after The Tripp finished their set.

A roar engulfed The Gardens as Jimmy Livingston and The Tripp left the stage. It seemed to take a few minutes to die down and then the roadies and stage hands started doing their thing. As our equipment moved forward on the stage I started to feel the butterflies take their rightful place in my stomach. Rob was standing just off centre- stage playing rolls with his sticks on a road case, while Roger walked calmly about backstage playing the chords to "She Ain't No Use To Me". Finally, all of us huddled together around Rob and I ran over the set list aloud. I pulled out my "A" harp and we checked our tuning. Bob MacAdorey walked up the stairs at centre-stage and slipped through the gear and up to the front, under the lights.

"O.K. ladies and gentlemen. This next band needs little intro-Duck-tion, as their first single 'Nothin' is still on the Charts! Please welcome, The UGLY DUCKLINGS!"

As the whistles and screams and hollers filled our ears and hearts we raced out front and waved to the crowd. Glynn plugged in first and started right into the opening of "Everybody Needs Somebody", and then Roger joined in, glorious and scratchy. Then, Rob looked over at John, snapped the first downbeat on his snare and kicked off on his bass drum and we were away.

We were floating on waves of cheers as I went into the same preamble to the tune as I did every other night. Except that on this night instead of saying *We're so glad to be home*, I said, *We're so glad to be a part of the music of this city, Toronto!* The crowd screamed approval. We couldn't see the audience because of all the spotlights shining straight at us and the hundreds of flashbulbs exploding all around, but I waved at the first ten rows anyway. We knew the approximate area where the gang from the Village were seated and acknowledged them right away.

The din was unprecedented.

After "Everybody" ended it was on to "Hey Mama" and we could hear the Charlie Brown's people singing along somewhere out in those first ten rows. When we went into "Nothin'" we could hear even more voices joining in and it gave us a huge lift that pumped a few more calories into already drained bodies. We were diggin' it.

When the final chord of "Nothin'" died down I stepped forward to the mike. "Hey everybody, this is our new single that's just been released. It's called, "She Ain't No Use To Me!" Rob hit the opening shots on the toms as hard as he possibly could and we got right into the meat of it. The crowd were hanging on every chord and when Roger and Glynn went into the middle eight we could hear a surge of whistles and hollers!

We had decided that "Ain't Gonna Eat Out My Heart Anymore" was as close to a ballad as we were going to get for the night. When Glynn strummed the opening build-up on the first "A" chord the crowd went nuts. It was another of our Charlie Brown's favourites and always reaffirmed our faith in the power of rhythm and blues. After that it was a thrill to get into "Somebody Help Me".

We had just discovered Spencer Davis and Stevie Winwood in the spring and had added a couple of their tunes to our repertoire. Next, we kept things moving right along and punched it up with "Route 66" and "Down Home Girl". They were staples that we could play in our sleep and they gave us confidence, because we could literally nail them to the roof of the gardens.

When those two were done I made a small announcement to the audience, telling them that we were going to feature our drummer Rob in the final song of our set. Rob raised an arm and got a huge burst of applause. Meanwhile, Glynn made the switch surreptitiously, replacing his Gretsch with the Harmony clone.

Roger stomped on his Zonk Machine and screamed out the intro and soon we were riding the crest of "I'm A Man", imbued with a sense of pride and a determination to give the fans a little more than they had bargained for. We were going to pull out all the stops, this time. Over the preceding five months we had choreographed the whole song, into an eight minute example of Ugly Ducklings performance art. We knew every cue and crescendo, *over, under, sideways and down*. But tonight we had decided to push the envelope a little farther than ever before.

Rob's solo had the audience on its feet stomping and shouting themselves hoarse and when it ended with Rob's cue for the rest of the band to join in, Glynn went back to his Fender Showman and gave the amplifier cabinet a sudden jab with the headstock of his guitar. Loud piercing feedback screamed out of the speakers. Roger was still wailing away in a state of total bliss switching between his bass and treble pick-up, trying to make his 335 sound like it was crying.

In the midst of all of this I was wailing away on my brand new Hohner Marine Band doing reverse bends on the upper three notes, sounding like some kind of crazy screaming banshee.

When Rob cued the final crescendo leading to the end of the song, everybody ran back to their amps and started banging them with their guitars. John took his strap off over his head, turned his bass up-side down and stood it on its headstock on the stage twirling it around like a spinning top.

Roger

Glynn

As Rob cued the final shots Glynn slid his guitar off and over his shoulder and grabbed it by the neck, swinging it in a wide arc around stage left. He raised it above his head and as the last drum-shot echoed through-out the gardens, he brought it down on the stage with all his might and it disintegrated into a hundred pieces, feedback blaring from the speakers of his huge Showman Amplifier.

Roger held his 335 just in front of the speakers of his Traynor Mono-Block cabinet until a siren-like howl pierced stage-right causing some members of the crowd to quickly cup their hands over their ears. Rob immediately kicked his bass drum over and knocked his snare right off its' stand, along with his two large crash cymbals.

The audience went bananas! They were loving it, and roared their approval.

The guts of Glynn's guitar lay on the stage, just a couple of feet from his amp, moving spastically with the tension of the lower bass strings and the vibrations caused by the strange buzzing sound emanating from the Showman speakers. Rob arose and came forward from behind his drums and we stood in a line across the stage and took a bow in unison, ala; The Beatles.

I looked over at the guys, but couldn't hear anything they were saying; the noise from the crowd was just too loud and the feedback still reverberated mercilessly behind us until Huard or someone had the presence of mind to cut the power to the amplifiers. In the end we waved once more to the crowd and then turned and ran down the darkened stairway to the backstage area, mission accomplished!

As Roger always said, "Give 'em something to remember!"

CHAPTER 12

RESOLUTION

The reviews for the show were positive overall, but really didn't fit with the stature of the performances. It was so typical of the media in Canada; not one writer was willing to exert enough mental strength or will to really hype or promote any of our own bands directly. It was as if a collective inferiority complex smothered everyone in the media. They always looked outside of our borders for their real inspiration.

Musically, I couldn't stand playing things safe and it made me wonder where this attitude came from with all of our entertainment writers. Certainly most of the musicians in T.O. were willing to put themselves on the line; so what was it with the journalists? It seemed to me that it was time to start tooting our own horn and to really celebrate some of the remarkable artists within our own country. Why was it necessary for them to become successful on the international scene before we could acknowledge them right here at home? I was beginning to understand why Neil Young had left The Village and headed for L.A.

Now that the school year had begun and "She Ain't No Use To Me" was working its way up the CHUM Chart the band suddenly got very busy with high school gigs. Whatever un-booked nights were left over during any given week, we filled up with gigs at Charlie Brown's. Each of the guys in the band was now drawing over a hundred dollars a week. It seemed like we had really arrived.

By the middle of October we were really needing a change, or at least some kind of new challenge. Scribner called us in to his office to announce that he had booked us a package of three high profile gigs in Northern Ontario and Manitoba at the beginning of November and that when we returned we would be opening for The Beach Boys at The Gardens. Our reputation was growing far a-field and new opportunities were starting to present themselves. This was going to be an even bigger deal than our last mini-tour. Not bad for a little band from Scarborough who had played their first gig only eighteen months before!

In the meantime Ken Porter packed it in as our road manager and we had to find a replacement before the trip out west. We left it up to Huard this time, and he selected a scrawny kid from Scarborough who was one of the Village fans who hung out in the back yard at Charlie's when we rehearsed. His name was Howie Smith and he had a class "C" licence and a clean driving record and was very determined to get the job.

He was going to come to rehearsal on Wednesday to meet the band, so I arrived early and sat out front on the stairs waiting to make his acquaintance. I sat there trying to be inconspicuous playing my "A" harp rather plaintively and quietly and as I sat, I looked eastward towards Bay Street and watched the morning air shimmering as heat rose from the black pavement of Cumberland Street and dissipated into an overhead blanket of blue sky. In the distance I saw an older black man with a guitar case over his shoulder walking slowly towards me. He had been watching me as I played my harp and as he approached he doffed his hat and asked politely, "You want to play a little blues, son?"

"What kind of guitar you got in there?" I asked.

He un-slung it from his shoulder, opened the case and pulled out an old well-worn Martin guitar that looked as if it had been through a war, and then some. Then he sat down on the brick wall that encased the flower beds below the bay window and picked a few notes. He seemed to be right in tune.

He mumbled, "Key of "E", O.K?"

"Sure," I said.

And away we went. Three chords of the sweetest blues that I'd ever heard.

He was a bit like Jimmy Reed, but *way* smoother and real classy sounding. His voice was like butter. Sensual and pure. He smiled whenever I copped a few lines on the harp and flashed a glorious set of sparkling white teeth that could have lit up a street corner at 3 a.m. I didn't recognize the songs he sang.

We must have played for five or ten minutes before we finally stopped.

"What's your name, son?"

"Dave, Dave Bingham; what's yours?"

"Lonnie Johnson. I used to have my own club here in The Village, 'til it folded a couple of months ago. You play around here?"

"Yeah, right here at Charlie Brown's."

He held out his hand. "Pleased to make your acquaintance, Dave. You play some sweet harp. Maybe our paths will cross again sometime. You see me playin' anywhere in town, you drop by, O.K? Love to have you. You can get up and play with me, anytime."

We shook hands and then he packed up his axe, donned his hat and headed further on up the road.

Howie showed up before the rest of the guys and seemed very personable and relaxed. I told him about my experience with Lonnie Johnson, but he didn't really understand what I was trying to get across to him. For me, it had been a surreal experience and it was difficult to explain. We had heard his name before, so we made a pact to buy a Lonnie Johnson record, to hear what he sounded like on vinyl.

When the guys got there we all had a ball, as usual. Rehearsal went well as always, and Howie performed his duties dutifully and had the rest of us in stitches on more the one occasion. He had a very unique sense of humour that fit in perfectly with our warped sense of reality. Glynn seemed to appreciate his humour the most and they got along favourably right from the get-go.

As October came to an end we prepared for the coming expedition to Manitoba.

The first gig along the way was on a Wednesday in Fort William, so we figured it would be best to leave on the previous Sunday morning. That would give us three and a half days to get there, which was cutting us a lot of slack. After our experience on the road to Chapleau we thought it prudent to be prepared for the unexpected.

We took a couple of days off before we left, to spend some time with our girlfriends and families. Sylvia and I went out on a couple of dates, and I took her to meet my parents in Scarborough. The Saturday night before we left she stayed overnight at my crumby little room at 15 Admiral Road. Our relationship was starting to get serious. In fact, all the guys in the band, with the exception of Roger were now romantically involved.

On the Sunday of our departure we left at 9 a.m. with plans to keep going until we got to Fort William and Port Arthur. Howie and Huard took the first couple of shifts driving, and then Roger took over in the late afternoon. We had added some extra padding over the equipment to make the drive a bit more comfortable and Roger had replaced our crappy little six by nine speaker with a brand new one from Canadian Tire. Now we could pump up the volume on our favourite tunes with little or no distortion!

At about five o'clock we passed the infamous spot where we had had our little Charlie King miss-adventure. It was on Roger's shift. As it turned out, the posts and cables had all been repaired and there was no sign that there had ever been an accident there.

As darkness fell we made it to Kapuskasing and pulled into a Harvey's for some dinner. It was time for Howie to take his second shift. We loaded up with some extra take-out fries and stopped at a Becker's store for some pop and chocolate milk and then hit the road. As we left Kapuskasing Huard pointed out how black the sky was. There was no reflected light. The night sky was a blanket of billions of stars. What a difference from the city.

We hurried on into the blackness.

At about six in the morning we pulled into Hearst.

Just before we got to the main drag of the town, there was a large truck-stop on the left side of the highway. There were five eighteen-wheelers parked out front, so we figured the food had to be good. We pulled in and parked across from the big rigs. The sun was low in the sky and blinded us as we walked toward the restaurant. As Bill opened the door I saw a hand written sign taped to the inside of the glass partition beside the door. "No Dogs & No Firearms".

Once inside we saw that two of the four main breakfast nooks were taken. One was filled with four burly truckers and the other was occupied by a Canada Post letter carrier and friend. At a table against the window at the front sat a lone Native Canadian with long black hair pulled back into a ponytail, dressed in worn denim and dusty cowboy boots. He glanced our way as we walked in, and gave us a smile.

We must have been a sorry sight. All those hours cooped up in the "Blue Goose" made us look a bit wrinkled and sickly. Some of us were probably still trying to wake up when the waitress came and doled out the menus. We ordered hastily and waited with high anxiety for our food. When it came we dug into it with great enthusiasm and our conversation lapsed into a pause and chew, speak and chew, kind of rhythm. During one of these pauses I looked over at the truckers, across the room and heard a muffled laugh followed by, "Fuckin' hippie queers!"

I looked at Glynn, "Did he just say what I thought he said?"

"Yeah, ignorant bastards."

Glynn reached in his back jeans-pocket and pulled out a brand new shiny comb. He looked directly at the truckers' table and then stuffed the comb into his mouth so that the two ends of it pushed his cheeks out in a grotesque caricature-like display. He had a look of glee in his eyes.

One of the truckers responded with, "You can't even tell if that blond one is a fuckin' guy or a girl!"

Glynn was on a roll now. He removed the comb, took a couple of big spoonfuls of egg and sausage and a nice bite of toast and chewed it up loudly, smacking his lips and humming contentedly. Then he lifted his plate to his lips and peered over the edge of it at the truckers as he regurgitated the mouthful of food slowly back onto it. The truckers looked away in disgust. Then Glynn ate his food quickly and efficiently and pushed his plate to the centre of the table. He pulled a nice grapefruit out of his knapsack and proceeded to insert the whole thing into his mouth, closing his lips around it until his teeth were no longer visible. He looked right at the truckers and launched it out onto the table with one giant exhaled breath.

One of the truckers rose from their table and walked over towards us. Another one of his friends followed.

"You fuckin' fairy! Who do you think you are?"

Glynn wasn't freaked, "I'm just a regular guy trying to eat his breakfast in peace, that's all."

Roger and Bill slid out of their side of the cubicle and stood up. Two more truckers stood and approached our table. Howie started spazz-ing out, pursing his lips and blowing air out of his mouth like a blow-fish, while he vibrated in his seat like he was having an epileptic fit.

John stood up beside Roger and Huard, Uh, excuse me fellas, could I just squeeze by? I think I've gotta go to the men's room." No one moved. John was trapped. The truckers were staring at Glynn, and Glynn sat perfectly still, looking dead-straight ahead.

"Well, you fuckin' pretty little faggot, you want to go outside, and get some fresh air?"

The trucker's words trailed off slightly as he turned to face the man who had just placed a hand on his shoulder and pulled him around gently. It was the Native guy with the black pony tail and dusty cowboy boots. He stood just slightly off to one side of our newfound friends. He was about six-foot four and around two hundred and thirty pounds with a massive neck and broad shoulders that reminded me of Steve Reeves in the movie "Hercules Unchained".

He spoke with a calm and reserved voice, "You fellas wouldn't want to take unfair advantage of these nice city boys, now would you? Seems to me they were just minding their own business having somethin' to eat, when you guys started making rude comments and calling them names. Now, if I was in their shoes I would have been righteously offended."

The truckers seemed to shrink a bit in stature and reconsider their aims.

"Well I never seen such a bunch of pantywaists in my life. Did you see what he did?"

Our defender answered, "Oh yes, I did see what he did and it gave me a few laughs. Maybe you guys should lighten up a bit and live and let live."

Two of the truckers turned and headed back to their table. The big cheese and his buddy hesitated a few more seconds before they turned and followed.

Huard turned to our friend "Hercules" and spoke first, "Thanks for the help, eh?"

"No problem guys, where are you headed?|

"Winnipeg, eventually."

"Well, my advice is to maybe stop at some burger joints and family style places. These truck stops attract a whole different clientele than you're used to dealing with. Time sort of stands still around these parts if you know what I mean. You guys really stand out from the rest of the crowd. I think they feel like you're a bit of a threat."

Huard extended a hand, "Thanks again." Then he walked over to the cashier and paid our bill.

As we pulled out of the truck-stop parking lot I felt a strange kind of re-affirmation of the human spirit. But at the same time I wondered; just what was it about us that seemed to bring out the best and the worst in people?

We were heading west on Highway 17 with the sun chasing us from behind, when Howie started vibrating in his seat again, blew out his cheeks like Dizzy Gillespie and suddenly became a blow-fish. He gripped the steering wheel hard, as his lips pursed and released air spasmodically and a strange language of uni-syllabic words were ejected from his mouth in rapid-fire succession. "Pooh, new, pooten, oooh, pooh, new!" He looked around at the rest of us and started to laugh. "Jesus Glynn, where were you when God was handing out the common sense?"

Glynn shot back instantly, "Who said I was common?" He laughed mischievously.

The rest of us started to laugh too, and slowly the laughter built until we were all chuckling and vibrating at the same frequency. Huard reached out and turned on the radio and got nothing but static. He dialled the tuner quickly, searching for a nice strong station and landed on something totally prophetic. It was Napoleon Bonaparte the Third chanting "They're Coming To Take Me Away, Ha Ha, They're Coming To Take Me Away"! Someone truly was watching over us. Howie "Blow-fished" again and we all fell into fits of laughter as we desperately tried to sing along.

We rolled the windows down to breathe in the clean fresh air and take in the incredible beauty of the northern Ontario landscape. The fall colours were gorgeous and the air was impeccably clear. It was the first time that any of us had been this far north and it was both an education and a revelation. We were blessed; lady luck still seemed to be on our side.

Six hours later we reached the outskirts of Fort William, found a reasonable Motel and checked in for the night. The gig was a day away and it was time for some serious rest and relaxation. Showers, T.V., refreshments and a cozy bed were all that was on our minds; after three days in a tin can all we wanted was to feel human again.

The next day fit the same routine that we had been following all year.

Check out the town, shop, eat and then drive to the hall where the gig was happening, to set up our gear. The exception this time was the beauty of the town.

You couldn't escape the fact that this town was on Lake Superior. The lake was visible from so many vantage points it was inescapable. There were some unbelievable sights to be seen, as well, not the least of which was the "Sleeping Giant", a huge headland that jutted out into Lake Superior and resembled a sleeping giant lying on his side. And the people were super friendly. Eye contact wasn't going to get you into trouble.

The audience that night was frantic. You could tell that they weren't used to having bands from "away" that often. They were very vocal and boisterous, shouting out requests and whistling and hollering their approval. And when we played "Nothin'" we got a big surprise when they sang along on the choruses, while a small group of fledgling guitarists stood directly in front of the stage and played "air guitar" along with Roger when he did his solo. Ah, the power of radio! Roger looked over at us with a huge grin on his face as Glynn punched out the chords to the finale with robot-like precision.

We got a number of requests for a slow dance and instead of the standard response of doing "Time Is On My Side", I changed it up to "That's How Strong My Love Is" by Otis Redding. It was a little bit slower, more soulful and was always a favourite of the "grinders"; those couples who just wanted to stand in one spot and get it on, on the dance floor. When we finished it we got a very large round of applause as quite a few couples left the dance floor to recuperate and cool down.

We moved through the rest of the repertoire with confidence and finesse. With every gig we just got tighter and tighter and were able to relax and enjoy the music and the people more and more.

"I'm A Man" as always, was the icing on the cake. By the time the end of the night had almost come, the audience was just waiting for us to trump ourselves. There was an expectation on their part that something special should happen, and when it did they felt elated and satisfied. We had never forgotten Roger's credo, "Make sure they remember!" After ten minutes of the organized chaos of "I'm A Man", performed with wicked musicality against a backdrop of coloured lights and a flashing strobe, they would certainly take home something to remember for a long, long, time!

One down, two to go.

Kenora was next on the agenda, but since it wasn't until Friday night we decided to sleep in on Thursday and get refreshed for the big drive ahead. The next morning we checked out of the motel at the last possible minute and then set out for Kenora. We made really excellent time on the road until we got to Dryden, at which time a strange whining and squealing sound started coming from under the hood. We had never had any problems with the "Blue Goose" before except for the accident, so it sort of freaked us out a bit. We pulled into a Supertest gas station with a huge sign by the highway that advertised Mechanic On Duty. There was a Harvey's about two hundred yards up the road. That cinched it. We pulled in and shut the truck off.

We all piled out of the truck in front of the garage doors and stretched and yawned as our eyes adjusted to the light. Presently, a large dude in blue coveralls came through the shop door and approached the truck.

"I heard you pull in. Pretty loud under there, let's see what's goin' on."

He reached between the grill bars with his right hand and opened the hood. There was a distinct odour of grease and oil as hot air wafted up out of the engine compartment. He reached in with his right hand.

"Well, there's the problem. No tension on the fan belt." He leaned in over the fender for a look.

"Hmmm, that's strange, there's no adjuster-bolt."

He reached out and grabbed something and pulled up-wards.

"Well, shit! The bolts broken off, right in the generator. Someone must've over-tightened it at some point."

Roger was watching closely and stuck his head partway under the hood.

"So what do you do, to get the bolt out?"

"Well, I'll have to take the generator off and drill it out, see if I can back it out of there with an easy-out tool."

Roger asked, "How long's that going to take?"

"An hour, maybe more."

"O.K. Can you do it right now?"

The mechanic smiled, "Everyone wants it done right now. How's about twenty minutes from now, after I get this other job finished, and then you guys can pick it up at about four."

"Sounds good. But keep it locked, eh? There's lots of valuable stuff in there."

The dude said, "Hey, I'll get the door for you, you can leave it parked in the other bay."

Lady luck was still smiling. Howie pulled the "Blue Goose" into the shop and then we all headed up the road to Harvey's for some beef and grease.

The mechanic was true to his word and the "Goose" was ready at four and after we picked it up and paid the bill we headed west to Kenora. The drive was uneventful but took us through some absolutely gorgeous country. After two hours on the road we reached the outskirts of Kenora and found a nice motel. Immediately upon our arrival Huard called the high school to see what time we could get into the gymnasium the next day to set up the equipment and was told four o'clock at the earliest. It looked like we were going to have to find something to do for the day. Bill called down to the front desk and asked the guy what we could do on a Friday around town and was told there wasn't too much, but that there was a new golf course that had just opened in the summer, west of town. The grass was a bit brown and burnt, he said, but they were still open for business and it was eight holes for three bucks a pair, everything included; balls, clubs and shoes.

John was the first player to step forward, "Hey, I'm in man. It could be a real blast. We can bring something to drink and some food. Hey, we can maybe get some sun and some real exercise!"

Glynn was more realistic, "Well, there isn't anything else to do in this town, so what have we got to lose?"

"Yeah," I said, "We can work out all the kinks from sittin' in that tin can for the last few days."

In the end it was unanimous; even Howie was into tryin' a few Arnold Palmer moves on the fairway.

Next morning after breakfast we headed out of town and pulled into the parking lot of the golf course just as the place opened. The sun was rising quickly against a blue sky and reflected with sparkling clarity off the seams of quartzite that ran in ribbons through the granite rocks that lined both sides of the fairway.

This was no ordinary course. It was more like an obstacle course than a golf course. It had been laid out between seams of granite shield that were millions of years old. Pink, grey, black and purple veins of granite rose from each side of the unnaturally green fairways. The retreating glaciers had left rolling ridges of rock with just enough space between them to fill in the small valleys with earth, creating these narrow and rugged fairways. Most of the holes were par five or four. There was nothing easy about any of them. As soon as Roger and John got a look at the course they brought out the vodka and poured a glass for anyone who was willing. I couldn't see seriously attempting the course so I joined them.

I paired up with Roger. My first drive hooked left about fifty yards out, hit some rock and careened weirdly over to the other side of the fairway, once again striking some rocks after which it launched itself upwards like a rocket and disappeared into the nether-land, never to be seen again. As did my second shot, and my third.

The comedy of errors that played out over the next three hours was far more interesting and varied than even the "Three Stooges". I lost count of strokes, lost ten or fifteen balls altogether, tripped on my own shoe laces and fell flat on my face, finally giving up after being brought to tears from too much laughter.

Roger didn't fare much better, or Glynn, or John. Rob was the best driver, managing to stay on the fairway on more than one occasion. Huard and Howie were better putters than drivers but broke out in incredible fits of laughter over totally inconsequential shots that seemed to never find their mark.

Everyone was so pathetic that it became a laugh-fest of the highest order. Two mickeys of Vodka disappeared as the number of strokes passed the hundred mark for each player and every drive or putt elicited uncontrollable laughter, the likes of which none of us had experienced in ages. We all decided that golf was the funniest game we had ever played. There was nothing else like it. We just couldn't understand why people took it so seriously; they were missing out on so much fun!

That afternoon when we got back we set up and in the evening we did our level best and put on a beautifully staged Ugly Ducklings extravaganza.

The night was a wild ride. During our show four fights broke out and had to be broken up by the teachers and the school prefects. The girls were more interested in us than the guys, and gathered around the front of the stage, giggling and holding their hands self-consciously in front of their bodies. The guys were another story. They seemed to be totally preoccupied with drinking until they were pissed-drunk and then picking fights with all of their worst enemies. Dancing was just a distraction for them from their real macho aim of male dominance and bravado.

The sense of foreboding and the air of violence that permeated the room definitely wasn't our thing and in the end we were more than happy to leave town.

We felt like crap as we drove away, but quickly decided that it was just the way that things were. We couldn't control everything. Every town had its own personality and character. Sometimes things would get away from us and the night would just stiff. It was human nature to feel bad about it, but we were learning to accept the fact that it wasn't our fault. We did our best and left the rest to fate.

Two down, one to go!

As we headed west on Highway 17 we wondered what was in store for us in Winnipeg. We knew it was the home of the Guess Who and that Neil Young had started out there before he made his way to Toronto. But what was it really going to be like? We cranked up the volume on the radio and tried to find some Winnipeg stations, but we were still too far away.

We had managed to get out of Kenora just after midnight, and Howie was pulling the first shift at the wheel. The sky was a blanket of black velvet with crystal-like stars filling the panorama of our vision, illuminating our journey. It was almost bright enough to drive with our headlights off.

At about 3 a.m. Howie pulled the truck over on to a section of wide shoulder and announced, "I gotta go, man." John and I were barely conscious and mumbled some weak acknowledgement. Howie opened the door, departed the truck and disappeared behind a thick stand of cedars. He returned about five minutes later and placed the roll of toilet paper on the dashboard. He saw that my eyes were open and then looked back at John.

"You guys want to see something incredible?"

I wasn't really cognisant, "Uh, whatta ya mean, man?"

"You won't believe the sky out here man, it's fucking incredible! There's nothing but stars, man. Nothing but stars! It's something that you never get to see in the city; sort of like you're already out there in space and the fuckin' stars are surrounding you. Just give it a try, man. It's only going to take a couple of minutes."

John propped himself up on one elbow to extricate himself from the bodies that were littered all over the equipment and slipped as he pushed forward. His knee hit Glynn in the head rousing him from a deep sleep.

"Where are we? What the fuck's goin' on?" We told him the story.

"Well, let's wake 'em all up. If it's really a once-in-a-lifetime thing, 'do it right!'"

Glynn gave them all a prod in the kidneys to bring them around and in a matter of moments the whole gang was standing outside the truck gazing up at the stars, complaining about all their little aches and pains.

Howie took charge. "Hey guys come on over to the ditch and check this out. It's way better when you can relax and hold your head still." He lay down on the crest of the ditch in the grass and stared wide-eyed up at the stars. The rest of us followed. Soon we were lined up like little kids making angels in a snow-bank.

"Holy shit, look at them!" Glynn was impressed.

Rob was busy finding the Big Dipper and Little Dipper, and pointing them out to us. They were the only familiar stars that any of us knew. We were aware that they pointed to other constellations, but none of us had ever paid enough attention in school to remember any of the others, or where they were in relation to different stars.

Howie wasn't worried about any of that stuff.

"Let's just concentrate and see if any of the suckers move!" He looked around for reactions.

Huard wasn't hopeful. "Not much chance of that, unless there's some meteorites coming in."

"Yeah, but wouldn't that be cool; actually seeing a meteorite shower!"

We all stared intently, taking in what little of the universe we could see with the naked eye, beholding it all with a new clarity that had never been possible before, simply because we lived in the city. It was an amazing sight.

Huard broke our reverie, "We should get going, guys. We could stay out here all night and never take it all in. There'll be other times.

Everyone agreed and slowly rose from the dried grasses and made our way to the "Blue Goose". Roger took the driver's seat and the rest of us chose our places for the long ride into Winnipeg and the unknown. Roger turned on the radio and moved the tuner across the dial until it landed on the first strong station, which was Duluth, Minnesota. The all night guy was playing British Invasion stuff and was just cueing up "Van the Man" and Them doing "Here Comes The Night". We all sang along as we raced westward toward Manitoba and whatever adventures awaited.

As the sun came up we rolled across the border into Manitoba. The terrain had already flattened out somewhat before we actually crossed the border, but once in Manitoba the trees started thinning out rapidly and the vistas quickly became more immense. With the daylight everyone started waking up and stretching, adjusting to the light and feeling like it was time for breakfast.

Huard was hungry, "Stop at the first restaurant, Roger. I gotta piss like a race horse."

"Yeah, Bill, you always gotta piss like a race horse. What's with your bladder anyway? Isn't it a bit over-sized for your body?"

"No it's not, I'm just full of it Roge', and I'm hungry."

"Yeah, we're all hungry Roge', let's stop as soon as we can." I was the band spokesman.

It was the same old thing. It was hard to adjust to a life on the road, cooped up in a little tin can with no room to move, minus all the conveniences. We were managing, but thank god it would soon end when we arrived in Winnipeg.

We stopped for a bite to eat and then got back on the road arriving at nine thirty. As soon as we checked into the hotel Huard was on the phone to all of our contacts in town. It turned out that the gig was in a large community centre and that we would be able to get in at six o'clock. In the meantime we were set to do an interview on TV on the Bob Burns Show at two o'clock, and an interview on CKY-Radio with Ron Legg at four thirty. CKY was the radio sponsor for the gig and Ron was going to be the MC for our show. We were impressed with the amount of hype the show was getting and wondered what size of an audience we were going to get with all of this promotion.

At one forty-five we arrived at the TV station, freshly showered and shaved and decked out in our best duds, ready to go. Bob Burns turned out to be a real music guy who wore horn-rimmed glasses and really knew his stuff. He asked us music-related questions and told his audience a little mini-history of the Ducks before he played "Nothin'" and "She Ain't No Use To Me" and hyped our show at the community centre.

On the other hand, Ron Legg was more open and let us ramble on about our own story with our own warped sense of humour. He quizzed us about The Village and asked if we had ever seen Neil Young perform, so I told him about that night at Chez Monique when Neil had sat in with "Just Us". At the end of the interview he played "10:30 Train" and "Nothin'" and we talked about the show that night and what we were going to play. We left the station feeling positive about the whole day. This was how it should always be. It was going to be a very interesting night.

The community centre where we were playing was a lot like the "Gouge Inn" back in Scarborough. Low ceilings, no windows, dark and warm. It was going to be a hot and sweaty night. We had set the gear up in record time and then had a great dinner reasonably early, so that it wouldn't affect our performance.

When we returned Ron Legg had just arrived and came into the dressing room to say hello. He told us that the place was sold out and it was going to be packed to the rafters. The other thing he told us, was that there were going to be a lot of Winnipeg musicians in the audience who were very curious about the band, having heard lots of rumours and stories from other Ontario groups who had come through town.

We took Ron's information into account and spent some extra time screwing around with the gear and doing a thorough sound check; with Huard and Howie standing at various points in the hall, monitoring the over-all sound. The community centre had supplied us with a drum riser for Rob that got him ten inches above the level of the amplifiers and they had also placed a big black cubical riser on each side of the stage, to elevate the speaker columns.

We decided to split the show into two one hour sets with a fifteen minute intermission. Normally we would do a one and a half to one and three quarter hour set and call it a night. But the characteristics of the hall pointed to the possibility of heat prostration and dehydration. Better to be on the safe side.

We retired to the dressing room to work out the sets and change for the night. Occasionally Huard or Howie would venture out front to see how the crowd was building, and what kind of a mood the room was in. The vibe was really important.

If the crowd was with us, Huard and Howie could feel it just by the interactions that were happening out front and the body language as people walked in. Every report was positive as show-time approached and we rearranged the sets accordingly. We wanted the night to be a slow-burn, so that the second set wouldn't be an anti-climax.

At five to nine Ron Legg walked up onto the stage and gave us a five minute introduction. When he was done

Glynn and Rob ran up onstage and immediately slid into the opening chords of "Everybody Needs Somebody To Love". There was a murmur in the crowd, (Where were the other guys?), and then every four bars another member joined the band until all five of us were riding the Solomon Burke soul-wave. I customized the intro-monologue as always with a recognition of the city of Winnipeg and got a surge of applause. With that we were away. We pumped it out with sheer joy and determination, moving through "I Can Tell, Hey Mama, Ain't Gonna Eat Out My Heart Anymore" and "Kicks", after which we slowed things down with "If You Need Me".

By this time the audience were sweating and starting to feel good. Every gig we played, there was always a turning point where a line was crossed and the crowd got on the same page as the band. This was it. It was the point where they really began to listen in earnest. From here on in we knew they would respond intuitively and the communication between audience and band had reached its highest level.

Any musician will tell you that that's the moment they live for. The ultimate connection. And that's what we felt at that moment. I switched the set around and did "10:30 Train" and "She Ain't No Use To Me", back to back.

Dave & Rob @ Boris's Nov.'66

The Audience checks us out!

As we were finishing "She Ain't...," I noticed a really cool-looking dude walking through the audience toward the stage with a briefcase in his right hand. He had dark flowing hair and a sparkle in his eye that showed an inner confidence, and he was wearing black suede Beatle-boots exactly like Bill Huard's. He stopped and stood at centre-stage for the remainder of the set. As I introduced "Nothin'" to end the set it finally dawned on me who he was and I nodded in his direction as we tore into the song. After Roger soloed I looked over and noticed that the "dude" had a huge smile on his face and was stomping his right foot as if he was playing along with the band.

When we finished the song there were waves of applause and we announced the intermission. As the crowd retreated for a break I walked over to centre-stage.

The "dude" extended his hand and introduced himself, "Hi, I'm Burton Cummings of The Guess Who, pleased to meet you!"

"Dave Bingham, likewise. Would you like to come back to the dressing room?"

"Sure."

We walked around the end of the stage and through the door of the dressing room into a mad house of activity, as the guys were all changing into something dry and busy tuning up for the second set. I took Burton around and introduced him to the rest of the guys, after which he announced to everyone, "If anyone is interested, one of the guys from The Fifth is having a party tonight and you guys are all invited. I'll leave all the information with Dave." Even when he talked his voice was mellifluous.

He shook hands with a bunch of people and then turned to me and said, "I'll let you guys get to it. The music is great, I'm really enjoyin' myself. Hope you can make it later. Good luck next set." As he walked out the door he turned and gave us the thumbs up sign.

The second set was entirely predictable. I probably lost three or four pounds and I know it felt like the sum of all the best gigs we had ever had, to everyone. "I'm A Man" was blisteringly psychedelic and lasted a good fifteen minutes. Howie used every trick he had learned with the lights and the strobe to alter the psyche of each and every audience member. The strobe light was particularly effective that night. On stage it felt like we were being hypnotised into some kind of a voodoo trance that was amplified by the incessant pulse of the music. We closed our eyes to try to soften the effect, but the light penetrated our eyelids and there was no escape.

When Rob finished his solo and cued the final eight bars, we collectively heaved a sigh of relief. The weight of the music had become oppressive; we needed to stop. There was nothing left but the end.

When the final notes died out and the lights came on in the hall there was another round of applause, and then the audience turned and left. A few people remained near the stage. I had a feeling they were musicians and turned to one of the guys who had long sandy brown hair, "You guys wouldn't be from The Fifth would you?"

"You got it! I'm the singer Ron and this is one of our guitar players, Johnny."

I got the directions to the party house and told them I would definitely be there, but that I couldn't speak for everyone. The night was just beginning.

After we had loaded up all the gear and dropped the rest of the boys off at the Hotel, Howie, Bill & I headed over to the Fifth's party. The directions we were given were right on and we arrived just before 12:30 a.m. When we knocked at the door we were greeted by Kurt, who whisked us quickly into the living room to introduce us.

"Hey, everyone, it's the guys from The Ugly Ducklings!" Kurt was already a bit under the weather and slurred the last couple of syllables as he ushered us over to a massive green upholstered couch, beside which was a giant Coca-Cola cooler filled with various coloured beer bottles.

"Help yourself guys, and have a seat."

People clamoured all around and told us how great the show was and how they had been waiting for so long for us to come to Winnipeg. It felt good to be appreciated and we told them we would be back for sure.

Howie gazed around the room, his eagle eye ever wary for lost or abandoned Femmes Fatale. Huard scratched his right side-burn and lit up a smoke. The guys from The Fifth all came over to the table to talk shop and we sat around for a good hour and a half discussing PA systems, amplifiers, fuzz pedals and the like while the rest of the revelers danced in the dining room and kitchen to the sounds of The Animals, The Kinks and The Stones.

At some point I noticed that Howie had disappeared. Our gracious hosts Ron and Johnny kept pouring rum & cokes for Bill and I and the room seemed to be getting hotter and hotter. Ron informed Bill that it was going to be minus 30 degrees F. for our trip back to Ontario and that maybe we might want to stock up on a few extra blankets to keep warm in the truck.

"Not a bad idea, Ron." Huard asked, "Is there somewhere we could stop on the way out of town to pick something up?"

Right then, at that particular second; the room started tilting and the back of my eyeballs seemed to catch fire and spin out of control, flashing purple and pink home movies on the inside of my eye-lids.

"Uh, I don't feel so good guys, I think I'm gonna be sick!"

Ron helped me to my feet and showed me to the back door.

"Just do it out there, Dave. But don't be too long, it's minus 25 degrees!"

I stood on the back porch for all of twenty seconds and then felt a wave of nausea propel me to the porch rail. When I was finished I stood there dazed and confused for a few seconds and then turned to go into the house. The porch was iced over and I reached out to grab the railing to steady myself and felt a warm sensation as my hand slid over the barf that had spilled onto the rail. I slipped slightly but grabbed on tight and steadied myself. When I went to open the back door my hand wouldn't let go of the rail. It was frozen to the steel like a wet noodle.

"Shit! What the fuck!" I felt like an idiot.

Off to one side of the door was a pathetic looking little shovel that I could just reach with my other hand. I used it to knock on the back door until someone came. After that it was a matter of warm water on the hand and a slightly bruised ego.

Bill grinned widely as I came into the living room, my frozen-and-then-thawed hand wrapped in a tea-towel.

"I think we better get a move on, Dave. It's a long way home and we've got to get a good start tomorrow."

"Yeah, you're right, Bill. Anyone seen Howie?"

Ron stood up, "I know where he is, I'll be right back."

In five minutes Ron came back with Howie who was accompanied by a cute little brunette. The two of them had contented, knowing smiles on their faces. As soon as Howie managed to extricate himself from the brunettes' grasp we all said our goodbyes and then the three of us piled into the "Blue Goose" for the trip back to the hotel.

Huard set the choke and turned the key and the engine groaned with a deep and pitiful rumble; turned ever so slowly, but then caught on the first revolution and started. We each breathed a huge sigh of relief.

Howie blew a little blow-fish whistle and then added seriously, "There are some outdoor block-heater plugs in the parking lot, Bill. I think we better plug it in when we get back. It's only going to get colder."

In the morning Howie went down and started the "Blue Goose" to warm it up and then came back upstairs to help bring all the guitars and bags to the truck. When we were all packed and settled in for the long drive Huard put the "Goose" in reverse and let out the clutch. The engine stalled. He tried again. The engine stalled again. Howie got out and stood watching.

"Try it again, Bill."

Bill tried again. Stall!

Howie came over to the side of the truck and checked the rear tires. He got down on one knee and took a good look. Then he got up and approached Huard's window. "The tires are frozen right into the ice, Bill. We'll have to get some hot water and free them up!"

After about ten minutes of running back and forth to the rear door of the Hotel kitchen with pails of hot water, the "Goose" finally broke free and we got on our way.

Three down and sixteen hundred miles to go! Bye-bye Manitoba!

When we got back to Toronto we played at Charlie's the next weekend and Glynn brought us a surprise that he had been working on. It was a spectacular Cartoon rendering of the Band in a pose reminiscent of the Stones on the front cover of their first album. Everyone loved it, and from then on we put it in the window while we played!

Glynn really was a talented artist. Our fans loved it too........

Glynn's Incredible DUCKS Cartoon

CHAPTER 13

PASSION

By the end of November "She Ain't No Use To Me" had slipped out of the top thirty on CHUM. Competition was fierce, as we were up against The Beatles, The Stones, Simon and Garfunkel, Sonny and Cher and The Byrds. Not to mention all of the up and coming acts within Canada. It turned out that on the east coast we were actually doing better than in Toronto, as a lot of stations there had put us into maximum rotation.

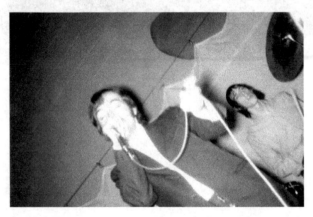

Dave Crooning

THE
UGLY DUCKLINGS

Here they are. Fresh from their smash hit "Nothin", the Ducks have come up with another nationwide hot one that's already being picked and charted from coast to coast. They're a real neat bunch of musicians and singers who have started the people in Canada thinking about the "new sound". John, Roger, Robin, Dave and Glynn are artists who think, talk and dream music. Onstage they're "out of sight". Watch for them better still, lend an ear to their big one.

"SHE AIN'T NO USE TO ME"

f/s

"10:30 TRAIN"

Distributed by Capitol Records (Canada) Ltd.
by arrangement with York Town Records
A Tommy Graham production

ON YORK TOWN - 45002

RPM Chart, Nov.'66

When we got back from Winnipeg we got right to work on new original material. If we weren't in the top thirty anymore, then it was time to cut another record. We rehearsed with a passion in order to get ready for our opening gig with The Beach Boys, and after every rehearsal we tossed around song ideas hoping that lightning would strike and reveal a true number one!

One Thursday night after a particularly long rehearsal at Charlie's Roger was screwing around with his Zonk machine trying to nail down a really wicked and cutting sound, when he accidentally played a simple riff that inspired Glynn to come up with the chords to "Just In Case You Wonder". At the time there were no lyrics, but I started mumbling along with what the two of them were playing and, voila; we had a song. Glynn and I went back to Admiral Road afterwards and we worked out the lyrics in a couple of hours. They were more basic and straight forward than anything else we had written, but we realized the focus of the tune wasn't the story, it was going to be the performance. The real test would be the arrangement. Glynn and I talked over how we envisioned it and memorized it in detail, for the next rehearsal. We knew exactly what we wanted; it had to be a showstopper for "Live" gigs; something that would distinguish us from the rest of the Toronto groups. We wanted to showcase Roger's psychedelic guitar style to full advantage and that meant letting him go for broke. We wanted him to cut loose just like he did in "Hey Mama" and "2120", except that this time it would be a solo in an original tune.

At the last rehearsal before the Beach Boys gig, we worked it up with manic precision until we were totally satisfied. Glynn and I sang a lot of the song in unison and Rob worked out one of his patented drum beats for the intro that really set the arrangement apart from other tunes of the day. Roger out-did himself with an over-the-top solo that was totally unforgettable and John's bass was a wall of sound. It was definitely an Ugly Ducklings song.

Our plan was to debut it at Maple Leaf Gardens.

November 20th finally arrived and we found ourselves at Maple Leaf Gardens once again, opening for one of the best loved bands in North America. We were becoming very experienced at this type of gig. We all arrived at the Gardens by six thirty and were finished with the set up in forty five minutes. Howie parked the "Blue Goose" back beside the entry doors and then we all stood around nonchalantly waiting for the Beach Boys to show up. Their gear had all been on stage and ready to go when we arrived, so now we waited for the guys themselves to show up.

At about eight-ten we decided it was time to change into our stage clothes and retired to our dressing room. Everyone had brought their best outfits from the Toronto Sound Show and the Stones Show, except for John, who had brought something extra special. He had a nice brown dry-cleaning bag stashed with his regular outfit and a big wide grin on his face.

"Wait 'til you guys see what I've got in here; you just won't fucking believe it!"

"Oh yeah," Glynn chided, "What is it, one of those weird Mohair Sam jackets with the piping on the lapels?"

"No man, it's something that Chris made for me to my own specifications."

Now everybody was getting really curious. Roger was impatient, "Come on, John, just open up the bag and let us see what the big deal is, eh?"

John was enjoying the mystery. He took his time dressing, putting on his slacks and shirt slowly and then pulling on his brand new black suede Clarke's Beatle boots. Finally he unzipped the bag very dramatically and removed a hand-made black and white striped *vinyl* jacket. The stripes were three quarters of an inch wide and flowed in a vertical direction, so that they ran the length of the arms. He swung it over his shoulder, slid one arm in and then the other.

Huard was impressed. "Wow that is so cool! Where did you get it?"

"Chris did it for me; she bought the pattern at a place on Spadina Rd."

Rob was impressed as well, "Touche' John! All the cameras are going to be aimed in your direction tonight."

Bob MacAdorey had just arrived and walked over to say hello. "Holy smokes that is really something, John! People are going to remember that tomorrow, for sure. I'll have to mention it on my show!"

Once we were dressed we walked back out to the back-stage area to see if the Beach Boys had shown up, just in time to see their arrival at the rear doors. Once inside the Gardens they got out of the limo and dispersed to their dressing room. They came out in a short time all dressed in matching striped shirts, white pants and sneakers.

Mike Love and Al Jardine approached our little crowd over at stage left and introduced themselves. They told us how much they liked Canada and Mike Love asked about

The Village. It seemed like the reputation of Yorkville was spreading around the world.

We told him all about the club scene and about the different bands who had made The Village their home base. He was impressed by the sheer number of bands and especially by the fact that there were over four hundred bands in the city; with almost twenty of them using Yorkville as a home base. Evidently, L.A. had the bands, but not enough clubs to keep them all working. We were really surprised. It didn't make much sense that one of the biggest entertainment cities in the world, would be short of music clubs for their musicians to play in.

We asked about Neil Young & Buffalo Springfield but neither one of them knew much about what was happening on that front. Evidently they had heard about a future possible signing of a record deal involving some recent Canadian immigrants from the Toronto area, but they were vague and unsure of any details.

A Gardens employee approached our little group and noted that The DUCKS had thirty-five minutes to show-time. We shook hands with Al and Mike, said our good-byes and headed back to the dressing room to get organized.

Roger was as always the instigator.

"We gotta remember to keep moving, eh? The stage is so big, if we don't move, it'll be hard for people to see us!"

John piped up, "Hey, well they're going to notice me for sure, eh guys?"

Rob was practising rolls and shots on a little practise-pad in the corner. "Yeah John, but they'll still notice you more if you're moving from side to side. Especially with all those coloured lights hitting that jacket!"

We had a half-hour set, in which we would fit all of our recent singles plus our latest creation, "Just In Case You Wonder". After that we would end the set with "I'm A Man" in typical "Ducks" fashion; minus the strobe light effects.

John's Custom Vinyl Jacket

There were plenty of Ugly Ducklings fans out front and they showed their unbridled enthusiasm at every opportunity. We moved around the stage constantly, egging each other on and interacting physically with the ebb and flow of the music.

From the opening chorus of "Nothin'" the audience were there singing along.

With each tune the band grew more confident.

Glynn was especially dynamic; crouching in front of Roger, grinning and punctuating the rhythm with stabbing chords and wildly accented glissandos. At the appropriate times he fanned his right arm out in a full arc and hammered his Gretsch Tennessean with a barrage of windmill-like strikes.

The response to "Just In Case You Wonder" was positive from the opening Fuzz-toned riff onward, and by the time Roger ripped into his solo we could hear screams and whistling over the strains of the music. John inverted his Gibson Bass during Rob's mini-solo in "I'm A Man", so that he could twirl it on its head-stock on the stage. The audience reaction was immediate, and sustained with whoops and hollers. By the end of "I'm A Man" there were chants of "Ducks", "Ducks", "Ducks" and loud whistles and screaming accompanied by loud foot-stomping and syncopated hand-clapping. We were really getting through to them. Roger was all smiles. I could feel the hairs on the back of my neck stand up as goose bumps covered my forearms. Rob hit the final cymbal crash and stood for a simple bow and we all bowed along with him.

We retreated backstage slowly, savouring the moment.

This was a sure sign. We were on a roll!

With the success of the mini-tour and our performance at The Beach Boys Show we felt inspired to start working toward putting out our first album. We held a meeting at Charlie's to work out the details of our approach. The first thing that was apparent was that we were going to need a few more original tunes. We became very determined to create as much original music as we possibly could. Glynn had grown more confident with the success of "Just In Case" and revealed that he was working on a couple of pieces and would be ready to show them to the band very soon. Roger was nonchalant in his response to Glynn's revelation, but seemed sure he could work up a few things.

Huard was not so casual in his response.

John – Bass-Twirling

"Uh, I think we gotta do this really fast, guys. We need a new single and then we have to have an album ready to establish ourselves as a real recording act. We can't just keep on releasing singles forever!"

Roger was pissed. "Don't get your shirt in a knot, Bill. We can do it. It's not like we don't have any ideas. We just have to get into rehearsing and let it all hang out. It'll come; I know it."

"Yeah? How about lyrics Dave?" Bill looked at me.

"Well, give me some chords guys and we'll see what happens!"

We knew it was going to come down to the work. When we really got into it deep, that's when the inspiration connected in a big way.

We set up a schedule of rehearsals that would give us a big push. It was decided that we needed to learn some new cover tunes as well, to refresh our stage show and give our audiences a surprise or two.

The next rehearsal at Charlie's we nailed "Home In Your Heart" by Solomon Burke and "Out Of Sight" by James Brown.

After a break for lunch we got back down to it and during a lull Rob started playing a funky snare and bass drum groove. Glynn asked what it was and Rob confided that it was inspired by a groove that Whitey Glann had played during sound check at the last gig that we had shared with "Mandala".

"Keep on playin' it, Rob." Roger walked over to stand beside Rob's kit and started playing some chords in synch with the bass drum. "Yeah, just keep goin' 'round and 'round with it for a while."

Glynn joined in. "What key is it, Roge'?"

"A."

"Oh, yeah."

Next it was John's turn.

All of a sudden we had a great groove going that felt like a sweet verse for a mid-tempo tune. I started humming along and wrote out some jumbled syllables on a piece of paper. All I wanted to do was to establish the cadence of it and map out the structure of a verse. The rest could come later. After twenty minutes of working with it we finally stopped. It was firmly implanted in our memory-banks now; we would be able to pick it up at any time in the future and keep going with it.

We felt good about our little creation, and after everyone else had left to go home, Glynn decided to show me one of the pieces that he had worked out on his own. He was a bit shy at first and botched a couple of bars of the intro, but as he warmed up his picking hand he settled into a nice groove with it. It was unlike anything I had ever heard before. All open strings and Gretsch sounds tempered with minimal use of the bigsby whammy bar. It sounded sort of mystical and dream-like to me and I felt a melody form in my mind immediately as he played it. I retrieved the piece of paper that I'd written my other notes on and added some scribbles to map out the cadence of Glynn's little beauty.

Wow, we were making headway. We headed home filled with anticipation for our next rehearsal. What was in store for us now? Only time would tell.

Before we could make it to the next rehearsal we all got a call from Huard.

He had gotten a call from Bob Johnson who regretted to inform us that we just couldn't rehearse at Charlie's anymore. Someone had complained to the city and evidently the club was only allowed to create noise (sic) in the evenings when other businesses in the area were shut down.

So, Bill had made enquiries and found us a new larger rehearsal space at 777 Warden Avenue, in Scarborough. It was upstairs over a small strip mall and would offer a lot more privacy. Below us was a small dance studio that closed at six o'clock. So we could arrive right after supper and stay as long as we wanted any evening of the week.

The first rehearsal there yielded "That's Just A Thought That I Had In My Mind" and "Postman's Fancy". Both tunes were complete departures from anything that we had done before. I had managed to write a set of verses for "That's Just A Thought" that gave us a real head start, so that it was totally arranged and finished by evening's end. Roger came up with a brilliant ending for it by playing a diminished minor seventh chord at the very end, and letting it fade off with a slight tendency to feed back.

"Postman's Fancy" was a different story. I had come up with one verse that Glynn and I used to show the rest of the guys the tune. John and Rob liked it but Roger was not impressed. "It's too wimpy Dave. It's like music from some other planet or something."

Glynn and I were still confident that it would evolve into something special and John was determined to write a bass part for it that would add to the other-worldliness of the song. Rob as always would come up with a drum part that was totally original. That was his job. He intoned us, "Just finish it off you guys, it'll come together when the story comes together in the lyrics."

Of course Rob was right. When it did all come together it was like a jigsaw puzzle that makes total sense as the last few pieces fall into place. But the tune just wasn't the type of song we could do in our "Live" show, so we never performed it at any of our shows.

Next up we learned "Ain't Gonna Eat Out My Heart Anymore" by "The Young Rascals" and "I Need Your Love" by John Mayall. We wanted some dynamic ballads for the show and both tunes fit the bill. Roger really got to show off his stuff in the "Mayall" tune and of course I got to emote authentically in the "Rascals'" tune. So, depending on the type of audience we had on any given night, we could come up with an appropriate ballad that would keep the show moving toward a dynamic finish. We always observed the ratio of girls to guys in the crowd to determine the feel of the set-list.

Within a very short time of moving to the Warden Avenue space we all became dissatisfied with the nighttime rehearsal thing. We needed and wanted somewhere that we could come and go as we pleased and make any amount of noise that we might manage. We sent Huard off on the prowl to locate the ultimate location.

In the meantime Glynn showed up one night with a wonderful chord progression all arranged and laid out in beautiful symmetry .We set to work on it immediately with real determination, as we were booked into Bay Studios the next week to lay down some tracks for the album.

In a matter of two hours the song came together lyrics and all. The words just fell out of my mouth and Glynn came up with the title chorus as we moved along through all the phases of feeling out the groove. Roger added some unique fuzz-tone lines between the verses that pulled it all together and as a result we had "Do What You Want".

The following weekend we premiered all the new songs at our high-school gigs and received totally positive feedback. They were accepted as "Ducks" songs just like all the rest and we felt a surge of excitement knowing that we would soon be in the studio.

Carol Pope (Of "Rough Trade") with Sylvia & Helen

Before we could move our gear back into Warden Avenue Huard found us a new space up on Midland Avenue north of Lawrence. It was a huge industrial plaza with twenty foot ceilings and truck ramps at each unit for loading and unloading. We were pumped. We could blast away all we wanted and rehearse whenever we felt like it. The first time we rehearsed there we set up all of the equipment as if we were on stage and ran through our whole stage show with Howie running the lights. Huard would watch the show and evaluate the set as it went by, noting where we could improve the flow so that it built to a climax naturally.

The next weekend we off-loaded our stuff at 2 a.m. on the Saturday night after a long drive in from Ottawa. We moved all the amps into their regular spots and got the place ready for rehearsal on Monday, as we were going into Bay Studios on Thursday to start recording. Before we left Roger removed his guitar from its case and sat on his amplifier.

"I gotta show you this thing that I was screwing around with when I was tuning up last night." He started strumming some chords, seemingly at random.

"Shit, what fuckin' key was it? Oh, I know. "E", "E" minor."

He started strumming away. It sounded a bit like a camp-fire thing. I reached into my harp bag and found my "A" harp and started playing along. Glynn was still bringing things in from the truck when he heard the chords and my harp. He put down what he was carrying, and then grabbed his guitar and started playing along, accentuating the two and the four while Roger laid out the tempo with his smooth flowing chords. Rob joined in playing a suitcase as if it were bongos.

It got to the point where words started falling out of my mouth. But there was still something missing.

Glynn was inspired, "It needs an intro Roge'. Some kind of line that starts it off and sets the tone."

Roger started screwing around playing lines on his lower strings until he did something that sounded ass-backwards. Glynn shot in, "Yeah, that one Roge' that's it!" They stopped playing and started over using the line the way Roger had just played it. Then I came in with the harp for a couple of bars and started singing.

Huard and Howie were standing back watching things unfold.

"Wow, that's cool guys. Where'd it come from?"

Roger looked up, "Last night tuning up."

Glynn grinned and put his Gretsch back in the case. "I've gotta get going guys, but we can work on this on Monday, eh?" We all looked at each other.

"You bet!"

"This week's going to be fun, guys. Relax tomorrow and get some rest, 'cause we're going to be really busy all week." Huard was the cheerleader as always but his voice had a more serious tone than usual.

We all headed home to get some sleep. This was going to be a really special week, and we all knew it.

So, Monday arrived and we started off by finishing the new song, which was titled "Not For Long". It evolved into something a little bit wimpy but it was O.K. because Roger had been the instigator and at least, in Roger's humble opinion it didn't sound like it came from a hit-parade on some other planet! Rob worked out some wonderful percussion parts for it that would be recorded in the studio using bongos. It was another tune that we never played "live" in any of our shows.

After we cinched the arrangement on the new tune we got down to meticulously dissecting all the songs that we were going to record. We timed them out and then decided what was essential or non-essential for the recorded version of each tune.

It wasn't easy. In our "Live" show we had nurtured and honed a lot of the tunes based on an emotional high-point that worked in a "live" setting but made the songs just too long for the studio. In the end we left some of the tunes alone because cutting them would have destroyed their appeal. Others were less delicate and adapted well to shorter versions. We decided against recording "I'm A

Man", just because it was so famous by "The Yardbirds". We figured we would get nothing but negative responses to it, no matter how well it turned out.

When Thursday rolled around we were ready. Everyone was on time and anxious to get going. As always setting up the gear was emotionally draining. The anticipation had built up so much during the last week that time seemed to stretch out to unimaginable lengths.

Finally we got to the point of running through some instrumental stuff to check out the levels and sounds. For this we used our old stand-by, "2120 South Michigan Avenue" by The Stones. It had evolved into something completely different over the last year or so and Ray Lawrence, one of our engineers, asked what it was.

Glynn replied, "It's our sound-check number. It started out as a Stones thing, but we don't really have a name for it." Because of the increase in the number of tunes in our repertoire we weren't even doing it in our "live" shows anymore. After we got all the levels and sounds adjusted we quickly forgot about it. We had to decide what to do first.

Rob was determined to work at the tunes with the idea of building up to the faster tunes as if we were doing a "live" show. That was how we achieved our "live" vibe, so we decided to give it a go in the studio. In the end we started with "Ain't Gonna Eat Out My Heart Anymore" and "Not For Long". Then we moved on to "Do What You Want" and "That's Just A Thought". For the latter we applied gaffers tape to the underside of Rob's snare drum to mute the effect of the snare-wires against the lower snare skin. It gave the track a different feel from the rest.

For most of the tunes I sang along "live" with the band, with the intention of re-doing the vocal if I screwed up. As it turned out it wasn't necessary. Instead, we doubled the vocal tracks or added harmonies. Sometimes Glynn and I added an extra track together. By early afternoon we had finished the major work on four of our new songs and decided it was time to do some covers.

At "Bay Studios", November 1966

We were all pretty loose and relaxed and Roger wanted to get heavy.

"I'm feelin' it guys. Don't know about you but I'm ready for a little funk!"

Huard was in the control room and came back to us on the phones. "Why not do "I Wish You Would" just to get into the swing of things!"

Everyone was cool with that.

Rob started off with the cymbals and hi-hat and then John came in with the bass. It was moving in synch right from the start. Everybody wound it up tight and let something loose. Only problem was, we hadn't come up with an ending for it. Huard stood in the control room and waved his hand in a circular motion above his head, indicating that we should just keep playing 'til we were played out. After four or five minutes it fell apart naturally and came to an end.

"Great, great guys! We can just fade it out sometime after the third verse!

"How about doing 'Just In Case You Wonder'?"

I knew what Bill was thinking. Roger was on a roll. This was definitely the time. We all looked at each other and heads nodded in agreement. Rob licked his lips in anticipation, "Sure, let's do it."

It only took four takes and everybody nailed it to the wall. Especially Roger. When it came time for him to do his solo I stood in front of him and played "air guitar", imploring him to reach higher and higher on the neck of his beautiful 335 until there were no more frets to render! When Ray played the track back we were ecstatic. Glynn and I added some more vocals on the last track and it was in the can.

We were getting a little winded by now and someone suggested a break. Howie decided to go out and get some food and took orders from everyone. We retired to the control room to listen to what we had put down. Listening to the tracks on the large overhead speakers was a thrill. In the past we had never had a chance to hear ourselves so clearly. We knew what the music *felt* like, but what it sounded like from out front was a different thing. When we rehearsed, Huard was always grinning and shaking his head after certain tunes. Now he spoke up.

"See what I mean, guys? It's powerful. Sometimes it just floors me."

Glynn was sitting quietly, thinking. "We've got to make it sound "live" like this in the mix. That's how it's got to be - like the listener is right there."

Ray was sitting at the console rewinding tape. "That's going to make it a lot easier for me to mix than it would be normally. The more you try to make it sound produced, the more difficult the mixing becomes."

Glynn asked to hear "Just In Case" again.

After another run-through he asked Ray to go back to the beginning. Right after the intro riff he motioned for Ray to stop the tape.

"We should put some acoustic guitars in the verses, right there. It would make it sound fuller and better!" Roger went and got an acoustic and started playing along. It sounded great.

"O.K. so what do we do, Ray?" Glynn was looking serious. Ray shot back.

"Well, we'll have to mix the bass and drums onto one track. Then Roger and Glynn's guitars onto one and then the vocals will have to go to one track, too. That way we'll end up with an extra track for the acoustics. We looked at Roger.

"O.K. by me. Right after dinner."

When Howie got back dinner went by very quickly. Everyone was eager to get to the task of building "Just In Case" into our new single. The recording of the acoustic guitars had to wait until we bounced the bass and drum tracks and vocal tracks onto two tracks. After that it only took twenty minutes or so and we were finished. We listened to the playback and congratulated ourselves on a job well done.

Jan.16,1967 CHUM Chart with Ducks Pic –"Just In Case" @ #30

It was eight thirty and we only had time for one or two more tunes. We picked "Hey Mama Keep Your Big Mouth Shut" as the finisher for the day. It usually ended a set, so it was a natural fit. We had always admired Bo Diddley and his tunes seemed to adapt well to our style.

Turned out it was the perfect choice. Rhythmically it was a stunner that Rob used to show off his hi-hat moves. Roger proceeded to blow everyone away with some frantic and lunatic solos, and then Glynn and I doubled the vocals once more. We were out of breath by the end and totally satisfied with the day's progress. We had filled one whole reel of tape. Tomorrow would surely be the icing on the cake.

The next day started off on a negative note, as Howie was late picking up Glynn and I in the village and we arrived almost an hour late at 11:30. The rest of the guys were all sitting around the studio ready to go.

Huard had planned out the day's activities meticulously in an effort to get all of the tracks recorded. Mixing was going to require a great many hours and would decide how the final product would sound. So, today was it; as far as recording was concerned.

"So is everyone on the same page, guys? Are we going to be able to manage?"

We all nodded or answered in the affirmative.

Rob started a roll on his snare and then swept around his toms ending in a huge cymbal crash, "What's first up?"

John interjected with a loud voice, "How about the James Brown tune?

I want to play some Fuzz Bass!"

Nobody had any problems with his choice, so Rob counted it in and away we went. We ran through it a couple of times while Ray got all his levels and created a nice Fuzz-Bass sound.

He came back on the talk-back channel. "Hey, Roger. Could you crank up the treble on your amp? Bill thinks it should be really grating on the nerves, sort - of." Roger turned up the gain and rolled off some low frequencies on his Traynor.

"O.K. Ray. Check this out." He played a few wailing lines.

"Great, Roge'," Bill came back over the phones.

We did three takes before we were finally satisfied.

Then Huard called for the Sam & Dave"tune, "You've Got It Made" and then Solomon Burke's "Home In Your Heart". They were of a similar feel and tone and we got through them in less than half an hour. Vocally and sonically they matched up in sound and Ray was pleased.

John had brought some rum and we took a little break to have a snack and a drink. No one was going to get looped but we wanted to come down a bit and mellow out for the next tune. We had been doing "Little Red Book" for quite a while and intended to do a special job on it. I was not really looking forward to it because of my propensity to screw up the tambourine tempo all the time. When we were doing a live show we could let it pass, but putting it on tape was another matter. Over-all it went quickly despite our nervousness about it. Even the vocals went by smoothly and within an hour we had it in the bag. Afterwards we followed it with "Somebody Help Me" by the Spencer Davis Group. It had always been a favorite at Charlie Brown's & Boris's. We all nailed it right off the bat and then Glynn and I doubled the vocals once again. We were having fun!

Now it was time to try "Postman's Fancy". Glynn set about getting exactly the right sound out of his Fender Showman, while John spent some time with Ray in order to come up with a rolling percussive bass sound. The rest of us sat around waiting.

I had the final lyrics written out on a sheet of foolscap paper and was memorizing them even though I would be able to read them as I sang. Rob busied himself fiddling around with his hi-hat sound while Roger sat on his amp slightly disgruntled. He didn't really like the song, but he had compromised and made peace with the fact that it was going on to tape. His participation was to be minimal, as he was only to provide a syncopated rhythm accent in the choruses.

When all the sounds had been previewed and set, Rob counted us in and Glynn started with a glissando strummed on the opening chord. John and Rob fell right in and we were away. It was something from *somewhere outside* our regular sphere of influence, but strangely it felt good. Glynn and I got a kick out of the convoluted lyrics and John's wonderful syncopated bass part. After some vocal doubling and simple harmonizing we were done and we broke for dinner. Tonight we were going to finish all the recording and some caloric intake was in order. Howie and I took orders and set off to Harvey's in the "Blue Goose".

The beginning of the evening was a chance for us to listen to a playback of what we had done during the day. We got Ray to crank up the volume and run through all of the tunes in order. Our spirits were lifted and reinforced as the tracks played back one after the other. We had never heard ourselves like that, at such an incredible volume and with such clarity. Recording "Nothin'" had been a gas, and so had "She Ain't No Use To Me", but in each case we had been dealing with two individual songs. This was different. It presented an audio picture that captured the sound and character of the band in a way that we hadn't experienced before. We felt as though we had really accomplished something special.

When all the tunes were finished we sat and contemplated what to do next. Ray solved our dilemma for us by suggesting that we do our instrumental sound-check number. At first there wasn't a unanimous agreement for it, but as we hashed out the idea it developed more and more appeal.

Huard posited the question. "What would we call it?"

"Yeah, it's got to be something that'll hook people's interest." John was idly drumming his fingers on the side of his amp. "Something spooky, or mysterious."

Huard stood up and said, "Let's not worry about it right now, maybe if we just get into it a little bit, then a title or a theme will come."

Everyone agreed and started to file out into the main room. Roger picked up his Gibson but then reconsidered and put it away and got out the Telecaster that he had borrowed from Tommy Graham for the sessions. He plugged it into his Zonk Machine and cranked out a few Fuzz licks.

"Wow, neat!" Glynn was impressed.

I was busy getting Rogers' old "Fender Princeton" set up so that I could play my Harp with a mike through an amp. After a few trial licks I managed to get a honking and horn-like sound.

After a few tentative starts we got down to the nitty-gritty of it and got a real groove going. I started playing some Paul Butterfield-inspired licks when it came my turn to solo and almost immediately John stopped playing.

"I know what we can call it guys!"

We all looked at him incredulously. "Yeah, so, what?" Glynn was impatient.

"Well, it's sort of sounds like a Chicago Blues thing, right?"

We all nodded, "Sort of, yeah, Uh-Huh"

"So we call it "Windy City". Get it?"

We all considered it for a moment; but only a moment. It was so obvious! Then we got back into the creation of the arrangement with renewed inspiration. We now had a theme to base it on and the ideas started flowing.

We kept building it over and over from the beginning, and Ray would come into the main room and adjust amplifier tones or volume or adjust the microphone positioning on Rob's drums. Huard grabbed the tambourine and maracas and played in a few special places.

We got Ray to record the first couple of minutes of the arrangement and then retired to the control room for a listen. Huard got excited right away and stood up asking Ray, "Have you guys got any sound effects records lying around here?"

"Yeah, I think there's a few in Tony's office."

"Do you think there might be any howling wind sounds?"

Ray was getting the idea, "Yeah, I'll bet there is." He got up from his chair and said he'd be right back.

Roger was thinking out loud, "Hmmm, maybe some other sounds, too; city sounds, Chicago-type sounds."

Ray returned with two sound-effects LPs and we spent the next hour and a half assembling and arranging "Windy City". In the end it was about five minutes of organized chaos. Roger and Rob created some great complimentary sounds and musical hooks that linked to the various sound effects that we inserted into the tune. We recorded all of the instruments to four tracks and then mixed them down to get an extra track for the sound effects. I had a great time playing with the amount of reverb on the harp track, making it change from an eerie wail to a funky sax-sound and then back again.

Huard and Ray worked together to drop the various "Sounds" that we had picked from the "effects" L.P.s into the appropriate spots and recorded them onto track four. Bill was using a turn-table, so he had to be careful not to allow the initial sound of the needle contacting the disc, to go to tape. When we listened to the playback we were floored. What a great final track for the album! It really captured the feel of a cold, bleak Chicago landscape and took the listener through a day on the docks and streets of the "Windy City".

Roger added a couple of over-dubs onto track four as well. He used Tommy's Telecaster to great effect to add harmonics and some searing, gut-wrenching, screaming guitar licks into the mix.

Roger with the Telecaster

Dave Harpin'

When we finished the last add-ons we still had half an hour of time left and Roger suggested we do the John Mayall tune "I Need Your Love". It would give both himself and John a chance to wind-it-up instrumentally. It was a real show-stopper in our "Live" show and we wanted to see how it would translate to tape.

We literally attacked it as though it was the last song on earth. No one held back. One take. One heart. One mind. When we were finished there wasn't even a chance to listen to what we had done. We had to tear down and get out of there. Not one of us would ever have guessed that we wouldn't get a chance to hear this one particular track again for another sixteen years!

CHAPTER 14
TRANSITION

Now that we had recorded enough tunes for the album we felt a bit more secure about the immediate future. The first thing on our agenda was to get into the studio and mix the two tunes for the next single. It was decided that everyone was to going to be there for the mixing and that everyone would vote on which song would be the "B" side of the single. We chose "That's Just a Thought That I Had in My Mind". There were no specific reasons. It just came about that it was the second-most favourite tune of all that we had recorded.

The sessions to mix the single took almost a full day. We started off with "That's Just A Thought" in the morning, and then broke for lunch and came back to do "Just In Case".

Because of all the bouncing of tracks we had done, "Just In Case" was the most difficult of the two. We got Ray to use the little six inch speaker box that he kept on the rear shelf of the board for play-back. Occasionally we switched it up onto the big Altec Lansings for full effect. Eventually we got a perfect balance between the two extremes and sent Huard off to Capitol Records with a reel of quarter inch tape to have it mastered and pressed for quick release. By the end of December it was at radio stations across the country and CHUM started to play it. The response was immediate. More demand for gigs and bigger pay-cheques. Ron Scribner was right. Being on the radio was the secret to success. The higher we made it on the charts the more demand for the band increased. It was a simple equation.

Just before Christmas we decided to record ourselves at our Midland Ave. space. We had been getting some requests to do interviews on the radio; most notably on the CBC. Also, Bob MacAdorey from CHUM had contacted us and suggested we might want to appear on a new show that he was putting together called "Talent In Toronto". He wanted to feature us on one of the first episodes.

Bill rented a nice two-track "Philips" Recorder and we set about organizing our equipment into a concert configuration where we could all see and hear each other without any great effort. He had also rented a ten-foot ladder and made himself busy hanging two Shure 57 microphones from the steel roof-trusses in various spots around the room. As we rehearsed he would record bits and pieces of our performance and then listen back in headphones until he was satisfied with the sound. After a few trial runs we found an appropriate positioning for the mikes and started recording.

We started off with "Little Red Book". After a couple of attempts at it we were pleased enough and moved on to "Home In Your Heart". This one was a newer addition to our repertoire and took a few extra tries to get it at the right tempo. Without much fanfare we moved on to

"Nothin'", which was the next tune in sequence as-per our "Live" set. The energy and tone of it came out just right and lifted our spirits.

Next we decided that since none of these tunes were going to be used for the album we would do "I'm A Man", and since it was strictly for our own use we left the arrangement alone and let Rob do his solo just as if we were doing a "Live" show.

To get us in the mood, Bill fired up the lights and turned on the strobe. After a couple of false starts we got right into the thick of it and pulled off some really inspirational performances. Rob's solo was absolutely polyrhythmic and the interplay between all of the guitars was as syncopated as we could get and sounded at times like a subway train screeching through an undersized tunnel, or a wailing banshee pursued by "The Hounds Of The Baskervilles". It timed out at over five minutes and ended orgasmic-ally in perfect unison.

Huard reached over and switched the machine off and clicked on rewind, but before the tape had totally rewound there appeared a pulsating red light at the front window and a sharp rapping at the front door. Howie got up and opened the door.

It was two of Toronto's finest. The lead constable presented his badge and asked if he could come in.

Huard walked over and stood beside Howie, "What's the problem officer?"

"Well sir, we received a call from a homeowner over on the east side of Midland Ave. saying that they observed a number of flashing lights and heard quite a commotion coming from this vicinity, and since it *is* after midnight our dispatcher thought it would be best to check it out. We've had a couple of fires in this particular plaza."

"Well, there's no fire as you can see, officer. We're just finishing up doing a little recording and pretty soon we'll be calling it a night." Bill was so diplomatic. But then again, that was what we paid him for.

The other officer stepped forward, "Yeah that's what we figured. We sat outside in the car and had a listen for a couple of minutes. You guys sound pretty good. What's the name of the band?"

Howie volunteered, "The Ugly Ducklings!"

The lead officer responded, "Well I'll be, we just heard your new record on CHUM, today!" He extended his hand, "Nice to meet you, guys!"

Everyone exchanged pleasantries and said their good-nights and the two officers left with an autographed eight by ten glossy and a large thank you from Bill. It was a heart-felt one too. It made us feel secure knowing that the police were on our side and that they were on-the-ball when it came to tips from our neighbours.

Bill played the tape back as we packed up and we all agreed that it sounded pretty good. After all of the recording we had been doing our confidence was growing and we were becoming more and more aware of our own sound. We knew it was good and it gave us a good feeling.

After spending Christmas with our families we played a few gigs around town and then had New Years' eve off. Sylvia and I went to see Luke & The Apostles and The Paupers at Boris's. It was quite a double-bill and both bands put on an incredible show. Luke especially was in top form. It had been a while since I had seen either band play, and it was invigorating. We sang "Auld Lang Syne" with the crowd and danced the night away.

The first few weeks of 1967 the band didn't play very much and the weather was cold and miserable. We sequestered ourselves at Bay Studios and set out to finish mixing all of the remaining album tracks. We would show up for a few hours of mixing time whenever there was a lull in regular studio business, and slowly but surely over the course of the first few weeks of the year the album came together.

We chose "Ain't Gonna Eat Out My Heart Anymore" and "Hey Mama Keep Your Big Mouth Shut" as the two cover tunes for the album. The other nine songs were all originals. We originally intended to include "I Can Tell" as the third cover, but we failed miserably in our attempts to fix the oh-so-slight mistake in the intro; where Rob had almost dropped one of his sticks. Ray and Dave tried to remove the flub a few times by physically cutting it out of the reel, but it was virtually impossible. The idea was to remove one bar of music, and thus preserve the tempo of the tune. But each attempt removed the blunder and left the remaining music hopelessly out of synch. In the end we gave up and passed on having the tune on the album.

Huard & Ray did some rough mixes of the other tunes from the album sessions and along with the "Live" stuff that we had recorded at the rehearsal hall, they put together a Demo tape that we could take to radio stations. So we now had something new to play for our fans on our up-coming interviews.

First up was a twenty minute segment on the CBC with Dave Charles. He was the CBC's youth commentator-of-the-day, and he really knew his stuff. We did five minutes of talk with him and fifteen minutes of music. The main feature of this piece was our five minute "Live" version of "I'm A Man" from our Midland Avenue Rehearsal-Hall session.

Next, we did a full one hour show on 1050 CHUM with Bob MacAdorey. It was a new show called "Talent In Toronto" that aired "Live" on Sunday nights at nine and it was revolutionary for the time, considering the lengthy format, the comprehensive nature of Bob's questions and the number of tracks we played on the show. We had a very friendly and informal relationship with Bob and with "Jungle" Jay Nelson from CHUM, so we thoroughly enjoyed every minute of our time on-air with Bob.

One strange and portentous occurrence from that show though, was that Bob kept referring to us as The Rolling Stones. Each time he let it slip we all groaned and laughed and when the hour was almost finished he finally cleared the air of his mind-addled fixation by explaining that initially (at least for that very first gig for our high school talent show) we had called ourselves The Strolling Bones. This was a little tid-bit of information that the record company had put in our press kit. No one had bothered to qualify the statement with an explanation of the circumstances. Thus, for evermore people believed that we had originally called the band The Strolling Bones.

Even though we weren't really a band at that point and the name had been an obvious tongue-in-cheek homage to The Stones, the reference stuck. We should have kept our big mouths shut!

The UGLY DUCKLINGS at The Cherry Street Spit, Jan.'67

The week after the CHUM show Sylvia and I went to the Uptown Theatre to see "How To Steal A Million" with Peter O'Toole and Audrey Hepburn. It was a good flick; light and airy with a neat plot and great photography and fashion.

Near the end of the movie Sylvia dropped the bombshell that she was pregnant. She was all tensed up and almost hyperventilating by the time she got the words out, but they were still words of excitement and wonder to me.

We knew the risks we were taking without using birthcontrol, but in our minds we must have made some silent decision, because the future still looked great and we felt at ease. We were madly in love and infatuated with each other. Nothing could have felt more natural. We walked back to Admiral Road slowly, discussing what our options were and how we were going to tell our parents. There was no doubt that we were going to get married. The only question was where and when.

We very quickly decided to get married first, before we told our parents what was happening. We went to City Hall, got a marriage license and made plans to do it before the band's next mini-tour.

On the 22nd of February we trudged down to Queen Street in the freezing cold with Bob Melbourne & Bill Huard as our witnesses and spoke our vows. That was definitely the easy part. The hard part was to come later, when we had to tell our folks. Or, at least, that's what we thought.

Eventually we gathered enough courage to approach both sets of parents and the deed was done with surprisingly less vitriol and hand wringing than we had expected. In fact, everyone seemed to accept our decision wholeheartedly. We felt vindicated. Things were looking up.

Meanwhile, totally unbeknownst to the band, there were discussions going on between Fred White and Tommy Graham, the owners of "Yorktown Records" and "Arc Records" of Scarborough. The object of said negotiations was to get us released from "Yorktown" and signed to a genuine recording contract. We were never privy to what exactly went on, or to what kind of negotiations were really happening, since we had *never even signed* a formal contract with "Yorktown" in the first place. All of the original arrangements for the release of our singles were based on a handshake and set up through Tommy Graham's connections with Fred. Obviously some money was about to change hands but we weren't invited to be part of it. At this point we still had not even received any royalties from Fred for "Nothin'" or for "She Ain't No Use To Me" and it really got under Roger's skin that all this negotiating was going on without us being involved. Roger was the only guy in the band that had an inkling of knowledge about business practices, but none of the rest of us paid much attention to his grumbling and criticisms. We were just happy to play our gigs and get a pay-cheque every week.

At precisely the same time that this was all happening John gave his notice. He was going to marry Chris Ruffle, Sylvia's sister, and he wanted to pursue a real job with some security and prospects for a future. Nobody argued the point.

New "Promo" Shot taken when Howie joined the band...

In any event, we didn't have to look very far for a replacement bass player. As soon as Howie heard of John's imminent departure he petitioned the band for the opportunity to audition.

He showed up at rehearsal with a rented Fender Precision bass and proceeded to blow everyone away with flawless renditions of the tunes. We couldn't stump him. Whatever we called for, he immediately played without hesitation. He had secretly been playing all of the tunes at home in the evenings, waiting and hoping that someday he would get just such a chance. The vote was unanimous. As of February 18th we had a new bassist. Things were changing fast and the changes were about to accelerate in the next few weeks beyond our wildest imaginings.

During this period we were trying desperately to get our album released and out into the stores. It was difficult because of the negotiations that were going on between "Yorktown" and Arc Records. In the end Fred White decided to release it on "Yorktown" since the deal with Arc Records had been temporarily put on hold. In late March we went into the studio and assembled the album with Dave Leonard, selecting the track sequence by band consensus. The final choice seemed totally natural and had a very familiar feel to it; like it had been a set-list for one of our shows.

The cover design was another matter. No one came up with any great ideas and Fred didn't really have any connections with any graphic designers. So we thrashed around aimlessly, accomplishing very little and getting more and more stressed-out about it as time went by.

Glynn and I wrote a couple of gnomish poems that we envisioned on the rear of the cover, somewhere amongst the liner notes. But the truth was that we still didn't have a title for the album and there just wasn't any real impetus in the band to get things done. We were so busy, that time slid by un-noticed until our window of opportunity reached critical mass.

Huard was our saving grace. He had finally had enough of our endless procrastinating and took things in hand to get the album finished. At an evening rehearsal he sat us down and told us we had to come up with a title, or else!

"It's now or never, guys. If you want the album to come out, you're going to have to name it! Tonight!"

There was a lot of mumbling and grumbling, followed by a sudden lingering silence.

Howie finally broke it. "What about the poems that Glynn & Dave wrote?"

Everyone responded, "Yeah, what about them?"

"Well, maybe if we're gonna have them in the liner notes, we could find something in them, for a title. You know, to tie everything together."

Glynn got his guitar case out and pulled out the sheets with the poems written on them. At this point neither of the poems had titles, but the first poem that Bill read had the concluding lines; "Somewhere Outside, outside your Mind, You'll find this group of five!"

Huard read them aloud, and everyone listened intently. When he got to the end there was a short pause and then Roger intervened.

"That's it, man. That's us, right? We're outsiders!"

We all looked at each other.

Howie immediately asked, "Outside Your Mind?"

Roger came back, "Na, Na, man. "Somewhere Outside", that's us, right?

Nobody can pin us down. It happens all the time. They can never figure out what category to put us in!"

Glynn smiled. I smiled. Rob smiled. We all smiled. It was meant to be.

"O.K. Bill, I guess you've got a title!"

Bill was satisfied and took Glynn's copies of our poems and headed out the door. "We'll have an Album cover before Friday, I'll be in touch!"

Bill was true to his word and he showed up at our gig on Friday night with a rough mock-up of the cover. It was a real surprise to us considering the instructions that we had given to him when he set off in pursuit of a designer.

We had wanted something that resembled the "Atlantic Records" releases of the day. Something that had a professional look to it, but above all, something with class that said we had finally arrived!

Instead we got a raunchy looking mess that looked like it had been assembled with typed quickie-notes pasted to an all-black cardboard background as a random assemblage of disassociated rectangles and squares. It was hard to believe that a graphic designer had really done such an amateurish job.

The front cover itself was more acceptable, although the photograph that it featured wasn't quite in focus. We all let Huard know of our disapproval but in the end Fred White allowed the cover to be used so that we could get it out and into the stores for the beginning of April.

As it turned out it was withdrawn within a week of release because of a fault in the master stamper that caused every copy to skip when it got to the middle of "Do What You Want". In an effort to save time Fred White had allowed Arc Records to cut the stamper. Bad move.

Front Cover of The Album – by "Gus"?

After sales of 330 albums the pressing was recalled and the tapes were then sent to Capital Records to have a master stamper created properly. The second pressing that hit the stores a little over two weeks later sported a newly designed coloured label and a much improved sound with less booming bass. Capital had re-used the original covers from the first run, rather than discard them; but when they got into the second run they needed to have more covers printed, so they altered the front cover by adding the "Yorktown" logo and serial number to the top right corner.

In less than a month there were now three different versions of the album released to the public. Sales were brisk and "The Record Villa" at Avenue Road and Yorkville Avenue was having a hard time keeping it in stock. It was a special treat to see the album in Sam's or A & A Records when we went shopping, and to be stopped and asked for autographs while we were in the stores. Hard to believe that so much could happen in such a short time.

But things were only going to get better, and what was coming was beyond what any of us could imagine!

Near the end of April, John married Chris, with much fanfare and the Band found itself featured on the front page of The Scarborough Mirror.

Our next item on the agenda was to find a new road manager to replace Howie. We had come to expect quite a lot from Howie, as he had provided us with a dedicated intelligent approach to the job. We didn't have to tell him what to do. He used common sense and intuition.

So we put the word out. We wanted someone with brains rather than brawn. Someone who could think his way out of situations and keep one step ahead of Huard and the band.

In the end we totally lucked out.

Kevan Staples, who was a friend of Carole Pope, had been coming to see the band at Boris's and The Red Gas Room for a couple of months. He approached Bill and asked about the position. His main question was about the remuneration, as he needed a certain amount to maintain his accommodations and to make guitar payments. We obliged with a suitable salary and were happy to welcome him into our musical tribe.

Kevan Staples

Glynn Backstage......

We were getting famous in our own little corner of the city. My mom and dad were really impressed! John and Chris headed off to New York for their honeymoon, and the rest of us got down to the business of rehearsing with our new Bass Player!

**Two Poems – Written by Dave &
Glynn for "Somewhere Outside".**

By & By

So in the wee, and by soos neck,
I on the sills percieved to peck.
By ridden trod-down nick and pack;
Foresoothe!
I spoiled the ghostly track.
And with a swarthy lip-lisped grin,
I mentally coiled the scrollment in.
Ah, with weak vigor by and by
I pricked the evil devil eye.
To slay the Satan on the ground
I nately turned his eyeball 'round,
And boiled him in oil!

SOMEWHERE OUTSIDE

Pouring from the tea-pot spout,
Five groobie cups of tea.
I looked from up the window out,
No hippies 'round to see.
And when the darkness came about
I lit the candle light,
And what should pop upside the ground but,
"Ugly Duckies" in the night.
Upon my sill I stealthily stood
With eyeballs bulging out
And brew a'spilling in my lap,
From inst the teapot - out.

In retrospect and here-to-forth,
And many waves of forethought,
I wined and dined and pranced and danced,
And then commenced to thought.
I dreamt I heard the music play,
And then a crier cried,
"Somewhere outside, outside your mind,
You'll find this group of five.

CHAPTER 15
GRADUATION

The following week we headed out on a small Maritime Tour. Scribner had arranged for us to play all the major cities, Down East, in a ten-day period. All of our singles had been played by the stations out there and had sold quite well. Now it was time to play in person and up the ante.

Frankly, with all of the tensions over negotiations with Arc Records and all of the bullshit that had happened with the release of our album, we felt relieved to get back out on the road. This would be Howie's first tour as bass player and he was almost giddy with anticipation.

We set out early on Monday morning and headed east on Highway 401. We had the new "Blue Goose II", a 1964 GMC Handi-Van that Huard had bought on spec at a Scarborough dealership. If we liked it, we could buy it. If not we could turn it in on something else. One thing that was nice about it was that it had a much more powerful radio than the old panel-truck. There was a big 10 inch speaker and more wattage!

As we headed east from Kingston around noon we cranked up the tunes and listened to The Young Rascals new single, "Groovin'". The DJ at the Kingston station was all ga-ga about this new song, and with good reason. It was a monster and destined to reach number one; at least that was my humble opinion. Kevan agreed. Roger thought it was a bit sappy; but of course everything was a bit sappy as far as Roger was concerned. He was far more interested in Bo Diddley's new album or Screamin' Jay Hawkins', "I Put A Spell On You". Roger loved the grind and the bounce. He needed the edges to be sharper and a little bit uncomfortable.

That evening after we got east of Montreal, Howie pulled a plastic bag out of his guitar case and asked pointedly if anyone would mind if he had a smoke.

"What the fuck is that?" was the big question that fell out of Glynn's mouth.

"Hey man, it's just a little weed, you know." Howie was quite calm and not the least bit defensive. "Haven't you guys ever tried it?"

No, no, no and no was the common refrain. We had all vowed when we moved downtown to Yorkville that we were not going to get sucked into the drug scene.

Rob was sitting beside Howie and asked to take a sniff of the bag. After a couple of sniffs he passed it back.

"Sort of smells moldy, or something."

Howie was quick to reply. "Yeah, it's really good stuff. Just a puff or two is all you need. Anybody want to try it?"

I motioned to Howie to pass the bag over to me and had a sniff. "How long have you been smokin' this stuff, Howie?"

"About a year."

Glynn was curious about Howie's consumption of the weed and its relationship to the weird comic outbursts that he would fall into at times; squirming and bellowing like a stuck pig and whistling at beautiful girls with a manic glee while bulging his eyes out like a mad Salvador Dali on uppers. He grilled Howie about a few choice incidents that had occurred in the last few weeks.

"Well, I think I might have had a few tokes for some of those trips, man. But the rest were just from the after-effects. You know what I mean?"

"No, tell me what you mean." Glynn wanted details.

"Well it changes how you think of things. How you perceive the world, you know. It makes the world a more enjoyable place. More fun and sometimes more paradoxical."

Roger grabbed the bag and had a whiff. He looked at Howie. "So, you don't feel loaded or whoosey from it?"

"Ah, no Roge'. It just makes you feel more in tune with things. It's hard to explain. One thing for sure is that it makes you more aware of how absurd some of the things in this world are. And it's very relaxing."

Everyone's curiosity was elevated by this point and Kevan volunteered to try it first. Howie was elated and immediately rolled a "joint" while everyone watched. He lit it and took a puff, then passed it over to Kevan. The smell of the smoke was sort of like a musky incense and it filled the truck in no time.

"Anybody else want a puff?"

I stuck out my hand and Howie passed it over. It tasted acrid and earthy.

Howie watched me intently and told me to try to hold the smoke in my lungs for a while. I did, and I did.

Rob's hand abruptly appeared beside my head and the joint quickly made its way to the rear of the truck.

Howie busied himself by rolling another one, which magically appeared glowing and lit just as the other one winked out after it had burned down to about half an inch in length.

Glynn was still hesitant. "Did you guys all forget what we decided about smoking dope when we first started playing in The Village?"

Roger had just finished taking his first puff and exhaled loudly as he replied, "Yeah, well I guess that was a long time ago, when we were all still afraid of the big bad wolf!"

Everyone chuckled.

"No, seriously Roge'. Didn't we say that we would be better off just sticking to booze and forgetting about all the other crap that's out there?" Glynn made his point and leaned back against Roger's Traynor stack, waiting for a reply.

"Well, yeah. But we know a lot more now, don't we?"

Howie turned around and faced everyone with a serious look, "Listen guys, nothing bad is gonna happen. Nobody's going to turn into an addict. Take my word for it, we'll all get a bit of a buzz and feel real nice and that's it. Relax and keep your mind open; the world isn't going to come to an end just because we had a little puff of marijuana!"

"Here, Here!" Rob made his point, and a slight giggle slid from between his lips as the words rolled from his tongue.

Glynn stuck out his hand and intercepted the joint as it made its way forward, "O.K. then, I guess I'm in".

Huard looked at him as he took a drag from the joint and finally spoke. "Well I guess if you're going to try it, I'll have a go!"

So the joints made the rounds as we rolled along and Howie rolled another and then, another. Huard was the first to notice how hungry he was. Then, as soon as he mentioned that it might be time to stop and re-energize, everyone started grumbling about how dry they were.

Rob was perplexed. "Man, I feel like my tongue is almost glued to the roof of my mouth!"

Roger passed out some life-savers as we motored on, all of us salivating as we anticipated some greasy burgers and fries. Kevan started messing with the tuner on the radio and came up with an American station out of New York State that was putting out some great R&B. As we pulled into a service centre to wet our appetites Wilson Picket came over the airwaves with his best to-date, "Mustang Sally". We were all transfixed. The little keyboard flip at the beginning of the song took us by surprise.

"Did you hear that?" Huard turned his head sideways. "How the hell did they do that?"

I heard it too. It sounded like the keyboard and amp was floating on water, or something.

Roger was miffed. "Hey, I thought everybody was hungry. Are we gonna sit here and listen to music, or go eat?"

Kevan looked at me, I looked back at Bill. "Hey you guys go ahead, we're gonna check this out!"

So, Kevan and Bill and I stayed back and listened to the whole song. We were amazed that it didn't sound like we remembered it. It was so much better.

We heard different parts in it, different sounds and aspects that we had never noticed before. As we walked across the parking lot to the restaurant Huard had an epiphany.

"Hey, you know something? All those kids in the village and at our shows; they're listening to us just like that. They're smokin' up and hearing us through a marijuana fog!"

"Yeah, sort of like an Alice In Wonderland collective experience," I mused. And then as we sat down to eat we re-hashed all the speculation about "Puff The Magic Dragon". When our food finally arrived we all got strangely quiet. Taste was suddenly a different experience. We cherished every bite. Yeah, the world was changing fast. We were going to have to adapt.

So we hit the road with a different attitude than before. We turned the radio up and were amazed at the sensory overload, as we experienced music as never before. We marveled at the green of the fields, the brightness of the sky, even the sharpness of the exhaust stench from all the trucks and cars on the road when we came to a halt at a traffic light.

Howie was right. We became more aware.

Just before four o'clock we pulled into Fredericton, New Brunswick. Our first stop on the tour. We checked into a motel and Huard immediately got on the phone to the local Radio Station. It had all been arranged that we would do an interview with the local drive-home-show DJ before our concert. So after a quick wash and change of clothes we headed down to the station.

We were still a little buzzed when we finally went on-air. But over-all the interview went well, without any major faux-pas and we enticed the kids to make it out to the show by dropping hints that we had a lot of new material we were going to lay on them. As we signed off, we introduced them to Howie, our brand new bass player and the DJ played "Hey Mama Keep Your Big Mouth Shut" from our album!

That night was a real experience. Dozens of local girls jammed the area right in front of the stage, entranced by our every move. Some of their boyfriends must have gotten jealous, as they started to heckle the band, calling us "girls" and then later on, "freaks" and "animals". We were perplexed. We'd always heard great stories about the incredible hospitality of people in the Maritimes. We put it down to a fluke and kept on playing, but it just got worse and worse.

Before the second set was over they started throwing things at us. The rest of the audience were just as pissed off with the situation as us, and started yelling at them to stop, but it made no difference. These guys were loaded and angry and there seemed to be no security people there who were willing to intervene on our behalf.

Before we started "I'm A Man" I announced that if the shit didn't stop, then we would. As Roger wailed through the intro the missiles started coming. We soldiered on. I think we made it about half way through the tune before I got hit with a piece of cardboard that whizzed out of the crowd like a miniature UFO. It just glanced off of my head as I turned to look over at Glynn.

That was it; I grabbed my harps and walked off stage. The rest of the guys kept playing, but I was done. So much for maritime hospitality!

Rob thundered through his drum solo and brought "I'm A Man" to a close a bit sooner than usual and the night ended. We were stunned. It was such a shock to be sabotaged by a bunch of fucking greasers in a small town, like that. This so obviously wasn't Toronto.

It had never crossed our minds to demand proper security for our shows. It was a lesson well learned.

The next day we were on the road to Antigonish, Nova Scotia.

When Scribner had laid the gig on us we were flummoxed. None of us knew of such a place and certainly none of us knew how to pronounce the name of it properly. It turned out that there were lots of "Ducks" fans there at The Sir Francis Xavier University and they had sent a letter to Ron, telling him that we should make it a stop on our tour if we ever made it Down East. Or, so he said.

The drive was pleasant enough and we were taking in the sights as we went along. It seemed to me that the countryside looked very similar to Ontario and that there wasn't much to distinguish these roads and fields from anything back home.

The guys told me to lay off the critical talk and mellow out. No one was in a mood for down-talk after the fiasco of the night before. It still bothered us. What the hell was that freak-out all about? Nobody had ever thrown stuff at us before with intent to harm.

Glynn had it figured, "They're just scared man. Things are changing fast these days. We represent something somewhere off in the future, and they don't want to go there. We're a threat to them. It's like they're feeling bad about themselves!"

Kevan was nodding his head. "Yeah, this isn't Toronto out here, they don't get to see and hear about as much of the world as we do."

Howie chuckled as he pulled a joint out of his shirt pocket and lit it, "Too bad we couldn't turn them on. Maybe they might finally be able to really see, instead of just looking around dumbfounded like everybody else!"

Roger took a poke and mumbled, "Come on you guys, forget about all this shit, lets just drive."

We were making good time and around five thirty we pulled off at a service centre to have a bite to eat. We'd finished four or five joints in the last half hour or so, and the munchies had set in. Smoke wafted from the "Blue Goose II" as we opened the doors and spilled out onto the pavement. We made our way inside giggling and laughing over some very rude joke that Howie had been performing for us in his usual manner.

We must have looked as if we had been starving for days as we devoured a half dozen burgers and a mountain of fries. The waitress was sweet and asked us if we were a band, "or something". Huard pulled an eight by ten out of his case and we signed it for her before we left with some coffee and soft drinks to go.

As we headed back out on the highway we felt elated and inspired. We cranked up the radio and grooved to some Stones and The Music Machine doing "Talk, Talk". We loved the groove and the volume. We kept it up for the next hour or so while we sang along like a bunch of punch drunk sailors. And then a very strange thing happened.

We went over this shining and glittering, silvery grey steel bridge. Right away Howie let out one of his empty wolf-whistles. He almost hyperventilated.

"Oh shit, man. Oh, shit!"

A chorus of, "What? what's up, man. Speak up!"

Howie didn't raise his voice, he just said in a very plain monotone, "We've been over this bridge before!"

Kevan took his foot off the gas and let the "Blue Goose II" drift off the road onto the gravel shoulder.

"Are you sure, man?"

"Yeah, I'm sure!"

Huard leaned out the window and took a look back at the bridge. "How can you be sure Howie? All these fuckin' bridges look the same!"

There was a crossroads about a hundred yards ahead and Huard told Kevan, "Pull up when we get to the intersection. Let's read that sign." When we got there the sign had an arrow on it pointing to the left, saying "Blair Lake 2 Miles". Just beyond that there was another sign that read "Amherst Next Exit".

Roger was intent, scouring the map. Then his eyebrows raised and his lips curled. "Son Of A Bitch! We just drove back where we came from by about forty miles!"

Glynn started giggling and a huge grin spread across his face. "So what the fuck do we do now?"

Huard was thinking; concentrating very hard. "O.K. we just came back forty clicks, and we had about seventy to go when we stopped. So, a hundred and ten. That's about two, two and a half hours."

He looked at his watch. "Oh shit man, we can't make it. The dance starts at nine and it's already seven-fifteen. We're FUCKED!"

We had screwed up royally. No excuses. No passing the buck.

Everyone sat there stoically, unable to process what had just happened.

Huard rubbed his forehead as if in deep thought, finally got a grip on things and then sprang into action.

"Hey guys, we just broke down, eh? That's all. The truck broke down. We've got to call and let them know what's happening. We can't tell them the truth obviously, because we'd look like a bunch of idiots. So, what do you think?"

I didn't want to look like an idiot; "Let's do it, Bill. We have to do something!"

Slowly it dawned on us that our reputation was at stake and we had to get serious. We headed back in the right direction and pulled into the first place that had a phone. Bill handled it all with grace and genuine dismay. He didn't have to put on an act. We were all pretty devastated that we wouldn't be able to play. We were going to lose six hundred and fifty bucks! We apologized profusely and accepted regrets from the folks on the student council at Xavier University where we were to have played, and the deed was done.

When Bill got off the phone we all stood around rather dejected, everyone at a loss as to how such a thing could have happened.

Glynn was the first to broach the subject of our direct responsibility for what had happened. "I guess there'll be no more smokin' in the truck, eh guys?"

We all sort of shuffled our feet and answered with quiet guilt.

"Yeah, I guess. Uh huh. I guess so, man. Yeah. Yeah, man."

What else could we say? We all had to admit we screwed up.

We decided to make it a rule. From right then, and on. There were certain parts of this life that had to remain business. Getting to gigs was surely the most important one. It didn't matter how great a band we were, or could be, if we couldn't get to the gigs on time!

Bill had one final brainwave, as far as preserving our reputation with Scribner and with our allies at CHUM, Bob Mac and Jungle Jay. He phoned up CHUM and taped a "DUCKS on Tour" segment with Bob, re-telling the story of our breakdown for all the fans back home, and eliciting sympathy from the guys at CHUM, as well. It was a master-stroke of promotion and self-preservation.

We grabbed some sodas and coffee and headed on down the road in the direction of our next stop, Prince Edward Island. We were booked in Charlottetown and after our Atigonish debacle it was decided we would catch the first ferry across, the next morning. So away we went.

As we crossed highway thirty four to "Unstable", Howie tuned in CKCL in Truro and "She Ain't No Use To Me" came blasting through the speaker at 105 decibels. It lifted our spirits, for sure. We weren't going to screw this one up.

The trip across on the ferry was special. None of us were stoned, as we had put *that* to bed until after the gig was played. The idea that we had screwed up so royally didn't sit well with any one of us. It was major guilt and recrimination time.

The sun was shining and the salt air was invigorating. Those of us that hadn't seen the ocean before stood enraptured on the foredeck watching the seagulls and terns and digging the salt spray as the bow of the ferry churned its way through the blue-black waves.

The gig in Charlottetown went without a hitch. We did an interview in the afternoon on the local radio station and then rocked on with illicit abandon for a good two hours at the local arena. We really pumped it up that night, to make up for our reckless behavior of the day before. None of the folks involved in the PEI show were aware of our major screw-up and we hadn't mentioned a word about it at the interview in the afternoon. Still, we were racked with a certain amount of guilt. Our pride was bruised and we had to atone for it in our own minds. I'm certain that I shed a couple of pounds that night!

Everyone was spectacular, culminating with Rob's drum solo which reached new heights of innovation and rhythmic intensity. We felt vindicated and retired to the hotel for some much needed rest and relaxation.

Of course the relaxation part now consisted of a few tokes of the wicked weed, provided by Howie Smith. We were very careful to only smoke on the balcony of our rooms so that no incriminating odors crept into the hallways.

Howie was the master of ceremonies for our exploration of the wonders of weed. The auditory enhancement of music was the thing that really got our attention. It was purely an emotional response to the effects of the weed, but it made us understand the attraction for all those "heads" out there who were turning on and thumbing their noses at the establishment.

Listening to The Beatles, or The Stones; classical music, Sinatra, the Blues; you name it. Anything you listened to, took on another presence, another aura and then wormed its way deeper into your psyche and your soul. It truly was a magic elixir!

Around midnight we got very hungry and Bill and Howie and I went out to get some treats. We were having great difficulty suppressing the laughter that seemed to follow every word that any one of us spoke. *Everything* seemed so funny!

On our way out we noticed that there were many prints of the famous "Group of Seven" artist's paintings, hanging on the walls of the corridors and the lobby.

Huard looked at one in the lobby and scratched his head, "Hey, look at this one. The reflection in the water is a perfect reverse image of the lake and the mountains!"

Howie wasn't impressed, "So? So what's the big deal?"

"Well. If you turned it upside down it would be the same thing wouldn't it?"

I could see what Bill was driving at. "Hey, what do think, you guys?"

Huard looked around. The night clerk was sitting behind the check-in counter reading a newspaper.

"We'll wait 'til we come back in".

Half an hour later on the way back in we turned three paintings upside-down. All of the ones that had reflections of water and mountains, forests or sunsets etcetera.

The next morning as we checked out of the hotel we all had a chuckle, as we noticed that all three were still hanging there in their upside-down state; no one having noticed; even though they were all hanging slightly higher on the wall because the wires on the back had not originally been strung at dead centre.

We had a good laugh as we scooted out the front doors and set off to Halifax and the grand finale of the tour!

Compared to our other Down East gigs, Halifax was like playing at Maple Leaf Gardens. The radio station people, the bookers and the press all treated us like royalty. The audience was ours from the get-go. The night was one of those supreme rock 'n roll blissed-out fantasy concerts. All vague and smudgy and seen through a fish-eye lens. We couldn't have dreamed it any better! We ended our set with the same "finisher" as always but we got a surprise. The audience promptly demanded an encore!

Having nothing left to play we automatically went into "Windy City" and wailed for the next five minutes.

That seemed to satisfy them and everyone was willing to call it a night. After we signed autographs and chatted up some major "Ducks" fans we retired to the hotel. Before we hit the sack Glynn and Huard announced that they wanted to fly home, as they were weary of the cramped quarters of the "Blue Goose II". We couldn't blame them; we would probably all have made the same choice if not for the expense.

So, the next morning we drove Glynn and Bill to the airport to see them off. Kevan waited in the truck with Roger while the rest of us headed inside to the Air Canada counter. Rob was curious to see how expensive the tickets would be.

After Bill & Glynn bought their tickets we headed for their departure gate.

When we were almost there we noticed a tall skinny dude hanging out in front of the international departures area. He looked vaguely familiar and was dressed to the nines in grey dungarees, cowboy boots and a floral shirt with epaulets. I had that de'jà vu feeling of having seen him before, but I just couldn't place him. As we walked along he carefully checked us out and then approached us before we could pass.

"Are you guys taking the flight to "London?"

Huard moved forward, "Ah, no man; we're heading back to Toronto.

We got a little tired of the road and decided to bite the bullet and fly".

The stranger extended his hand, "Well hi guys, I'm Scott Mackenzie. I sort of pegged you guys as a band. I guess I got that right".

I inadvertently blurted out, "I knew I'd seen you before! You were just on "Shindig" a couple of weeks ago, weren't you?" I knew my memory wasn't screwing with me.

"Yeah, I'm just heading over to Europe to do a bunch of promo spots for the single. What's the name of your band, man?" He shook hands all 'round as he waited for an answer.

Glynn responded, "The Ugly Ducklings".

Scott raised an eyebrow, as if something in his memory clicked. "Yorkville, right? Seems I heard something about you guys and Yorkville. Is that Village scene all that it's cracked up to be?"

We were floored. Huard filled him in on the scene, as the rest of us interjected tidbits of information here and there. He was a real gentleman and it made us feel great that people out on the west coast knew about us and about the Toronto scene. It figured that word would spread, seeing as how a substantial number of musicians from the Village had made the pilgrimage and settled in L.A. and San Francisco.

We wished him well with "If You're Going To San Francisco", said our goodbyes and left Glynn and Bill at the departure gate. The rest of us headed back to the "Blue Goose II" for the long trek home. The world seemed like such a small place.

CHAPTER 16

DECEPTION

By the middle of May the deal was done between Arc and Yorktown and we were called into Arc Records to meet Bill Guilliland, their head of A & R and production. He was very forthright with the band and informed us that he had listened to all of our demo tracks and was not impressed by our recorded output to-date. He said that the level of musicianship in the band left a lot to be desired and that we should work hard to get in shape for some serious recording in the future. The company was offering us a standard recording contract of five years during which time we would record a minimum of five albums. If we couldn't manage to cut the mustard in the studio, we would be expected to allow session musicians to take our place, in order to keep recording costs down.

He explained that this would be of benefit to us as well as to the company, since all artists were expected to repay their recording costs from their royalties from record sales. Thus, the more costs incurred during recording, the longer we would have to wait to receive royalties.

We didn't give a shit about all of the financial in and outs of the business.

We told him that as far as we were concerned the business end of things was his problem. We just cared about our own personal integrity, and we made sure that he understood where we were coming from. An Ugly Ducklings album was going to be exactly that. No substitutions and no misrepresentation as to who played on our recordings.

Guilliland stood at the head of the table and looked incredulous. "Listen guys, this is a just a standard recording contract, we're not making any special requirements of you. These contracts are universal in the industry. If you want to make a living in this business, you'll just have to accept it. Otherwise, your inexperience as musicians, especially in the studio, will cost you your chance at a music career."

He was being honest and up-front, but we just weren't interested.

Glynn stood up first, "This is bull-shit, you know how I feel, guys." He turned and headed for the door.

Howie followed and then Roger and Rob stood and looked at Huard.

"We better schedule another meeting, Bill. Something's going to have to give, or this isn't going to happen."

Huard looked at Guilliland and then at me. "Yeah, Bill. Maybe we should sleep on it for a few days. No sense talking any more right now. This is a big deal as far as we're concerned."

I looked at Guilliland, too, "We've got this far by playing on all of our own records, Bill, and our fans seem to like it. Maybe you should re-think your position and come back with some kind of compromise. The whole music business is changing. Maybe Arc Records could use a few changes too!"

He shuffled the sheaf of papers he'd been holding in his hands and tamped them lightly on the table to align them before placing them back into his briefcase. The corners of his mouth were turned down and he had a slightly stunned look on his face. He watched as Roger and Rob headed towards the door.

"I'll talk it over with Tony DeMaria and the guys tomorrow and get back to you after the weekend."

Huard and I turned and joined Roger and Rob. We walked to the parking lot in a daze; visibly dejected. We were sort of in a bind, now. We were pushing the envelope. We didn't know anything about the negotiations between Arc and Fred White. It wouldn't do to get locked into a major dispute with the company that was going to be promoting all of our recorded output. This was going to be like a poker game. Only it seemed to us that maybe all the cards weren't on the table.

Less than two weeks later we had reached a compromise. Guilliland and the boys weren't going to screw up inking a deal with the hottest band in the city. They knew that we had something special, even if they couldn't quite put their slimy little fingers on it. In the end Arc agreed that we could play on our own recordings, but we relinquished the right to choose our own producer. They would pick a producer for us, someone with advanced musical and arranging skills, who would mold us into a primo record-ing outfit. We were willing to do this because we realized our limitations. We didn't know anyone in the business in Toronto and we had no real experience in the studio, beyond what we had done for our album. So it was to be a marriage of convenience.

We would still write and choose our own material but they would have first right of refusal. We had enough confidence in our writing skills and our choice of cover tunes that we didn't see that this would present any major challenges.

It was a classic affair of give and take and everyone walked away happy. We looked forward to the events of the next few months as the beginning of a major phase in our career. We were ready.

Who could know what tomorrow might bring?

Over the next couple of weeks not much happened.

Finally, on the third Monday after the meeting Guilliland called me in to his office at Arc Records. He had a proposition for me that he said would give me a little extra spending cash and at the same time introduce me to Bob Halley, a great producer from New York City.

Evidently The Stitch In Tyme, who had also just signed to Arc a month before us, were going to New York to record a song that was to be used for a Miss Clairol Hair Colouring commercial and he wanted me to go as a fourth voice and for Huard to tag along as our Road Manager/ P.R. guy.

I would be able to make some extra bucks and at the same time get some studio experience and Bill would get some liaison experience by handling the business end of things for everyone.

I asked about our gig situation, since we were booked to play on Thursday night in Fort William, Ontario, which was quite a long way from T.O., and he was proposing that we fly down to New York on June 20th for the session.

He scratched his left ear and assured me that my flight down to New York would be covered by the advertising company's expenses and that they would book us a connecting flight to Fort William on our return to Toronto.

For an expectant father who had just started looking for a new apartment and was certainly in need of extra cash, it was almost too good to be true. I talked it over with the guys and with Sylvia and everyone agreed it was the thing to do. The guys would have a couple of days off, before driving to Port Arthur and Sylvia and I would get our first and last month's rent out of the deal, to secure a new apartment.

Next morning Bill and I were on an eight o'clock flight to the Big Apple with Donnie Morris, Bob Murphy and Grant Fullerton from The Stitch In Tyme. It was a short hour and a half flight and as soon as we landed we grabbed a cab and headed for Bell Studios in Manhattan. It was the same studio that The Four Seasons had recorded all of their million selling hits at and the same one where Ronnie Hawkins had recorded his self-titled debut album for Roulette Records. John Hammond Jr. had also used it to record "I Wish You Would" and "I Can Tell" for his Redbird Records single release. When we walked into the office we were in awe. There were photos of The Four Seasons and dozens of other fifties vocal groups lining the walls.

A studio employee came out of an office, welcomed us and escorted us to room "B". He said this was the big room where they could fit a small orchestra if they had to. We peered through a ten inch square window into the "big" room and then were ushered into the control room where we were introduced to Bob Halley. This was the man Guilliland had told us all about.

He was a dapper looking dude, just under thirty years old, wearing a beige cashmere sweater over a powder blue cotton shirt. He smiled right away when he saw the bunch of us come in and shook hands with everyone as Huard introduced himself and then the rest of us; one at a time.

He gave us a little background on what was happening with the track at that particular moment, commenting that most of the musicians in the studio for the day were from the Tonight Show Band. Then he motioned for us to go into an adjacent room where we could rehearse our vocals, which he indicated would be needed in about an hour.

Donnie had brought along a demo acetate of "New Dawn", the tune that we would be singing and he put it up on a turntable that was set up in one corner of the room. We started warming up right away.

It was definitely *not my thing* but the melody was O.K. and it was made for great four part harmony. Donnie worked with me, helping me lay out my part.

At any time we could cut the audio for the turntable and switch over to the audio that was on playback in studio "B". It was very tempting, as we could feel the pulsation of the bass and drums coming through the floor from the next room. Whenever we took a break it was very encouraging to hear the power and the clarity of the backing track that Mr. Halley was putting down with the guys in the "big" room. A couple of times we even sang along with it.

Sure enough after a little more than an hour had passed we got the call to get into the studio. They split us into pairs and placed us in small vocal cubicles; pairing me up with Donnie and Grant with Bob Murphy.

For almost two hours we fought with the intricacies of the harmonies for "New Dawn". There were three different versions that had to be recorded. A one minute spot, a thirty-second long version, and then the full-song version that was going to be used for one of the "Stitch In Tyme" singles.

Bob Halley called a time-out for lunch and told me that he wanted me to meet someone. I was all ears and eager. We went over to studio "A" which was a much smaller room and I was introduced to a tall skinny black dude with a stubbly unshaved face and a huge wide smile.

"Dave Bingham meet Carl Spencer", Bob Halley introduced us formally.

We shook hands and I looked at Bob with a quizzical look in my eye, hinting that I'd like an explanation.

He was up front. "Carl is a songwriter, Dave. He's got a tune that he'd like you to hear. He also drives a cab and he sang his tune for me a few weeks back when he picked me up at the airport".

I still looked dumb.

"We cut a demo of it last week with a few of the guys. If it's O.K. with you Carl's going to sing it for you right now, to the demo track. It's called "Gaslight".

Weird title; I was really getting curious now. "Sure, yeah go ahead, Carl".

Bob leaned over the console and turned on the small turntable and cued it up. The tune started with a cracking snare introduction followed by an incredible guitar phrase that led right into the verse. Carl sang it right away.

She don't really want my love, but she won't set me free, she want's to hold me. She's gonna make me blow my mind, if I don't get away, my doctor told me".............I'm walkin' around talkin' to myself...... "

Carl laid it out for me from beginning to end, sounding like a very soulful black version of Eric Burdon. I sat there stunned and enthralled by the simplicity and honesty of the lyrics. You couldn't get much clearer than that. The power of the choruses was inescapable. I was gaga.

Bob Halley must have been intuitive. He leaned towards me. "Hey Dave, you think that's cool? You should hear the arrangement that we've got worked up for this tune. It's like nothing you've ever heard!"

I was dumbstruck, I didn't know what to say.

"Yeah, I can imagine it might be pretty powerful."

"Right on, man. We're working on it after lunch. How'd you like to give it a go?"

I was caught slightly off guard. It hadn't really dawned on me that this was all for my benefit. I reasoned with myself silently, my thoughts racing at the speed of light. It wasn't that it would be such a bad thing; if I did it. I had never expected the opportunity and now here I was in New York City with a bunch of guys from The Tonight Show Band, all set to start to record this incredible song by a great singer and songwriter who was ready to teach me the ins and outs of *his* song! My answer sort of caught in my throat and then slid out sideways.

"Well, I don't have anything else to do right now. What is there to lose?"

Bob was pleased, he looked at me with a more serious expression, "I'll leave you here with Carl, then Dave. He can show you the ropes on the song.

You guys can work on the performance, and I'll send in your food."

He disappeared.

After lunch Huard came over to studio "A" and brought us back to the big room. We sat behind the big console with Bob and he pointed out the various musicians scattered out on the floor.

"Most of these guys are super pros, Dave. The Tonight Show Band is as good as it gets in this town. Except for the guitar player, Hugh McCracken; they're mostly jazz guys with a penchant for R&B. This kinda stuff really gets them going!"

He called on the talk-back. "O.K. guys, everybody got their lead sheets set? We ready for a preamble?" Everyone answered in the affirmative and the drummer counted down. The first run through was just to establish Bob's intentions for the feel of it. A few adjustments and additions were in order.

The next pass was starting to get some balls to it, but still had a few faults and bloopers that had to be worked out. There was quite a bit of talk-back to Bob and then a pause while everyone made notations on their charts.

The third pass was when it started to get heavy. Listening to the playback at full throttle it was mind blowing. The dynamics were perfect and they didn't even have a singer singing a demo track in their headphones. They just knew where things went. They *knew* how it would eventually feel.

Afterwards Bob slowed the pace and talked to the drummer and the guy on the kettle drums and told them how to hit their accents. Then he called up Hugh on the talk-back, "We need a couple of bars coming back into the third verse there, Hugh. Give us some "Cropper-isms", something funky, OK?"

Hugh came back, "Give me a minute will you, Bob?"

It was almost like Bob counted backwards from sixty seconds. Time was up before we knew it and they were into the next run through. Only this time Bob cued the tape operator for a take. When the time came for Hugh to do his little segue into the third verse everything went perfectly. Then he gave the guys a break and let them hear what they had done.

"What do you think guys? Want to hear it again?"

No takers. Silence.

"O.K. I agree, that was pretty damn good. Ed, how about really punching it on the kit right after Hugh does his thing before the last chorus comes in?"

"Sure thing, Bob". The drummer looked up, adjusted his earphones and then counted in once again and away they went, everyone wrapped in the sound and the power of it. Huard glanced at me, pointed at the drummer and then he phonetically mouthed the name "Shaunessy". The next three minutes seemed to last for an eternity, but a small miracle had happened. All thirteen of them had managed a perfect performance. Bob was excited. He pumped his arms in the air to keep them thumping it out on the tag-out at the end and then finally broke it off as echoes of the horns reverberated from the big Lansing Speakers as the last note faded.

Bob was really keyed up, "Man, that was hot. Let's hear it". He motioned to the tape operator.

Everyone sat motionless as the track played through. My heart was in my throat as I sang along in my head and I imagined what the final sound of this track could be like. It was like I was in some kind of dream. Two days before this I could never even have imagined this day as a possibility.

Bob was almost certain that this was the final take, but he had the engineer run it through a couple of more times, so that he could lower the volume and pull various tracks in and out to check for mistakes.

There were none. Wow, the sixth take! Shit!

"O.K guys take five. Dave, you feel like doing a run through? I just want to hear your voice on it, to see if there is anything else we might want to add before we send the rest of the guys home."

I readily agreed and was ushered into one of the vocal cubicles.

Carl sat beside Bob and led me through the tune. My chops weren't really happening yet, but Bob was satisfied and called it after a few passes.

"I think we've got to get some vibes over that turn-around phrase between the verses guys, and maybe get

Hugh to do some more Memphis soul guitar as counter-point to the vocal lines in the verses."

He came on the talk-back, "Dave, stay in the room there, O.K? I want you to sing with the track so that Hugh can get a feel for the guitar."

Hey, I was game for anything. "Whatever you want, Bob."

Over the next hour, Bob added the finishing touches to an incredibly powerful backing track and I learned the finer subtleties of the cadence of the lyrics from Carl.

Bob had to juxtapose the various overdubs into the open spaces that were available in the four tracks he'd recorded. Later on in the evening, before we laid the vocal down he would have to mix the tune down to three tracks in order to free up a track for my vocal.

That night was even more of a dream-world experience. It was so hard to get my head wrapped around the fact that all of this was really happening.

Huard and I had gone out for a walk on 42nd street after going out for some dinner, and he had bought a beautiful counterfeit watch for ten bucks off a huckster in a pork pie hat. The guys arm had been like a jewelry display case when he hiked his jacket sleeve up past his elbow. Bill knew it wasn't genuine, but bought it anyway, as a souvenir of our journey.

As we walked in the door to the studio I asked him the time and he crooked his arm and looked at the watch. The second hand wasn't moving.

"It says six thirty, but I know that's definitely not right".
He held it up to his ear.
"No ticking, hmmmm. Maybe it's screwed".

We walked into the office and asked the receptionist if Bob Halley was there yet.

"He's been here a while, guys. He said he'll meet you in number two".

We walked down the hall. As we approached we heard an incredibly thunderous sound emanating from behind the padded door of the control room. Bob was mixing down the four tracks to three, in order to free up a track to record my vocal. We entered and sat against the back wall of the room, enveloped by the sound and totally, utterly flabbergasted.

The power in the rhythm section was phenomenal. Our ears were filled with pure pleasure. Neither of us could speak.

After a couple of run-throughs Bob was satisfied that he had what he needed and turned to greet us.

"Well Dave, do you feel ready to give it a shot?"

I had been thinking about how I was going to get into the groove for this and had decided that there was no way to force things, I was just going to have to relax and take it in stride. All of the Duck's best performances had come when we least expected them because *we weren't thinking*, we were feeling it! So I was going to just go with my intuition and see what happened.

The story that was in the song was pretty universal. Some poor guy was getting the gears from a girl who really knew how to push all the right buttons. Hey, that sounded just like all those experiences that I had had at Cedarbrae Collegiate in Scarborough. I had lots of memories to draw on.

"Yeah, I think I'm ready Bob. I'll need some water and I think we should turn the lights off in the booth; I don't want to be distracted."

We were all set in ten minutes.

The first couple of times we ran through it I was holding back, but at a certain point I told Bob to start recording. You never knew what might happen. By the seventh take we were making headway. On the eighth I really nailed the choruses and Bob came right back in the phones.

"Come on in, Dave. You've got to hear this!"

As the tape rolled by Huard choked up and blurted out, "Holy shit Dave this is a fucking monster!"

Bob shushed him up and calmly said, "Just listen, Dave. Decide what you really like and what you want to re-do. This is something that's going to last forever."

We spent the next half hour fixing up a couple of lines in the verses that weren't up to snuff and then putting down a nice scat over the ending. Huard and I left the building in a daze, toting a four inch reel with a rough mix of the day's work. Bob was going to come to Toronto with the four-track, where we would do the final mix at Bay studios.

Bill and I headed to the hotel knowing that we had to be at the airport for the flight home at seven in the morning. Restless sleep and a five thirty wake-up call. Another day in the life of The Ugly Ducklings!

We really were on cloud nine as we descended out of the skies and touched down in Toronto. We had a lay-over of an hour and a half before we boarded a flight for Fort William. When we finally took off and headed north-west over Lake Michigan we wondered aloud what we were going to say to the rest of the guys when we arrived.

We concluded that the truth would be our best bet. Our only problem was how we would begin. It all seemed like a dream.

Would they believe our story?

CHAPTER 17
REVELATION

When we landed at the airport in Fort William we found Kevan in the arrivals parking lot, waiting for us in "The Blue Goose II", our snappy new gun-metal-blue GMC Handi-Van. We loaded up our bags, hopped in the van and sped off to the gig.

Kevan immediately started asking probing questions about New York, but both Bill and I answered with vague descriptions of our shopping expeditions and treatises on recording vocal harmonies, courtesy of Stitch In Tyme. We had decided that we weren't going to say anything about our further escapades in New York until after the show, when we had been paid and we were safely on our way to the next gig in Sudbury.

After a rabble-rousing gig, replete with an incredible Robin Boers drum solo during "I'm A Man", highlighted by an inspired light show courtesy of Mr. Huard, we finished packing up and hit the road by twelve thirty.

By two a.m. we were a hundred miles out and most of the guys were starting to nod off. Heads were falling forward and low rumbling snores were emanating from the rear of the van. Howie lay on his side with his denim jacket pulled up over his head, making hog-like grunting sounds alternating with intermittent gasps for breath. Bill and I sat up front while Kevan drove.

Roger, Rob and Glynn drifted in and out of consciousness scrunched up against the seatbacks and Glynn's Fender Showman speaker cabinet.

"So what really happened in New York guys?"

Kevan was a mind-reader.

"There's something about the way you two have been acting. And you've been walking with a really light step, if you know what I mean."

Bill looked at me.

I didn't want to lay it all out, so I told a little white lie. "Well, I sang on a demo of a song some guy brought in to Bob Halley."

"Oh yeah? What kind of song?"

"Well it's sort of mid-tempo, you know. Kind of like an Animals thing."

Huard glanced over at me and interjected, "Yeah, we're gonna have a preview of it for everybody at the studio next week." Bill really was great at shooting from the hip. Brilliant. This was precisely what we were going to have to do, anyway. What better way could there be to lay it all out? Get everyone in the studio, lube them up with a few drinks, get them in a good mood and then just let it rip. Let it wash over them with those giant Lansing Speakers; and then watch their reactions! Touche¢ Bill!

Kevan seemed satisfied for a moment, but then asked us who wrote the song; whereupon Bill told him the story of Carl Spencer and how he sang the tune to Bob Halley in his cab on the way to Bell Studios after picking the guy up at the airport.

Kevan grinned and seemed content with that. After all, it was a great story; and wasn't that the way Rock 'n Roll was supposed to happen? We'd all heard it so many times. Another rags to riches tale. It was so totally appropriate.

We headed on to Sudbury and played another memorable night fuelled with vodka and bravado. Sudbury just seemed to be our town. The people were pretty raunchy and seemed to bring out the raunch in us.

The next week we set everything up with Bay Studios and arranged for the band to meet one night after supper. Bill Guilliland was there with Ray Lawrence and Tony Dimaria. Ray set up the tape so it was ready to be played and we all sat around the control room having a catch-up conversation with Guilliland about his efforts to promote the band and publicize the launch of Arc Records' new label, "Yorkville Records".

The last person to arrive was Roger, who had been having some work done on his car.

Now we all looked at each other expectantly and Huard took over the proceedings.

"O.K. guys, we brought everybody here today because we've got something really special here. This song has the potential to take the band to the next level, as far as our Chart success is concerned. When Dave & I were in New York with The Stitch In Tyme Bob Halley played a demo for us of a special tune. A tune that he thought would be really suited to The DUCKS. When we heard it, we knew we couldn't pass it up."

Howie sighed and Glynn shifted his weight on the stool he was sitting on, his face showing a slight grimace. Roger looked over at me tentatively with a look of betrayal on his face. I just looked back at Bill.

"So Dave sang it. We put it down with some guys from the Tonight Show band and we did a rough mix of it. It's just like a real DUCKS song. So, pay attention and everybody listen carefully. You can all be the judge."

Ray reached over and hit the big red "play" button on the Ampex four track. When the drum intro exploded from the speakers I watched as everyone casually re-adjusted their stance. Rob grinned happily. This was more than he was expecting.

Glynn looked over at me incredulously as the verse settled in and I began to sing. Then the first little Steve Cropper-ism slid by and he couldn't help a big smile from overwhelming his face.

Roger and Howie were rocking in their chairs, their ears open and their minds hooked on the groove.

So many hooks.

So many riffs.

So much soul and angst.

Everyone felt it. As the fade-out faded there were requests to hear it again. Ray complied after a quick re-wind. But before he hit the play button, he turned and calmly announced, "I've got reel to reels for anyone who wants one. Bill figured you'd all want to be able to listen at home".

He hit the button and we all relaxed and had another listen. This time no one moved. Ears were open and intent on taking it all in.

Afterwards, Guilliland sat on the edge of an unused rack and laid out the labels' plans for our release. After a few minutes he summed up.

"So that's the bare bones guys. There's more that has to be done, but man what a foundation! I know you guys were dead-set against using studio musicians, but I think Tony and I have been vindicated. We really only intended this to be a demo of the song, but as you just heard there's a hell of a lot more there than just a demo. We think we can make this track a real contender for the top ten right here in this city. And with the right promotion we might take it right across the country.

Glynn as always asked the most pertinent questions.

"So you're saying it's a great foundation. What are the plans, then? It sounds pretty fuckin' good to me. What's going to make it any better?"

Guilliland was pumped. He stood up and walked around the room, totally in his element. "Well, we've just hooked up with a young producer from out east, named Brian Ahern and we want to get him involved. Maybe we'll do some of Dave's vocal over again. Not that there's much wrong with it, but the stronger the final product is, the easier it'll be to hype it. The very next thing, though, is for you guys to start rehearsing and get ready to promote it like crazy."

Howie was looking really strange and reserved and wasn't his normal self.

He looked at everyone and said softly, "This is the one, this is the one that can really do it!" He puffed up his cheeks and did an empty "Howie" whistle.

Roger agreed, "Yeah, man. That track sounds just like we played on it. We can nail it down so close no one would ever know that we didn't record it." Guilliland raised his eyebrows a tiny bit and a sly grin washed over his face. He said nothing.

After another listen on the big Lansings, everyone slowly drifted out the door and headed to the parking lot, with a reel to reel in their hands. There weren't a lot of words said; just a whole lot of quiet contemplation.

Glynn and Roger slowed down as they reached Roger's Pontiac. They were really eager to get into the rehearsal room and work it out.

"Hey, Roge', I think I want to do that little lead thing in the middle".

Roger shot back, "Fine with me, Glynn; long as I get to do the fuzz-lead intro I'll be happy!"

Rob looked at me and then at Huard and just licked his lips. He always did that lip-smacking thing when he was shifting the grey matter. It was a sign that he was thinking. As he slid into the back seat of Howie's Renault he popped the obvious question.

"So, what are we going to put on the flip-side of this thing?"

Huard countered, "Don't worry guys we'll cross that bridge when we come to it. Something will present itself, it always does!"

The next week at rehearsal we worked very hard at learning "Gaslight". Each time we ran through it, it seemed even more like such a perfect fit for the band. There was no end to our love for the tune.

There was one problem though. The key that I sang it in, in the studio was definitely not going to make it on stage. We had to change it by moving it down a couple of steps. Since we were never going to start a set with it, we had to consider that I might get winded or that my throat might get a bit raspy and I wouldn't be able to hit the high notes.

Once we got the song in the right key, though, we slammed it for a good half hour and everything was fine.

After that, we had to make the decision on where we would debut the song. As I still had work to do on the vocal in the studio, we reluctantly put it on the back burner for a while and kept it to ourselves. It felt strange and unnatural to be playing gigs and not be able to do the song, or even talk about it. But we still walked around confidently, knowing that we had a giant ace up our collective sleeves!

We had a difficult time trying to get back into the studio before the end of June. The end of the school year meant that our itinerary was jammed full of high school graduation dances. These gigs were very lucrative and always a treat because of the students' appreciation for the band and their unwavering determination to have one final blow-out party! We had a great time doing the gigs and promised everyone that we would have a big surprise for them by the end of the summer.

Finally, with a couple of days off, I got into the studio and met Guilliland's new *producer-prodigy* from down east, Brian Ahern. He was in his mid-twenties with an aura of self-assuredness and the look of an English country gentleman. His handshake was firm and his manner cordial and precise. We sat down at the console in the control room and re-listened to the four-track of the song. Brian was full of enthusiasm for the song and immediately described to me a string chart that he had written for the second verse that he was sure would turn the track into a monster contender for the top ten.

He said he was already in touch with some players in Toronto who were willing to lay down the parts.

But first we had to nail down the vocal track.

There wasn't really much that was wrong, according to Brian. The inflections that I had used were the right ones, it's just that I didn't push the lyrics the same way in the choruses as I had in the verse. He said I was going to have to own them for the listener to believe them.

I knew he was right. The track was right at the limit as far as my voice was concerned, and I needed to really get a lot of air behind the lines of the choruses.

Stamina. That's what I needed. I had to get into the right mind-set.

I imagined those hot and sweaty nights at Charlie Brown's where we had played until we all felt like falling down. I remembered that feeling.

It was always just one more song, just one more verse; just one more solo, to wind it up.

Roger's credo, make it count, make it real, kept running through my mind.

Brian was clued into my daydream, but he didn't mind if I was in some kind of altered state, as long as I was working it. He coached me as we went through the first two verses and then suggested a short rest before we went for the last chorus and the scat that would take us out of the song. We were going to go for it as long as the track played and then fade it out later.

"This is the clincher, Dave. This is where it gets real. If you can nail this down we'll have a classic; I promise you!"

I didn't need any prodding, I knew what I wanted and just went all out. It felt like sparks were going to jump from the ends of my fingers. Sort of like the prelude to a really good orgasm. When we were satisfied with the whole performance we listened one last time and then Brian invited me back on the following Monday night to hear the results of the recording of the string section.

I walked out of the studio in seventh heaven.

What else could possibly happen? Could anything be more right? I would soon be a father, and I had just given birth to an iconic song; something that was definitely going to out-last me.

On Monday night I got the answer to my question.

Yes!

Bill Guilliland was in-studio with Brian, and the string players had just left after completing the session. I walked into the control room and Bill looked over at me with a huge grin on his face. Something was up. He was literally happiness personified.

Brian picked up some charts and placed them out of harm's way. "We've got something really special here, Dave. One of the string guys came up with a great idea for the fills where the vibes are, just before you come back into the verses. It takes the track to another level. We've got things all set here for a run through to give you an idea of the mix."

He reached over and punched the play button. Everything sounded familiar until I started singing the first chorus; whereupon I thought I could hear some pizzicato strings hitting the accents with the guitar chops.

Then when the lyric ended the strings played an incredible sliding glissando that started at the highest note, in key, and ended three octaves lower; to bring in the second verse.

And then behind the second verse a mournful, soulful string section wrapped itself around the vocal and grabbed the listener's heart-strings and gave them a great big tug! It was classic. No doubt about it.

I was blown away. I didn't know what to say. Brian and Bill looked at me quizzically, but I was speechless.

Guilliland walked over and gently placed his hand on my shoulder, "What'd I tell you Dave?"

I looked at the two of them, stood up and extended a hand. "Thanks guys, I really don't know what to say."

Brian smiled, "We couldn't have done anything without you, Dave, thank yourself; both of our prayers have been answered!"

I walked home in a daze, a permanent smile etched into my face. From now on no matter what happened in my life, no one would ever be able to deny the essence of that track.

It was a killer!

Ray @ Bay Studios

Rob & Glynn Listening

The next thing on the agenda was to get a "B" side happening, so that we would have everything ready for a quick release. As soon as an evening was available we called everyone together for an after-hours session at Bay Studios to record our new instrumental, "Rimb Nugget".

It was a bluesy take on "Stormy Monday" with a major-minor progression, lots of fuzz-tone and wailing harp. It was one of the only numbers in our repertoire that was really a jam session. It came out sounding totally different every time we played it. Once we got all the gear set up and finished a sound-check with Ray, it was a matter of laying it down a few times and then choosing the best take. After we picked what we thought was our best performance, Ray noticed Rob seated at the piano playing along with the play-back and had him add a few piano chords to it, going "live" to tape as we mixed it down.

We had walked into the studio at about eight-thirty and had the track recorded and mixed before midnight. As an added bonus Ray put "Gaslight" up on the four track and we all listened to a straight run-through of the basic tracks. There was no need to perform much of a mix; it was all there with it's raw power and all the finesse of Brian's strings and Bob Halley's arrangement. We all knew it was a killer.

Kevan Staples, who had basically been out-of-the-mix throughout all of the "Gaslight" sessions was dumbstruck. As we tore down the equipment and lugged it out to the cars he calmly repeated over and over, "That's gotta get into the top ten. If that doesn't get in, then there's something really rotten in the music business in this city!" Huard looked at him and smiled one of his wicked, knowing smiles, and said, "We'll see, eh guys? We'll see."

We all headed home in a state of bliss.

CHAPTER 18
INSPIRATION

The Saturday of that same week we had a rare night off, and although we were playing in town on the Sunday, I decided to go see a special performer in Yorkville. Mike McKenna had informed me that Junior Wells was going to be playing at The Riverboat on Saturday night with Buddy Guy playing lead guitar. The news from every blues freak in the village, was that their new album was incredible. I hadn't heard the album yet, but I knew in my heart that I just had to go.

Sylvia was almost eight and a half months pregnant and getting quite large with our little "package" and so she bowed out. I quickly phoned around, and arranged for Huard to meet me just before the club opened.

It was a fantastic opportunity to see an incredible harp player up close and personal and I literally floated through The Village after I got off the subway.

Of course I got there early, and so I ended up waiting outside by The Grab Bag munching on potato chips and sipping Vernors Ginger Ale while I was waiting for Bill. I kept my eyes open and when I saw a couple of guys walk down the stairs into the club, I quickly followed. The place was empty and I saw Bernie Fiedler, the owner, near the back of the club turning on all of the lights. He saw me standing at the front and walked over. I introduced myself and asked if we could get seats right beside the stage.

Bernie replied that he knew of the Ducks and had heard us playing on occasion when he walked by The El Patio on the way to work. As far as he was concerned there was no problem. I left my chips and Vernors on the table and paid him the cover charge and then headed out the door to wait for Huard.

Half an hour later I was feeling pretty dejected; having not seen even one familiar face. I concluded that all our musician friends were probably playing at their own gigs and we were plain out-of-luck. After all, it was June and this was the weekend that all the kids were getting out of school. Every club and every high-school dance would be booked solid. The fact that we had a night off was strictly an anomaly.

I headed back to The Riverboat and arrived just as Bill sauntered up. He grabbed the hand rail and effortlessly glided down the stairs, ducking his head slightly as he went through the door.

There were maybe half a dozen people there, picking out the choice tables. We watched as the rest of the crowd made their way in. About ten minutes from show-time Gordon Lightfoot slid smoothly in the front door with two friends and made his way to a table at the south end of the little raised balcony across from the stage. And almost immediately afterwards Ronnie Hawkins made an oh-so-grand entrance flanked by two hulking guys who looked like they were bouncers from Le Coq d'Or Tavern. They sat at the north end of the balcony directly across from us. We were right beside the stage at the north end, hoping to be able to witness every nuance of Junior's performance.

At nine-twenty the band all made their way to the stage in single file. Buddy Guy was a good looking skinny-rake of a dude, who looked like his Fender Stratocaster was weighing him down. He deftly swung his axe behind his back and reached behind his Deluxe Reverb amp and flipped the on-switch. A slight hum was audible throughout the room.

I had always enjoyed seeing artists here, the ambience was perfect. You could hear the musicians on stage as they talked with lowered voices. Bill and I were ten feet away from Junior, but we had to crane our necks to see Buddy, who was on the other end of the stage, closer to the door.

Then Junior plugged in his harp mike and a tiny piercing feedback note screeched and howled throughout the room, piercing and penetrating everyone's eardrums. People scrunched-up their eyes and raised their shoulders. A few ladies winced.

I just got excited; because I knew exactly what was coming.

Junior tweaked a few knobs, tapped his knuckle gently on the face of his mike and then pulled a sweet warbling, sexy, and latent, bent note. It had just enough gain on it that it could be heard. But certainly not by the folks at the back tables.

He reached over and twisted a couple of knobs once more, and then stepped up to the mike.

"Hope you people like the Blues, because we really been feelin' 'em tonight!"

Junior mumbled the count out of the side of his mouth and then they were off. They sailed right through a pumping, relentless version of "Yonder Wall" that left Huard and I breathless and then they slowed the tempo down with a funkified version of "Early In the Morning".

The whole time they were in it, I was studying Junior's technique, trying to figure out his vibrato and single-note quaver. It was hopeless. Every move was so fast and furious. Every quaver was different, with a slightly different attack or release. I was constantly behind the moment and stupefied. I gave it up and just sat back and enjoyed the rest of the set.

After thirty five minutes of pure joy the set came to an end and the audience roared their approval with loud whistles, furious hand clapping and boisterous table knocking with ashtrays and empty drink holders.

Huard got up to go outside for a smoke and I sat at our table in a minor state of bliss contemplating the next set. As I sat in bewilderment, Bernie Fiedler passed by me and went over to Gordon Lightfoot's table and sat down. He waved to Mr. Hawkins and his bodyguards in the opposite corner and then chatted cordially with Gordie and his friends.

I ordered another drink and waited for Bill. When he returned we passed the time by looking around the room, picking out people at various tables, and speculating as to their vocations. Some of them just didn't seem to look like real blues enthusiasts. Of course we would never know the accuracy of our guesses because we would never get to meet all of them. But still it helped to pass the time.

After a half hour break Junior and Buddy returned with the band for the second set. Right off the bat they launched into "Messin' With The Kid" and I was back in that never-never land of trying to figure out Junior's technique.

Hopeless. It was hopeless. I couldn't make out anything he was doing. His cheeks alternately filled with air and then collapsed as the notes whizzed by in a dazzling flash. He was the Dizzy Gillespie of the harp.

Suddenly the tune was over and Junior approached the mike, after getting a few quick breaths.

"Hey folks, Mr. Fiedler just told us while we were on our break, about a young harmonica player who is here tonight in the audience. Seems he opened for The Rolling Stones last summer when they came to Toronto."

He looked over at our table.

"Mr. Dave Bingham, would you like to come up and join us for a tune?"

I was in shock. I looked back and saw Bernie standing near the entrance to the kitchen, a big wide grin on his face. He motioned for me to get up by moving his arms up and down.

I was feeling a bit shaky and my mouth was suddenly as dry as dirt. Huard looked at me with a grin too and stood up so that I could get around his chair.

The next thing I remembered was hearing Junior ask me what key I would like to play in.

"A", I said, "I like "A", it's my best key." I was lucky to get that out.

Junior smiled, "My favourite, too!"

He turned and looked at Buddy and then said, "Hoodoo Man Blues."

Away we went, and then for the next five minutes I was trading licks with Junior, interspersed with beautiful guitar fills from Buddy.

It was so strange. I felt like I couldn't feel my tongue or connect any of my thoughts with what was actually happening. Every time it came my turn, Junior would look over at me, lift his elbow and tap my arm. Then he would break out in a big wide grin, showing off an incredible set of gleaming white teeth. He sang with perfect grace and glanced at me, watching as I wailed a few licks in between each of the lines of the verse as he sang.

It seemed to last forever, but in fact it was over so very quickly. I had no idea how I had sounded and I could only hope that I had risen to the task. When the last note sounded and the drummer slapped that last snare shot, I was spent. I looked out at an audience that I could barely see because of the proximity of the stage lights and heard a spontaneous burst of applause. Wow! People liked it. I must have done alright!

I turned and shook Junior's hand, nodded towards Buddy and the rest of the band and then exited the stage in a daze. Another visit to cloud nine. I felt like one of the luckiest guys on the planet!

After a blazing set of sharp R&B-tinged funky blues, Junior and the band took another break and disappeared into various corners of the club. I got up and went to the washroom where I bumped into Junior on my way out.

"That was some cool playin', dude. You been taking lessons from Mr. Butterfield, or something?" Junior had actually been listening to me.

"Uh, well, I play along with a lot of different records, and that's definitely one of them. But I play along with yours too, and Charlie Musselwhite, as well!"

He put his hand on my shoulder, "You got the gift, man. No question. Now you just got to find your soul. Get some more vibrato, man. Deep stuff. You need the deep stuff, you know? And don't shake it so fast. It's like makin' love, man; you gotta just draw it out and make it cry."

He smiled the most incredible mischievous smile and then headed off into the kitchen.

When I got back to the table, Huard was chatting up a sweet looking blonde who was sitting just behind us. Before I had a chance to sit down I was approached by one of Ronnie Hawkins' bodyguards. He motioned for me to follow him to Ronnie's table.

I thought to myself, "Why not?" The night was young and I liked meeting people. When I got to the table I extended my hand, "Pleased to meet you, Mr. Hawkins."

His handshake was strong and firm.

"Just call me "Ronnie, son."

He sat back and gave me a wry look. "Where you from, boy? I get this feeling that we've met before."

"I'm from Scarborough, Ronnie. I met you and Levon a few years ago at "The Disc Shop" at Cedarbrae Plaza, in Scarborough. You showed up in your Porche and signed a bunch of autographs."

"Well son, I remember that place but you sure woulda looked a whole lot different then, I expect. You've got a band in Toronto, eh? Can't say as I've heard any of your stuff on the radio. Or maybe I have and I just can't place it. But now, opening for The Rolling Stones though, that rings a bell." He pulled a toothpick out of his shirt pocket and bit it decisively.

"That was some mighty fine harpin' there my friend. You were drivin' right down the white line! You know what I mean?"

"Thanks Ronnie, I don't get to jam that much these days."

"You makin' lots of money in this band of yours?" He took a sip of his drink and didn't even give me time to answer. "I'll give you a hundred and sixty bucks a week to come on over to my band. And you can have the first three songs in every set for your own show!"

Jesus! I didn't know what to say. I blanked out and hesitated.

"Hey listen, man. If that's not enough I might be able to go as high as one-eighty."

I was in shock, but it somehow gave me extra nerve. I decided to just speak my truth. It was so amazing to be in this position only three short years after the "Disc Shop" autograph session. It was time to pay my respects.

"No Ronnie, it's not the money; the money's fair. It's just that, well, we've just finished recording a new single in New York and I really feel like it's going to make a bit of a splash, you know? My wife is expecting and my life is just at a point where it's all coming together. So I've gotta pass, man. I mean, you were one of my biggest musical influences, Ronnie. I can hardly believe that this is really happening!" I took a deep breath and composed myself.

"Thanks a lot for the offer man, but I just can't do it."

Ronnie looked back at me, smiled graciously and then said, "Hey, all's fair in love and music, eh kid?" He grinned profusely and chomped down hard on his toothpick.

We watched the rest of Junior's set together and when the night was finished Ronnie walked over and introduced himself to Huard. He reached out and shook Bill's hand, placed his right hand on my shoulder and then announced with great sincerity, "Just in case this here record of yours does a big nose-dive boys; remember you're always welcome in my shop. You need a gig, Dave, you come see me. I'm always lookin' for new blood. You know where to find me."

He waved as he stepped out the door.

Bill and I just grinned and headed over to Avenue Road. Life really was stranger than fiction.

The week after my adventure with "Junior" we added another member to our management team. A slightly older Dude who had previously worked for Bill Guilliland approached us with Huard's blessing and asked to join our little family. He had been following us around town; checking us out on the advice of Mr. Guilliland himself. He already knew about "Gaslight" as Huard had filled him in, and he had heard one of the tapes that Bill had brought back from New York.

His name was Ross Atchison and he said he wanted to help promote and book the band. He was really smooth and we all liked his style and his forthright manner.

Glynn asked him if he was "As full of shit as all those other jerks at Arc Records" and he replied, "That depends on what kind of shit you're lookin' for Glynn. There's the good shit and then there's the bad shit. You get the bad stuff, it's a piece of shit. If you get the good stuff, the world is your oyster! So, I'll give you the good stuff; and I'll never let you down. You can count on it."

The guy was a rock and man he could talk. Even Huard was in awe of him. We figured it would be good to have another voice that could connect with all those program directors out in Radio Land. So we brought him into the club. It was going to be quite interesting to see how people reacted to this brand new Ducks organization, as well as to "Gaslight".

It was summer in the city.

Glynn & Dave on-stage @ "The Gouge Inn"

CHAPTER 19

EXPANSION

The next week Bill Guilliland and Brian Ahern worked on the mix of "Gaslight" until they were satisfied that they couldn't possibly make it any better. Bill called a band meeting at Arc Records in Scarborough to go over our touring schedule and discuss the release of "Gaslight".

It turned out that only Roger, myself and Howie made it there. Our new friend Ross Atchison was there sitting in as an observer, just to get up to speed on Guilliland's plans.

Roger was suspicious of almost anything that Guilliland did and therefore had to be in on every meeting. Howie, on the other hand, was anxious and just wanted to push to get everything moving ahead much faster than the tortoise-like pace that Arc seemed to be pursuing.

Guilliland was a bit pissed that the other guys weren't there, but forged ahead, outlining his plans to hype the release across the country and to try a limited release in upper New York State. He had hooked up with a small U.S. distribution company to get the single into stores in Buffalo, Syracuse and Rochester. Since all of these cities were capable of receiving signals from CHUM and CKEY radio, it only made sense to try and capitalize on the fact.

It was a novel approach and worth the effort.

We were happy with all of Bill's plans but the band was more interested in the final release date for the single. We wanted to start playing it "Live" and see what people's reactions would be.

Guilliland informed us that it was due to be released on the 3rd of August. Up until that time he intended to hype the band and the record in as many industry and trade publications as possible. He reminded us soberly of the kind of competition we would be going up against.

"Remember; The Beatles and The Stones, The Beach Boys, Spencer Davis; all these bands that are monopolizing the charts right now, are going to be bringing out their best stuff during the summer. Our idea is to hold off a bit until they've all made their moves. Then we come in with a top-notch effort and hopefully make people sit up and take notice. Ross is going to be working closely with us to inform every program director across the country of the strength of the record." Ross smiled.

It was all pretty boring stuff.

We just wanted to play the song.

Howie was always the edgiest one in the band and that day was no exception. He took the initiative and turned to Bill just before we left and asked point blank. "So, we can start playin' the tune now, right Bill?"

Guilliland was nonplussed. "It's your song now, guys. You can do whatever you want. It's out of my hands. Tell all your fans when it'll be coming out. Build it up. Try and create expectations. Don't hold back. Whatever you do can only help!"

At the next couple of gigs at the beginning of July we played "Gaslight" and announced the release date each night. It made us feel good that we could hype it and get it out there. But the audience weren't as receptive to it as we had imagined. They hadn't heard the record yet. We knew it would be different after the single came out and they had the mental image of the tune dancing around in their heads.

Music was like that. A lot of the fascination with it was because of its connection to memory. Sometimes it was *how* you heard the song, or *where* you first heard it. It would connect to the feelings that accompanied those memories and forevermore take the listener back to a particular time or place and more than ever to that first associated feeling. It was transformative. That was where we were going to be with "Gaslight". It was a simple song with a simple story and enough hooks to take you right back to it hundreds of times. Whenever I heard it, it would take me back to that first day, in New York and to Carl Spencer's incredible smile as he taught me the melody and lyrics of the song.

Bob and Carl had played the demo for Gene Pitney only two weeks before and he had turned it down. I would forever be in his debt. I could just thank my lucky stars that he had passed on the song. It was all synchronicity anyway. To this day I can't imagine what it would have sounded like with him singing it. I think that I was *meant* to sing it.

One Friday night after playing in The Village I decided to stop at Webster's Restaurant on Avenue Road for a bite to eat. It was a warm summer night and all the street lamps shone with a vivid orange glow. I was really in an "up" mood and my head was filled with positive affirmations and expectations about the coming release of "Gaslight".

I strolled into the restaurant in a half-dream state and headed for my favourite table at the very back, near the entrance to the kitchen. As I turned the corner I was surprised to see David Clayton Thomas sitting there at the table with sheets of foolscap and a dictionary spread out before him. We had recently become label-mates on "Yorkville Records". He looked up and a sly smile crossed his face.

I spoke first. "Hi David, what's up"?

"Oh, just figured I'd stop in on the way home and go over some lyrics to some of my new tunes. Guilliland wants me to demo some stuff for him".

He had his lyric sheets in a nice bundle, tucked in the sleeve of a leather binder.

I was curious. "What'cha working on"?

He pulled a sheet from a couple of spaces behind the top and passed it over to me. The title was, "Spinning Wheel". I read it quickly and was totally surprised. It was so different from the tunes that he had recorded with "The Shays", that it stunned me. I had become a fan back in the beginning when he had recorded his version of "Boom Boom" by John Lee Hooker, and of course I was blown away when he eventually came out with "Brainwashed".

He reached over for the sheet and sang it ever so softly for me while reading the words. The cadence was perfect. The structure of the song was really impressive and I immediately heard so many different possibilities for arranging it.

"Wow, that's really neat, David. Have you rehearsed it with anyone, yet"?

"Not so far. That's the next step, I guess. What do you think, what kind of feel"?

I didn't have a clue. I suggested, "It should be slightly funky and straight-up but have a few little dog-legs in it, you know? It has to be your own thing. Something that no one else would do".

He pondered that for a second or two. "Yeah, I think you're right, Dave. What you're saying is that it has to be iconic. Yeah, that's where it's got to go".

He reached to grab his coffee and inadvertently knocked a lyric sheet to the floor.

I reached down and picked it up and read the title; "Processions of MABS".

"What's this one, David"?

"Oh, that's a little psychedelic thing I've been working on. Don't really know if that's a direction I want to go, though".

I ordered coffee and a rice pudding, and we sat and talked shop for half an hour, discussing our favourite writers and performers. I was surprised to find out that he was really into Dylan and John Lennon, as I had always associated him with straight R&B and Blues. His parting statement to me was a mantra for me for the next couple of years.

"Keep it open, Dave. It'll come through you. That's what I'm trying to do – just let it flow. Words, music, thoughts, and feelings. That's what it's all about"!

His words repeated over and over in my mind as I walked home. But in the back of my mind I realized that it really helped if you could sing like an angel!

The second week of July we had a gig in Peterborough. It was always a huge party when we played there and this weekend the weather was going to be hot and sticky. Ninety degrees in the shade. The crowds would be large and in major party mode.

Sylvia was really quite big and the baby was due at almost any time. At the last visit to the doctor everything had been A.O.K. and he had said it was hard to judge the exact date but that the baby was healthy and getting ready to make a grand entrance. Things were getting really exciting and it was a total drag to have to leave Sylvia to do the stupid gig. We figured I was only going to be gone for about twelve hours, or so. Considering the speed with which the last nine months had passed, it would pass by in a flash and things would return to normal.

Jim Oliver was coming to see the band for the first time in a long while. He was going to be driving his '56 Oldsmobile 88, so he had arranged to pick up Bill and me and take us to Peterborough. I had to tear myself away when Huard knocked on the door. I gave Sylvia a big hug and a kiss and promised to be back as quickly as possible. The three of us took off in the 88, headed north-east on Kingston Road with all the windows rolled down and the radio blasting.

It was a long, hot and sweaty day. A day when air-conditioning seemed like the most prescient invention of all time. The drive to Peterborough was uneventful but glorious, in its own way. The main impetus was to keep above sixty miles an hour, so that the air that blew through the open windows would be sufficient to dry the sweat from our skin. Of course the resulting noise meant that we had to keep the radio cranked even louder than normal. So, for the next hour and a half we listened intently to CHUM and then CHEX as we bombed along ploughing our way through air as thick as custard.

On arrival at the gig we were met by some fans who wanted to help us set up. Well, by all means guys. By all means. Glynn and Rob weren't there yet so it was a big help to us and very considerate. With help from our dedicated fans, Kevan easily had everything organized by seven and we sat and waited for the rest of the guys.

The first set was at nine and despite the heat we managed to put on an incredible show; although we all lost a few pounds in the process. Each of the next two sets left us panting and thoroughly drenched and we constantly changed into new t-shirts every half hour and drank copious amounts of water so that we wouldn't pass out on stage.

The audience suffered as much as we did and showed their appreciation by calling out for their favourite tunes as we valiantly motored along. During the final set we got a phone call from Sylvia saying that she was heading to the hospital, as her contractions had started!

Shit! Trying to finish that set and get on the road back to T.O. was pure torture. The crowd just didn't want to let us go.

In the end, Bill, Jim and I left before the band had finished "I'm A Man". As soon as Rob was into his drum solo I was off the stage and packing. We went to the manager of the club and got paid for the gig, exchanged pleasantries, shook hands and were on the road heading down Highway 115 before eleven thirty. Jim put the pedal to the metal while Bill and I kept our eyes peeled for black and white OPP cruisers.

The minutes passed achingly slowly. We cranked up the radio and tuned in the loudest R&B we could find on the dial. The Olds rocked and rolled to the funky strains of Arthur Connelly, James Brown and Van Morrison as we made a bee-line for the 401, the ribbon of black-top that would take us straight through to University Hospital and a chance to see my daughter or son be born!

We had decided on a name for a boy the week before. *Sean* was our first choice. We had bought one of those trendy "name" books at Zellers that had lists of hundreds of names in it. It had been our focus for a few nights. We would sit around the kitchen table reciting names, seeing how they sounded and felt, as we pronounced them aloud. But we hadn't chosen one for a girl.

Now, as Bill and Jim and I sped at eighty and ninety miles an hour towards the presentation of the final act, I was going over names in my mind, thinking to myself; it's fifty-fifty. A fifty-fifty chance. Boy? or Girl? But very soon there would be an answer. The final result. A new human being was going to join us and enter into the light, forever changing our lives.

As we pulled into the driveway of the hospital, my heart almost pounded its way out of my chest and I felt like I could barely breathe. The girl on the front desk directed us to Sylvia's room and we headed straight there.

When we got there Bill and Jim waited outside and I went in to see how Sylvia was doing. She was awake and smiling. "Oh, Dave he's so beautiful! You just missed him. He arrived about forty five minutes ago!"

I held her hand, and cried. I couldn't help it; I was such a sentimental klutz.

"When can I see him? When?" Sylvia looked at me with a big smile, "Why don't you go ask the nurses?" I gave her a big hug and a kiss and headed down the hall. Huard and Jim Oliver followed quietly behind me.

The nurses were all smiles, too, as they led us to the nursery and arranged the three of us outside the glass windows. One of them went inside and brought a little bundle of white over to the window, pulling aside a corner of fleece to reveal a wide eyed strapping boy with dark black hair. His eyes were scrunched up in the light, but somehow he must have perceived movement or something because his eyes opened for a second and he peered up at the three of us, as we stood there, motionless, in total awe. We gazed into the eyes of a strong and curious fellow. He smiled and rubbed his nose with a tiny little hand. Sean Harrison Bingham had arrived!

The weekend after Sean arrived we were booked into The Stratford Arena for a big summer bash. As it turned out, it was just as hot and muggy as the previous week. But this weekend Ross Atchison had decided to come along for the ride with Bill. He brought along a bundle of pre-rolled joints for the trip down the 401, and a nice new slab of hashish to provide some inspiration for the concert later that night.

The drive to Stratford was loud, boisterous and hilarious. We were party central. Roger drove the Pontiac with Huard and Glynn up front while Ross joined Howie and me in the back seat. Rob was in the Blue Goose II with Kevan. As soon as we passed the Airport we proceeded to fire up the first of the joints in Ross's tight little bundle. Howie immediately did his freaking-fish routine and had everyone in stitches for the whole trip.

We were in a great frame of mind by the time we arrived, but we were literally soaked with sweat and feeling like grubby cowhands after a one hundred mile cattle drive. Once there, we headed straight to the washrooms to clean up.

But in the end we couldn't contend with the effects of the heat. By eight o'clock when we had finished setting up everyone was thoroughly exhausted again and headed back to the washrooms. It was still ninety five degrees and we decided that we were going to have to hit the stage shirt-less. There wasn't much else to do. Heat prostration was a real possibility and we had all been very close to it at other times during the summer and wanted to avoid it at all costs. We took off our shirts and went outside to cool off, as the humidity was a bit better outside where there was a bit of a breeze.

A half hour later we were happily leaning against the "Blue Goose II" and Roger's Parisienne, shooting the shit and trying to cool down. Ross had just pulled out his slab of black hash and had started to peel off a couple of slices into his pipe when a black & white O.P.P. cruiser pulled up outside the Community Centre parking lot and slowly made its way over to the entrance, as the two officers inside it observed us closely.

Ross calmly walked around to the front of the Pontiac and deposited the slab of black hash on the top of a worn and weathered cedar fence post that was part of the fence that enclosed the parking lot. He then bent over and slipped the smallish jade soapstone pipe into the arch of his left running shoe and continued on past the "Blue Goose II" to the centre of the parking lot to greet the officers as they arrived.

As the cruiser came to a stop the sound of crunching gravel grated on everyone's nerves. The engine died. The two officers slowly extricated themselves from the car and walked forward to greet Ross.

There was a lot of tension in the air, but it was somehow diminished by the oppressive humidity. The officer who had driven the car spoke first, removing his hat and wiping the sweat from his forehead.

"Howdy boys. I guess you're the band that's gonna be playing here tonight in the arena. We just got a call from a lady that lives across the street here sayin' that there was some lewd activity taking place over here in the parking lot."

Ross smiled, "Well Officer that would almost be a compliment if it wasn't so funny. We just took our shirts off to try to cool down in this heat."

The officer sort of grinned at that. "You boys wouldn't be drinking in a public place would you? You're not con-cealing any liquor, or some such thing?"

Glynn raised a can of Pepsi up where everyone could see.

Ross took one step forward and said, "Officer, there's really nothing much going on here. Just eight guys hanging in a parking lot trying to cool off before having to go on-stage tonight in that sweltering arena over there. It's a good five to ten degrees cooler out here than it is in there, and things aren't liable to get any better. If you'd like you can check the vehicles, but there's nothing to find."

At that moment my stomach jumped inside my chest and Howie pursed his lips, ready to do his mad fish impression. I glared threateningly at him.

Ross was as cool as a cucumber.

The two officers looked at each other and then the leading officer spoke.

"I don't think that'll be necessary fellas. Sometimes these little old ladies might give us great tips, but other times I think maybe their imaginations sort of get the better of them. Doesn't look like there is anything shameful going on here. You boys carry on, and have a good show."

With that they got back into their cruiser and left the parking lot.

When they were safely down the road apiece Ross reached down and pulled the little jade pipe from his left shoe, grabbed the slab of hash from the fence post and asked, "Anyone like to have a poke of this now?"

The third of August came very quickly and CHUM Radio jumped right on the band wagon with "Gaslight". They loved it; both as a great song and as a great production.

The next week I happened to run into Bob MacAdorey at the Dundas Street Subway Station and he said, "There's never been a Canadian record with as much balls as "Gaslight", Dave. And I mean performance-wise and also production-wise! Man, what a treat. It makes me feel proud every time I play it on the air!" He placed his left hand on my shoulder and pumped my right hand. There was a huge smile on his face. "Keep up the good work, Dave, see you soon!" He turned and disappeared in a flash up the stairway to Yonge Street.

The next week when the CHUM Chart came out on Monday I went down to Sam's and picked one up. We weren't on it; yet. My guess was that the record had come out too close to the end of the week.

By the next week though, we entered the chart at number 39 against some pretty stiff competition.

It was good news. Huard had just informed us on the weekend that we had been confirmed to head-line at EXPO '67 in the first week of September. Montreal was a new city for us. It was something foreign; something mysterious and culturally different. We were all ready for a challenge even if it felt a bit scary for us.

The scene in Montreal was very diverse and thrived in English and in French. We wondered how our music would fare against bands like The Rabble and The

Haunted. We had heard of "The Haunted" on our travels to The Ottawa Valley and we definitely appreciated their single 1-2-5 which had been released on Quality Records in Toronto, but we had never seen them play. Who knew, maybe that would change?

The response to "Gaslight" was incremental. The second week on the charts it managed to get to number 33, but by the third week out it was up there at number 23! We were doing alright, and making progress against some great competition.

The fact that The Beatles' "All You Need Is Love" was riding high on the charts, and that Van Morrison's first solo outing "Brown Eyed Girl" was chasing them towards number one, sort of put the brakes on "Gaslight" for a while. If we were going to get into the top ten we were going to have to have some real staying power. Fortunately for us the switchboard at CHUM was constantly inundated by kids phoning in to request us. And we were still selling albums, as well, although at a slower pace than at the beginning.

By mid-August Roger and I had emptied the well as far as our song-writing was concerned. I had written a new tune with Glynn called "My Watch" and another one on my own called "Epilogue". We had demoed the two of them at a rehearsal at The El Patio, but it remained to be seen if either one of them could be made into as strong a record as "Gaslight". Things were not looking good for a follow-up.

It was hard to get Roger in the writing mood. Over the summer we had had lots of heated discussions about the way the music business, and music itself was slowly changing. I wanted to learn something about music theory so that we would be able to work more easily with other musicians, both in the studio and out of it, but Roger resisted at every turn.

I saw the emergence of Cream, The Who, Traffic and Procol Harum as a harbinger of the direction that music was going to be taking in the next few years. Along with the explosion of bands on the west coast of the U.S. and Canada, the shift to a more melodic and less simplistic musical base was a portent of what was to come. The level of sophistication in music was growing every day. Even Motown was adapting to the changes and reflecting peoples' new musical tastes back at them. The Beatles had literally sprung the lid on a magical music box and in the process had changed the game forever. I didn't want to be left behind.

As Labour Day approached Roger and I came to an impasse and our song-writing was effectively stalled. I really couldn't understand his reticence. I didn't want to change his vibe or undermine his creative impulses; I just wanted us to understand what we were doing, so that we would be able to continue in a more informed way.

I wanted to understand what made our music great. It was all right to feel it, but I wanted to realize the structure and get right into the heart of it.

The last weekend of August we headed up to Sauble Beach on the shores of Lake Huron to play at an *end-of-summer* bash at the local beach pavilion. By this time I had decided that I was going to ask Roger to leave the band. I was absolutely petrified by the prospect of confronting him with my feelings, but I had been building up my courage and resolve for the week before we left.

The drive up there was muted and strained and sabotaged by an undercurrent of anxiety. There just wasn't a lot of laughter. Everyone avoided talking about our lack of suitable recording material, or about "Epilogue" and the possibility that it might be our next single. By the time we arrived at the gig you could cut the tension with a knife. It was very obvious that something was going to have to give.

As a consequence our show was particularly uninspiring and not up to our usual standards. We were giving it everything that we had, it's just that we didn't have that much to give. Our energy level was at an all-time low and our altered state left us feeling edgy and disconnected.

After the gig we headed back to the motel and Howie pulled a mickey of lemon gin out of his kit-bag.

"I don't know about you Dave, but I'm going to have a couple of shots of this, and maybe a toke or two to bring me back to reality. You're welcome to join me."

Huard came in the door at that moment.

As visions of the coming confrontation with Roger flashed through my mind, I decided to join Howie and Bill; against my better judgment. My prior experience with gin had clued me in to its numbing qualities, and my racing heart needed something to slow it down. So I eagerly wolfed down a couple of shots and had a couple of tokes as Howie passed a Rasta-sized joint around.

I should have asked him what it was.

It wasn't that it took that long to find out - it's just that I might have had second thoughts.

As the warm buzz of Howie's Maui-Wowee cocooned my addled brain, the impact of what I was about to do became crystal clear.

I hadn't told anybody about my intention to ask Roger to leave. I felt it was a personal thing between Roger and me. If we couldn't reach agreement about the direction that the band was going to take, or find a way to continue to write songs; then there wasn't much point in soldiering on.

After the second toke I felt a bit woozy and excused myself to Howie and Bill and went out for a walk on the beach. Unseen waves crashed softly off in the distance and the night sky was awash in slate grey and gunmetal blue clouds that slid transparently across a silver moon.

I racked my mind for the right words to say to Roger, but they wouldn't come. I couldn't think of any easy entry to the conversation, or any way to even take the conversation where I wanted it to go. In the end I decided that it didn't matter how it went down. It was going to be an end.

It would be the end of our partnership, but I didn't want it to be the end of our friendship. We had a disagreement. We were at an impasse. There was no way out. It was that simple. When I got back to the motel Roger was sitting out in front of his room with Howie. I greeted them and waved through a gin-soaked haze and then slid into my room, with my tail between my legs.

The confrontation would have to wait for another day.

We set off for Montreal and "EXPO" in a grand mood. We were holding our own against The Beatles and The

Stones! It was like being in a dream. Not like having one, but somehow like living inside one.

Sean was seven weeks old now, and growing like bamboo; putting on weight and sprouting about half an inch a week; or so it seemed. It was difficult to leave him, but Sylvia had things organized at home and assured me she would be O.K.

All through the summer we had been playing double bills with The Mandala and Roy Kenner and The Associates. Arena gigs, mostly. But there were a few that we had played at a smaller club in Scarborough called The Gouge Inn. We watched these guys closely and admired their professionalism and dedication. They were our ultimate role models as performers as well as musicians, and they had a certain fashion sense, or style. They had been influenced by many R&B acts from the U.S. and the Motown bands that passed through Toronto and seemed to be on T.V. almost every week. They wore custom suits that set them apart from the rest of the pack and gave them a unified look on stage.

Watching their shows every night had a profound effect on us. They were a couple of years older than us and consequently had started playing earlier. As musicians they were already at the top of their game. George Olliver would inevitably give me a round of goose-bumps on any given night, and Domenic Troiano would blow my mind with his wickedly intense solos and incredible stage presence.

Eventually their thing rubbed off on us and we decided to clean up our act somewhat. The Carnaby Street look was just coming into vogue in the U.K. and we decided to incorporate it into our act to spruce up our image. We got our hair trimmed and got identical hounds-tooth stove-pipes and charcoal black blazers.

We looked like a unit! Suddenly we had some class and a bit of sass.

So, this is how we set off for Montreal. We were no longer going to be the bad-ass-bad-boys with the shaggy hippy-dippy look that people had come to expect. We were moving up in the world and we were going to let it show.

CHAPTER 20
ELEVATION

Expo 67 was a monster of a show and presented us with a new challenge to be even more professional in our attitude than ever before. We were booked to play in the Canadian Pavilion in a huge room with a rotating stage that rose out of the floor from floor level, to a height of three and a half feet. There were also three accompanying pillars that rose in synchronization with the stage, set at 120 degree intervals around it. These were for the go-go dancers.

So, as we started playing our set we would have our backs to part of the audience and then later on as the stage slowly rotated we would eventually come to a point where we faced them. Nifty!

It was a strange feeling to see the audience move as we played. Because the stage rotated so slowly, it seemed that they were the ones who were shifting position and we were stationary. But we did get used to it. The go-go dancers each had room to rotate as they danced, so they tried to keep in time with the rotation of the stage. It was all pretty high-tech, but not intimate in any sense of the word. Not a waste of time but certainly not to our taste.

One great thing about the gig was that we were finished by seven o'clock at night. This left us free to explore the Montreal club scene. Bill and Howie and I decided after our Thursday appearance to go to The New Penelope Club to see a new band from California called The Mothers Of Invention. We had seen and heard their debut album at Sam The Record Man's before we left, but other than that, we didn't know much about them.

We took a walk on St. Catherine's Street and stopped at a great little restaurant for dinner. Then we walked around checking out head-shops and clothing stores to kill time.

Just before nine we arrived at The New Penelope to find that we were very early. People in Montreal didn't come out to play until ten o'clock. It was kind of a drag; we didn't feel like waiting around and headed back to our hotel in a slightly foul mood.

The next day Huard was on the phone to Scribner and was informed by Ron that "Gaslight" had made it to number 13 on the CHUM Chart! We were literally gob-smacked. Wow, only three full weeks into the chart and we were at number 13! We went out to a nice restaurant for lunch and had a few drinks to celebrate. Things were looking pretty rosy. The most challenging part of our dash for the top ten, of course, was the competition. Van Morrison had been in the top ten for almost a month with "Brown Eyed Girl" and The Box Tops were hanging in there as well with "The Letter". Bill Guilliland had been very calculating in picking the 3rd of August as our release date. The Beatles "All You Need Is Love" and The Doors' "Light My Fire" were just dropping off the charts when we came along. But we needed some room to get in there, and things didn't look too promising with Bobbie Gentry stuck in the top ten with "Ode To Billie Joe" and The Rolling Stones coming on strong with "Dandelion/We Love You".

There wasn't much that we could do, except to urge our fans to phone in to CHUM and request "Gaslight" at every opportunity. Every call counted. It was a game of wait and see.

The week after we got back to Toronto from Expo, "Gaslight" made it to number five and we were finally in the top ten! But it was a hollow triumph. Roger was still unhappy and stubborn about his desire to keep our music ragged and primitive. I just knew deep down that after "Gaslight", that approach wasn't going to fly. I knew we couldn't follow it up with a clone, either. That had been proven to be a recipe for failure by many Motown bands of the day. Our best chance at success was to keep pushing the envelope in our own original way. Pretty tall order for a musically uneducated band of gypsies from Scarborough.

In the end it was Bill Guilliland who noticed the rift in the band and called us to order. He somehow sensed the tension; just in his phone conversations with Huard and myself. He arranged for a band meeting.

The very next week we moved up to number three!

Three!

It was ever so close but still not there. We looked at the chart and at the other songs that were at the top and crossed our fingers. At least things were moving in the right direction, but it seemed like we were in a long distance race against the world champions. We were definitely the underdogs. Just two digits more and we would be there.

The "DUCKS" in August of 1967

Guilliland was in heaven. His hunches had been substantiated and he was sitting on top of the world. Roger and Glynn didn't show for the meeting on this particular night, but we forged ahead anyway.

Bill wanted to use Brian Ahern to produce our next single and he arranged for Brian and I to get together at Bay Studios on Thursday to go over some tunes and try to come up with the next step in the Ducks master plan. Howie and Huard were open to whatever we could come up with, and both Howie and Rob were eager to get back in the studio. That was my feeling as well. I loved it in there; it was such a special environment and there was always an air of possibility there that energized me. I headed home to work on the two new tunes to get them ready for Brian. At this point I had decided that I couldn't count on Roger to come up with anything substantive and I was determined to move on.

The meeting with Brian was as I thought it might be. He didn't care much for "My Watch" but he was very enthusiastic about "Epilogue". I sensed that it was the melodic content of the song that hooked him. He made a copy of the demo tape and took it home. He promised to come up with something over the weekend, so that we might get to work on it the following week.

The next Tuesday we were called into the studio to start on the backing track for it. Brian had the arrangement written out on paper in "tab" form and hurried us through set-up so that he could teach us the sequence.

It was slightly different from how I had perceived the song, but still within the realm of possibility for the band. Roger was duly pissed. There was nothing for him to play except for a few accent chords in the choruses. Glynn was instructed to play certain chords in strategic points of the tune after setting the vibrato on his showman to a slow speed with lots of depth. When Brian started recording stuff to tape he made three or four trips out to the studio floor to reset the speed of the vibrato so that it was in time with the drum fills that Rob was inserting in critical parts of the verses.

Most of the real recording work was done with Howie and Rob, in order to accentuate the interaction between the drums and bass. It was painstaking and slow, and something that we had never attempted in the studio before. Brian kept telling everyone that there was nothing to worry about. All of the holes in the arrangement would be filled appropriately with other instruments that, for the time being resided firmly in his own imagination. He must have said, "Trust me, guys" a dozen times during the session.

That was a leap of faith that Roger just couldn't countenance. After his meagre contribution to the track, he sat in silence and stewed. I could tell he was bored. After a couple of hours into it he got up, packed up his guitar and headed for home. The rest of us soldiered on, curious to get some idea of what Brian was up to. By the time we all left for the night, there was definitely no consensus on the viability of the tune as a sequel to "Gaslight". There wasn't enough on tape to even get the gist of an idea of what it might sound like in finished form. It was a wait and see thing.

Brian promised that by the next session he would have the track in a sufficient state of completion that we would be able to understand where he was going with the arrangement. I trusted him. No one else had worked with him before, but I knew there was a method to his madness!

The next week was almost gone when I finally got a call from Brian. He wanted to know if I knew anyone who had a Sitar. The only person I knew who had one was Mike McKenna.

Brian was relieved; I could tell by the sound of his voice.

"Do you think you could get him to come into the studio tomorrow night at about eight o'clock?"

I was really curious as to what he had in mind and I posed a few questions. His reply was evasive but pretty straight ahead and simple. "Don't worry about it, I'll have some other surprises for you when you show up. Just make sure you bring him here and tell him there won't be lots of money; that all we'll have is some great food, great hash and some awesome wine!"

I got right on the phone to Mike and set it all up. He really did have a Sitar.

He had bought it on impulse while he was out shopping for clothes to wear for the final Luke and The Apostles gig at The O'Keefe Centre. Whether or not he could play exactly what Brian was thinking of, was another matter. But he was game and he loved to party.

When Mike and I strolled through the doors into Bay studios the next night, we were met by Brian and a grinning munch-kin-like character who reminded me of Michael J. Pollard from the movie Bonnie & Clyde.

Brian introduced us. "Dave and Mike, this is Bill Speer who is here to play some wicked clavinet on our track tonight." We all shook hands and then continued into the room. We noticed that the lights had been dimmed and someone had lit a stick or two of incense. It made the studio feel comfy and warmer than it really was. Good move.

Bill was already set up with his gear in the centre of the room and had been doing run-throughs with Brian before we arrived. Mike and I retired to the control room and sat in a couple of wheeled armchairs to listen as Bill did the next run through. As soon as the track started I was stunned. There was now a beautiful bass piano part right underneath and mirroring the bass part that Howie had put down for Brian at the first session. Together, the two instruments created an other-worldly kind of bass sound that was positively church-like. After the final verse Bill started playing his thing. It was simply spectacular. He looked like a mad classical genius as his fingers flew absolutely and precisely over the keys.

When the interlude ended Brian called him in and we all listened intently.

I got goose-bumps. I'd never been that close to someone while they played such magnificent stuff. Bill was a wonder.

He sat quietly, listening. He reached up and grabbed his chin, rubbed it slowly and then raised his hand and motioned for Ray to rewind. We listened again until Bill finally stood up and walked out the door and back out into the studio.

He spoke oh-so-quietly, with a mischievous gleam in his eye, "One more time should do. I want it to really come to a conclusion in a twisted sort of way. You'll see!"

This time was truly even better. Bill had created his little classical interlude along with Brian and had added the most demented suspended 4th harmony (or whatever) on the last chord. When he heard the play-back he just grinned.

Mike had been listening as all this was going down and I had noticed a kind of questioning façade fall gently over his face. He was having a hard time letting his imagination lead him. He looked apprehensively at Brian.

"So, ah, where do you want me to put the Sitar thingie, Bri'?"

Brian smiled. "Right in the last bar before Bill comes in on the clavinet. You're going to take us into it. It'll be really seductive and sensual."

Brian grabbed Mike's arm and gave him a tug toward the studio. They went out and immediately started tuning Mike's Sitar. Brian sat at the grand piano and punched an "E" octave while Mike set about tuning all of the notes that made the chord, plus all of the resonating harmonies that made the Sitar sound so full and distinctive.

After fifteen minutes Brian was satisfied with the precision of the tuning and asked Ray to roll tape. At the appropriate time he pointed at Mike and said,

"O.K. tune up."

Mike responded as he had been for the last fifteen minutes and almost played the figure that Brian was looking for. It was his turn to crack a big smile.

"Now I get it. It's just like a baroque strum of the chord. I'm the grace note!"

They tried it four more times until Brian was satisfied, and it was on tape. Then Brian put me into a cubicle and told me he wanted a really good quality guide vocal for the string players to relate to. Hey, whatever: I was always game to try anything. We worked it for ten minutes or so, and then I put down a "keeper".

"That'll give 'em the idea, Dave. We'll get the strings on it next week!"

Strings? Strings? What strings?

I just couldn't imagine it. But hey, I didn't even know what a diminished chord was; what the hell did I know? I was still learning.

Eventually, by the time we had finished the song, we had added acoustic guitar, inserted some backwards harmonica, added a three-part string section and two backing singers, and then a final vocal track with input from Brian on the precise inflections that he liked in all of my performances. The result was totally unlike anything that any of us had ever heard. No one could classify it; which left us all feeling a bit uneasy. It didn't really fit into any genre. It was just psychedelic and trippy; but so right for the times! With a haunting melody and a splendid introduction by Brian himself on his beautiful Martin D18, it took the listener on a journey through love, and loss.

We had recorded my harmonica playing along to the sound of the *reversed* beginning (tail-out) of the tune. Then, Brian learned to play the reversed melody on the guitar as a finger picked intro. We then recorded that sequence and we mixed it with the backwards harp. We continued the acoustic through the second verse and, voila, we were finished!

Now all we had to do was mix it. Brian assured me that it was no problem; all he needed was a good night's sleep and some time away from it. When I got home that night I couldn't describe the vibe of the track to Sylvia. It was beyond my musical vocabulary.

I had a hard time getting to sleep, as all the various parts of the track worm-holed themselves into and through my melody-saturated brain.

The following Wednesday Brian called us into the studio in the evening to hear the final mix. We all met in the parking lot just outside the studio and Howie passed around a couple of joints to lighten the mood.

Things started off quiet. Glynn was indifferent but still his jovial self and keeping an open mind. Rob was eager to hear the drum sounds that Brian had promised him, and Bill and Kevan were glad to finally be in on the action, as they had been absent from the sessions. I had told Bill what to expect, but Kevan had been totally out of the loop and I was counting on watching his response to the track.

When Brian played the track there was total silence and awe. It was totally unique. No one knew what to make of it.

Brian was just as flabbergasted as any of us. He looked around at us as the tune faded out, and leaned against the console. "I had something definite in my mind when we were putting it down, guys, but this is way beyond what I expected. It's up to you guys. If you put it out, you'll have to be able to play it "live". I don't know……" He looked concerned, "What do you think?"

Howie motioned for Ray to play it again. And then again.

Howie spoke first. "Hey, it's pretty psychedelic, man." He crossed his arms and leaned back in his chair. "I don't know if we'd be able to do it justice on stage."

Glynn had a half-smile on his face. "Hey, we can play it, man! It's pretty simple.

Rob and Howie would definitely shine in this one, they were right up front in the mix. Rob shifted in his seat and mumbled something about tuning his floor tom like a kettle drum. Enthusiasm ebbed and flowed. Bill and Kevan liked it but wondered how "Radio" would relate to it. I wasn't sure we could pull it off, but I wanted to give it a try. We agreed to leave it for a while and see how we felt after a week-end away.

It was strange but this was our creation and we didn't know how to react to it. We had made the sounds, but Brian Ahern had painted a musical painting with them. It was difficult to recognize and accept someone else's vision and we were having a hard time getting used to it.

I had a hard time sleeping that night. I couldn't make up my mind about it.

Kevan liked it. He thought it was "of the times". But I was torn because I knew it would change how people thought of the band. And for sure some of the fans were bound to resent it.

A couple of nights later I decided to get out and get some fresh air. I wanted to get my mind off of it. I didn't want to think anymore. I wanted to experience something; anything. I just wanted to turn off my mind, relax and float downstream.

I went downtown to Sam's and A & A's browsed for a while and bought some new albums. Then I headed back to The Village.

After I exited the subway, I turned left onto Yorkville Avenue and headed west. Then, as I passed Bellair Street, I heard the most incredible sound of harmonized guitars coming from this new club across the road from The Flick, called The Strawberry Patch. It sounded like Jimi Hendrix & Eric Clapton were having a wailing contest!

I was drawn like a fly to capers. The sign said, Tonight – INFLUENCE.

So, I let my feet follow the sound that filled my ears and man, did I get a surprise! As I walked into the club the band introduced a tune called "Pieces Of Me". It was a wide open sound, all abstract and impressionistic. The drumming was superb, and totally original in concept, setting up a loping, stride-influenced tempo. (Ringo couldn't have done any better!). The harmonic structure of the song was malevolent and the two guitars sailed together across a dark, foreboding and operatic back drop. I just loved it!

Then they announced the last tune of the set, "Mad Birds Of Prey". And again they literally destroyed everyone in the audience. I looked around and saw lots of large smiles and noticed stifled laughter as their keyboard player Bobo Island, "played" all of the characters that he sang in the song. It was like a Gilbert and Sullivan mini-opera.

As he neared the end of the tune he sang, *Lonely, I smashed the idols to myself....* and as he did, he poured the remnants of a coke over his bare chest, grabbed an ashtray off of his Farfisa Organ and spilled the ashes and butts all over his sticky torso. The audience roared. His eyes then turned manic as he channelled Little Richard for the finale of the song and finished with a screaming, *A wop bop a loop bop a-lop bam boom!*

I floated on home in total amazement and to this day that performance is still etched permanently in my mind. OMG!

CHAPTER 21
EMOTION

Through the next couple of weeks we wrestled with the prospect of accepting a new direction for the band. Everyone was torn, but still willing to listen to each other's point of view. I knew where my choice would lie. I wanted to move ahead. I knew deep down that we couldn't stay in one place musically and survive. Big changes were coming and I wanted to ride with them, not fight them. I wanted us to stay the course but become better musicians, individually as well as collectively. Roger just withdrew and got more and more obstinate.I talked with the other guys in the band to get their take on things, and came to the conclusion that no one wanted to rock the boat. It was hard for all of them to imagine the band without Roger. It was disheartening to be on my own, but there was no support from anyone other than Kevan Staples, who truly understood that it was the future of the band that was at stake.

His advice was simple and straight forward. "You've got to compete, Dave. You may not like it, but there is nothing that will destroy the band more than indifference. Music is changing and you guys will have to change with it, or you won't be around for long anyway!"

Roger and I had started the band, so there was the dread of reneging on the commitment that we both had made in the beginning, to be loyal to each other and to the music that had turned us on.

But that was just it. The music that had inspired us was changing. The heart of Rock 'n Roll was evolving and becoming a different thing. I didn't want to be left behind.

People were writing about things that really mattered. It wasn't simplistic teenybopper music anymore, or dance music. It was more than American Bandstand. It was serious stuff and critics were taking it seriously. The Beatles were being compared to Cole Porter and George Gershwin! Eric Clapton was being compared to Freddie and Albert King and in the U.K. he had been declared a god! There was a new expectation that each song would be better than your last, and that as a band you wouldn't repeat yourself. I wanted to live up to that; I wanted to grow.

The next weekend we had a gig in the west end of the city. I had been on the phone with everyone and finally informed them of my desire to ask Roger to leave the band. Everyone relaxed when I told them. They had all seen it coming. They all said they could feel it from the vibes emanating from Roger and I on stage and in rehearsal.

We decided that it should be sooner rather than later. I didn't have any confidence that I could actually manage it on my own when it came down to the crunch and the rest of the guys wanted no part in it. So it was agreed that Huard would break the news to Roger when he drove him home after the gig.

I don't know what kind of force takes over people in situations like that, but the music was fantastic that night. Every riff and cue was solid and precise. The band was as tight as a drum and as single-minded in composure as we had ever achieved. Everyone put their hearts and souls into it and took it way over the top.

When the night was over, we signed autographs and chatted with fans as we tore down the gear, but we were unusually quiet amongst ourselves.

After the drive across the city, Bill dropped Glynn off first and then Rob & I and then he headed for Scarborough with Roger. When he had almost reached Victoria Park Avenue he dropped the bomb.

"The guys have voted you out of the band, Roge'".

A slightly taciturn grin spread across Roger's face as he turned and looked at Bill with a calm resignation and replied, "Yeah, I sort of figured something was up, Bill. It's O.K., I'm O.K. with it."

"Well, I......"

"Don't worry, Bill. We had a good run. It's O.K. I can handle it."

They drove on in awkward silence listening to each other breathe until they reached Mason Road. Bill dropped Roger off across the road from his mom's place. Roger got out of the car, opened the back door, grabbed his Gibson and then leaned down by the passenger window as he walked by Bill and said, "Call me". He slapped the roof of the car, turned and walked across the road.

I couldn't sleep that night. I tossed and turned until four in the morning with the thought of facing Roger the next weekend running over and over again through my mind like a skipping record. I could only guess at how the other guys felt. My guts ached.

I needn't have worried. Huard promptly cancelled the gig for the following weekend, which gave us ten days to get a replacement guitarist and rehearse. I got on the phone to Mike McKenna. I offered him the job right off the bat. He sounded relieved. After The Apostles break-up he had just been jamming around town and hadn't really figured out where he was headed.

"Hey, thanks Dave. This is going to be a lot of fun. I've got a real good feeling about it."

We talked for half an hour about what we would play. Mike was a stickler for playing the right material. He was concerned about which "Ducks" songs would fit with his style of playing.

I assured him, "Hey, you just show up at rehearsal and we'll work that all out. Make a list and we'll just try stuff. And don't worry about our songs. We'll do whatever sounds best." I knew it was going to be a blast. Hell, it was going to be new and it was going to be a challenge, musically. It was just what the doctor ordered.

The next week at rehearsal we tore through all the tunes that we could manage. It was a matter of finding out which ones would have a common feel that suited everyone. Mike was a rock as far as "time" was concerned. He never wavered. You set him off at one speed and he just kept going. He *never* lagged behind or got ahead of the beat.

Tunes like "Little Red Book" & "I Wish You Would" that were common to both The Ducks & The Apostles took almost no effort and grooved right away. We decided to do "You Can't Judge A Book By The Cover" as a replacement for "I'm A Man" at the end of our Show. Mike had it down to a tee and it felt totally right the first time we nailed the arrangement.

"Nothin'" didn't cut the mustard. Mike's style just didn't mesh with the tempo, the tune or the treatment. On the other hand, "Gaslight" was a full blown gas. Glynn and Mike totally integrated all of the hook-ish parts of the arrangement to suit their individual styles and it came off sounding even more powerful than it had been before.

After two days we had eighteen songs. Hardly enough for a full show. We decided it was time to do some newer material. The weekend was coming up and it was the last of our free time before we had to debut the new line-up of the band. Everyone brought tunes to rehearsal for us to try.

By the time the first gigs came around we had added an original Mike McKenna blues called The Blues Fell This Morning, plus covers of; Foxey Lady, Ain't Superstitious, Hey Joe, Crosscut Saw, Nadine, Spoonful, Leavin' Trunk (ala: Taj Mahal) and a reworked version of Zip-A-Dee-Do-Dah (by Bob B. Soxx & The Blue Jeans).

In advance of the rehearsals Mike and I had started working on some new original material as well. At my instigation we had gone over almost every piece of music that he had in-the-works, so that I would have a general idea of what there was to work with.

It was a total surprise to me, but Mike had a lot more up his sleeve than just some twelve bar blues and various foot stomping ravers. He had some introspective pieces and some surprising up-tempo pop. Well; not really pop, but Mike McKenna style pop; featuring his own unique R&B influenced guitar styling's.

The first weekend went by quickly and with gusto. People missed Roger dearly but truly loved Mike. We were certainly a different band (with a slightly different sound); although the basic foundation of the music was the same.

Roger had been more ragged. Mike was much more precise. And that was something that the audience was going to have to adjust to.

"The UGLY DUCKLINGS" September 1967

For those who hadn't seen us before the enthusiasm was straight-forward. If they were fans of "Gaslight" then for sure they would be satisfied. For those who were died-in-the-wool Ducks fans it was a no-brainer. If they had loved Mike in The Apostles, it was easy to like him in The Ducks. Their only real disappointment was the fact that we no longer performed "Nothin'". We made up for that fact with super-heavy renditions of "Foxy Lady" and "Ain't Superstitious". The interplay between Mike & Glynn on guitars was truly something to behold. Glynn stepped up to the plate and worked his custom Les Paul and his Gretsch Tennessean to the max, through a brand new Fender Showman amp. The two of them were having a great time. It was a new experience for Mike and gave him the freedom to stretch out and experiment much more than when he shared the rhythmic chores with Peter Jermyn in The Apostles.

Less than two weeks after Mike joined the band "Gaslight" made it to Number 1, pushing The Rolling Stones & *We Love You / Dandelion* out of the top spot. It had taken a long time to get there, but it was finally a reality!

	this week	last week	
1.	GASLIGHT	Ugly Ducklings Yorkville	2
2.	NEVER MY LOVE	The Association WB	4
3.	LITTLE OLE MAN	Bill Cosby WB	5
4.	WILL YOU LOVE ME TOMORROW	Bunny Sigler Decca	8
5.	DANDELION/WE LOVE YOU	Rolling Stones London	1
6.	GIMME LITTLE SIGN	Brenton Wood Apex	6
7.	THE LETTER	Box Tops Quality	3
8.	HOW CAN I BE SURE	Young Rascals Quality	12
9.	HEY BABY	The Buckinghams Columbia	22
10.	PEOPLE ARE STRANGE	The Doors Allied	29

GASLIGHT #1, October 1967

For the next month we travelled all over southern Ontario and introduced the new Ducks to our hardcore fans. All was well. The band grew musically and the fans were on board for anything we did.

The split with Roger was much less complicated than I had thought it would be, and he was a true gentleman as far as wrapping up all of our business obligations and such.

But he didn't come to see the band. That would have just opened up a mess of bad feelings and I think we all sort of felt the same way. We didn't want to go there. Rest assured though; we still lived and played by his credo. It was always in the back of our minds.

"Give them something to remember and never hold back!"

CHAPTER 22

TRIBULATIONS

In October we made it Ross Atchison's job to really set about ramping up the promotion of the band, with an eye to increasing our profile nationally. Up until this point he had been working with Huard on day-to-day business stuff. Now he was going to make the big push. "Gaslight" had made it to Number 1 in Toronto, so Ross decided to get the media across the country a little more interested in the band. It was time to tell our story.

Through November we played in and around Toronto, and at various High School gigs just outside the city. At the beginning of December we played in Oshawa at the Jubilee Pavilion. It was a great gig, as The Apostles had been very popular there and the fact that Mike was now in the band drew us an even larger crowd. It was always a gas to play there and see the photos of Dennis and Jerry Edmonton plastered all over the walls of the dressing room. Their parents were the owners of the Jubilee and were very proud of their sons' achievements in Steppenwolf and their earlier work with Jack London and the Sparrows.

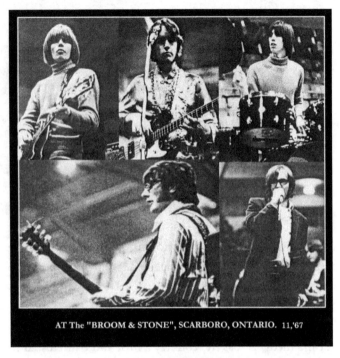

AT The "BROOM & STONE", SCARBORO, ONTARIO. 11,'67

The "New" UGLY DUCKLINGS, Nov. '67

After another gig at The University of Toronto, Hart House, we were to head to Winnipeg once again. We had done very well for ourselves in the 'Peg and the paycheque for this next mini-tour was going to be the biggest yet. The plan was that we would do an after-Christmas gig in Winnipeg proper and then scoot out to Brandon Manitoba for a big New Year's Eve bash.

Just as we were getting organized to head west Kevan Staples decided that the trip was a bit much for him. He wanted to spend time with friends and celebrate the New Year at home.

After a slight scramble to replace him, Howie hooked us up with one of his old ganja connections and we ended up hiring Rene' Clodo to be our substitute roadie. He had the kind of personality that fit right in with the band. Way out in left field, but still right behind home plate. He was the only person outside of the band members who I had observed reacting positively to Howie's warped sense of humour. So, all in all he had great qualifications for the job.

We celebrated Christmas with our families and then on Tuesday at eight A.M. we set out for the 'Peg on our fourth sojourn. The band members all took the good old CN-Rail train across a wintry, bleak and grey Ontario and Rene' and Huard left a day earlier driving the Blue Goose II at a sober pace with lots of rest stops along the way. Rene' and Ross Atchison had supplied us with a bundle of fifty or sixty joints for the trip which the seven of us had divvied up and consumed along the way with great satisfaction and discretion. Huard and Rene' stayed tuned to the best Rock 'n Roll they could find on the dial and thanked God that the temperature remained humane for most of the trip.

The rest of us rode in style, drinking in the Bar-Car and smoking our doobies between cars where the adjoining bellows allowed for maximum ventilation and zero risk of detection.

We were Masters of our own fate; chomping at the bit and ready to set the music world on fire. We sat back in our seats on the second level of the rear observation car and took in the vast panorama of the Canadian hinterland as we made our way west at a comfortable sixty mph.

Once again we were interviewed on Ron Legg's radio show and he played "Gaslight" after an over-the-top introduction and then introduced our brand new follow-up single "Epilogue". Huard had brought along a Radio Station Promo copy, as it had not yet been released. Ron was a great guy and was a major supporter of Canadian talent. Because of his efforts and the support of hundreds of die-hard Ducks fans, the first gig in the 'Peg was a huge success and a gas. It was on a Friday night and yet every musician in town came out to see us and at the end of the night they gave us a rousing send-off to Brandon by forcing us to play two successive Encores. We headed back to the hotel to get our six or seven hours of sleep before heading west to Brandon.

So on the last day of 1967 we were driving west on Route 1, a hundred and thirty miles or so to Brandon on a cold, crisp, minus twenty degree day. The sun shone like a diamond and cast shadows that followed us, as long strips of grey that floated over the stark white drifts of snow blanketing either side of the highway. We were pointed due west, so that the sun never blocked our line of sight unless we inadvertently gazed into one of the rear view mirrors. Loud rock 'n roll blared constantly from the front radio speaker and bluish-white marihuana smoke filled the air.

Magically, eight hours later we were rolling eastward, back down the Trans-Canada Highway at sixty mph, approximately forty miles west of Winnipeg. The gig had been an unmitigated smash! The music was bliss and the audience had definitely been an audience from heaven. It had been totally exhilarating. At the stroke of midnight we chose to usher in 1968 to the exotic sounds of The Ugly Ducklings pumping out an extended *Foxy Lady* at one hundred and twenty decibels!

And then we scrammed right out of there.

Home was a long, long, way away.

Mike & Glynn had decided before we even left for Brandon that they didn't want to travel in the van. They figured twenty-something hours cramped up in the "Blue Goose II" was more than they could handle.

So they had grabbed a taxi for the trip out, and now they loaded up their gear in the same taxi and sped off into the night to catch an early morning flight back to Toronto. The rest of us had finished loading up the "Blue Goose II" and hit the road by twelve fifty-five.

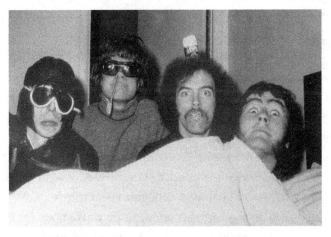

Howie took this shot the night before New Year's Eve, in The 'Peg

As of now, it was two thirty-five a.m. It was thirty-eight degrees below zero and it was hard to believe, but

Howie had just noticed that the gas gauge was almost on empty, with only forty miles left to go. We had just aced the biggest paying gig of our careers and now it looked like we had also managed to initiate our biggest blunder as well!

A sort of ominous feeling of dread crept over us. It was hard to believe that this was really happening. Why couldn't we have just *filled* the tank when we pulled into Brandon? Would that have been too difficult to manage?

My guess was that we were so stoned at the time that we'd just forgotten. Or maybe someone had looked at the gauge and figured that there was enough to make it back to the 'Peg. No sense in putting the blame on anyone, though. It wasn't going to make any difference now.

So anyway, reality was right here, right now! The big question was, what were we going to do? We all just sat there, eyes looking straight ahead listening to the insistent, thrumming drone of the engine.

I'm normally the optimist so I jumped on it. "I guess we just keep driving guys. Let's see how far we can get. I remember someone told me once, that when the gauge reads empty, you've really got a couple of gallons left. Sure would be nice."

We hadn't seen another car for an hour or so. It looked like we had the whole road to ourselves! Come to think of it, who would be insane enough to be out here on New Year's Eve anyway? At this temperature you're taking your life in your hands as soon as you head down the road.

I looked over at Howie and heard him talking to himself under his breath, "This truck better keep on moving. Pooh, noo, too, noo, pooh, noo!" He puffed his cheeks out and released one of his patented blow-fish whoops.

At that very moment the engine skipped a beat and the carburetor then sputtered and coughed. A strange hissing took over inside the truck and there was no sound of exhaust anymore. No drone, no whine; just the hissing and the monotonous crunching of the tires on the frozen, snow encrusted blacktop.

Howie threw the truck into neutral and slowly we drifted to a stop. It was dead calm! Not a sound out there. Just our own shallow breathing and nervous mumbling.

It soon became apparent that the heat wasn't going to last very long. There isn't much insulation in trucks. Just metal, metal and more metal. Within ten minutes we could see our breath.

And no one was dressed warmly at all. City boys just don't know that they should be prepared for any eventuality out here. We looked up at the stars and then straight ahead at the pencil-like vanishing-point of asphalt as it disappeared into a moonlit sparkling white wasteland.

Everybody's teeth started chattering uncontrollably. Then suddenly it sunk in, and it seemed that gravity had increased by a factor of two. It was raw fear. Pulling us down. We could feel it in the pits of our stomachs. This was serious SHIT! And suddenly we realized that we had better start to deal with the situation.

And Now!

Nobody was philosophical.

"Let's be practical," Rob said. "It looks like someone will have to go for help."

"It's just like in the movies," Rene' said. "We'll draw straws, and whoever gets the short straw will have to go!"

Silence returned. No one wanted to admit it but he was right. There was no other way.

"Damn", I said silently to myself, "I could have gone back to Winnipeg in a nice warm car with Glynn and Mike and be flying back to Toronto first thing in the morning! We're supposed to be rock stars. So, why are we riding with the damned equipment, anyway?"

The tips of my fingers were starting to feel numb. I piped up, "Let's just get on with this!"

Rene' took a used chocolate bar wrapper, pulled out the hard cardboard support and tore it into strips. Five of them. Four long ones and one short.

Rob was really starting to shake and managed to stutter, "Jus...jus...jus.. just do it, man!"

Rene' took the strips and rolled them between his palms so that they rolled over each other and ended up akimbo. Nobody wanted to go first. He lined the pieces up carefully between his freezing hands without observing which was which.

Finally I got tired of waiting and reached out and grabbed one, pulling softly so as not to tear it. It came free. - Long!

"You lucky bastard!" blurted Huard.

"Who's next?" I asked.

Huard got filled with bravado and piped up, "I'll do it!" He reached across in front of me and grabbed the closest strip. It slid out of Rene"s grasp. - Short!

"Well, I guess it's you, Bill," said Rob. "You've got the most clothes on anyway. Lucky you wore a suit and vest, eh?"

Rene' passed Bill his ear-muffs, "These will help a bit."

Then Huard lit a smoke and traded jackets with Howie, and said, "If I'm not back with help in an hour, you guys can kiss your asses goodbye!"

"Don't be so melodramatic," I told him. "If you can't find help in half an hour, get back here so we can all freeze together."

"Yeah, you never know. Somebody might come along, stranger things have happened!"

Then everyone patted him on the back, the door opened and he was out. We watched as his silhouette slowly merged with the eerie shadows cast by an indifferent moon. Our prayers were with him.

So now there were four of us, waiting. We started massaging each other's backs, rubbing our arms and shoving our hands into warm armpits. Howie pulled out a joint and lit it. "We might as well feel good when we pass out," he mumbled, coughing and wheezing.

"How long do you think he can last out there?" Rob asked of anyone.

"Who knows?" I replied, "He's a pretty tough cookie, he never complains much." The joint made its way around. Rene' tried to Bogart it a while.

"Hey, pass it on, will ya?" Rob whined.

Howie busied himself looking out the windshield at the stars.

"Holy shit, that star is moving!" he exclaimed. Everyone leaned forward, craned their necks and peered upward. Nothing. Not a damn thing.

"You're stoned, man," someone mumbled.

We got back into massage mode trying to keep our circulation going. All of us were rubbing and shaking vigorously. All the heat was finally gone from the truck and the glass was frosting up on the inside, forming incredible snowflake patterns. Howie was sitting quietly, staring at one of these beautiful works of art on the driver's side window, when he noticed a black shadow moving towards us on the road. His voice was excited, "That can't be Huard. He's only been gone fifteen minutes!"

Rene' scraped the frost off his section of window and peered out into the void. "It sure as hell is him!"

As the figure ahead moved closer everyone recognized Huard; but he was somehow different. He wasn't wearing the same clothes. He had on this huge parka with a fur trimmed hood and some kind of mukluks or something on his feet. And he was carrying a large can of something in his hand!

"Hi guys," he spit out, "look what I've got!"

It was a can of gasoline, one of those old wartime ones with white letters stencilled onto khaki paint.

Un-fucking-believable!

Bill came around to the passenger-side door and I slid back into the rear on top of Glynn's Showman. He sat in the passenger seat and placed the gas-can between his boots and looked around at everyone.

"Hey guys, wait 'til you see the place I got this from! It's this old hermit's shack beside the highway about a quarter of a mile east of here. He says we can drop in to get warmed up once we get the truck going."

We were all looking at him incredulously.

"So what's the hold-up Bill? Let's get gassed up and get on the road!"

"Uh, well there's only one thing guys; we don't have a nozzle or a funnel for the gas. That's why I was gone so long. We tried to find one, but we came up empty. So we're gonna have to improvise!"

Rob was curious, "Yeah, so how Bill. What's the idea?"

Bill reached around behind the seat and got his brief-case. He reached inside it and grabbed a couple of our eight by ten promo shots and then gently rolled them into a trumpet-like funnel shape.

"That ought to do it."

Rob said, "You might want to add a couple more, Bill. And somebody is going to have to hold them together to keep the whole thing from unravelling."

"Man, it's almost minus forty degrees out there, that'll be torture. Nobody's got any heavy gloves or anything." Rene' was looking scared. "We'll have to draw straws again. Man, this ain't gonna be any fun."

So, we went through the whole process again and this time it was my turn.

I didn't really give a shit. I just wanted to get the truck going and get warm again!

Rene' gave me his leather gloves, which were unlined and I put them on. Then Huard and I scrambled to the back of the Blue Goose II and removed the gas cap. Huard handed me our improvised bull horn funnel and I inserted it, and then he began to pour.

Of course some of the gas was going to leak out of the gap where the paper folded. This happened right away. But it took a little time to seep right through Rene"s gloves. When it did, the pain got excruciating. It was only a two gallon can, but it seemed like it took forever to empty it.

When we were done I peeled the gloves off and chucked them into the ditch beside the road. By this time I couldn't feel my fingers. We capped the tank and jumped back into the truck.

Howie set the choke and said in a very quiet voice. "Okay everyone, don't make a sound; I've got to hear the sounds of the engine."

He turned the key and the starter groaned mercilessly. Howie knew the Goose better than anybody, and he just let it go round and round. On the third revolution the engine roared and he gave it a few pumps of the throttle and then set the fast idle speed with the choke.

Everyone yelled and whooped. Howie did his Blow-Fish impersonation. Rene' whistled and Rob and I clapped our hands like madmen. We were back in business.

After a few minutes of warm-up time we set out for this hermit-guy's shack. When we got there Huard got out and went to the door and knocked. Rene' pulled the truck up a little closer as Huard turned around in the doorway and motioned for us all to come in.

It was a tiny place. Maybe two hundred square feet. But right in the middle of the room was a glowing red-hot woodstove that was pumping out many, many British Thermal Units of wonderful, wonderful heat!

The owner of the place was an older guy with a slightly unkempt look and a huge smile. He introduced himself as Jimmy and shook hands with each of us. "Happy New Year boys; looks like the lord has been covering your asses tonight! There's some hot coffee percolating on the stove and I just found half a bottle of "Jack" after your pal here left with the gas, so sit down and warm up a little bit and we'll get a good old New Year's toast goin' on here, in a few minutes."

We sat on a couple of chairs and some orange crates and waited for the drinks, thanking our new-found friend for his gracious hospitality. Alternately, we stood hands outstretched toward the woodstove as a warm feeling of gratitude filled the room. It was a great feeling. It was something that made us all thankful for being human.

This guy didn't have to do this. He could have just sent us on our way, but he didn't. He was a gentleman and a comrade. He spoke once more to Bill. "I got you a bit more gas son, and I found an empty plastic bleach bottle we can use for a funnel. That'll make sure you can make it into the 'Peg!"

He was our saviour.

We all drank a toast together to the New Year of 1968 and then we gassed up a bit more and hit the road. Jimmy gave us an old thermos with the remains of the coffee and "Jack Daniels" for the trip back. Huard gave him fifty bucks for saving our lives, and then we all thanked him profusely and shook his hand as we left.

Generosity and gratitude. There's just no denying the human spirit!

Amen.

After we returned to Toronto we found out that Glynn and Mike had endured the same deep-freeze adventure as we had. Their taxi had broken down half way between Bandon and Winnipeg and they had to get out of the car and push it over to the side of the road. Then they had to sit and wait for their own semi-dramatic rescue, after their driver had radioed for another cab in desperation! They made it back to Winnipeg just in time to catch the first plane that was leaving that morning for Toronto!

CHAPTER 23
REVISION

A week later Glynn walked into our first band meeting of the New Year and said that he was leaving the band. This was totally out of left field and really hard to take. We tried to talk him out of it, but he was absolutely certain and had made up his mind. He wanted to get into graphic arts and he wanted to take personal control of his life. No one could argue with him. He was a fabulous artist and everyone knew it. We knew that he would be successful; there was no doubt about it in our minds. But it was sad to see him go.

So now what would we do?

We decided to just chill and not worry about it. We rehearsed with just the four of us and decided it was O.K. and that there was no rush to do anything.

In fact we started rehearsing almost every day, working on new original material. We had found a new rehearsal room on Danforth Road just north of Kingston Road before we had left for Winnipeg and we could use it twenty four hours a day, seven days a week. It was right around the corner from where Sylvia and I had moved into our new apartment on Fishleigh Drive. I could walk to work. My old friend Ernie Pope and his wife Carol had recently moved into an adjoining building and Ernie had told me that there was a vacancy in one of the buildings at a recent gig at Charlie's.

One morning while walking the half mile to rehearsal I had had an epiphany and a whole new song just dropped into my befuddled brain. It was called "Hangman". I had been watching a lot of Canadian politicians on T.V. debating the new law to abolish Capital Punishment in Canada and somehow the conversation had permeated my whole being. By the time I made it to rehearsal I had guitar lines, drum fills and lyrics all spinning around in my head. We put it all together over the next two days and we were confident that we had our next single in the bag.

Huard was ecstatic. "Man, this song is so fuckin' heavy it'll blow people's minds! Where the hell did this come from, Dave? Are you channeling something, or what?"

I didn't really know, and I didn't care. But I loved the fact that it just dropped into my lap like that. That was so cool. That's what songwriters call getting into the zone. Like when Roger & I had hit on "Nothin'" and just pumped it out in twenty minutes. When this happens, it's almost like you're not really creating it; you're just sort of letting it come through you. And strange as it may seem, you can't will yourself into this state. You can only create all the conditions for it to happen; wait for the mysterious door to open and then go with the flow.

Mike got all wound up by the experience. He called me up and told me to come over to his place on Walker Avenue so we could get to work. I was game. Next day I was over there by eleven thirty and we worked all afternoon. We outlined two songs. "Playgirl" and "Rise To Your Calling". Two *great* songs. They were built from Mike's doodlings on the guitar. Every guitarist does that same thing when they plug in and tune up. They mess around. Well, we turned two of Mike's favourite messes into songs!

Acoustically they sounded wonderful; but translating them into a full electric sound was going to be a challenge. We were looking forward to it, though. We couldn't wait to get to work.

At the beginning of February Ross and Bill got us a spot on "Through the Eyes of Tomorrow" a Toronto CBC Production that was broadcast across the country. Since we were going to be lip-synching for the video shoot, we had to go into a little three-track studio at the CBC and pre-record the audio tracks. We chose "Can't Judge A Book" and "Hangman" as they were the two most popular numbers in our "Live" show at that moment.

It seemed like it was a good session, but there was no way for us to tell for sure because we had nothing to do with the mixing. The next afternoon when we went back in to the Studios to do the videotaping, the CBC engineers proudly played the tracks for us. They were good. They were right where they needed to be. We felt quite confident and did what we thought was a great performance as we filmed the video. The same situation applied, however. We would have to wait for the show to be aired to see the final cut. There had been three cameras on the shoot and the production crew had a bit of work to do before air-date. Ah, what the hell; it was what it was. No worries, no hurry.

Promo Shot of "Through The Eyes of Tomorrow"

Next up: the boys got us an opening slot for Albert King and The Animals at the Queen Elizabeth Building at the Exhibition Grounds. We were on a roll. It was a shame that we didn't have a new single release out there to promote. But the guys at the label seemed indifferent and not even really interested in coming to see us play.

It was a fabulous night opening for Albert and Eric. The ride of a lifetime.

Mike was in awe of Albert and when we finally met the man backstage we were all knocked out by how humble and sociable he was. He was a true southern gentleman and he chatted with Mike about Mike's new sunburst Les Paul. Albert said he liked the Les Paul but that The Gibson Flying "V" was the *ultimate*. He said it was much better for him because of the fact that he played it upside down and backwards and he therefore needed the double cutaway. Besides that, they had really similar electrics and he dug the slightly different tone of the "V". Couldn't fault him on that one! After we did our set Albert complimented us as we came off stage. "Good job, boys! Righteous playin'. You got the silver, and that's for sure!" He gave us a big thumbs up.

And then Albert got up and played his heart out. He sweated buckets and never, ever laid back. He just gave it all, and the audience gave it all right back to him. He saved "Born Under A Bad Sign" for the end of his set and got a thunderous ovation.

Backstage @ The Queen Elizabeth Building

Eric Burdon and the "New" Animals arrived backstage in the middle of Albert's set and were escorted to stage left. There was no way for us to approach them, but they did acknowledge us with a wave, realizing that we were obviously the opening act. They watched Albert along with all the other folks backstage and nodded and clapped in all the right places. Their set was simply majestic. Sky Pilot, San Franciscan Nights, Don't Let Me Be Misunderstood; all those incredible Animals hits. Just about everything they did had the audience singing along with them. I didn't know it at the time, but those songs were going to be worm-holing their way around my music-addled brain for the next few weeks! They were indelible.

Albert Ripping It Up!

Over the next month we rehearsed our asses off and put together ten new songs for our new album. Once we felt confident enough with all of the basic arrangements we decided to rent a good two-track tape machine and demo the stuff for the A&R guys at Yorkville Records.

Kevan Staples had returned to the fold as our Road Manager and Huard was the maestro. He organized each day's recording schedule and called the shots as we made our way through all of the material. There were endless adjustments to be made to each of the instruments and to the vocals, as we laid down each tune. Bill supervised and Kevan moved around the room, constantly changing microphone placements and adjusting volume and tone settings on each of the guys' amplifiers and the P.A. system as we recorded.

After a week of work we had a tape that we could play for the guys at Yorkville. That job was deemed Bill's responsibility. He took them the tape and laid it on them. He wasn't there when they eventually got around to listening to it, so he had no explanation for their negative response to what we had done. He was just told that the music wasn't up to snuff, it wasn't what the A&R guys were looking for and we should re-think our musical direction and where we wanted to go!

We should have realized that these guys were in a different head-space than us right from the start. They were always nice, and very polite, and went to great lengths to fit in whenever they were around us. But, they never once came to see us play. Not once! To me, that would have been a major pre-requisite. Audience reaction was definitely a precise indicator of record sales, was it not? It really pissed me off that they were never there to see any of our triumphs. And after "Through the Eyes of Tomorrow" aired on the CBC they never once mentioned anything about our performance, or the show itself. It was as if we didn't exist.

By April things were very, very bad. Our morale was at a low point. We had been getting incredible response wherever we played, and the audiences were especially digging the new material. "Hangman" was even as popular as "Gaslight" and was called out for encores at the end of the night. We just couldn't fathom where our A&R guys' heads were at.

To lift our spirits Huard called a meeting and asked for ideas. After a few hours of discussion we decided to try out some keyboard players. Mike wanted more room to maneuvre within the arrangements and we all thought that adding the keys might make the sound more amenable to Tony and Bill in the A&R department at Yorkville

The parade of keyboard guys at the auditions was a lot of fun. Each player had their own little idiosyncrasies and tried in their own ways to fit in with our sound. Except for Bill Speer. Huard had called him, remembering his eclectic contribution to "Epilogue" and invited him to try out.

He was a godsend; a totally intuitive player with his own harmonic sense and an ability to merge seamlessly with just about anything we did. He had a wonderful old Hammond M3 organ and his memory was impeccable, to boot. We only had to rehearse a number once and it was stored forever in Bill's lock-tight memory bank.

It was a done deal.

The next month and a half we had a ball playing all around Southern Ontario and in fact, it was probably the most musically intuitive band that we had had up until that point. But there was still the matter of the next recording, and the guys at Yorkville still weren't happy. They wouldn't budge. It soon became apparent to everyone that what they really wanted was another "Gaslight". I got the impression that they wanted to have their own little Canadian version of Motown Records. They wanted to mold us into a nice little cookie-cutter outfit that would spit out one "Gaslight" after another.

But that wasn't what we had in mind.

We had a band meeting about it and Ross Atchison suggested that maybe we should hire a lawyer and try to get out of our Recording agreement. We all agreed. There was nothing to lose and as far as our musical direction was concerned, we had no intention of starting over.

After we hired the lawyers and started the process we became aware that we were really in a "business". We had never considered ourselves as such. We might have thought of the band as a partnership, but we didn't want to get into the legal implications of what we were doing. We wanted to be free to create whatever we could musically, without being burdened with being conscious of the hype and the contracts.

Well, we were about to get an indication of that burden. Within three weeks of our lawyer's petitioning Yorkville we had our answer. Yes, they would release us from our contract, provided we paid them the princely sum of $7,500! Although we had never received so much as *one* royalty payment for *any* of our recorded out-put, they had still found a way to charge us astronomical fees for our recording sessions. Plus, according to the contract we had signed, we owed them 15% of all of the monies from our "Live" performances. This was a surprise to me, and it had no-doubt been hidden in some obscure clause in the contract.

Our lawyers had examined the contract and advised us to pay.

We were devastated. There was no way to come up with the money and therefore no way out. The guys at

Yorkville had mistakenly assumed that there was another Record Company who had approached us about signing a deal. They thought they had a good chance at cashing in their chips so they had padded the expenses and assumed someone else was going to foot the bill.

Wrong move! You can't squeeze money from a stone.

Two weeks later Mike left the band. He wasn't into hanging in there through a long legal fight. Who could blame him? He put an ad in a local paper to solicit guys for a new band, and within a month McKenna Mendelson Mainline was born.

We, on the other hand, had to find a new guitarist.

We put the word out and placed ads in the newspapers, on Long & McQuade's bulletin board and at the Musician's Union, Local 149. We were swamped with applicants and set up the trials for the next week at Danforth Music.

Depending on the players, the individual auditions might have lasted an hour or maybe as little as twenty minutes. It went on through the middle of the week with little resolution until a fellow named Dave Burt showed up. As soon as he started playing we liked him right away. He had a good ear and great tone and could jam without much verbal communication. We asked him if he would like to join the band, but he declined. He was perturbed by the fact that we smoked the weed.

It had never occurred to us that pot could have a negative influence on the outcome of the auditions. To us it was a way to relax and cut the tension, so that we would have a chance to hear the true personalities of the players. But it was a lifestyle that some people didn't respect.

We carried on.

On Friday a skinny rake of a guy showed up and removed a beautiful Gretsch White Falcon from a beat-up old case that was plastered with many, many place-name stickers. His name was David Kindred and we had been told he was from Down East.

We were used to Telecasters and Les Pauls, Stratocasters and Gibson SG's. We hadn't seen a Gretsch since Glynn had left the band. And we had never seen anyone other than George Harrison who used one for Lead Guitar.

When we ran through the first tune we were blown away. Jaws dropped.

I had asked David to do a boogie-woogie number in "E"; something that we could all get into and experiment with. I asked him to start it up and he took off like a psychopathic version of Les Paul on speed! Wow, did he wail! We all joined in and stomped it out for a good five minutes.

Bill Speer's face lit up with a big grin as we finished the tune. "You got some more of that stuff up your sleeve, or what?"

Howie puffed up his cheeks and did his blowfish routine.

Rob looked very satisfied and relaxed, which was his normal positive reaction to anything.

I broke the ice a little more. "Hey, what do you say we have a little smoke break and then we'll try one of our original tunes?"

David looked cool and calm. "Sure, whatever you guys want."

I was thinking of "Hangman". What would it sound like with this monster guitar guy? There was only one way to find out.

The "new" UGLY DUCKLINGS" June 1968

Howie pulled out a wad of pre-rolled joints and lit one up. We passed it around and David had no problem with it. In fact he held on to it for a little while. The room was filled with a pungent bluish haze as we went over the chords to "Hangman". David had some ideas of his own about how he was going to play them and that suited us just fine. We wanted someone who would be confident enough to volunteer some input.

Half an hour into the song we locked into it and we finally came together as a unit. One collective mind-set played the song. Everyone, including David knew the final decision. We all smiled. It was mutual and unanimous.

Music is like that; it's a matter of knowing.

CHAPTER 24
MUTATION

So, once again we had a straight five piece set-up. Keyboards, guitar, bass & drums. But, with the addition of David Kindred we now had the capability of playing in any genre that we chose. Theoretically, we could now do almost any type of tune that we wanted. Our new-found Mr. Kindred was an amateur guitar historian as well as a player, and he could easily demonstrate the guitar styles of almost any famous guitarist we could name. It was especially uncanny how he could channel Chet Atkins, and get him absolutely to a tee.

The other unique thing about his playing, was his ability to get almost any kind of sound out of his magical White Falcon. He couldn't replicate other guitars with it, but he could get damn close.

We rehearsed for a week and by the following Friday he was fully integrated into the band and ready to play. We added some Dylan (Just Like Tom Thumbs Blues), a Beatles (Eleanor Rigby) and a Jeff Beck (Ain't Superstitious).

Bill Speer was a great arranger, and took all of our arrangements to another level. It was nice when the tunes were less predictable. We let him have a go at "Hangman" too, after we had mastered his incredible arrangement of "Eleanor Rigby".

The new "Hangman" was tighter and less showy than the older arrangement and eliminated the spoken-word gambit at the end of the tune. It had been a fun part of our show for almost a year, but Howie and I were getting tired of it anyway, and everyone liked the way Bill changed it up.

In November we got a chance to perform both of these mainstays of our repertoire on What's Happening, a local CBC Television show. It was hosted by Shawn and Jay Jackson and The Majestics, one of the hottest R&B outfits in Toronto and it alternated with similar shows from three other large Canadian cities, in the five thirty evening time-slot on CBLT- TV, Toronto.

Local DJ, Joey Cee of CKEY Radio introduced us as the band that had that great big hit, "Gaslight"! For us the show was a big success. We managed to perform with flash and integrity and the audience was with us, as always. No one saw it coming, of course, but that show was our swan song, of sorts.

Two weeks after it aired Bill Speer gave his notice, in order to join Anne Murray's new touring band; and then Howie surprised everyone by handing in his resignation. He was determined to travel around the world by sail and his plan was to make his way to the west coast and eventually build his own boat and make his dream a reality.

Bill departed right away, but Howie felt more of an obligation to the rest of us and gave us a bit of time, agreeing to stay on until we finished playing all of the gigs that we were contracted for.

It was all too much! It was becoming a bit of a chore; always working a new member into the band. The game was losing its allure. Rob and I were exhausted and decided that we had had enough. We just ran out of steam.

We decided to take some time off to consider all of our options. The whole summer and fall of 1968, since Mike had left the band, had been like being on a merry-go-round with all of these players coming and going. It made it very difficult to book the band and was really destroying whatever confidence that we still had.

What did it take? Why could no one commit?

One benefit of our sudden stop was that we had a Christmas and New Year's Eve at home for a change, and that was nice. We watched Saturday Night Hockey for the first time in four or five years!

Man, we almost felt like regular people.

I phoned Rob and David and told them that the band was on hiatus and that they could pretty well do whatever they needed to do, to survive. I needed a break.

After New Year's I went out and got a straight job as an apprentice Insurance Salesman. I had to do something. There were bills to pay and mouths to feed. Sean was almost a year and a half old. I wasn't a very good salesman; but as an incentive to take on the job, Prudential Insurance provided all their new trainees with a trial period of two months and a guarantee that you wouldn't be let go until you had at least put in that much time. So I could provide for a few months at least.

I went out and got my driver's license in January as well, because I knew I was going to have to stop relying on other people to get around. It was obvious that regardless of what happened in the immediate future, I had to be mobile. I also bought a used 1965 Volkswagen Beetle. It was the biggest purchase I'd ever made and it made me feel all grown up. Strange; being married and having a child couldn't bring about that special feeling. But having your own car was somehow the definitive sign that you had arrived and you were now a serious adult?

What a pile of bull. It dawned on me that I had been unduly influenced by mass marketing and advertising. It wasn't a nice feeling. It made me feel awkward and uncomfortable in my own skin. This wasn't me. I knew that I wasn't meant to be a salesman. It was all a bad dream that I hoped and prayed would soon come to an end.

Also during this time Sylvia and I were having difficulties communicating our feelings. She was an incredible mom and tuned in to every nuance of Sean's behaviour and development and she wanted me to be a responsible provider.

I was up to the task and obviously I had made the sacrifice and gone out and landed a job. But deep down I wasn't really committed.

I was dying inside. All of my thoughts were of getting back into the game and putting another band together. As I drove around Scarborough to meet with clients, I was constantly writing songs in the car, memorizing the melodies and writing out the lyrics in my client book.

Sean was what kept the two of us grounded. He was our inspiration.

We bathed him in the kitchen sink sometimes and marveled at his adaptability and his steadfast and easy going personality. Nothing riled him. He could sleep through a thunderstorm, digest almost any substance known to man, (which he often did) and scream louder than a seagull caught in a blender. We took him for walks around the block, during which he would examine and taste anything of interest that he found in his immediate vicinity.

Life had become a constant roller coaster ride, and we were stuck on it and somehow it seemed we couldn't get off.

In a five month period we moved three times. We were trying to find a nice place to live at a reasonable cost; but with little satisfaction. And soon, as time passed it became apparent that I was definitely not going to be a Prudential Insurance Man.

My boss called me into his office for an evaluation after I completed my first eight weeks on the job. His conclusion was that I wasn't cut-out for it. I couldn't have agreed with him more, but I dared not admit that. I asked him for a couple of more weeks. I told him I just needed time; but truth be told I had nothing else up my sleeve and nothing left to give. When I went home to Sylvia and Sean there was no way I could hide my fears. The next two weeks were hell on earth and after a lot of acrimony and soul-searching, in the end it was decided that I should leave. If music was to be my life; it would have to be without them in it.

The physical act of walking out the door was the hardest thing that I had ever done in my life, up until that point. I loaded up the Volkswagen with all of my clothes, my amp, my harps, and my record collection and then headed straight downtown. I had to pull into a few strip mall parking lots along the way to recover from major tearing-up. More than once the tears had become so bad that I couldn't see to drive. But in the end I sucked it up and regained my composure. I knew who I was. I knew I couldn't change, and I knew where my future lay. And deep down inside I knew that Sean & Sylvia would always be a part of my life. There was a soundtrack playing in my head that just wouldn't stop and I had to find out what the final chords were.

I managed to find a room in a rooming house at 122 Kendall Avenue, which was within a few blocks of the Village. When I knocked on the door to inquire about the room I was greeted by a nice looking young East Indian man. He introduced himself as Kai and showed me to a room on the third floor at the front of the house. It was a keeper. I thanked him and then gave him a month's rent and moved in all my junk. As soon as my phone was connected I set about getting another band together. Of course I called Rob and David first and once they gave the thumbs-up the hunt was on for a bassist and a keyboard player.

It took some time, but within two weeks I had hooked up with Dennis Pendrith, (formerly of Luke & The Apostles) on bass. He had just been through a very short sojourn with Bruce Cockburn and Colleen Peterson in 3's A Crowd.

On keyboards was a new acquaintance, Ray Nowak, whose name had been given to me by Danny Marks of Edward Bear. Danny and I were always bumping into each other at Long & McQuades or at various booking agents' offices. We talked shop and music a lot and tried to boost each other's confidence.

Right off-the-bat, I secured a gig at The El Patio; so that we could rehearse in the afternoons and get it all together. With four days of rehearsal we had covered all of the Ducks material that David knew and then we added a few more numbers that Ray suggested. We had almost enough for three complete sets and then I came up with the idea of having a theme song that we could use as an intro or tag, to each set. I looked at David and told him to play that same boogie number that he had laid on us at his Ducks audition. He pulled out all the stops and started wailing his "Boogie in E" and then I came in with the harp. After a few solos David inserted a little Homage to the Canadian National Anthem into the mix, and we were all set. A new tune was born. Howie had always referred to it as that "Psychedelic Armpit Boogie" thing. So we adopted the title. It was a great number to really get a crowd moving and for the rest of the summer we put it to good use.

When it came time to advertise the gig we had to decide what we were going to call ourselves. The situation that had developed with all of the various musicians coming in and out of the Ducks was deeply troubling and had really affected the way I felt about the demise of the band. It seemed that The Ducks existed in the past tense.

This new incarnation of the band sounded nothing like any version of the Ducks had ever sounded and the inspiration for the music had changed as well. We still played the blues but it wasn't our only source. Our musical foundation had expanded. So we opted to change the name. We truly were a separate entity and we felt it was no longer necessary to have any connection to the Ducks. There was still all of the unfinished business of the split with Yorkville Records as well; so this choice really simplified matters.

Finding a new name was another matter. It was getting harder and harder to come up with something original. There were probably half a million bands in America and Europe who were all vying for attention and every conceivable name had surely been taken. We were just another new band, trying to get an edge. In the end we settled on GNU. No "the"; no plural. Just GNU. (Pronounced "new", as in the Asian animal species).

It was a simple statement, but most people (and certainly all of our Ducks fans) didn't like it. They liked the more traditional approach to naming bands. We decided to stick with our choice and continued writing more and more non -Ducklings type material. David and I hit it off right away, as far as writing went. I was fascinated by his melodic sense and I loved the lack of pretense in all of his music. Within two months we had enough material for an album.

GNU's First Promo Shot – In the middle of "Avenue Road"

Our piece-de-resistance was the new arrangement that we had come up with for "Hangman". It rocked! David's guitar playing on it was majestic and powerful beyond words. All of the real "stoners" in our audiences just loved it to death and would immediately jump up and start dancing around like grateful "Deadheads", whirling and vibrating as if they were possessed.

Dennis and I even managed to write a tune together called "The Sage". We were all into reading about eastern religions and spiritualism at the time; and had become intent on experiencing a major creative surge. So one afternoon after a long and particularly inspired rehearsal the song just fell into our laps. Dennis was just as surprised as me.

Rehearsals had become a lot of fun. David kept coming up with the most supremely outrageous hooks and riffs and our challenge was to find a way that we might incorporate them into the music.

One Saturday night at The El Patio while we were playing to a packed house we noticed a dapper well decked-out gentleman at one of the front tables who seemed to be very involved with the music. He smiled persistently and made little notes in a booklet that he pulled from his coat pocket.

After the set he introduced himself as John De Nottebeck, an aspiring new producer on the scene in Toronto. He wanted us to do a demo recording. When we asked him what other bands he had done, he told us that at this point he had only managed to record one local band. They were called "Zooom" and they featured an incredible new guitarist from Sarnia named Kim Mitchell. David and I were impressed. We had heard great things about "Zooom" and Mr. Mitchell from all of our friends in Yorkville. They had played at The Patio earlier in the year, and blown everyone away.

We made an appointment to meet with John at his office at I.P.S Recordings on Hazelton Avenue and thanked him for his appreciation of the band. Ray was particularly excited at the prospect of recording with him, having heard great things about him from other musician friends.

Before we met with John though, I had to take my beloved Volkswagen back to GMAC credit in Etobicoke. There was no way that I could afford to make the payments on it anymore, and I really didn't need it because I was going to pick up the "Blue Goose II" from Huard later the same day. Our business arrangement with Ross

Atchison and the rest of the Ducks management crew was now finished, but Huard assured me that he was still interested in staying on to see how this new project would turn out.

Loyalty was one quality of human friendship that I was now coming to truly appreciate. Bill was there, always. And Rob was a rock. Somehow we were a unit, and we three were inseparable. It was hard to imagine that so much had happened to us in just five short years.

When we met with John De Nottebeck at his office, he had already booked time at Hallmark Studios for us to record our demo. We had eight days to rehearse the tunes and get ready.

The plan was to do a "live" recording of the band and then perhaps add a few overdubs afterwards. Our confidence in the level of musicianship in the band was pretty high and we didn't anticipate any problems. We just put our noses to the grindstone and worked for those eight days to get the music as together as possible.

When the day finally arrived we were more than ready. We were polished and shone. The music was our lifeline and served to inspire our day-to-day lives and in a way it justified our existence. We lived and breathed every verse and chorus, every riff and every solo. Putting it all down "Live" was going to be a pleasure.

We arrived at the studio right on time and were escorted into the big room. This wasn't what we expected but we were not going to complain, under the circumstances. John obviously had his reasons and no one was going to question them.

"GNU" Behind the "El Patio"

On Stage @ the "El Patio"

We said hello to our old friend and mentor Terry Vollum who passed by in the hallway. He wasn't doing our session but paused to say hello. Then it was time to get down to business.

We were used to the process by this time, and set about getting all of our levels set appropriately and then we worked on cooking up some nice drum and guitar sounds before we started putting things to tape.

The first tune we did was a new one that David and I had written only a few weeks before, called, "I'm With You, Babe". It only took a few takes and we nailed it to the wall. It was one of the new songs that had a somewhat country feel to it, and David played it in his most emotive and gentlemanly style. Because it came off so well we decided to continue with the others that were in the same vein and we laid down two more tunes with a similar vibe; "The Telephone Song" and "Nervous Tension".

After a short break we started to run over the new arrangement of "Hangman" that we had rehearsed the week before. Dennis had worked out a whole new bass & drum thing with Rob that complimented and fit ever so tightly with David's new heavy-funk guitar arrangement. Every time the band line-up had changed, the feel and the sound of "Hangman" had changed as well and it seemed it was always for the better.

This newest version was the heaviest yet and we were really looking forward to hearing what it would sound like on tape. While we were running it through for the fourth time, the sound of David's amplifier changed drastically and the speakers started breaking up horrendously.

Everything ground to a halt. John had been working on the sound of David's guitar and came running out to see what was happening. David was beside himself. We didn't have a spare amp or any spare tubes.

"Man, this amp has never, ever given me a problem! Why now?" He sounded really despondent.

Huard immediately began rummaging around the studio to see if there were any guitar amps hidden in any corners, but came back empty-handed.

"Too bad, if there was almost any kind of amp we might have been able to borrow a power tube. So what do you think, David?"

David was busy readjusting all of the controls on his Concert Amp.

"Well, I should be able to get it set so that the lower volume stuff is reasonably clean sounding, so that it will only break up when I really start to push it hard. Like, the more gain I give it, the raunchier it will sound."

Huard liked that idea. "Sounds good, Dave. Then the lead stuff will sound like you're using a fuzz tone, or something!"

John DeNottbeck was standing off to one side of our little cluster of equipment and he approached David and smiled. "I like a positive attitude, Dave. Way to go. I'll get back to the board and we'll see what we can do with the sound".

Next time we went through the tune it had a really dirty edge to it. John clicked on the talk-back. "Hey that sounds really gritty Dave; just leave it like that and we'll see how it sounds with some reverb and compression."

We soldiered on through "Hangman" and all the remaining tunes, and in the end the sound was quite suitable for the material. David did a fantastic job of controlling the distortion so that it only came into play where it contributed to the vibe of the remaining tunes.

We managed to finish nine tunes in six hours, total. John was conscious of the overall mix as the tunes went to tape, so that there wasn't too much fiddling around with levels when it came to the final mix-down. We went home with two copies of the session. One for the band and one for John.

The result was an excellent quality demo reel of the band and as we left the studio John promised to arrange a meeting within a week at I.P.S.

But it was not to be.

A week later Dennis gave his notice. He was going to hook up with Bruce Cockburn who had just dissolved his current band and was about to set out on a solo career.

We were all dumbstruck. We had just got a new thing going and here we were back at square one. David was more destitute than anyone else and was determined to keep things happening. His brother Peter had recently made the pilgrimage from New Bruswick to Toronto, so he suggested we incorporate him into the band to see if it would work. He didn't have a lot of experience as a bass player, but we had nothing to lose. We had one upcoming gig at The Hawks Nest that was a week away, so we decided to go for it.

David and I worked with Peter at my place; going over the tunes with just an acoustic guitar and a steely determination to make it happen. But Peter wasn't really up to it. He was a novice player and even when we played the tape of the session for him, he had a lot of difficulty trying to cop all of the bass parts.

There was no turning back though. We needed the money. We were surviving on a shoestring budget.

I phoned Ray and Rob and told them the situation, without glossing over any of Peter's deficiencies. It was decided that we would do the gig regardless of our doubts. It was a Thursday night thing anyway. Chances are that there wouldn't be a huge crowd and we could fake it.

The afternoon of the gig Ray and I went out and bought a couple of bottles of wine. We needed some cheering up. Starting at dinner time we hit the bottle(s). By the time we went on at nine o'clock we had finished one of them and were deep into the next one.

The result was one of the worst gigs we ever played (minus of course Rob's contribution, which was always excellent). But even Rob couldn't make up for the lack of cohesion and the sloppy execution of the rest of us. It was a devastating night that pretty well ended the whole thing for all of us.

Rob was pissed, David was distraught, I was ashamed of our lousy performance and Ray was totally depressed.

It was over. GNU was no more. I called John DeNottbeck and gave him the news. He was really disappointed but accepted that this kind of thing was part of the whole Band experience. It wasn't easy keeping four or five people all on the same wavelength and he hadn't really spent a huge amount of money to do the demo.

So, everything was kaput and there was no next step. It was time to move on. The future was a mysterious enigma and none of us had an inkling of where we were going. One thing was for sure though, we were at the very bottom and the only place left to go was back up.

CHAPTER 25

DESOLATION

Facing the challenge of whatever future lay ahead, was a scary prospect.

We knew that adapting to a straight life would be a complete about-face for all of us. But in a way it was something that was an unavoidable eventuality. We knew it was going to happen, so we decided it might be interesting to find something else that we really loved to do, that we could make a living at. Being on the road wasn't all it was cracked up to be, there had to be a better way.

Rob decided that he would head to California to see if he might be able to ingratiate himself into the scene there. We all knew that there was a large Canadian contingent in L.A. who were making a name for themselves. He felt that it was worth a shot to go there and hook up with whoever might give him a chance.

David and Peter decided to go back home. The whole experience of GNU had left a bad taste in their mouths. I tried to temper their disappointment with a pro-Toronto-music-scene pep talk, but it was to no avail. They were truly homesick. Being with family and friends was what they really needed right now.

Ray was at a loss to decide what he was going to do, but he was certainly not going to jump right into another band. There were other ways to make a living and he was determined to find something.

As for me, I was single-minded in my desire to continue on. I called everyone I could think of and checked all the ads in the newspapers and the Long & McQuade's bulletin board to see what was happening, but there was nothing worth the effort. Most of the musicians I knew were in stable bands, or had already started a new band. I was pretty dejected.

And then I got a call.

Joe Agnello, my bass playing buddy from the band, Leigh Ashford called me up to say that they were recording an album with producer Jack Richardson of Guess Who fame. He said that they needed some help. They were doing their own version of "Hangman" and they were having problems getting a suitable vocal on the track. Their drummer Dave Cairns who normally sang the tune was in the hospital with appendicitis and another drummer, Wally Cameron, who had played with A Passing Fancy was substituting for him for the sessions. No one could sing it. They needed a voice.

I told him I was in, and two nights later I was at RCA Studios on Mutual Street being introduced to Jack Richardson. I was suitably impressed. What a gentleman.

He extended a hand and smiled broadly.

"That was some performance you did on 'Gaslight', Dave. You know, that's Burton's favorite Canadian Single of all time. He was completely blown away by it!"

I was shocked. I never would have guessed. Of course, one never thinks of things like that; so it's really a nice treat when you find out that one of your contemporaries appreciates your work.

"Well, thanks Jack, that really means a lot to me." I sat down in one of the plush armchairs in front of the console. "So, what kind of performance are you looking for, for this track?"

He explained that he wanted it to be dark and foreboding; that it had to have a desperate tone to it and convey a feeling of resignation and fear.

He had summed up all of my original intentions for the tune. I understood.

Perception was the root of all great performance. The singer has to get into the character of the protagonist in the song. This one was a little different than "Gaslight", but it was the same basic premise. Get the feeling across. Bring the listener into the story.

Jack sat back in his comfy leather producer's chair and had the tape operator cue up the track. When it started to roll I was caught off guard. It was nothing like any of the versions of the tune that I had sung before (and there had been many).

It was as pure an example of The Toronto Sound as I had ever heard. People had been talking about this particular signature sound (that somehow typified Toronto) for the previous two years. It had grown out of the local R&B community.

Mandala and Roy Kenner and the Associates along with Bobby Kris and The Imperials were all progenitors of the basic concept. It grew out of the interaction between bass and drums and the emphasis on sevenths, ninths and thirteenths when accenting and accentuating chord structures with the guitar and the keyboards.

The track I was listening to now was about as psychedelic a roller coaster ride as a band could create with this particular vibe. It was a manic extension of the original concept of the song; all far-eastern and exotic in texture and overtly dramatic in its execution.

It was hard to sing to it. I kept getting distracted by all of the various elements of the arrangement. In the end though, it came together as a perfect example of the adventurousness of the times. Leigh Ashford's guitarist Gord Wazeck played the most inscrutable guitar solo that I'd ever heard in my life. It sounded like he was a mad guitar player from "Tralfamador". The imagination and soul that went into it was beyond words.

When it was finished we all sat and listened, stunned.

Jack got up from his chair and said, "You know fellas, this isn't exactly a commercial song. It's sort of like a Picasso. It's cubist. I don't think it could ever be played on Top Forty radio."

Gord stood up and interjected, "Yeah, but its O.K. Jack. There's other more singles oriented tunes on the album. 'A Country Place' is a good singles tune. There's lots of other stuff for us to draw from."

Jack agreed, "You're right Gord, of course. I'm just hoping that this track doesn't get overlooked. It's like an abstract painting; sort of make's your imagination work overtime!"

The night ended with handshakes all around, and I thanked everyone and headed back to Kendall Avenue.

Leaving the environment of the studio was a drag. It felt like I really belonged there; it was where my soul felt complete.

CHAPTER 26

RELAXATION

When the end of the month came I didn't have any money left for my rent.

I was sort of in a quandary. I felt strangely separated from the music. I had never thought of it as a business before, but now it was very apparent that that's what it was. Because I had no money! Music had always been my provider, but now it was letting me down; albeit gracefully.

To keep from starving I went down to the welfare office and copped enough money to pay my rent and buy some groceries. It was degrading to me. I had always been able to pay my own way.

Realizing that I didn't have any real prospects for the next month, either; I went home to visit my folks. They were far more understanding than I had ever given them credit for. They offered to let me stay in the basement of the house until I could get something happening.

They didn't preach to me this time. They respected me and gave me some space and time, and left me alone to figure things out for myself. It was so strange not to hear the familiar phrase "I told you so". I knew deep in my heart that it was Mom. She was behind it. She was keeping Dad reined-in.

It must have been tearing Dad up a million ways to Sunday to not be able to get his two cents worth heard. But I had to give him credit too. He stayed back and kept mum. I was going to come out O.K. so why screw things up with a useless mess of hyperbole and condescension? I appreciated the restraint and actually got out of the house most days before nine a.m. looking for work.

The second week that I was back at home, I met my best friend Brian Ross as he was pulling into the driveway next door to visit his parents. I told him my predicament.

"Hey, why don't you drop in and see the guys where I work at Convertible Pools, they're always looking for good guys to work on one of our teams."

That sounded weird. "Teams?" I said.

"Yeah, you know. Like sports teams. Everybody works with everybody else to get the job done. It's the only way to run this kind of company, Dave. All kinds of shit keeps happening all the time. You've got to be able to depend on people."

He looked at me with a questioning glance.

"Yeah, yeah, O.K. can you set it up for me?"

"Na, just give the boss Jack Bannerman a call. He's a straight-ahead guy.

He'll talk at 'cha for a few minutes and then get you in there. Hey, you know who works for us?"

I looked blank. No clue.

"Dennis Cook and Bob Aitken!"

"Holy shit, Dennis?" I was intrigued by that. Dennis building swimming pools? This I had to see. And Bob. He had always been so quiet and private. I especially wondered what kind of bee had gotten under his bonnet.

Next morning I was on the phone to Jack Bannerman first thing, and then a half hour later I was sitting with him in his office telling him the story of my life - up to this point. What was different with Jack was that he actually listened.

"Ever had any experience in construction, Dave?"

I had to answer in the negative.

"Ah, well we won't worry about minor inconveniences like that, you'll do fine. How about concrete, ever wheeled a wheelbarrow-load of that stuff around?"

I had to be truthful. "No."

"Well don't worry, man. We'll break you in gently. Don't want to discourage you from a career in the trades, eh? We'll let you work up to the heavy stuff. Be here tomorrow at seven a.m. sharp. Oh, and remember to bring lots to eat and to drink. You're going to be one hungry son-of-a-gun after you get a few hours of training under your belt!"

He stood up and reached across his desk for my hand. We shook, and I walked out the door in a state of amazement. I hadn't even asked how much money I was going to make. Strange. What kind of guy could have that much of an effect on people?

Next day, and for the next eight months I found out all about Jack, and about all of the other guys on the "Team". I got an education in concrete forming, pouring and construction and in installing cedar decks and heating and plumbing for swimming pools. In eight months I learned how to construct a swimming pool from scratch. I learned it all; from digging the hole in the backyard, forming the shape of the pool, trowelling the concrete, to installing ladders and diving boards, drains, filters, heaters, and Saunas.

I ate like a horse and drank like a fish and put on fifteen pounds and I gained a healthy respect for labourers. I discovered that there was a good deal more to building things, beyond the heavy lifting and grunt-work. You had to know what you were doing at every step along the way. There were rules and there was also an awful lot of knowledge that was a necessary prerequisite for the job.

I found out that Dennis and Bob were both floaters. They managed the different pool sites, ordered materials and concrete and pitched in on the crews when extra hands were needed. Their job was to keep things moving.

After a long hard day, Jack and his partner Sandy Amodeo would gather all of us back at the showroom for a swim in the display pool and a few shots of Rum or Scotch. It was a long hot crazy summer and I had a great time and made a bunch of new friends and loads of cash.

It made me feel good to be able to send Sylvia money to look after Sean. I didn't get to see him much, but I got news on how he was doing from John Read.

On one occasion near the end of August I delivered Sean's payment directly to Sylvia's door. She was amazingly friendly and seemed surprised by my newfound healthy appearance. We had a few laughs and I left with a smile. I almost felt like a grown up. God forbid.

In November we took Sean to see the Santa Claus parade together and had a great time. He was learning to talk now, and I noticed that he just couldn't stop asking questions. He had to know about everything. Previously, he had just needed to know how everything *tasted*. Now, he wanted to know *how* it worked, *why* it worked and *when* it worked! Sort of made me feel a bit inadequate, in that I couldn't always come up with an answer for him.

Maybe all that propaganda about pot destroying your brain cells and frying your memory was really true. I truly hoped not, because if that was the case then I was definitely screwed!

The first day that it snowed and there was ice on the puddles in the road, I asked Brian what was going to happen, as far as building pools went.

"Oh, no problem. We're going to keep building right on through to the spring!"

I said, "No, really Bri', what's going to happen? Do we get laid off or what?"

"Well, no Dave; we're really going to keep going right through the winter. Jack's got a plan. We're going to put up a rigid vinyl tent over the back yards and just continue building underneath them. You know, we'll heat the space with portable propane heaters!" I really didn't know if he was pulling my leg or not.

But I remembered once in October I had stopped in on a job-site where Brian was supervising the installation of a backyard Pool Cover. It was a massive ten foot high metal-framed vinyl cover mounted on metal tracks that ran down both sides of the pool deck. It worked like a giant accordion that was normally all compressed at one end of its length. When the weather got cold, you just pulled it out taut, so that it covered the whole pool and then turned on the pool heater. The heat from the water kept the air warm inside.

This was evidently where Jack had had his epiphany. One day on the job he had looked around and saw the future staring him right in the face. We could build all year! It was all so clear! From that day on it was a foregone conclusion and Jack decided then and there to make his dream a reality.

Ah, if only it had been that easy. If only the winters in Canada would not sometimes dip down to -30° F. If only vinyl didn't turn to cardboard once the temperature dipped below 60°. If only there was some way to predict whether or not there was an underground stream in someone's back yard. If only!

I remember one specific day, in mid-December, when John and Yoko were traveling around with Ronnie Hawkins on the peace train. They had hired a Cessna Plane from the Island Airport to tow a huge "Give Peace A Chance" sign all around downtown Toronto and back and forth along the shore of Lake Ontario from the bluffs of Scarborough, to Port Credit. I had the portable transistor radio tuned in to CHUM, with the volume cranked, listening to reports on John and Yoko's exploits. I was at the top of a 12 foot ladder trying to thread a vinyl panel into a galvanized extruded frame rail. My hands were bare. The temperature was 10°F. There was no other way to do it. Because each vinyl panel was edged with encased rope it had to be fed into the extrusion with bare hands and then pulled along between the extruded frame rails from one side of the pool to the other. Each panel was 28 inches in width, and 20 feet long. There were 18 altogether. After three of them I couldn't feel my fingers anymore. Neither could my partner Lenny. We had to stop, climb down off of the ladders and warm up in front of the propane heater.

The only thing that Jack hadn't really considered in all his musings, was the fact that we were sometimes going to have to put these tents up - over people's backyards - in arctic conditions! Our first installation at the beginning of December took five days. If it had been a regular tent we could have done it in two days. But of course; then we would have had to use lights inside to see what we were doing.

So, vinyl it was.

We did get better at it.

We got so we could dig the hole and install the cover in four; maybe five days. A miracle! But still a lot of pain and suffering.

After a winter of installing these ridiculous plastic domes, I had had enough. I had a wad of cash in the bank, a bad attitude and I was yearning to play music again. I had been going out to see a lot of my old friends play at all of the best clubs in Toronto. When I would get up to sing a tune, or sit in and play the harp, the old juices would start flowing and I could feel a strange energy radiate through my whole body.

It was intoxicating.

I knew I was ready for a change.

As the Ides of March approached, I gave my notice.

Freedom!

CHAPTER 27
RESUMPTION

There was no turning back now; nothing to do but think of the future and all the possibilities that lay ahead. Once I had given my notice I called up my brother Dale.

We had a conversation about sharing an apartment. On several earlier occasions we had broached the subject in passing, but now an opportunity presented itself. Neither one of us had any possessions to speak of, other than a massive stereo and a more than ample record collection, but we knew we could be resourceful and work around those kinds of inconveniences. I still had that big wad of money in the bank, so a first and last month's rent wasn't a problem.

We eventually found a place in Scarborough near the Golden Mile Plaza and moved in at the beginning of April. The two of us started working with a temporary agency, filling in at O.H.I.P. in Don Mills for employees who were sick or on vacation. It was a reasonable gig and certainly not as physical as building swimming pools. We spent the summer hanging out in clubs and going to Outdoor Festivals.

Early, after the beginning of September we arrived at work one morning to find Keith, one of our co-workers and a huge music fan, sitting at the table in the mail room with his morning newspaper and a face as white as a ghost.

Dale reached out and pinched the top of the newspaper with his fingers and asked, "What's up Keith?"

"It's Hendrix, man, he's dead. He was found dead in his Hotel room this morning, in London."

"Oh shit, man, not Jimi!" Dale was genuinely distraught and sat down in a chair and took a long deep breath. He looked at us with a strange expression on his face, and then he just sat there, silently, as the rest of the people arrived for work. Their reactions were as varied as their personalities and temperament, but the overwhelming feeling that everyone shared was one of sadness. I was stunned. I didn't say much all day. I just withdrew and meditated on what had happened.

Jimi was a major inspiration to me, but also to so many other musicians and I felt sure that his death would have a profound effect on the collective psyche of the global music business for a long time to come. We headed home that evening in a daze. Life was too strange.

As winter approached I was becoming very dissatisfied with my current arrangement with Dale and he had pretty well had it with me. It became apparent that we just couldn't get on the same wavelength about anything. Even things like organizing our grocery shopping became a bone of contention and the cause of bad feelings. So, after many heated arguments and a few anxious discussions we decided to look for alternate accommodations on our own.

Near the end of October I heard about an apartment for rent in the Yonge and Bloor area, downtown. One of the girls at O.H.I.P. had a girlfriend who was moving out of an old one bedroom, just around the corner from Yonge Street and Mary Street. The next day I was down there in a flash checking it out.

It couldn't have been more perfect. It was located at 65 St. Nicholas Street directly behind Yolles Antiques. The Yolles building was on Yonge Street just south of Mary Street and actually abutted the four-plex on St. Nicholas Street. When I opened the windows in the kitchen of the place, I looked out onto the roof of Yolles. The only drawback to the place was the miniature size of the living room; but it was duly compensated for by a huge kitchen with a large dining area and a perfectly suitable bathroom and bedroom. And the rent was a paltry $90 a month.

The super was a skinny, grizzled old codger who informed me that he played the organ nightly at The Hungarian Village, which was a restaurant just around the corner on Bay Street, north of Wellesley. I gave him a hundred and eighty bucks up front and asked if I could use the remaining days in October to re-paint. He was agreeable, so I worked my butt off for the next week and totally transformed the place just in time to move in at the beginning of November.

The Friday before I moved in I gave my notice at the temp agency. There was no way I was going to be making a trek out to Don Mills every day for the amount they were paying me.

I started scouting for musicians and began making plans to start up another band. I promised myself it would be different this time. Nothing was going to happen until everything was in place.

One afternoon I had gone in to Long & McQuade's to buy some new harps when I noticed an ad posted on their bulletin board for a singer. A band from Port Credit called Papa Grey were looking for an experienced singer to replace Eddie Spencer, who had just left them to go solo. The prospect of not having to go through the rigmarole of assembling and auditioning musicians was very tempting.

I had no idea who they were or even what type of music they played, but I had heard of Eddie Spencer and I knew that he was well-regarded amongst the Toronto music establishment. So I wrote down the number and called as soon as I got home.

I phoned the number and spoke to their manager Doug Greer, who immediately proposed that I come out to Port Credit and check out the band for myself. It wasn't hard to convince me that there was really no other way to see if we would be a good fit, other than to try it out. He told me that the musicianship would amaze me and that the biggest plus about the band was their creative energy.

I was intrigued and set up a jam session for the following Tuesday. I arranged to meet them at the Go-Train station at Southdown Road in Mississauga after which I would be driven to their rehearsal space.

It turned out that their space was the basement of the drummer's parents' home and that they had two of the hottest guitarists that I had seen in years. But they were so young! When I talked to their manager, I hadn't even thought to ask how old they were or how long they had been playing.

They were all eighteen or nineteen years old and very inexperienced as far as gigging was concerned. Despite that fact, their proficiency on their chosen instruments was exceptional. They had been together as a band for approximately fourteen months but hadn't really had a chance to play regularly enough to be noticed.

But I was sure that that would change. They were very intuitive and tuned in to each other's playing. As we jammed I noticed a lack of flash and a healthy attitude toward the over-all sound of the band. They were definitely a unit. One for all and all for one.

I told them it felt pretty good and that I was willing to give it a shot.

The drummer Wayne Baguley was a tall skinny dude with a Robert Plant hairdo and a Mitch Mitchell smile. He was capable of some wicked Mitch Mitchell inspired beats and fills, too. Not too shabby. His rhythm partner, bassist Tom Fryer was sly and confident and constantly grinning with anticipation with every new number that we laid down.

The two guitarists were very enigmatic. John Bride, who persistently cracked wry jokes and never took anything seriously was a perfect foil for Ed Pryla, who was the shy guy in the band but liable to explode with passion whenever his turn came to play a lead.

After just two weeks of rehearsal we felt ready to play and gave the go-ahead to Doug to rustle up some gigs. By this time we had started to write some pretty heavy tunes and our confidence was growing. Doug had visited The Music Shoppe, which was a new agency that had evolved from the remnants of my old booking agency. He hooked us up with Wayne Thompson who was one of the principal bookers there along with his partner Ray Danniels, who had just started working as an agent. Evidently my reputation with The Ducks and Papa Grey's connection with Eddie Spencer, was enough to get us on board. The agency was relatively new and was taking steps to move ahead.

We did a couple of high school gigs that went quite well and then Wayne placed us on a bill at The Global Village with a new band called, A Foot In Coldwater. They had formed out the disintegration of Nucleus, who had just recorded a very unique album with Mainstream Records in the states. Despite glowing reviews on both sides of the border the album had failed to take off and the band had subsequently imploded.

My old friends Danny Taylor and Hugie Leaggat of The Lords Of London fame had failed to make their mark with Nucleus but had forged ahead and put together an incredibly funky and heavy outfit that expanded on the quirky vibe of Led Zeppelin. I had seen them downstairs at the Embassy Tavern on Bloor Street and walked out amazed by their precision and tightness and by the incredible playing of their guitarist, Paul Naumann. We were asked to open for them and gratefully accepted.

The Global Village was distinctive, in that it was a theatre in-the-round with seating that emulated a Roman Forum. The audience were all around us, spread out in an arc of slightly more than 180 degrees.

The visual impact of this set up was impressive, but the audio problems it created for the bands was its eventual downfall as a music venue. It was so difficult to hear yourself play that playing off of each other and improvising was a major problem. Even the best monitoring systems failed to correct the difficulty.

As a performance theatre it was wonderful. Actors didn't even have to have their voices amplified.

That said, both bands put on a spectacular show despite the deficient acoustics and Wayne was pleased enough that he gave us a gig in Port Credit opening for a new emerging band called Lighthouse.

Lighthouse was Skip Prokop's new band that he had formed after the dissolution of The Paupers. He had conceived it as a Canadian version of Chicago or Blood, Sweat & Tears. Massive sound and super musicianship!

Tom *John* **PAPA GREY 1971** *Wayne* *Ed*

When I had known him in The Paupers his style was straight ahead and built on pulsating rhythm. Their whole shtick had been to blow the audience away with an onslaught of percussion.

Now, he was the leader of a full-blown mini-orchestra with a line-up that was capable of doing almost anything, musically. They had gone through a slew of personnel changes over the last couple of years but had recently reached a stable point with the addition of Bob McBride on lead vocals. They had an all powerful sound and we knew we were up against the wall as their opening act.

We decided to go for broke and hit the audience with "contrast". We went back to the Ron Scribner playbook and decided to emphasize our differences. If they were to be big and expansive, we would be small and loose. If they were to be loud and profuse, we would be dynamic and precise. There was nothing better than "contrast" according to Ron to really make an audience sit up and take notice. We had nothing to lose.

And of course when the evening finally arrived we played it to the hilt and it worked like a charm. The audience loved our set and responded positively to the personal nature of our music. We still did some stuff that was totally flash, but we kept that to a minimum and laid it on heavy with some wanton blues; such as Mike McKenna's "The Blues Fell This Morning" and a new ballad that I had written called "I Just Can't Shake This Feeling".

Our strategy worked perfectly and we held our own against the power of "Lighthouse" and the very engaging voice of Mr. McBride. Their set was truly magnificent and featured tunes from a new album they were working on which was soon to be released, called One Fine Morning.

We were rewarded the next day with a totally biased review from the local Port Credit newspaper that suggested that we had stolen the show! It was a little over the top but it was a big ego-boost nonetheless.

Over the next nine months we worked ceaselessly in the basement of Wayne's parent's house, writing and arranging more than a dozen original tunes. Sometimes we were joined by members of the band's best friends' club. They would drop in and observe the goings-on, giving us encouragement and support. Among them was a young blues singer and harp player named Chuck Jackson who would soon have a band called Madison Street Walkers and who would eventually become the lead singer for The Downchild Blues Band. He was particularly helpful with arrangement hints and even contributed a few key phrases to some of my lyrics. All of the fans who hung out with the band were supremely loyal and took pride in the fact that the "boys" all came from Port Credit.

Every rehearsal was a party.

During this time we recorded sixteen demo tunes and shopped them around to all the Major Record Companies in Toronto; but we didn't get any action. It was very disheartening for everyone. The guys put everything they had into the music, as we rehearsed and then toured all over southern Ontario through blinding winter snow-storms and incessant summer heat. There was absolutely no slacking, coasting or procrastinating. It was a total one hundred percent effort on everyone's part.

But the inevitable dissolution eventually came to pass. There is only so much rejection that a person can take. It seemed that the record companies in Toronto just weren't into blues based rock. It didn't make sense when you looked at what was happening on a global scale, but it was a time of change. And change was something that the music industry in Canada was not ready for.

In the end we gave it more than was warranted for the response that we had received. But no one in the band was willing to bang their head against a wall forever.

In just ten short months it was over.

I guess you could say that I was a bit depressed by the chain of events.

I holed up in my apartment like a recluse and sort of withdrew from the scene.

I needed some cheering up. And lo' and behold, one of my old buddies from Convertible Pools, Lachlan Clement called on the phone and suggested we go to a new club at The Dovercourt Tavern called On The Bar to see Rick James and his new band, The Great White Cane.

Now that, was just what I needed!

I was expecting something special that night because I knew most of the musicians in the band & they were all quite good. Especially Denny Gerrard from The Paupers, who played bass. But nothing could have prepared me for the power & the majesty of such a great band!

We arrived at the Dovercourt early and I went back-stage to chill with the guys. Denny was there floating around the dressing room like a Hobbit on speed. I spoke with Ian Kojima (sax), Nick Balkou (guitar) and Norm Wellbanks (drums) who had played with a Scarborough band called Milestone. Along with Denny they were the heart of the band and were augmented by keyboardists Ed Roth and John Hughes.

Rick saw me talking to Ed in a corner of the room and called me over to a table where he had just laid out six lines of cocaine on a brand new copy of Time Magazine.

"Help yourself, Dave. There's lots more where that came from!"

I had never snorted coke before and was caught off-guard, so initially I hesitated; but not for long.

I tried to sound non-chalant, "Don't mind if I do, Rick."

I took the rolled up twenty dollar bill from his hand and killed one line. It was a real eye-opener. No one had ever told me what to expect. There was no rush and no apparent effects, but boy did it clear my sinuses. So I did one more!

Rick passed the bill around to anyone else who was willing to take a hit, but not everyone was interested. Other folks were passing around joints of some nice fragrant weed and others sipped from an open mickey of Jack Daniels.

I looked around the room and saw Mike McKenna chatting with Denny Gerrard near the doorway. It was getting close to show-time and friends and hangers-on started drifting out to the front of the stage. I followed them out and joined Lachlan up near the bar. We stood out front and took everything in. The band's gear was impressive. Way impressive! You might say it was the best that money could buy; and as it turned out, there was a reason for that. The reason of course was; quality begets quality.

These eight guys were on a mission! The band was so precise & tight that the whole club danced and moved as one entity all night long and screamed in appreciation with every new tune! Rick's song-writing & his on-stage presence and performance were extraordinary. It was simply inspirational. I went home that night, literally drenched in sweat, humming the choruses to songs that I had never heard before. And over the years I've never forgotten them. The most memorable of them was a tune that Rick wrote with Mike McKenna called "You Make The Magic". For my money it was far superior to anything that he did in his later career.

The next day I started planning my next band in earnest. I was going to have keyboards this time, and there would be no limitations on the kind of material that we would do!

Rick and the guys had really inspired me, but over the next couple of months as I tried to get something happening, I became pretty discouraged. There just wasn't a good pool of musicians available to choose from. I was now paying rent for my new apartment on my own so there wasn't much choice when it came to finances. I didn't want to watch my savings all disappear, so I called Brian Ross to see what was up in the swimming pool business.

It turned out that he had just started his own company and he was in need of help. So, the next week I was back at it and enjoying every single minute. It felt great to have another way to make some bucks and I felt really good watching my bank account grow and grow. And this time I didn't have to deal with the pain of installing those huge vinyl covers over someone's backyard in sub-zero arctic temperatures. Spring was already here and I was happy as a lark to just build the pools and get back into good physical shape again.

Things just rolled along smoothly and life was treating me very well. I worked at decorating the apartment a bit. I bought some clothes. And of course I found time to add to my record collection.

Near the end of June, Brian called my whole crew into his office early in the morning before we left to go to the job site.

"I've got a real surprise for you guys this morning. Just thought I'd let you know that we signed a deal yesterday to build a pool for Paul Henderson of The Maple Leafs!"

"Wow! So when, Bri', when do we start?" I was eager, as Paul Henderson was probably my most favourite hockey player of all time.

"Next Monday, or whenever you can finish up what you're workin' on right now."

Laurie, our chief concrete guy spoke up, "Wow. This'll be really interesting, eh? They're announcing the final picks for the Canadian team for the Canada-Russia series next week too! What if he gets picked?"

Brian answered, "We talked about that and it's not a problem. He'll be off at training camp for a while before they leave. There'll be lots of time."

Well it turned out that there was lots of time and Paul did get picked. Then the weather got really shitty and things slowed right down as the rains turned Paul's backyard into a mud-bog. Suddenly time was of the essence. Paul wanted to get everything done quickly so that his wife would be able to use the pool in the summer while he was gone.

So he called up some reinforcements. Friends Dave Keon and Frank Mahovlich came over and pitched in, helping to move concrete and earth around the yard and loading and unloading materials from our truck whenever we arrived on site.

As the deadline for the beginning of the series neared Paul approached me and expressed reservations about the conditioning of the Canadian Team.

"Have you ever watched those Russian players skate, Dave?"

"Well, yeah, I guess so. But it's hard to really study them when you're watching on T.V. and they're zooming by at thirty miles an hour!"

"Yeah, that's true. And the thing that you can't see on T.V. is their conditioning. They can go full out for fifteen minutes and not get winded. They hardly break a sweat. It's really intimidating for the opposing team, you know? We've got some guys on our team who haven't seen it up close. It's worrisome. They don't get it that the Russians practice thirteen months of the year, if you catch my drift."

I said, "Well, you're lookin' in good shape, Paul. You guys are haulin' ass with the best of them when it comes to moving concrete."

"I hope you're right, Dave. But I get this feeling that it's all in God's hands now. There's no turning back. Everything's been set in motion and it's going to come down to character. People; that's what I'm putting my faith in."

I never forgot those words. How prescient.

The rest of the summer was golden and exciting. We all watched as the series see-sawed back and forth and then finally tipped in favour of the Russians as the eighth and final game drew nearer.

On the night of the eighth and final game I visited Ross Atchison at his mom's place on Broadview Ave. just north of Bloor Street. The beer flowed and the pressure mounted as the game progressed. As the third period wound down the tension became unbearable and then "the miracle" happened.

It was Paul. He had an epiphany. He had a vision and he pushed his way over the boards and onto the ice and he scored!

He not only scored, but he scored the most famous goal in the annals of Hockey. And Ross and I knew the whole story. We knew about all the reservations, the doubt and the fear.

The two of us just sat there stupefied.

Oh my God! This was going to go down in history!

CHAPTER 28

REJUVENATION

I had been pretty devastated when Papa Grey ended, but by now a certain passivity was creeping into my psyche. With the Ducks there had been a special bond that brought us together. It was an unconscious thing; something you could never really put your finger on, but nevertheless it was there. And there was a sense that it was ephemeral or in some way inevitable.

And now I felt that that was gone. Now, all of the connections I was making with other musicians were simply alliances. There was no longer an underlying commitment to a greater endeavor. I didn't want music to simply become just another job. It had to be more than a way to pay the bills and make a living.

All of a sudden I had been cut loose. Adrift. I felt like a fish out of water. But at least I was safe now and I was comfortable enough in my own skin, that I was still absolutely determined to get another band going.

Having an alternative vocation had given me the ultimate freedom.

After work on Fridays I would head over to The Village or down Yonge Street to the clubs to see whatever bands were playing. A favourite place during this time was The Gasworks at Yonge and Dundonald Streets. It had just the right kind of vibe and de'cor and suited the feel of the music that was emerging in Toronto at that time. The bands that were continually booked there were on the cusp of a musical resurgence that was changing the face of Canadian music.

My two favourites were Max Webster and Rush. Both bands were just starting to really get established and both were evolving their own sound and style. Max Webster had the edge though in the song-writing department and I was constantly amazed at their musical and lyrical creativity. Watching Kim Mitchell perform was a pleasure. I had seen him of course, when he first arrived in Toronto from Sarnia with his band Zooom and I was already a fan. But as I watched him now; I just knew that he was committed. Every note was played with real passion and authority. He had teamed up with Terry Watkinson from Dee And The Yeomen and had started writing songs with Pye Dubois, who was a supreme lyricist. And just recently they had teamed up with our old compatriot John DeNottbeck to do some recording! I knew their success was inevitable.

Rush on the other hand were far more experimental and in a way, less melodic. But they had a sense of purpose and a drive that was consummate and totally set them apart from other technical bands of the day. They were definitely more technical than Max, which was not my preference. But their emphasis on technique was tempered by an obvious flair for melody in their individual playing, and in Geddy Lee's singing. And Geddy's voice was so high! The other unique thing about them, of note, was that they were managed by Ray Danniels of The Music Shoppe. Ray would soon be a force to be reckoned with in Canadian music.

I don't think I was ever bored by either band. They always gave the audience their all, and it was obvious that they both had that ever-elusive spark; the indefinable link that held each band together as "one".

I was envious.

I had also discovered a band called Fingerwood who featured a guitarist named Mike McDonald who was a master of the Gibson SG. They played quite often at a club at the southern end of the Yonge Street Strip, downstairs at The Colonial Tavern, called The Meet Market. One of their premiere songs was a Jesse Winchester tune that I had never heard before called "Twigs and Seeds". To this day their arrangement sticks in my brain; as I learned the tune and the lyrics to it by watching them play at every opportunity.

As I say, Mike was a master of the SG. In its day it was a very distinctive guitar with a very recognizable sound and Mike worked wonders with it. Quite a number of guitarists from in and around Toronto would stop in to check out a couple of sets on the weekends and watch his every move.

Along with the really creative and original bands that were emerging in Toronto at that time, most of the clubs regularly booked cover bands to fill out their schedules. Checking out some of the better cover bands turned out to be a great resource for me for finding musicians once

I finally got around to putting my next band together. I made it a priority to meet and greet any players that really impressed me and returned to see them perform whenever possible.

Sometimes I would be joined by Lachlan Clemente or my brother Dale and we would hit more than one club a night. We could walk to almost all of the most well-known clubs from my place, so we would generally meet at 65 St. Nicholas and have a drink before we set out.

On one such sojourn Dale and I met a fellow Scarborough native over at the Gasworks named Bob Matheison. He was a big music fan and enjoyed the same bands as us, so eventually he started coming along on our music-quest nights.

I would work at Scandia Pools all day, starting at seven a.m. and then beat it back to St. Nicholas Street in time to clean up and change, and then head over to The Gasworks or The Piccadilly Club to meet Bob and Lachlan for a night out. Eventually it wore me down physically. I was sometimes getting only five or six hours of sleep before I would have to head out for another day of hauling concrete or installing decking and fencing.

As the end of November approached I was faced with the same choice that had presented itself while working for Convertible pools. Did I really want to deal with the ravages of winter, once again? Maybe I wouldn't be called on to install pool covers as before, but the prospect of working outside when the temperature dipped below freezing was anathema to my psyche.

The first week of December I gave my notice.

I immediately began calling musicians to see what everyone was up to and I was surprised to find that there were lots of guys looking to play. Rick James' band had folded in L.A. and most of the members had returned to Toronto. The first guy I called was a drummer named Dale Hutchinson who I had seen play at the Gasworks in the summer. His band was finished, so he was eager to get something going. Next, I called Matthew Dennington who had been the organist in Milestone. Same deal; he was in.

I was feeling good at this point and gave my old buddy Ed Pryla, from Papa Grey a call. He was eager, too. He had been out of the loop for six months and simply said to give him a call when I had a probable band all set to go.

It looked like it was a close thing so I called Ian Kojima from Rick's band White Cane and asked what he was up to. He said he wasn't sure he wanted to jump into something new so soon after returning to T.O., but he said he would consider it and give me a call back.

Well, the very next day he called back and said it was a go, and that he also had found a bass player for us. I asked who that might be and he said that he had called Norm Wellbanks, the drummer for The Great White Cane who had volunteered to take over bass duties, seeing as how the drumming spot had already been filled!

Within a week we were rehearsing and getting a repertoire together.

Things moved along at a frenetic pace and I was totally amazed at the level of professionalism and experience shown by everyone. Norm turned out to be a wonderful bass player, and Ed held his own as the "young dude" in the band. We planned on establishing ourselves as a good bar band in the beginning, before we set out to do original material and try for a recording deal. We were all in need of a steady income to make things work. No one had any desire to be a starving musician anymore. A new reality and mind-set had come into play.

Evidently Rick and the guys had experienced major deprivation in Los Angeles while trying to get The Great White Cane album recorded, and it had left a bad taste in their mouths.

We started off band life as Mix, which we figured was as good a name as any other for a bar band. We did a very eclectic blend of tunes. Everything from The Stones to Steely Dan to The Band, Dylan, Dr. John and Leon Russell. We weren't exactly Top 40, but we did enough chart stuff to get booked at most major clubs.

The whole scene had changed in the past couple of years. The age of majority had been reduced to nineteen from twenty-one; so that a lot of young people were hitting the bars. Forged, or borrowed I.D. was rampant and hard to combat. High school dances became less and less successful because the kids wanted to drink and they were very adept at finding ways.

In January of '73 I negotiated a residency at Yonge Station Tavern which was on Yonge Street just south of Bloor Street. It had originally been The Brass Rail and had been renovated and up-dated to compete with the other bars that were becoming prominent on the Yonge Street Strip.

We were contracted to play twenty-one full weeks of the year, with an option to do weekends on the other weeks that we weren't otherwise booked. It was a great opportunity to work regularly and have time to write and rehearse and get our act together. But it was also grueling work. The contract called for four 45 minute sets a night, plus a matinee of 3 hours every Saturday afternoon. Almost as bad as slavery!

Ed Pryla was the first to leave, having no desire to work so many hours per week. He was replaced immediately by Nick Balkou, who had been the guitarist in The Great White Cane with Rick and the boys. The next to depart was Ian who was finding things a bit too demanding as well. To replace him we enlisted John Bride as a second guitarist, instead of trying to find another horn player. The two guitarists really played off each other well and it was with this line-up that we built a reputation and started really drawing crowds; especially for the Saturday Matinees.

We would have special guests such as Skin Head Vinson, Paul James and Danny Marks drop by, and they would get up and jam, which really livened up the afternoons! John Bride's reputation as a seminal Blues Guitarist in Toronto grew by leaps and bounds during this period and many Toronto musicians would come to the Saturday matinees to check out his playing.

The first Saturday in March was a day off for the band. We had played a successful high-school gig on the Friday night and I had arranged with Bob Matheison to get together and hang out on the strip. We hit the Gasworks first and watched part of the first set, but the band was pretty uninspiring and we soon headed up the street to Yonge Station to see what was up.

The Ugly Ducklings" @ City Hall, Toronto '73

The band that was playing were pretty non-descript and didn't get much of my attention, but after only a few minutes of hanging out we spied two gorgeous blonde girls sitting at a table against the wall across from the stage.

After much discussion and procrastination I was the first one to make a move and approached their table and asked "one of the most beautiful women in the world" if she would like to dance. To my surprise and relief she said yes.

Her name was Jane Lillie and she was an absolute angel. In her presence I immediately became a basket case. She was so delicate and soft that I felt awkward and stiff holding her as we danced and then I became very self-aware and began to feel that I looked like a slob, dressed in my grungy jeans and bleached denim shirt.

We danced for perhaps ten or fifteen minutes, making small talk and getting past the anxiety and the initial tendency to hyper-ventilate as we spoke. As we started our second slow dance we noticed that Bob had finally asked Jane's friend Janet, to dance. By this time I was in a semi-dream state.

When we finally retired to the table to sit down and drink I excused myself, telling Jane that I would be a few minutes. I high-tailed it home to St. Nicholas Street, changed into some nice glen-checked pants and a wool sweater, put on some Old Spice after-shave and returned hastily to the club.

When I walked up to the table Jane smiled a huge smile. I knew that I had made the right decision. For the rest of the night we danced and talked as if there wasn't enough time for us to waste. Our eyes stayed glued on each other not wanting to stray away, or lose contact. We were oblivious to Bob and Janet almost to the point of discourtesy, caught up in the excitement of our own self-discovery.

At the end of the night it felt uncomfortable to leave each other, so we made a pact that we would meet the following Saturday. We exchanged phone numbers and then Bob and I escorted Jane and Janet to the Bloor Street Subway Station.

As the train pulled into the station we stood on the platform, held each other tightly and exchanged a life-changing kiss.

Bliss was now a word that truly belonged in my vocabulary.

The next Saturday, Jane and I met at The University Of Toronto to see a band from Sudbury called Aaron Space. I was interested to see them because of the fact that two of the members had been in a band called Buckstone Hardware that had briefly appeared in Yorkville during the Summer of Love in '67. At the time I was really drawn to their funky-folksy brand of Country Rock. They were a few years ahead of the curve.

We had a great time at the concert, dancing and talking and then walking hand in hand around the grounds of the University. The evening was unusually warm for March and the moon was almost full, lighting our way with a pale blue-white light.

We walked back to my place on St. Nicholas in a velvet fog, mesmerized by our infatuation for each other and the synchronicity that had brought us together. We drifted up the stairs and through the door and into each other's arms and then we made love.

It was a new beginning for both of us.

CHAPTER 29

REALIZATION

Something truly possessed us from that first night together. We just did not want to separate for any reason. We got up on the Sunday morning and felt gloriously happy. The sun streamed from the east through the kitchen windows warming us as we cooked fried mushrooms and cheese sandwiches and devoured them as we sat around the kitchen, lounging in our underwear.

We talked about living together. We made love again in the early afternoon and then we got dressed and went out to The Charles Promenade for coffee and Black Forest cake.

And for the rest of the afternoon we kept on the subject of cohabitation. In the end we decided there was no use in postponing the inevitable. We felt that we had something going that was more than just a mad infatuation. And so it was agreed that I would pick up all of Jane's worldly possessions at her parent's place, the following weekend.

But of course that presented quite a challenge, as I had not yet met her folks. She assured me that it would be O.K. if I met them when we went to get her things. According to Jane they were very reasonable and they would surely appreciate me and understand the seriousness of our situation. I trusted her judgment and ultimately in the end she was proven right, as we had a great time with her mom and dad when I went to meet them.

Her mother, Mae, was as sweet as a peach and had the most lovely smile and demure presence. She exuded warmth and hospitality and seemed to have a genuine knack for conciliation. Her dad was an engineer, the same as my dad and totally pragmatic and logical in his approach to our predicament. He asked for assurances that I would cherish his daughter as much as he did; which I dutifully gave him. Together we made sure that they both understood that we didn't take lightly what we were about to do and that we would be seeing them on a regular basis and keeping them informed of our adventures.

We stayed for four or five hours and then Doug, her father, helped as we loaded all of Jane's earthly goods in the van. We gave her mom a big hug and kiss and then I shook Doug's hand before we finally jumped into the truck and drove away, waving our goodbyes out the window and honking the horn.

So, in just two and a half months I had established a completely different life for myself. I had a brand new band and I had a brand new love. Everything had changed. Everything that a man really needed, I now had.

Love and purpose.

The test now was to make it all work. I knew for sure that I was lucky in love; the question was, where would this new purpose in life take me?

The next week I got a call from Wayne Thompson at The Music Shoppe. He had heard through the grapevine about the reputation that we had cultivated at Yonge Station and he wanted to talk. I walked up to see him that afternoon and we discussed the band signing with The Music Shoppe as our exclusive agency. His one prerequisite for signing would be that we immediately change our name back to The Ugly Ducklings and pick up where the band had left off.

Up to this point I had been booking all of the gigs myself and I asked for one concession, which was that the Agency would relinquish any claim to agent's fees for bookings that I managed to find myself. I had established quite a few contacts on my own and I didn't feel it was fair to give up a fifteen percent fee on whatever money we earned as a result of my own efforts to book the band. In return they would have first right of refusal for any dates that they could supply us with a gig, other than the dates we had already contracted for at Yonge Station. They agreed!

So we now had a house gig in town with no agent's fee at Yonge Station and after we signed we would pay commission only on whatever outside gigs that The Music Shoppe could provide for us. Wow, it was a sweet deal! We planned a coming out Showcase gig at The Station that we could use to promote the re-emergence of the band.

But before all this could happen, we lost Matt Dennington. He departed for basically the same reason as all the others had; he was getting tired of so much work.

I immediately called Jim Oskirko who had played with Jay Smith and the Majestics and we had him rehearsed and in the band by the time the Showcase thing came around. He was more of an R&B kind of player than Matt had been and his vibe just seemed to fit the band naturally. His temperament was so suited to everyone else's personalities that I was beginning to think that we might soon implement the original music part of our plan and start writing some new tunes of our own.

The "DUCKS" John & Nick & new organist Jim Oskirko

The Showcase was a special gig that everyone showed up for. All of the band's girlfriends came out, along with all of our old friends from The Village and all of the past members of the band who were still living in town. It was a musical extravaganza of epic proportions and all the members of the band were in the zone and played right on the money that night, as the expression goes.

Nick Balkou's girlfriend Wendy, who he had met in California, had finally arrived in Toronto, and she and Jane got along famously. A few old Papa Grey fans from Port Credit made it in to the city to see John Bride do his thing with The Ducks. Even a few lesser-known journalists came out to bear witness to our new-debut performance.

The general consensus was that everyone had a great time and that things were looking extremely good for the band. Wayne Thompson was unquestionably impressed and was set to put us back on a sure footing, gig wise.

Jane and I got busy decorating the apartment and while doing some simple maintenance work I inadvertently got a part-time job working at Yolles' Antiques on Yonge Street.

I had climbed out one of the windows in our kitchen to repair one of the hinges that was not allowing it to close properly. While I was out there on the roof I noticed that the steel frame for one of the skylights on the roof of Yolles, had buckled the previous winter, and the glass was cracked and coming apart in a major way. It hadn't fallen into the building because it was double paned and had a wire-mesh in between the two layers of glass.

I reported the problem directly to Mr. Yolles, who was long past the normal retirement age, but still came in to work every day. He was suitably impressed and we struck up a conversation. Before I left he offered me a tempo-rary job compiling an inventory of all of the furniture that they had stored in various parts of the building. I accepted unconditionally, not realizing how much work I was getting myself into. As it turned out, they had four various sized rooms and a full basement that were packed from ceiling to floor with chairs, tables, sideboards, bed frames and numerous other specialized antique wardrobes and odds and ends.

After the first day of examining all of the storage space I reported back to Mr. Yolles the approximate numbers of the various pieces of furniture that he had accumulated. I estimated that it would take at least a week to organize it all and to itemize it. We agreed on an hourly wage and I reported for work the next day.

In the end it took me a good two weeks to do the job and along the way I found some priceless Louie XV dining chairs with sideboard, some very valuable American Arts and Crafts pieces and two ancient bushel baskets full of silver and gold jewelry, that had long since been forgotten and abandoned. The baskets had been hidden in the basement for so long that all of the silver and gold in them had turned black and a thick blanket of dust had covered them to a depth of half an inch.

So, when I eventually finished, Mr. Yolles was pleased enough that he gave me a bonus of a hundred dollars above my wages and thanked me personally for a great job, well done.

I was feeling pretty self-satisfied around this time and determined that it was time to buy a new car. Not new new, mind you; but new to me. The long hot summer was almost on us and I wanted to be able to go to my parent's cottage up near Bancroft. And also, I had a nice fat wad of cash burning a hole in my pocket.

So I started looking around at various Used Car lots on Danforth Road and on Queen Street East. Not much impressed me. Most of the cars were pretty beat up or burdened with high mileage. The ones that weren't were expensive.

I whined to mom about all this while I was talking to her one evening and got a call back from her twenty minutes after I got off the phone. She and dad had also decided it was time to buy a new car and they were offering their Chevy Impala to me for five hundred dollars. It was a good car; a '68 with low miles. I told Jane all about it and the next weekend we visited and took it for a test drive.

Sold, sold, sold! No doubt about it. We were riding in style.

On the music front, we were building the reputation of the band back up to what it had been. We were making good money and had started writing original material again. Nick Balkou and I were the instigators. He had a treasure trove of material that was left over from his experience working with Rick James. Most of the tunes he showed me were eighty percent complete, so they were relatively easy for us to finish. And then I started writing again on my own.

We booked time at Sound Canada Studios and recorded a three song demo on a warm and sunny day near the beginning of June. The three tunes were, "I Don't Want To Be Loved Anymore", "Strawberry Wine" and "The Band Played On". We shopped them around to the Record Companies with no success. One A&R guy told me flat out that his label was looking for a "teenybopper" act. I asked him about *our* music and he said it was really great stuff, but it wasn't what "they" were looking for at the moment.

I don't think "they" really knew *what* they were looking for. They weren't exactly breaking any big acts at the time. Things were sort of stagnant with the over-all scene in Toronto and it seemed like the music-biz was going through a major transitional period.

The second weekend in June we headed up north to Lakefield, Ontario to do a High School gig. Last bash of the year. We arrived early and got everything set up rather quickly, so we decided to have a pick-up basketball game in the gym. Dale Hutchinson had found an errant basketball in a storage room and we tossed it around and ran back and forth dribbling the ball with various degrees of finesse and miss-placed machismo.

Dale was the tallest guy in the band and the best dribbler. After half an hour of wheezing and sweating he managed one last manic burst of confidence. He ran an outside route around everyone, forced his way into centre-court and planted both feet with massive force intending to lay out a long jump shot.

He crumpled to the floor like a sack of flour.

Everyone ran over to him to see what the matter was. We held out arms above and beside him and helped him try to stand up. He seemed to be dazed and he would immediately fall back down to the floor.

He seemed confused and spoke quietly, "There's no strength in my legs or my feet. They just quit. They're not working."

We carried him shoulder to shoulder and sat him down in a chair by the stage.

"What do you want to do, man?" Nick was looking pale.

Dale was baffled. "I can't move my feet, man. I think maybe I better go to a hospital or something. It doesn't feel right. I can't move them!" There was a desperate tone in his voice.

Norm went to the staff room and called an ambulance and when it came he went with him and Nick followed in Dale's car. They left him at the hospital and came back, faces white as a ghost.

Norm was literally shaking as he spoke, "Hey, I don't know what's going on, but Dale's knees were swollen up like balloons by the time we got there!"

We all sat there stunned and fearful. Silence and dread filled the room as we realized the serious nature of what had just happened. We didn't know exactly *what* had happened, but it was serious shit and it meant that things were going to change, once again.

We played the gig without a bass player, with Norm playing the drums and with the guys giving it the best that they could under the circumstances. I could barely sing.

I had no wind. It was like someone had kicked the crap out of me and I was breathing through a wet towel.

We phoned the hospital after the gig and they told us that Dale had been transferred to Toronto General. He had severed both his Achilles Tendons when he had planted his feet and pushed off, and he would be lucky if he ever walked again! There wasn't anything positive in any of that. I hated the way that they passed judgment on Dale as if they were Gods, and they could see into the future. I hoped and prayed for his sake that they were wrong, and I cursed them for their insensitivity. (*In the end he proved them all wrong with a 100% recovery. He was playing the drums again six months later!*)

We enlisted the help of our former road manager-turned-drummer, Kid Carson, to fill in for a few gigs until we could find a new drummer, but as it turned out it wasn't necessary as Rob Boers had just returned to Toronto and he gave me a call. He wasn't aware of our situation, but when I informed him of what had happened he immediately suggested a return to the fold. But it wasn't to last. Rob started gigging right away, but two weeks later John Bride and Norm Wellbanks left to join Shooter, who had just secured a Record Deal with GRT Records. So much for loyalty! But I could hardly blame them, they almost doubled their salary.

We now had no bass player and only one guitarist. I was getting pretty disheartened by all the changes but decided to push onward and upward.

Bob Abbott at Long and McQuade's knew of our situation and told me that Bob Jennings who had played bass for Fingerwood was just out of a job and had been in the store "looking", so I called him up. He joined the band in a matter of days and we were right back up to snuff, even though we lacked a second guitarist.

For the rest of the summer we forged ahead, playing regularly at Yonge Station and shuttling all over Southern Ontario to numerous high school and club dates. We played some wicked music, satisfying our own needs to keep it in the groove and entertaining audiences far and wide with all of the moxy that we could muster.

But it wasn't the same. The experience of playing music was slowly losing its luster and I was starting to feel that I really didn't need it anymore. I hadn't lost my love for music but I gradually became aware that keeping a band together was the real focus of my work. Music was secondary.

In the fall more changes took place. Bob Jennings and Jim Oskirko departed and I finally got to play with an old friend Ed Roth, who had played in L.A. with Rick James, and who I had first met when he played with Bobby Kris and The Imperials. We added a second guitar once again; this time hiring John Pimm from The Rabble, out of Montreal. For bass we brought in Rob's new bass player friend Ron Cameron. We even got to jam with Nick's old nemesis Rick James himself at The Running Pump Pub in West Hill.

Rick showed up at midnight on a Saturday night and we got him up to sing on "Honky Tonk Women" and "Tumblin' Dice". There were probably ten or fifteen people left in the audience, but we had a blast.

*Nick   Ron   Rob   **The DUCKS 1974**   Dave   John   Ed*

We carried on right through the winter until the spring of 1974 and that was when the hammer finally came down.

I came to the realization that I was no longer getting any Satisfaction!

I knew I wanted to spend more time with Jane.

But most of all I determined that I didn't want to end up playing in bars for the rest of my life.

I made the decision to go back to school to get a trade and I knew exactly what I wanted to be; a Mechanic. I loved cars, especially old ones. I loved everything about them. The look of them, the smell of old leather, the styling and the speed of them. But more than that I wanted to be mobile and free to move around. I thought I was being immensely practical.

Hey, a mechanic could get a job just about anywhere, right? And everyone knew that mechanics never had to put out tons of money for a car. They always had a decent ride and they had real job security.

I figured that most of all I needed security, so that I could get to know myself again. I had gotten lost in all of the shuffling around and the constant instability of the last couple of years and suddenly I wasn't who I thought I was, anymore.

But now the future was going to be different, I had true love and a reason to believe. I was going to get my groove back!

CHAPTER 30

RESURRECTION

After the band had broken up and I made the decision to get an education of some sort, I enrolled in a special quick-run apprenticeship program that would allow me to start working as a mechanic after only ten months of schooling. I bought a 1950 Plymouth Special Deluxe upon getting a tip from my old friend Steve Propas from the Propas Agency who had just started managing Chilliwack and had set up his own Record Company, Solid Gold Records. He knew I had a thing for old cars and he phoned me up as soon as he heard it was for sale.

After my initial ten months of schooling I got a job as an apprentice at Ontario Chrysler at Bay Street and Wellesley. It was just a two minute walk from our front door!

I hauled the Plymouth out of storage and restored it in my spare time and got it painted and licensed at work. All through my last round of trade school I drove it out to the campus every day in Scarborough.

After I'd been at Ontario Chrysler for a while, the shop foreman found out about my affinity for old automobiles and started sending "special" jobs my way. In the spring he got me to do a cylinder-head job on a 1937 Packard Straight "8" convertible coupe. I didn't mind the finicky work that was required and actually enjoyed the challenge of trying to do the job the way it was intended. I usually took longer than the job paid, but that was O.K. because I was still an apprentice and hadn't been assigned to "piece-work" as of yet. Then in May, or June, I got a really nice assignment.

Malcolm Tomlinson, who had just signed a record deal with A&M records, showed up at the service department with his very own 1951 Plymouth. It needed a bit of work. Nothing major – just a bunch of little things that had added up over the last few months, to make his life miserable. Jack, our most esteemed service advisor thought of me immediately because of my mission to restore my Special Deluxe.

Malcolm had just put together an incredible band and was about to produce his first album and over the following days that I worked on the car, they dropped in with Malcolm to see how things were going. Two old friends, Danny Marks, from Edward Bear and Scott Cushnie, were in the band and gave me little tid-bits of information about what they were recording.

It all sounded like so much fun. I was envious and wished them well. Although, with the line-up that they had I was sure that the results would be fabulous. In the end I was proved right. The album, which was called Comin' Out of Nowhere was a perfect gem of Toronto Canadiana, and still stands as a major achievement.

Jane got involved in the automotive business too, by getting a job as a receptionist at Addison Cadillac on Bay, which was a five minute walk from our front door.

We got married in 1975 and set our sights on buying a place *somewhere outside* Toronto where we could live a relatively relaxed lifestyle. With the combination of our combined income and an unusually low rent for our apartment we started salting our money away in the bank, waiting for the day that I would receive my Mechanic's License and we would be free to move out of the city.

By the middle of the year in '78 I had put in enough working hours and I had passed my final exams. At the end of June I was finally granted my license and we started looking in earnest for a house. One of my classmates at school, Doug Stanton, had just bought a place in Fenelon Falls, on the Trent Canal and suggested we go there and have a look. Evidently the prices were great, the town was beautiful and totally laid back and there were a lot of places currently up for sale.

The first place we looked at was a classic. It was a small cottage-style house, on a hill overlooking the town with a third of an acre of land, including beautiful maple trees and an incredible mature weeping willow that was the centre-piece of the yard. It was in need of a lot of renovating, but we didn't hesitate. We had to accommodate the renters who were living there by agreeing to rent them the house until they could find another place, but it was still our little slice of heaven, and we knew that we would soon be there!

Two months after we moved in, in March of '79, I got a call from Roger Mayne. I was flabbergasted. During the life of The Ducklings he had never, ever called me. I had always been the instigator. In fact he never had that much to say to me and unless he was under duress he was normally very quiet and reserved.

Well, all of that was history, now. The new Roger was a mover and a shaker. He had his own T.V. Commercial Distribution Company called Cine Service and he had just started his own Record Label and recorded Toronto's most notorious Punk band, The Viletones. He talked my ear off, telling me of all of his exploits, to-date; those of his business dealings and those that dealt with his new-found passion for Punk Music.

Central to this dialogue was his incredible adventure in New York City, where he had gone to secure a distributor for his label Razor Records and where he had met Bleeker Bob of Bleeker Bob's Records in Manhattan.

Roger had just met Bob, to discuss placing The Viletones disc in the store. After all, New York was the centre of the new Punk Music scene in North America. He figured this was where their record should be.

He was making conversation and had just mentioned in passing that he had played in a band in the sixties called The Ugly Ducklings, when Bob excitedly jumped up, left his office and returned in a few minutes with a copy of our album, Somewhere Outside. It was like-new and was still in the original shrink-wrap.

"This is your album, right kid?"

Roger was totally surprised, "Yeah, yeah that's it alright. Where'd you get it?"

Bob looked at him quizzically, "Can you get any more copies, kid? You wouldn't have any in storage or anything, would you?"

Roger was baffled. "No, I think I might still have an extra one kicking around at home."

"Well listen kid, this one is for sale for $250 bucks, see? Still sealed. Never played. Fuck, I can sell a scratched up copy for $50 or $60; you know what I'm saying? Kids go nuts for this stuff! Do you own the masters? Hell, we could sell a couple of thousand copies in a month at $30 a copy, you know what I'm saying?"

Roger said that Bob was a straight ahead guy. None of his information was bullshit. There was a real market and a genuine fascination with our music among the Punk Community in New York. They identified with our attitude.

Original 45s of "Nothin'" were selling at Bob's for $25 a copy.

Roger was energized. He wanted to get the band back together, with the original line-up. I really had never anticipated anything like this, so I didn't know what to say. I told him to phone the other guys to see where they all stood. If everyone was "in" then I said I wouldn't throw a monkey wrench into the works.

Jane was truly puzzled. How had these kids in New York discovered our music? It was a question that a lot of music journalists and DJs would ponder during the next few years, but one that no one would ever get a clear answer to. It was called word of mouth, and it could be a really powerful thing.

Of course everyone in the band was into it. It made us all feel as if we had really accomplished something special. We had never thought much about where we fit in, in the scheme of things. The sixties had sort of galvanized a new generation of artists to explore different forms of creativity and expression. But we had never considered the roots of our music or the inspiration for it, to have been artistic. We were aesthetic innocents.

Roger phoned me back in three days and confirmed that everyone was on-side. The next step was an organized rehearsal, but first we were going to have to get a hold of some amplifiers and a small P.A. system. John Read didn't even own a bass guitar anymore, so that was an obstacle to be overcome. I still had my microphones and my little Gibson Harp amp that Tom Fryer had built for me while I was in Papa Grey, so I was all set.

Roger managed to get a rehearsal organized right away. In order to facilitate everyone's travel time (except for mine), he rented a space on Queen Street west near Bathurst Street. It was close to everything and had lots of parking near-by, which was essential.

From the first moment we plugged in and started playing, it was a totally intuitive experience. For everyone. It felt like hardly any time had passed. Our music was forever embedded in our memories like Christmas carols or Coca-Cola jingles. We had played all of the tunes so many times that with almost no effort they came right back. John was the only one who had difficulty, but it was strictly because he had lost all familiarity with his instrument. He had rented a Fender Precision Bass for rehearsal, and yet he had never played one during his whole tenure with the band. He was used to a Gibson Bass and he therefore had to adjust to the difference in size of the Fender, as well as to a completely different neck design.

On the other hand Rob had never quit playing and had become a much sought after drum-teacher since the band had imploded. He was a rock! His solid playing kept us focused and energized through every tune regardless of whether it was one of our own, or one of the many covers that we had become known for. When we finally got around to doing our version of "I'm A Man" it was like de'jà vu and all of the various cues that we had used to navigate through the complex arrangement of the tune, all came back in a rush and we nailed it first time! The first weekend of rehearsal was a gas.

The sound was exactly the same. It was twelve years since we had played together but nothing had really changed; because we were essentially the same people and related to each other in the same way. Roger and Glynn hadn't really moved on to other music or to higher levels of musical development. In fact Glynn hadn't picked up a guitar and played since 1974. So the context of what we did remained the same, all of the instruments and the equipment *were* the same and the spirit of our music of course, was the same.

The other thing that came back without any effort was the interaction between everyone in the band, both musically and on a personal level. Our personalities had developed and expanded, but none of us had changed enough to effect a change in the dynamics of the band. All our egos were intact and in the same space they had been. We all still fit like five fingers in a glove.

We set about rehearsing quite seriously; our strategy being to play at one of Toronto's newest and most popular venues, The Edge, before the end of June. It was slightly ironic, because Jane had worked there for a short stint as a waitress while we were saving up to buy our house. At that time it was called Edgerton's, but in essence it hadn't changed much. It had recently become a showcase club for New Wave bands. We chose it, for its size and for the fact that it was so much like many of the clubs that we had played in, in Yorkville.

We wanted to do some new material before we played as well. Roger had a few ideas and I had still continued to write tunes during our hiatus. It was a matter of finding material that fit our persona. Over the next few weeks we tried a bunch of tunes that included some that I had written with Nick Balkou in the last version of The Ducklings. We added them to our sets carefully, taking care to make sure that they fit and that they complimented our other material.

One of the first tunes we nailed was "Just Another Rock 'n Roll Band" which I had written with John Bride, in Papa Grey. Glynn and Roger soon made it their own and it fell into place as an essential Ducks tune. The same thing happened with The Band Played On. In the 1974 version of The Ducks we performed it as a laid back lament for the sad state of the music business in Toronto. But Roger assaulted it with a totally aggressive ferociousness such as he had only brought to bear previously on "Just In Case You Wonder" and "Hey Mama" and in the process he transformed it into a raving love-hate rumination on the state of Rock 'n Roll and record companies.

We also learned a new autobiographical tune that I had just written called "Reality". Although I had written it as a mid-tempo Reggae piece we decided to do it as our one and only ballad, in the style of an Otis Redding slow soul scorcher. Just one slow song to celebrate all those times that we had done "Time Is On My Side", "That's How Strong My Love Is" and "Cry To Me".

Roger and I did write one tune together in time for the gig, and it was the one tune out of all of the newer material that everyone in the band contributed equally to. It was called "Scarred" and the irony was that it was a Reggae influenced song as well. All of us had been inspired by Bob Marley through the seventies and it was a natural thing for us to try to do. We didn't know how our fans would react to The Ducks wailing on a Reggae beat, but we were willing to risk it. Roger and I created the chord progression together and because of the way it was created I got to play little bits of lead guitar through-out the song. That meant that I would have to play "live" on stage to make it work. In the past that would have been a daunting task, but now I looked forward to it as a challenge that would make the whole experience of playing again more exciting. Glynn, John & Rob added their own personal touch to the arrangement as well, and it sailed along on a delicious groove every time we ran through it. We couldn't wait to do it "live".

The night of our "comeback" gig finally arrived after much publicity and speculation by the media in Toronto. Roger had managed to get us mentioned on "The New Music" on CITY-TV and ads had been placed in all of the major newspapers. Various DJs at the FM stations in T.O.

had questioned whether we would still have our chops and suggested that we might crash and burn in a blaze of irrelevance and fuddy-duddieness. Really?

It was all fabulous publicity. Stuff that you would pay through the nose for if you were trying to launch a new band or a new record. We soldiered on and organized every little detail of the show to the point where we almost had our set memorized.

Roger had managed to get our old compatriots and chart-mates The Last Words to play an opening set for us and all these years later I was still impressed with their tunes and their musicianship. Graham Box had been warming up on his acoustic guitar when Glynn and I had walked into the dressing room earlier in the evening.

Every musician we had known back in the day was either in the audience or hanging out backstage. Carol Pope and Kevan Staples, who were starting to make a name for themselves with Rough Trade had dropped in and were relaxing, chatting with band members and journalists. Most of our close friends had taken our advice and arrived extra-early so that they could get up close to the stage. We waited patiently in the dressing room while friends of Roger re-arranged the stage after The Last Words' set ended and then we did one final tuning. (It was the first time that any of the guys had used electronic tuners at a gig!).

Carol Pope & Kevan Staples of "Rough Trade" @ The Edge

At the appropriate time we all formed a line and walked through the hall and the club and made our grand entrance. The noise was deafening. As we walked through we were never more than two feet from the crowd. It reminded me of taking the stage at Charlie Brown's in The Village.

We started off the set with "Everybody Needs Somebody to Love" as we always had, and the crowd went nuts. It was pure de'jà vu! (All over again). The band was just as euphoric for the audience as the audience was for the band. Our fans were never shy and on this night they let us know what they liked.

We never looked back. They were with us for each and every song and they sang along with every chorus they knew. There was no containing their enthusiasm or their energy. When we performed "Scarred" they danced with all their hearts to an Ugly Ducklings reggae beat and suddenly all of my anxiety over playing the guitar simply vanished. When we slowed down the tempo and presented them with "Reality", they danced "the grind" as enthusiastically as if they were back at their senior prom in high school! And at the end of the tune they howled their approval.

When Roger finally started the first three chords of "Nothin'" they went berserk and then they sang along with a real genuine passion, so that we could physically hear the words being sung back at us in unison *from the audience!* They sang it so loud that I couldn't hear myself sing. What a rush!

It was the kind of gig that would forever-after be hard to top.

We didn't worry about it though. We just thanked our lucky stars for the opportunity and then thanked the crowd for their love and patience.

And we promised we'd be back, and soon!

And we did return almost immediately. In mid-August we played the El Mocambo to a sold out crowd and afterwards Roger announced that he was going to finance the recording of a brand new Ducks album. He had set up a partnership with two of his friends, Henry Powmer and John Dale, who were willing to invest some money in the band.

Over the next five months we recorded and produced our new album, Off The Wall at Nimbus Nine Studios in Toronto. It was engineered by Grammy Award winner Jim Franks and mostly produced by Roger, who really had no idea what he was doing. Roger and I had our differences about the how and the why of the recording of the new album. I wanted to do as much as we could "live" off of the floor to try and capture the feel of one of our "live" shows; but that entailed lots of rehearsal and finesse.

Glynn, Rob & me @ "The Edge" 1979

A montage of shots taken @ The Elmocambo 1980

It was deemed that because everyone was working now, we didn't really have the time that would be needed. And besides, the standard recording procedure of the day was that tracks were recorded separately, which helped to achieve good stereo separation. So doing things the modern way was inevitably our final choice. I think things might have worked more in our favor if we had had a real producer who could have guided each of the guys through the process with an ear towards the final mix. To me it seemed redundant to disassemble our sound and then put it back together again. What was the point?

The result was that all the spontaneity in our music was lost. Although there were some great moments on the album, it failed to excite anyone and didn't chart.

We played a couple of gigs in the summer of 1980 to help promote it, but in the end there wasn't much that could be done. It was a failed opportunity. In my estimation if we had released an Extended Play of the best tunes from it, we might have fared a lot better. One thing that had been a treat, though, was to have Scott Cushnie come in to play piano and to have Ian Kojima and friends record the horn section on "Reality".

In 1981, Ahed Music released an "Ugly Ducklings Greatest Hits" album collection to try to cash in on the current resurgence of the band. Much to our surprise it charted and made its way to number 86 on RPM's National Album Chart, before it finally sank into oblivion.

Also, in 1981 I recorded a demo with The Cameo Blues Band. I had established a rapport with the guys in the band by racing down to The Hotel Isabella to sit in with them after almost every Ducklings rehearsal over the previous two years. It was directly on my way home and I would always stop in before I got onto the Don Valley Parkway to head north. I loved watching the interaction between Chuck Jackson and John Bride and I couldn't get over the marvelous grooves that Omar, Sonni and Ray consistently laid down.

An Unused "Cover Shot" for "Off The Wall"

The Izzy was a landmark club in Toronto and part of the success of the place had to be due to Cameo's reputation. There was never a dull night in the joint, and certainly never a night that Cameo didn't give it everything that they had. That summer I recorded six tunes with them that The Ducks had passed on for one reason or another. I released one single from the sessions called "Rock 'n Roll To The Rescue" which was actually played a few times on CHUM - FM by DJ Bob Mackowycz. Thanks Bob!

In the summer of '82 with interest in the band still reasonably high, Roger phoned everyone to see what the general consensus was about playing. The response was positive with all of us except for John.

His wife Susan really didn't want him to be away rehearsing and playing all the time. So he bowed out. I felt sorry for him because I knew how much it meant to him to get out and play with the boys. It was a cause that made you feel that you were genuinely part of something that was bigger than yourself. Sometimes it felt good to fit in as a cog in a big machine, when you knew that the machine couldn't go anywhere without you. It gave you a sense of belonging.

So for the second time John left us without a bass player and the very first replacement that came to my mind was Ron Cameron. I could recall many a wonderful night grooving with the incredible rockin' Rob 'n Ron rhythm section, in the very last version of the Ducks in 1974. I got on the phone to Rob and he agreed to call Ron and pop the question. By the following Tuesday it was a done deal and we were on track for some hot fun in the summertime!

The gigs at The El Mocambo and at Ron Scribner's Cafe' On The Park that summer were probably the most fun that any of us had had since 1966! We just rocked! There was no way that we could have been more in the groove than at those gigs. We added two more original songs, "Moment of Madness" and "War Babies" and we got Glynn to sing *lead* and play *lead guitar* on "It's All Over Now". The audiences were great and very supportive and made every gig a very special treat. Any musician will tell you that they would rather have 100 people who are hanging on every note than 1000 who are totally indifferent. Well, we never had an indifferent soul at any of those gigs. It's simply a joy to play when it's that comfortable.

@ The Elmocambo, July 2nd 1982

There was more music to come in the eighties, but sadly the gigs would be without Rob. There was a major problem with our situation because of the fact that Rob was playing in three different bands at the time; (a jazz band, a rock band and a pop band) and he was teaching a multitude of students as the head instructor at the Ontario College of Percussion And Music.

It was literally impossible to work around his schedule, so we called up our old friend Kid Carson who had become a very competent drummer and he joined the band. He had his own sound company and had a lot of free time on his hands.

In 1986 we did a charity concert at The Diamond Club in Toronto. It was a very difficult time for Glynn, as his father had tragically been struck and killed by a drunken motorcyclist only three days before we played. He persevered like a real trouper.

In 1988 and '89 we did two outdoor concerts in Yorkville that were organized to raise money for various charities. All three of these gigs were highly successful and drew enormous crowds, especially the concerts in Yorkville. We played in the parking lot at Yorkville Avenue and Bellair Street on both occasions and the irony of that fact was not lost on any of the audience. By this time the gentrification of The Village may have been complete, but for these two occasions it was as if time stood still. Long lost friends from The Village showed up and old friendships were renewed and new ones forged. Tears flowed and laughter filled the air.

Both shows were truly extraordinary. The first year the show was opened by our old buddies The Stitch In Tyme and we got to hang out together with them for the first time in twenty years. The next year Robbie Lane and The Disciples took the opening spot and warmed up the crowd, and when they finished their set Robbie gave us a particularly bold and flattering introduction and got the crowd to bring out their lighters and light our way to the stage as if it was 1967! It felt just like home.

The Ducks "Live" in Yorkville, 1988

Back in Yorkville 1989

CHAPTER 31
INTERMISSION

During the nineties the band existed in a state of suspended animation. We kept in touch, and even saw each other occasionally; but there was no impetus to bring us back together to play. Everyone had their careers going in full swing and the focus was on work.

In 1990 after gigging so much with The Ducks I felt a desire to play again on a regular basis and set up a weekly Blues Jam on Sunday nights in Lindsay, Ontario at a place called Crackerjacks. I had been following a lot of local bands from Lindsay and Peterborough and the surrounding area and had made quite a few good friends among all of the blues players there.

By pure chance I met the owner of the club, Gord Phillips, at an outdoor concert in the spring and during our conversation I proposed that we get his club rockin' on Sunday nights. I had stopped in at the club on a Saturday afternoon the previous weekend for lunch and met Phil Marshall who was managing the restaurant for Gord. He had just moved up to Lindsay from Toronto, where he had previously managed Sneaky Dee's, and he inadvertently planted the seed in my mind about a jam night while talking about his experiences in T.O.

So, on this sunny afternoon while watching a young band wind it up in the park, I was just shooting from the hip and not really that serious. But it struck a chord with Gord because Sunday nights were usually the slowest night of the week for him. He was totally open to the idea.

"Hey Dave, let's give it a shot. We've got nothing to lose but our pride. If this works out even half-ways decent you can have the night for the whole summer! See what you can put together!"

The Crackerjack Blues Band

John   Phil   Gary   Dave   Brian   Stevie

So I phoned all the guys I knew whose playing inspired me and within a week or two we were all set to go. We had the place to ourselves on Sunday afternoons for rehearsal and it all came together with very little effort.

We had a rock solid bottom end with Brian "Fergie" Ferguson on drums and John Steele on bass. Two guys from Lindsay, Ontario with an absolutely intuitive feel and an ear that could carry the band through whatever might possibly happen on stage.

We had two guitarists; "Little" Stevie Fralick from Hamilton and my newly enlisted partner-in-crime, Gary Hornbeck. Two players as different as night and day. Which was exactly the way I liked it. I had always remembered what Ron Scribner said to me back in the day. "Contrast son, you gotta have contrast!"

And up front, sharing the vocals with me, we had Phil Marshall; our resident manager, singer and unshakable Master of Ceremonies. Phil worked a crowd with deft precision. He could make people move despite themselves and he ran the Jam Session part of the show like Johnny Carson on uppers. There was almost nothing that he wouldn't say or do to get the audience's attention.

We tore it up for a good nine months working the back room every Sunday at Crackerjacks and then things suddenly changed. It became more than just a weekly blues jam.

I got very involved with Gary Hornbeck, writing a fair number of tunes with him that had a great deal of promise. Real promise. They weren't just blues tunes, but they were challengers for the top forty of the day. The old song-writing "spark" had been re-ignited and Gary and I were looking to record in the future. We rehearsed and played some of these tunes with The Crackerjack Blues Band, but weren't really satisfied with the results.

At the end of November we started putting a serious unit together to record and promote our songs. We were very intent on putting our best foot forward and so we set about getting the best singers and players that we could possibly find.

We stuck with "Fergie" on drums but added Blind Whitey Somers on bass. He had played lead guitar with his own band in Fenelon Falls, but we wanted his stage vibe and his voice. He was an exceptional harmony singer, who played a great bass and contributed his fair share in the song writing department; as well as inspiring us on and off-stage.

For a second guitarist we added Marty Hepburn; an incredibly talented singer-songwriter and musician from Port Hope, Ontario, who possessed a deep husky voice. I had known him and appreciated his playing, for five years.

Sleight Of Hand – 1991
Gary   Dave   "Styx"   Marty   Whitey

Collectively we called ourselves "Sleight Of Hand" and together our intention was to play original music and take a serious stab at securing a recording contract. It was the first time I had ever been involved with a band that had four really competent singers. Having four strong voices with harmonies really added to the impact that the band had in concert, and the fact that everyone could really play their instruments was a huge bonus.

At one of those Crackerjack's jams in the spring I had met a great keyboard player who had just moved up north from Toronto, named Rick Lamb. He was currently playing with the new version of A Foot In Cold Water, who had just re-formed and were starting to gig around southern Ontario. I invited him over to my place in Fenelon Falls and we started writing together. He was a very melodic writer and player and he totally inspired me. So with partners Gary and Rick I was now totally re-immersed in the vagaries of song writing.

During the summer of '91 we opened for Jeff Healey, Doug and The Slugs, Lee Aaron, Edgar Winter and King Biscuit Boy. We always put on one hell of a show and garnered legions of new fans along the way.

In the early summer the band had hooked up with a young dude, Dave Sandy from Janetville, Ontario, who had his own Eight-Track recording studio. We were a very determined lot. Over the next ten months we played a multitude of gigs, hired a new drummer from Toronto, Mr. Dave "Styx" Bourque, and inexplicably managed to record a complete album and shop it around to a bunch of Canadian record companies.

But in the end it was all for naught. It was the nineties, and no one knew, or even understood the direction that music was taking. None of the record companies, with the exception of a few independents had any idea of who to sign. Budgets were drying up, staff was shrinking and artists were being purged or downsized.

We ended up duplicating the album on tape ourselves and selling it at gigs, but of course that wasn't going to lead us anywhere. So we entered some of our tunes in a couple of Radio Station contests; at Q107, in Toronto and at CKPT, in Peterborough. We got into the top ten at both stations and our tunes got on the Contest CDs, but there were no real prizes other than placing our tunes on their Discs. Neither station played our tunes more than once on the air, which was very disappointing.

After that the inevitable break-up came all too soon. It's a sad fact that nothing lasts forever. Even the best things come to an end.

And, so it goes.

But I wasn't in any mood to stop. I was still writing music and I was very interested in the talents of another one of the contestants in the CKPT Contest.

I had known him for almost ten years at that time, but only seen him perform with Joe Hall and The Continental Drift and with Loose Change, another band from Peterborough that featured an up and coming young Blues singer, named Rick Fines.

This guy's name was J.P. Hovercraft and I had never contemplated performing together with him before, but had always admired his bass playing. After he won the CKPT Contest with a monstrously funky tune that he wrote called, "Drownin' In Blue", I approached him about writing together and we formed a partnership.

In the beginning it was just the two of us, but within a few months we added the former keyboardist with Loose Change, George Bertok, and we became a trio.

At first we called ourselves Innocent Bystanders, but we soon changed our name to ReDucks after another band from Buffalo, NY, took the Bystanders moniker and managed to release their CD first. We paid homage to The Ducklings by calling ourselves ReDucks and continued to write and record two album's worth of material while sending out numerous demos to labels and publishers.

At first I found it difficult to take all of the rejections that came back with regular precision, but at some point - I think it was after about the 25th rejection letter - I realized that there weren't any real A&R people left at most of these labels anymore. They were hiring high school students and housewives to come in and listen to the mountains of submissions, as a screening mechanism to weed out all of the crap. There was just too much music and not enough knowledgeable A&R people to screen it all.

Every now and then I would get a letter from a real music person, who I could tell understood exactly what the three of us were doing. It was usually in the form of an apology for the fact that they were actually looking for genre specific music to try to maintain a presence on Much Music or MTV. Music that was aimed at an older mature audience was doomed, because it couldn't be promoted on T.V. anymore, and wasn't getting played on the major radio stations. Some of these people would advise us to release our material independently, but it wasn't like the sixties anymore. You couldn't just release a single. The expense was too great. Who could afford a Video?

It was a situation that I knew couldn't last. Older audiences had a lot of money to spend and they tended to be very loyal to artists and labels that they liked. So sooner, rather than later, there was going to be an emergence of younger artists and record label owners who aimed to please the older fans out there who were hungry for new music.

By 1997 we were spiritually exhausted and we finally decided to call it quits. It was a sad day all around but it never diminished the pride and the satisfaction that we each got from creating the music. It was our vision and our dreams that we laid out for everyone to hear and it will always endure; just as it has with The Ducks, Papa Grey, The Crackerjack Band and Sleight Of Hand.

We painted an audio picture in all of our songs with our music and lyrics.

It was up to the listener to fill the empty film-screen in their minds with their own little mini - movie. Imagination is so much more fun than MTV or Much Music!

ReDUCKS in 1993

CHAPTER 32
REDEMPTION

In September of '97 I got a call from John Bride. He wanted to inform me that Long & McQuades and a whole mess of Toronto musicians were getting together a party to honour Pete Traynor for his contribution to the advancement of music in Toronto and in Canada. It was only fitting. His amps were known all over the globe! They were having plaques made up to give to him as a show of thanks for creating all of the amplifiers and accessories that bore his name, over the years.

Along with John Bride, Domenic Troiano and Freddy Keelor were there. Tom Fryer, Ray Harrison, and Danny Marks showed up along with various other musicians. Bob Abbot from McQuade's presented Pete with the awards and then everyone had a few drinks and jammed blissfully into the evening hours.

The next week I got to play at Maple Leaf Gardens and at The Royal York Hotel, with my new song-writing partner James Owen Bush. We had met in Lindsay at the dealership where I worked and I had teamed up with James to write a handful of tunes. James had won the most promising Male Vocalist award at the 1996 Canadian Country Music Awards. He had then met Ron Ellis, from the Toronto Maple Leafs at a summer golf Tournament and Ron asked him about writing a song for the 25th Anniversary Party and Celebration of Team Canada '72. The game & party was coming up near the end of September. It was a tall order, but Ron gave us some personal inside information on the feelings and fears that the players experienced during the series and with this "inside" information James and I managed to create a song that would satisfy the players as well as the fans. There was also a possibility that our tune might be used for the new DVD Boxed Set of the series that was due to be released before Christmas.

John Bride, Domenic Troiano & Me @ Pete's Bash

So, I had rehearsed with James and his band and then played once more in my old haunt, The Gardens. This time there was a twist, though. The band played from up in the stands in the north end of the gardens. Because of the ice surface the stage area was simply not available. We set up our gear in the afternoon and then we got to watch the Anniversary Game, which was only two periods long. We played during the one and only intermission and for the last song of the show we performed the song we had written, which was called, "Team of The Century". The crowd roared their approval and the teams came back on-ice for the grand finale.

As if this was not enough, we were invited to play at the formal dinner for the players that was being held at The Royal York Hotel. Watching them play and skate was one thing, but getting a chance to meet and greet with them was another. All of us were truly excited.

When the evening finally came we put on a splendid show and finished it once again with "Team of The Century". We got a standing ovation from the players and their wives and friends and then left the stage to mingle before the dinner was served.

I walked over to the table where Paul Henderson and his wife were sitting, along with Yvan Cournoyer and Ron Ellis. I approached the table, but hesitated, not knowing what to say. Paul looked up and caught my eye and a quizzical look came over him.

"I know you, don't I"?

I said, "Well, I just played harmonica in the band."

He looked at me once more and then said, "No it's not that, it's…………..it's the mustache. Take away the mustache and you're…….you're the guy that built our pool!"

I said, "Hi Paul, yeah it's me, Dave. And I'm the one who wrote the lyrics to your song, too. I guess you could say I was sort of qualified - in some strange way!"

"Well pull up a chair Dave. This is my wife Eleanor and I guess you know Ron and Yvan."

I sat down, and we chatted for five or ten minutes before the food arrived, during which time I found out that Paul and Eleanor had sold the house in Mississauga. But both of them made it clear how much they had enjoyed the pool and how that whole summer of '72 was still so vivid and clear in their minds.

I had bought a commemorative book on the series and I got a bunch of the players, along with Paul, Yvan and Ron to sign it before I left. On my way out to my car I lugged my amplifier to the elevator and waited for the doors to open. When they finally slid back into the walls, I was immediately confronted with the presence of Rex Murphy; looking as if he was all set to do his nightly report on The National on CBC.

I pinched myself mentally. I was a huge fan and suddenly, here I was riding the elevator down to the mezzanine with him, not knowing what to say. The man has such a giant intellect that I was throttled. What would be appropriate?

I needn't have worried. When the elevator door opened he stepped aside and motioned with his hands for me to leave first.

He spoke first. "Nice performance tonight, Dave – great song too. Congratulations."

I drove home totally satisfied.

A month later I got a call from Roger Mayne who was developing a new Television program and wanted me to help him write a theme song for it. He knew what the visuals for the intro to the show were going to be and he sort of had an inkling of an inspiration for the music. Sort of. I told him I was game to try anything, but that I certainly wasn't going to drive all the way to Toronto to experiment with his musical ideas.

So I arranged that after we finished our conversation he would call me back and record what he already had in mind, directly onto my little answering machine. It worked like a charm and after a few calls back and forth we worked out the theme to his new show which was going to be called "Madam X". We used the name of the show as the title for the song and he coached me on the lyrics, painting a picture of "Madam X" and how her character related to the show and to the audience, so that I had a frame of reference to write by.

Eventually he decided that we should record it, which meant we would need a drummer and a bass player. So Roger called Kid Carson in to play the drums and I called up my best friend J.P. Hovercraft to play the bass, and we reserved some studio time at Manta Sound in Toronto.

It was a very odd combination of players, but it showed me just how professional Roger could be when he was dealing with his own business. He knew exactly what he wanted out of the tune and he directed us all towards his own personal vision. The session lasted about six hours from start to finish and the result was totally Roger's dream, 100%. I didn't really see it as a "Show" theme though. To me it was like any other Ugly Ducklings song that we had written. It rocked. It was raw Rock 'n Roll and it rocked!

At the same time that all this was happening I was negotiating with Amherst Records out of Buffalo, New York, who had *supposedly* bought the rights to the Ducks back catalogue. I got an oral commitment from their lawyer, a Mr. Larry Silver that I could re-master and re-release all of our records. But according to him the original master tapes had all been lost and if I was going to do this I would need to do it from some pristine vinyl.

I spoke to Roger about the situation and found out that he had made copies of all of the original masters back in 1981 when he was helping the guys at Ahed Music Corp. put together our Greatest Hits Album. How convenient!

So, when we booked time for the "Madam X" sessions, we also took along Roger's copies of the tapes and transferred them to High-Speed VHS so that I could work on them with J.P. Hovercraft at our leisure in his mini-studio in Peterborough.

During that winter we restored all of the Ducks original material to the best possible condition and then arranged to have everything re-mastered by Peter J. Moore whom we had met through Jan Haust of Other People's Music. Jan had approached us about releasing our album on CD. We had decided by that time that we wanted to have ultimate control over the whole restoration and re-mastering process, so we had turned him down.

But Peter had won a Juno award for his production work with The Cowboy Junkies' Caution Horses CD and his mastering skills were unparalleled. So we called him up and eventually he did a fabulous job of mastering all of the tracks.

In the spring we were finally ready to go when we got a rude awakening. Amherst Records suddenly announced that they had sold the Arc Records catalogue to Unidisc Records in Montreal.

Ah, what nice people Record Executives are! I should have known that in the Music Biz the only thing that counted, was signing on the dotted line! And as always, money was the main motivation; the *bottom* line. Integrity was a rare commodity of little concern; especially when it got in the way of a modest profit.

We had already worked out an agreement with Pacemaker Records of Toronto to release our stuff once it was all re-done and they had made a verbal agreement with Amherst as well. After they were notified of the sale, their lawyers advised them to go ahead with their impending release on the strength of their original verbal agreement with Amherst.

So, in 1998 three Cds of The Ugly Ducklings material were released almost simultaneously. It created quite a buzz about the band and I started getting phone calls and Emails from various people in the media.

Some journalists phoned to complain about the disparity in the sound quality of the various releases. The "Pacemaker" release was deemed to be O.K. by the majority of music reviewers, but the Unidisc releases definitely *did not* cut the mustard. I had to explain to them that Unidisc didn't have the original masters, and that they had redone our stuff from vinyl using Pro-Tools or some kind of digital program to enhance and supposedly re-master our tunes.

They had absolutely no knowledge of, or understanding of our music and had butchered our sound in the process; so that what they ended up with almost sounded like a musical caricature of the band. They destroyed my voice by soaking it in digital delay and reverb, and in our most famous tune "Nothin", they left Roger's notorious lead guitar barely audible in the mix. And to really show their lack of knowledge and understanding they used the *wrong mix* of our biggest hit "Gaslight". The mix that had gotten to Number 1 on CHUM in Toronto and in the top twenty across the country, was nowhere to be heard on either of the Unidisc releases!

Another of the many calls was from a Documentary Producer who was contemplating doing a film about the heyday of the Yorkville Village music scene.

He was a great conversationalist and was very enthusiastic about the subject material of the proposed film, having been inspired by the "vibe" of the place when he was a younger man. His name was Paul Asplande; his Company was called Vipro Productions and he asked cordially if he could come over to my place to shoot some interview footage. The whole idea was entirely agreeable to me, so it was all arranged.

While he was at my place I gave him as much contact information as I could find for all of the other players that I was still in touch with. We shot the interview and I didn't hear from him again until the spring of 1999.

When he did call it was to discuss the idea of putting a revival show together at a venue in Toronto, so that he could film all of the bands "live" in concert. Evidently he had had very little success in locating "live" footage of the majority of the groups from The Village. I wasn't surprised at that. Most of the television networks had done very little, if anything to preserve the history of Canadian Music from our era. If a band couldn't afford the cost of having a Video-Tape copy made of their Television performance, then there was no guarantee that it would ever be preserved for posterity.

But Paul's idea had a different vibe to it. He was going to get all of the bands from one very specific scene, and present them together at one gigantic show! So of course the classic question would ultimately arise.

Could they still play? Could they still sing? Did they still have what it takes? All of the usual speculation that people brought forth, would only help to promote the show and bring in the crowds. Human beings were so predictable!

I called Roger and we mulled it over. The show was going to be billed as The Toronto Rock 'n Roll Revival and it was going to be promoted heavily by 1050 CHUM Radio. We didn't want to let any of our fans down and we wanted to be able to pull off a really incredible set. So once again, we brought in Kid Carson. Kid's vibe was always positive and jovial and making music was fun when he was around. Plus, he always made time for the music, and he got things done.

Then we phoned our old buddy Stan Endersby, who had recently done some "voice-over" work with Roger on a couple of C-L-R Miracle Cleaner commercials. Stan was the ultimate showman and had been in twenty bands, at least five of which had existed during the Yorkville era. He was normally a lead guitarist but we offered him the bass player spot, and he accepted gracefully. Then we phoned Glynn and told him the news and he gladly came on-board. So we had a dedicated team. Five friends who were willing to do the work, but still determined to have a good time.........

We rehearsed at least once a week and sometimes two. We gave it our utmost attention and commitment knowing that in the end it was all going to come down to how we performed for the thirty minutes that we were onstage for our own particular set! There would be no excuses and we knew it. And there definitely wouldn't be any second chances because it was all being filmed "live", direct to tape.

Whatever happened we would own it!

The big show was Sunday May 2nd, 1999 and when we arrived we had to be careful that it didn't turn into an old home tail-gate party. A substantial number of the musicians hadn't seen each other for many, many years and consequently they had a lot of catching up to do. For me it was a real treat to see Donnie Morris and Bob Murphy from Stitch In Tyme. We had shared a lot back in the day and it had been ten years since we had seen each other at the first Yorkville Reunion gig.

There were so many people to say our hellos to. We all knew each other to some extent, so even if we didn't have a chance to talk, there were an awful lot of smiles in the building that afternoon. Big, warm, genuine smiles!

At a certain point the show got organized and each band found out their place in the sequence of events. The

Ducks were slated to appear at about eight o'clock and when the time came we gathered together in the dressing room and psyched ourselves up for about ten minutes before we hit the stage. Roger gave us his little pep-talk about "making sure they remember us" and then we just went out and nailed it. There were a lot of our old fans in the audience. Folks from Charlie Brown's, Boris's, The Gouge Inn and The El Patio. So many familiar faces; all with sparkles in their eyes and diamond-lit smiles.

We gave them all of *our* favourites and the biggest hits, including "Nothin" and "Gaslight" and they responded affectionately with unbelievable applause for each and every tune. It was a mutual admiration society. We couldn't have asked any more of them.

Roger & I on stage @ The Warehouse, May 2nd 1999

After our portion of the show was finished I cleaned myself up, changed clothes and in due course made my way out front to watch Domenic Troiano perform at the centre of both versions of Mandala and as the leader of Bush. Seeing George Oliver and Roy Kenner simultaneously on the same stage with Dom was very special. George sang "Opportunity" with absolute authenticity, soulfully telling the amazing story of Mandala's pilgrimage to L.A. and then Roy came on and gave us his two iconic hits of the sixties, "Loveitis" and "I Can Hear You Calling".

After seeing Stitch, Luke and The Apostles and then Mainline and Domenic with the boys, I felt pretty satisfied. I hadn't been able to see all of the bands, but I had certainly heard them all, as the stage-sound had reverberated tremendously through-out every nook and cranny of the building.

Reviews for the show were positive over-all and we could only hope that the film of the show would reflect the reality of it. Paul Asplande assured us that he would be in contact with us, to let us know when, and where the Film of the Concert would be aired on Television. Roger and I felt uncomfortable about not having any input into the mixing and editing of the film, but we resigned ourselves to the fact that we would have to put our trust in Paul. The next week was a bit of a let-down for us. Everything had gone according to plan, but now there was nothing to look forward to for the future. We had put two months of rehearsal into the show and had enjoyed ourselves so much that we didn't want to stop. So we decided to press on and see if we could secure some more gigs. There were a lot of venues in Toronto; surely we could find somewhere to play.

Roger had started to write again and one evening he phoned me to say that he had a bunch of ideas and why didn't I drop in to his place sometime and we could work them up into some new tunes? So that part of our relationship began to flourish again. In a matter of a few weeks we had a half dozen tunes as well as some more ideas that we could present to the other guys to try and finish at rehearsal. It was exciting to go to rehearsal and work on something brand new.

Everybody had a chance to contribute and as a result the songs just kept on coming. By the fall we had half of what we would need for another album. By the fall we had half of what we would need for another album. We tried to keep the tunes consistent with an Ugly Duckling vibe and avoided any subject matter that was too esoteric or political. We took time off for Christmas and welcomed the new millennia with our friends and families.

Right after New Year's Roger phoned me with a proposal for another gig. It was another fund-raiser at a place on King Street called, Peel Pub.

Our aim was to play and enjoy ourselves and this gig sounded just right. We would have another act open for us and then play one long set and we would be joined in our fund-raising aspirations by former boxing champ George Chuvallo, who was lending his name and his presence to the event. Roger's cousin Fred Calvert came along and video-taped the whole night so that we could evaluate our musical progress. It was all good, and it went off without a hitch, building our confidence in the process.

We continued on into the spring, writing and rehearsing almost every week at Kid's space at Cherry Beach

Studios. For Glynn and myself it meant a 2 to 3 hour drive each way, depending on traffic; which would leave us 3 to 4 hours for rehearsing. But it was energizing and usually left me with a buzz for the drive home.

In May we did a gig at The Horseshoe Tavern in Toronto. It was a treat to play in a club that had played host to so many incredible bands over the years. It had a similar vibe to The El Mocombo and was another landmark we decided we had to try. The night was warm and hazy for May and the crowd were into Ducks.

After the first set a small-ish cool lookin' dude dressed in black jeans and a black western shirt with white piping, approached the stage and introduced himself.

"Hi Dave, my name's Cleave Anderson from Blue Rodeo and The Screwed and I've been diggin' The Ducks music for twenty five years!"

We shook hands. "Wow; that was a great set. When did you guys start writing all the new material?"

I told him about the Warehouse Gig and how we had been inspired to write again and then we had a great conversation about sixties music and the "Garage" and "Punk" scenes in Toronto. He loved raw, visceral music and he thought of us as the originators of the style in Canada. He boosted my ego for the second set.

Ugly Ducks
top retro bill

TORONTO ROCK REVIVAL, featuring **STITCH 'N' TYME, THE UGLY DUCK-LINGS, KENSINGTON MARKET, MAINLINE, LIGHTHOUSE, ROBBIE LANE AND THE DISCIPLES, DOMENIC TROIANO** and **CROWBAR**, at the Warehouse, May 2. Tickets: $20. Attendance: 1,700. Rating: **NN**

As soon as openers **Stitch 'N' Tyme** started into the mop-top covers, the nostalgic tone of the evening was set. Their perfunctory stab at the Righteous Brothers' You've Lost That Lovin' Feeling was just a buildup to an even more dreadful crack at the Beatles' Got To Get You Into My Life.

Luke and the Apostles padded their set with covers, too, neglecting to perform their one great original tune. Been Burnt, in favour of lame versions of familiar blues and R&B numbers. Never has Billy Boy Arnold's Wish You Would sounded so much like Don't Sit Under The Apple Tree.

As always, it was left to the **Ugly Ducklings** to shake things up. A clean-shaven **Dave Byngham** walked onstage beside original guitarists **Roger Mayne** and **Glynn Bell** without any fanfare. Then, just three minutes after launching into a sneering She Ain't No Use To Me, the oldies-but-goodies vibe had vanished.

The mighty Ducklings were not content to toss off a couple of quick covers for old times' sake. When Mayne slashed out the intro to Nothin', you could tell by the way Byngham shook with each note that he was committed, and his tin-roof-rattling shout confirmed it.

Somehow, the Ducklings' performance didn't seem like any kind of backward glance — they were far too confrontational for that.

TIM PERLICH

Now Magazine Review

Promo Shot from the Summer of 2000

As we went on stage for the next set we were accosted by a bunch of guys directly in front, who lobbied us hard to do "I Can Tell". It turned out that they were a band from Hamilton called The Deadly Snakes and they were huge Ducks fans. We hadn't really rehearsed "I Can Tell" that much but we agreed to do it and it came off rather well to their delight, and was followed by lots of whoops and hollers! Folks from Hamilton were some of our staunchest supporters and we felt obliged to give the guys what they wanted. Hamilton was the one city where we had never played anything less than a sold-out concert!

Reviews for The Horseshoe were positive and we played again that summer at the end of July for a street dance on Yonge Street. The irony of this particular night was inescapable, as we played on a gigantic stage right in the middle of Yonge Street just half a block south of the Mighty CHUM building!

We slowed down considerably for the rest of that summer as Jane and I concentrated more on her Pottery business. I had left my job as a mechanic and taken some courses in mold-making so that I could help build Jane's hobby into a full time career. I learned how to cast and trim clay pots and for the rest of the summer we took her pottery to Arts and Crafts shows all over southern Ontario.

After Labour Day the band resumed rehearsing.

Roger phoned me at the beginning of October to say that he wanted to go into the studio again. I was in agreement, but stumped as to how we were going to get there. Roger put forward the idea of talking with Jan Haust and Peter Moore. I asked if he really cared about making any money and he just laughed.

"Money? You gotta be kidding, Dave. Naw, I just want to make a great album; something that really kicks ass and sounds good!"

I felt the same way. There was no use flogging a dead horse. Our chances of ever making any money from our music were slim at best, or non-existent.

So I called Jan; Roger didn't get along with him and didn't feel up to it. I told him right up front that we just wanted to make a great album. Money was not an issue.

"Hey, well that's a relief Dave, because you know there isn't very much to be made if you only expect to sell a few thousand units! You'll be doing it for the love, not for the money." I told him that's all we ever did it for!

He talked it over with Peter Moore who was going to be his partner on the project and they called me back to say that everything was a go. They just had to locate a studio and sell off some old gear to raise some funds for studio time and tape costs. In the meantime they wanted to come to a rehearsal and hear some of the tunes.

It was all good.

Actually, it was all good until the two of them actually came and checked out one of our rehearsals. They listened intently as we performed two of our new tunes that were our favourites at that time. One was called "Don't Bug Me" and the other was our newest, "No Brains Today". They loved both of them.

Kid had been recording what we played onto a "DAT" machine and Peter had noticed and asked if they could borrow the tape to take it back to his studio and make some copies.

Kid didn't like the idea and became very protective of our songs. It was a totally unnecessary freak out. One that I suspected was motivated more by Kid's dislike of Jan and Peter, than by the circumstances. It was embarrassing for Roger and myself and created a distinctly unnerving situation to finish off the evening.

Jan and Peter went home empty handed and Roger and I felt like there was someone trying to pull the rug out from under us, to turn us away from our main goal. It was a minor betrayal of trust.

We knew what we were doing with Jan. We had initiated it. We trusted him. Everything was above board and out in the open. My God, he was selling off some of his older recording gear in order to finance our project!

So suddenly the even flow of our evolution was rudely interrupted and we were faced with an untenable state of affairs. How were we going to manage the entire process of recording a new album with a veil of mistrust and tension hanging over the whole project? I got a knot in my stomach just thinking about it.

I mentioned my predicament to my friend George Bertok one evening on the phone and he said simply, "Why don't you get someone else, Dave?" It was such an obvious solution.

So my next thought was, "Who?" And of course right away the answer was staring me in the face. What was Rob doing? Did he have the time, and would he be able to commit?

Unused Promo Shot for S.N.A.F.U. 2001

I called him the next night and told him our plans and that everything was almost ready to go, as far as recording the album.

His questions were simple. "How many tunes have you got, Dave?"

"Ten, maybe eleven."

"So where can we rehearse for a couple of nights?"

"Maybe Roger's place, I don't know."

He was pretty sure that we could get it together in a couple of nights. I said, "So, a couple of nights?"

"Yeah Dave, I can do charts for all the tunes, O.K? So even if they're not rehearsed to perfection, I'll have the charts for the studio."

This would be something new for a Ducks recording session. I didn't say a word to Roger about the charts. It might have spooked him. He would find out everything once we started rehearsing anyway.

It was up to Roger to break the news to Kid. I had a lot less experience in that department than he did and he had intimated that it would be best if it was left to him. I didn't envy him. I knew how much the gig had meant to Kid.

So, around the beginning of December we ended up in a nice 24 track studio in a loft somewhere on Queen Street West. It was a nice space with wood flooring and acoustic tiled ceilings.

The production of the album was a revelation for us all. Peter Moore had initially thought that it would be swell to record us "live" off the floor, as a band. I quickly put the kibosh to that idea. We had a discussion about time constraints and creative inspiration.

Our final process involved recording all the tunes "live", but without solos and vocals. We knew that we needed the "live" energy in the backing tracks, but we left the finesse of soloing for overdubs. My vocals were done spontaneously at whatever time I felt ready to do a particular track. That way I never felt pressured and the performances were real and un-strained.

Everyone contributed equally to the final sound. Peter Moore was truly amazing. He puffed on his pipe constantly, walking around the studio, listening intently to each and every little sound and part. His ear was impeccable. And his knowledge of all the gear was unmatched.

When it came time to record Roger's solos, I would stand in the studio with him and conduct his playing like a conductor guiding an orchestra. It was the same method that I had used over all the years that we had recorded and it worked like a charm.

Once the album was in the can it was a matter of waiting for Peter to mix it and master it. He transferred all of the tracks from tape to his digital suite and went to work on it. In February of 2001 it was done and we played a CD Release Gig at The Horseshoe. Suffice it to say that with very few exceptions, our new music was not welcomed, nor played on radio. But we weren't really that surprised. We were still untouchables.

Our next gig was at Blues On Bellair, a new club in Yorkville that had been opened by Peter Jermyn, the organist from Luke And The Apostles. It was a special gig organized by my friend Scott Kennedy of Dixie Rumproast and Kensington Market, to honour the contributions of Andy Frost of Q107 FM, to the cause of preserving Canadian Rock Music for posterity. Andy's show, Psychedelic Psundays on the Mighty "Q" was a mainstay of classic Canadian rock in Toronto that had helped to keep our music alive, and we felt privileged to honour him.

The Mike McKenna Band, Greg Fitzpatrick and Keith McKie opened for us and the audience was enthusiastic and lovin' every minute of it! We had a ball.

So much so that we booked another show at Peter's for September 15th and 16th during The Toronto Film Festival. We figured we might get a really great international crowd by performing right in the heart of Yorkville.

Dave & Scott with Andy Frost in front of "Blues On Belair"

But fate intervened and the whole weekend turned into a disaster as the world watched the horror of 9/11. The remainder of the Festival was cancelled and we found it very difficult to play that weekend. We had zero energy and no faith left in humanity. The world was in a state of shock. What more can be said?

That was pretty much it for playing for a while. We all settled back into our regular lives and tried to recover a sense of purpose, or at least some normalcy. Then the world fell into a quest for revenge and we had to adjust to a new reality. It was a month before we got our groove back.

On October 4th we were at The Docks in Toronto playing at a Fundraiser for the victims of 9/11. On the bill were Lighthouse, Foot In Cold Water, Santers, Goddo, Bob Segarini, Alan Frew (Glass Tiger), Moxy and my old label-mate from the Yorkville Records days, Ronnie Hawkins. The whole gig was one big party and a mutual admiration society. It was fantastic getting to play that kind of show, with all of our friends and former colleagues. Seeing Godovitz and Skip Prokop, plus all the guys from "Foot" was a total blast! But it was the last time I saw Rick Lamb alive, as very soon after the gig he was diagnosed with lung cancer.

The next gig we did was in May of 2002; once again at The Docks in Toronto on Cherry Street. It was organized as a fund-raiser for another charity of some sort and was to feature a lot of the same bands that had performed at The Toronto Rock Revival in '99. But there was a difference this time. A *huge* difference. There was absolutely no involvement on the part of any of the major Radio Stations in the city.

It was almost 3 years to the day after we had done The Warehouse Gig and it was the biggest let-down that most of the bands had experienced in their careers. There was almost no promotion and no publicity and as a consequence there was almost *no* audience. There were less than two hundred people there to see ten bands.

It was nice to meet up with all of the bands again but the circumstances sure brought everybody down. I felt sorry for Pinky Dauvin from Stitch In Tyme because it was his daughter who was the major organizer and had to bear the responsibility for the failure of the show. The Stitch had travelled all the way from Halifax to do the show and Crowbar had flown in from Calgary. A lot of people lost quite a sizeable amount of money. It was an indignity that we all suffered in silence.

But it wasn't a totally unique event. All of us had played gigs before where we weren't paid, or where the promoter reneged on part or all of their promises. It was a reality of the business that came with the territory. But in this case it was just an unfortunate chain of events that led to utter failure on the part of the promoters. It was inexperience and an *unfounded* confidence in the power of the internet as an instrument for promotion. It was such a shame it had to happen to all of us at once, when our intentions had been so good and our cause so noble.

But as Mr. Vonnegut would say, "So it goes".

That whole episode sort of knocked the wind out of us permanently and we went into a deep hibernation. There wasn't much to keep us going.

Momentum is a funny thing; when you start running downhill you seem to gain more and more of it. And then of course you ultimately reach the bottom where everything comes to a final, screeching halt. I didn't want it to be that way.

It was better to go quietly than to flash out.

Roger did call me occasionally to get my feelings on playing a few gigs here and there, but in the end there wasn't much satisfaction to be had by us playing even the best club gigs in Toronto. For The Ducks to play it had to be an event. There had to be a reason. And there didn't seem to be many reasons on the immediate horizon. Time just slid by so effortlessly.

And then on the morning of September 29th, 2004 I received a phone call from Stan Endersby who rarely, if ever, called. He said, "Hi Dave, its Stan". His voice cracked almost imperceptibly. He hesitated for just a second and then said, "It's over, Dave. Roger passed away last night. We have no guitar player."

Roger had had a massive heart attack the night before and went very fast. He was such a powerful person with such a strong will and stalwart personality; it was hard to imagine that he would leave us that way. But he did. And I miss him very much, to this day.

The following is a message I sent to Andy Frost at The Mighty "Q107" the very next day and it pretty well summed up my feelings. Andy read it "live" on-air on Psychedelic Psunday on October 1st, 2004.

> "Hi Andy,
>
> Just a note to let you know: Roger Mayne, our lead guitarist and my inimitable song-writing partner, suffered a massive heart

attack last night and passed away in the early morning.

We are all in shock and deeply saddened. Roger was a total original and the "engine" that drove the band. He loved the fact that you guys still played our stuff and delighted in the fact that our survival and longevity repudiated all of the critics of our day who belittled our sound and our music.

As a guitarist he was totally original and spontaneous. He never played the same lick twice. He was Canada's progenitor of the Fuzz-tone Guitar and augmented his playing with enormous energy and wry wit.

We will all miss him very much, but are comforted by the fact that we will always have his music. Thanks to all at "Psychedelic Psundays" for playin' our music over the years!

Rock and Roll will never die! Yours In Music,
Dave Bingham, The Ugly Ducklings."

That was "The End" for me and for everyone. There could be no thought of playing without Roger. He was the core. It was his baby from the very beginning and with his passing the curtain came down.

I still miss him, and so do many, many others. His smile could light up a room and his guitar playing could make even the most depressed of us break out in a foolish grin.

One of the last promo photos of the band

Later that year in November of 2004 I got a call from a true gentleman, Mr. Larry Fitzgibbon, from Nepean, Ontario. He had some amazing and interesting information for me. He told me that he was in possession of the *original* Acetate of "Somewhere Outside"! I was a little bit skeptical and to tell the truth, more than surprised. It was miraculous to say the least!

How had this happened? Where did he find it? It seemed so improbable after so much time had passed. I had so many questions.

But as it turned out, Larry had all of the answers. He was genuine and for real. He was a major record collector and music historian specializing in Garage Music and he had acquired the acetate in the 70's at a record convention. He told me he had felt guilty about hoarding it, ever since. Somehow, the news that our Masters had vanished had filtered through to him and he became extremely uncomfortable with the fact that he held the solution to our problem.

He offered to give me back the acetate if I would give him credit for finding it and restoring it, on any further releases. The restoration part was something that intrigued me. What was that all about?

Larry explained that he had acquired the acetate in a damaged state and had therefore, paid a good price. He explained that it had a kink in it. It was a fused aluminum-cored acetate with a vinyl covering, but it had been bent at some point, so that it was no longer playable.

While he was at a Record Convention in Ottawa he was talking to a prospective customer about the disc and told him about the kink. It turned out that the customer was an airplane mechanic and knew of a solution.

Evidently, very fine aluminum aircraft panels are routinely straightened out using a special press which does not compress or mar the aluminum.

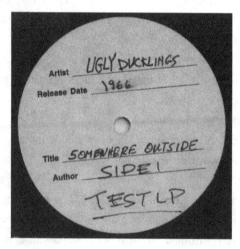

Acetate Side 1

Acetate Side 2

So an arrangement was made and this guy really did it. He brought the disc back to a playable state. At that point Larry enlisted the aid of his music partner, a Mr. Dave Sampson of Ottawa, to make a transfer of the album from the acetate to the digital realm and subsequently I received new Digital Files of the *original* album. They were pristine, with very little noise and surprising audio quality. Dave had used his noise removal programs to clean them up as much as possible.

I was inspired by his efforts and immediately acquired some more digital restoration software and spent four months perfecting the tracks, bringing them back to life as I remembered them. It was a true labour of love.

I sent the files off to Sundazed Records in New York State, who had contacted me the previous year about doing a Vinyl release of the album. So, in 2005 almost 40 years from it's original release date, a new authentic re-creation of "Somewhere Outside" came out on Beat Rocket Records a sub-label of Sundazed, and in a matter of weeks the pressing of 1000 copies was sold!

After Roger passed away I continued to play and perform in a much more subdued fashion, choosing gigs carefully and purposefully.

The "New" Crackerjack Blues Band 2004

In 2004 while shopping at Long & McQuade's in Oshawa, I had met a great guitarist, Norm McMullen from Lindsay, Ontario. My old band-mate from Sleight of Hand, Marty Hepburn, who worked in the rental department in the store, introduced us to each other. Norm had played in the 80s with a band out of Toronto, called New Regime. They had recorded a couple of albums with producer Terry Brown and had minor success; releasing two videos to Much Music as well. Together we decided to form a new version of The Crackerjack Blues Band. Along with my old friends J.P.Hovercraft (bass) and Brian Ferguson (drums), we played for almost a year at Norm's restaurant and bar in Lindsay, "The Electric Tomato".

Then in June of 2009 I received an invitation from Cleave Anderson and his band The Screwed, to participate in a gig at The Cadillac Lounge in Toronto, with their other special guest Gord Lewis from Teenage Head. It was the kind of treat that I just could not afford to pass up. It was to be on July the 9th, which was timed just right for me, as Jane and I didn't have any Craft Shows lined up until the 15th.

A week before the gig I got a call from Radio Host and Blogger "Psychedelic" Pete Ahrens who wanted to arrange an interview on site at the club. After the long drive to the city, the night of the gig flashed by in what seemed like minutes. There was a sold-out crowd and many of my old friends from the west end dropped in to see the show. Pete conducted a wonderful quirky interview outside on the sidewalk as the Queen Street West crowds strolled by in the warm July breeze.

It was a special show featuring one whole set of Ducklings and Teenage Head tunes. I had to learn the Head's tunes and then nail them with no rehearsal. It was a gas and of course everything worked out just fine. The boys were all true gentlemen.

A local Video Production company came out to the club and filmed the whole performance and agreed to send me copies of the tunes that Gord and I participated in.

So, now they are up on Youtube for posterity.

Screwed Poster

Me with Cleave after the Show

With "Rhythm Pot Pi" - 2009
J.P. Hovercraft, myself, Frank Watt & Chris Hiney

After The Screwed gig, I hooked up with J.P. Hovercraft's new band Rhythm Pot Pi and jammed on Thursday nights with J.P., Chris Hiney, Frank Watt, and Brent Farrow at The Coach & Horses in Lindsay, Ontario. The music was all very informal and un-pressured and it was a great way to let off steam after a hard day in the pottery studio.

Also, it was a pleasure to play with such great and intuitive musicians. The interaction on stage was exhilarating. Chris Hiney was a wonder to behold and has one of the most innate Blues guitar techniques I have ever heard. And Brent Farrow's melodic sense was the perfect foil for Chris. There it is again, eh? Contrast – you gotta have contrast!

Later in the summer we did a Local Cable TV Show at CHEX in Peterborogh. It was another guest appearance, with myself and Cris Cuddy joining the band for a full half hour of music. Videos of this performance are all up on Youtube.

Later that year while on vacation in San Miguel De Allende, Mexico, I met Ken Basman, a phenomenal guitarist who had played with B.B.Gabor in the eighties back in Toronto. Ken had joined B.B's band just in time to play on his second album, under the direction of producer Gene Martinyk. Gene was famous of course for playing guitar with Kensington Market. He had started a whole new career for himself as a producer, by producing a number of Bruce Cockburn albums and then moving on to produce discs by other contemporary artists.

Ken and I hit it off very well and since then I have been gigging sporadically every year in San Miguel with Ken and his partner in crime, drummer Rick Shlosser. Rick is one of the most accomplished and successful session drummers of all time and has played with Van Morrison, Rod Stewart, Diana Ross, John Mellancamp, James Taylor, Lionel Ritchie and a list of artists as long as your right arm. Ken and Rick introduced me to Antonio Lozoya, Scott Mason, Bobby Kaplan, Doug Robinson and many other great musicians around town. We jammed at Tio Lucas Restaurant and played some gigs at La Malinche, near the Jardin in 2010, calling ourselves The Lost Chords.

In July of 2011, I got an Email from Greg Godovitz of Goddo asking if I would like to come to Toronto and do his radio show, along with my old mentor, Ronnie Hawkins and his friends, The Partland Brothers. Greg now had a radio show on 1010, CFRB where he inter-viewed musicians who were passing through town or releasing new CDs. I was pumped to do the show with Ronnie, as I hadn't seen him since 1994 when he had given a free concert in Peterborough. My old friend John Bride had played on some of the Partland Brothers' recordings, including their hit, "Soul City"; so the line-up was a match made in heaven, and I told Greg so.

After a nice comfortable drive down the Don Valley Parkway I scooted into the studios of 1010 and was greeted by Greg and his producer Bob Reid. Ronnie and The Partlands arrived a few minutes later.

Greg did a masterful interview with each of us and then opened the phone lines, so we could take questions from the audience. It was a total hoot. Ronnie, of course, was in fine story-telling form and kept everyone in stitches for the entire duration of the show. I laughed so hard my stomach was sore.

Afterwards we posed for photos, said our goodbyes and then headed back home. Greg and Bob had been gracious hosts and given us each thumb drives, with a recording of the show. It was a real treat for me, because Greg and I had done a duet of "Ten Thirty Train" live on-air. Fun, fun, fun! Ah, the life of a musician......

"RockTalk" *Back row:* Me, Greg Godovitz & G.P. Partland, *Front row:* Bob Reid, Ronnie Hawkins & Chris Partland

Before we all pulled out of the parking lot I asked Ronnie if he still remembered the time that we had met at The Riverboat in the Village, when I had sat in with Junior Wells and Buddy Guy and he had offered me a residency in his band.

He looked at me and said, "Dave, I've got so many memories now, that I've got to forget some of 'em in order to remember the other ones. You know what I mean? Seems to me you had a full head of hair back then, and I wasn't sportin' a beard at the time. Hmmm, it's all a little fuzzy – but one thing I do remember, is that you just wailed on that harp. I wasn't goin' to replace The Biscuit with just anybody!"

We shook hands and he hopped into the cab of his pick-up.

I waved and turned to walk to my car, and then he was gone.

In the spring of 2013 I returned to San Miguel and together with Ken Basman, Rick Shlosser and former Pila Seca bassist, Danny Beltran, we re-formed the band The Lost Chords and played every Friday night at VC & Friends at the invitation of owner and music lover Jorge Levario. Jorge's club was really the closest thing to a true Night-Club that I had ever played. Before I left to return to Canada, we recorded an EP of songs at Ken's studio with the Chords, called "Into The Sun". The songs had all been written by Ken's cousin Mike Usiskin and his wife Jean. I had met them the year before and was stunned by the quality of the songs that they had written together. Mike joined us in the studio to add his guitar stylings into the mix.

The LOST CHORDS 2013

Rick   Dave   Danny   Ken

Back home in Canada in the early summer I got an Email from my old pal and Crackerjacks partner Norm McMullen. He was recording and writing again in a big way. He had bought a lot of new recording gear and a Top-Of-The-Line MAC-BOOK loaded with some incredible recording software. He was also full of fresh new song ideas. I sat down at the computer and listened to the MP3s that he had sent me and was totally inspired and immediately began to write melodies and lyrics to the tracks.

Norm's vibe was really close to mine and we clicked immediately. We started working at writing and recording right away and by sheer will and determination, we managed to complete an album of ten brand new songs. I headed south to San Miguel with a brand new album of The Road, called "Driven", in my suitcase.

The ROAD *2014*

Norm McMullen @ The Electric Tomato

In February when I finally arrived in San Miguel, The Lost Chords recorded four more of Mike and Jean Usiskin's tunes at Ken Basman's studio. So that all-together with the six tracks we had done over the previous year we had finished a complete album!

After I returned to Canada, in May, Ken's former keyboardist, Doug Robinson, got involved in adding keyboards to the four new tunes that we had recorded. I had met Doug in 2012 when I had filmed his fusion band, Mo' Ritmo at El Sindicato in San Miguel and uploaded Videos of four of the group's tunes to Youtube.

The four new tunes with keyboards really added to the depth of the album. I was ecstatic and so were Mike and Jean.

So strange – all this creativity just in time for the *major collapse* of the Music Industry! A lot of people had seen it coming; of course, but I think the full implications of streaming and file sharing had never been fully realized.

But the one thing that amazes me, is the way that young people keep creating music; along with new ways to make it work for them. It's comparatively much more expensive to record and tour today compared to what it used to be, even ten or fifteen years ago. And yet the true music freaks still find ways. And they thrive.

I'm gigging again in San Miguel with a new-found music partner, Mr. Tom Driscoll from up-state New York. We play every Friday night @ Dean Martini's Little House of Blues. If ever you're in San Miguel, check to see if we're there! And do drop in. No cover & no pressure – just loads of fun!

At this point in time, after completing The Ducks' story, I have made the decision to put up all of the *original* music that I have recorded over the years on my SOUNDCLOUD Page, and make it available for FREE to the public. I've uploaded all of my music in 320 kbps, MP3 Format, which is as close to loss-less as you can get in an easily downloadable file. All the music is FREE and easily downloadable! Including the new Re-Master of

"SOMEWHERE OUTSIDE" from the original Acetate, provided to me by Larry Fitzgibbon! Note: *Cover Songs* are not included on SOUNDCLOUD!

Simply go to
– https://soundcloud.com/djbingham-works

Also; you can go to
– https://www.youtube.com/user/nothin66

On my Youtube Channel you can view Videos of many of my Original Tunes, as well as performances by The Ugly Ducklings, Papa Grey, The Crackerjacks Blues Band, Sleight of Hand, ReDUCKS, The Road, The Lost Chords and many of the other Bands I have written about on these pages. There are also Videos of some of my favourite Artists and Groups from the Canadian Scene, and some personal Videos of other friends and favourite artists, that I have created.

My FACEBOOK Page is
- https://www.facebook.com/dave.dj.bingham

Go there to see more photos, Links to Music & Videos and

Announcements of current Events & Gigs

Thanks for coming along on this ride – the pleasure has been all mine!

Below are photos of me with "Musical Friends" from my Personal Photo Album

with Danny Marks & John Finley 2009

with Hawksley Workman 2011

Jammin' with Mike McKenna, 2009

Jammin' with John Finley, 2001

w/ Mickie de Sadist of The Forgotten Rebels 2001

w/ Danny Marks' Band   @ Jeff Healey's 2007

w/ Jerry Stone, (2013) the Fan who wrote,

"She's like a dog without the fleas!"

Tom Driscoll & myself, Gigging in San Miguel

GNU

THUMP & TWANG

MISSISSAUGA JAMS

ROCK 'N ROLL TO THE RESCUE

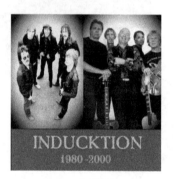

IN"DUCK"TION

TOPSY TURVY WORLD

EDGEWISE

ETCETERA

INTO THE SUN

DRIVEN

VALIDATION & ACKNOWLEDGEMENTS

In 2006 I received an Email from Bob Mersereau, a host on CBC - Halifax and a Music Historian and author. He outlined to me how his company Goose Lane Editions was putting together a new book called The Top 100 Canadian Albums.

Bob and his accomplices polled nearly 600 musicians, critics, journalists, DJs and retailers to come up with a ranking of the country's best-loved discs for his book. Each of the people polled had to pick their top ten albums. Each list was then assigned points, as in 10 points for #1, 9 points for #2, 8 points for #3 etc. and on down to 1 point for #10. Then the points were counted and the final list was calculated.

"Somewhere Outside" came in at number 72! It was something that I knew Roger would have been very proud of. The very fact that there were less than 1900 copies of the album pressed (see statistics below) was a testament to the longevity and appeal of the band.

In 1967 there were probably very few people who would have predicted that our music would have endured over the decades. But if they had stopped to think about it, it really was genuine unadulterated music and unquestionably came from the heart. There was no pretence and no condescension. We respected the integrity of our audience and I think that's where we made the crucial connection.

The next year Bob released his Top 100 Canadian Singles book, and in it, "Nothin'" came in at number 33! Astounding; considering that when it was released it only got to number 18 on the CHUM Chart and number 70 on the RPM Hot 100 national chart. Strangely, it had made it to Number 1 in Saint John, New Brunswick! Maybe the folks in Saint John understood something about it that the rest of the country couldn't fathom. But the fact was that it had something that people didn't notice back then; it was original in every way. The sound, the feel, the story and the musical performance were like nothing else, before or since. It wasn't The Beatles, but it didn't have to be, and it was absolutely real. Roger would have been very proud.

MANY THANKS TO:

Larry Fitzgibbon, Dave Sampson, Piers Hemmingsen, J.P. Hovercraft, Bill Huard, John Read, Rob Melbourne, Kevan Staples, Carol Pope, Mike McKenna, Johann Lowenberg, Glynn Bell, Rob Boers, Kid Carson, Andy Frost, Roger Ashby, Frank Manley, Nicholas Balkou, George Bertok, John Bride, Ed Pryla, Tom Fryer, Dave Sandy, Wayne Baguley, Doug Greer, Wayne Thompson, Bill Munson, Ed Green, Marty Hepburn, "Blind" Whitey Somers, Joe Agnello, Brian Ferguson, Brian Ross, John DeNottbeck, Doug Robinson, Bill Speer, Danny Marks, Tommy Graham, Cleave Anderson, Bill Guilliland,

Brian Ahern, Bob Halley, Sean Scoffield, Ray Harrison, Ray Montford, Gary Hornbeck, Henry Powmer, John Dale, Larry LeBlanc, Ken Basman, Kenny Brown, Scott Cushnie, Rick Shlosser, Al Black, Rick Fines, Larry Rogers, Danny Beltran, Norm McMullen, Ernie Pope, Rick Levenston, John Steele, Chris Hiney, Frank Watt, Jan Haust, Mark Miller, Stan Endersby, Ed Roth, Peter J. Moore, Carny Corbett, Ivan Clark, Tim Perlich, Willy Wilson, David Kindred, Dennis Pendrith, Ian Kojima, Matthew Dennington, Dave "Styx" Bourque, Tim Livingston, Rusty Prowse, James Owen Bush, Psychedelic Pete Ahrens, Nicholas Jennings, Kevin Brown, Tom Driscoll and Photographers; George Shagawatt, Villiam Hrubovcak, Gord Beattie and Gary Scoffield - for so many great Photographs! Also, thanks to Daemon Moore @ Friesen Press for his guidance, and a very special thank you to Peter Byker for his diligence in proofreading my initial manuscript.

UGLY DUCKLINGS DISCOGRAPHY —
and Number of copies sold.

Nothin' – YT 45001 - summer 1966 – 4,229 copies

She Ain't No Use To Me – YT45002 - fall 1966 – 1,274 copies

Just In Case You Wonder – YT45003 - Christmas 1966-67 – 2,981 copies

Postman's Fancy – YT45005 – unreleased (500 pressed)

Album - Somewhere Outside – YT50001 – March 1967 – 1,885 copies

Gaslight – YV45013 – summer 1967 – 25,040 copies

Epilogue – YV45017 – fall 1967 – withdrawn from circulation (unknown pressing)

Just Another Rock 'n Roll Band – RZ002 – 1980 – (500 pressed) – sales unknown

Album - Off The Wall – RZ003 – 1980 – (1000 pressed) - sales unknown

Album - S.N.A.F.U. - OPM-2126 – 2001 - pressing and sales unknown

Thump & Twang – PACE-087 – 2011- (500 pressed)

Somewhere Inside – PACE-086 – 2011 – (500 pressed)

UGLY DUCKLINGS ALUMNI –
1965 to 2004

Over the years I've sat in with a lot of bands and played hundreds of gigs with the bands that I have fronted. Everywhere I went I met people who knew someone who had played with The Ugly Ducklings. I had never heard of the *vast majority* of them!

So, here is the definitive **List!** If their name doesn't appear here, then they never, ever, ever played with the band and they have just been telling you stories!

Lead Singer & Harmonica - 1965-2004, Dave Bingham (Byngham)

Lead Guitar – 1965 -'67, 1979-2004, Roger Mayne

Lead Guitar – 1967-'68, Mike McKenna,

Lead Guitar – 1968 - '69, David Kindred

Lead Guitar & Vocals – 1973 -'74, Nick Balkou

Lead Guitar – 1973, John Bride

Lead Guitar – 1974, John Pimm

Rhythm Guitar & Vocals – 1965 – '68, 1979 – 2004, Glynn Bell

Bass Guitar – 1965 -'67, 1979-'80, 1986 – '89, John Read

Bass Guitar – 1967-'68, Howie Smith

Bass Guitar – 1969, Dennis Pendrith

Bass Guitar – 1973 -'74, Norm Wellbanks

Bass Guitar – 1974, Bob Jennings

Bass Guitar – 1974, 1981-'82 Ron Cameron

Bass Guitar – 1999 – 2004 Stan Endersby

Keyboards – 1968 – '69, Bill Speer

Keyboards – 1973, Matthew Dennington

Keyboards – 1973 – '74, Jim Oskirko

Keyboards – 1974, Ed Roth

Keyboards – 1980, 1988, Scott Cushnie

Drums – 1965 – 1969, 1974, 1979 – '82, 2000 – 2001, Rob Boers

Drums – 1973 –'74, Dale Hutchinson

Drums – 1974, 1986 – 2000, Kid Carson

Peter Kindred played Bass for 1 gig in1969 and John Hamilton, Drums for 1 gig in 1982.

UGLY DUCKLINGS SONG LIST —
Italics - Denotes "Original" Songs

10:30 TRAIN

2120 SOUTH MICHIGAN AVENUE

AIN'T GONNA EAT OUT MY HEART ANYMORE

AIN'T SUPERSTITIOUS

ALL DRUGGED OUT

ALIMONY

AIN'T GONNA EAT OUT MY HEART ANYMORE

AIN'T NO SUNSHINE

AMERICA NEEDS YOU

AROUND AND AROUND

ANY OTHER WAY

ALL DAY & ALL OF THE NIGHT

BETTER LUCK NEXT TIME

BLUE SKIES

BOOM BOOM

BOTTLE UP AND GO

BRING IT ON HOME TO ME

CAN I GET A WITNESS?

CAN'T JUDGE A BOOK BY THE COVER

CHANGES MADE

CHINA GROVE

CONGRATULATIONS

CRAWLIN' UP A HILL

CRY TO ME

CROSSCUT SAW

CRY YOURSELF TO SLEEP

DANCE DANCE DANCE

DANCIN' IN THE MOONLIGHT

DIDDLEY DIDDLEY DADDY

DO IT AGAIN

DOIN' FINE

DOMINO

DON'T BUG ME

DO WHAT YOU WANT

DOWN HOME GIRL

DOWN THE ROAD APIECE

EARLY IN THE MORNIN'

ELEANOR RIGBY

EMPTY HEART

EPILOGUE

EVERYBODY NEEDS SOMEBODY (TO LOVE)

EVIL (IS GOIN' ON)

FOXEY LADY

FREE RIDE

GASLIGHT

GET OFF OF MY CLOUD

GIMME THAT HARP

GIRL OUT OF TIME

GLORIA

GOIN' DOWN

GOIN' TO NEW YORK

GOT MY MOJO WORKIN'

HANGMAN

(NO) HARD FEELINGS

HEART OF STONE

HERE COMES THE NIGHT

HEY BO DIDDLEY

HEY JOE

HEY MAMA (KEEP YOUR BIG MOUTH SHUT)

HIGH HEELED SNEAKERS

HOME IN YOUR HEART

HONKEY TONK WOMEN

I CAN TELL

IF YOU GOTTA GO (dylan)

IF YOU NEED ME

I KNOW WHAT TO SAY

I'LL FOLLOW THE SUN

I'M ALRIGHT

I'M A MAN

I'M FREE

I'M READY

I'M WITH YOU, BABE

I NEED YOUR LOVE

IT'S ALL OVER NOW

IT'S ALRIGHT

I WANNA BE YOUR MAN

I WISH YOU WOULD

JOHNNY B. GOODE

JUMPIN' JACK FLASH

JUST ANOTHER ROCK 'N ROLL BAND

NOT FADE AWAY

NOT FOR LONG

NOTHIN'

OFF THE HOOK

OH CAROL

OUT OF SIGHT

PAINT IT BLACK

PEEPIN' AND HIDIN'

PLAYGIRL

PLEASE PLEASE PLEASE

PLAY WITH FIRE

POISON IVY

POSTMAN'S FANCY

PSYCHEDELIC ARMPIT BOOGIE

RAG MAMA RAG

RAMBLIN' MAN

REALITY

RIGHT PLACE AND THE WRONG TIME

RIMB NUGGET

RISE TO YOUR CALLING

ROADRUNNER

ROLL ME OVER

ROUTE 66

SATISFACTION

SCARRED

SHE AIN'T NO USE TO ME

SMOKESTACK LIGHTNING

SOMEBODY HELP ME

SPOONFULL

STRAWBERRY WINE

SUCH A NIGHT

SUMMER IN THE CITY

SUMMERTIME

SURPRISE, SURPRISE

SWEET LITTLE ROCK 'N ROLL

TALK TALK

TELL ME

THAT'S JUST A THOUGHT THAT I HAD IN MY MIND

THAT'S HOW STRONG MY LOVE IS

THAT'S WHAT YOU SAID

THE BAND PLAYED ON

THE BIRD IS THE WORD

THE LAST TIME

THE MIDNIGHT HOUR

THE ONLY ONE

THE PAIN IS ALRIGHT

THE SAGE

THE SPIDER AND THE FLY

THE TELEPHONE SONG

TIME IS ON MY SIDE

TIRED OF WAITING FOR YOU

TOO MUCH MONKEY BUSINESS

TUMBLIN' DICE

UNDER THE BOARDWALK

USE ME

WAR BABIES

WELL RESPECTED MAN

WHAT A SHAME

WHO DO YOU LOVE

WHO'S THAT GIRL?

YOU REALLY GOT ME

YOUR MAMA DON'T DANCE

YOU'VE REALLY GOT A HOLD ON ME

YOU'VE GOT IT MADE

ZIP-A-DEE-DO-DA

ABOUT THE AUTHOR

Canadian singer-songwriter and harmonica player Dave Bingham has been part of the Canadian music scene for forty-eight years. His career highlights include opening for the likes of The Rolling Stones, The Animals, The Beach Boys, Wilson Pickett, Sam the Sham & The Pharoahs, The Grassroots, Gary Lewis and The Playboys, Jeff Healey, Goddo, Mandala, Lighthouse, Mahogany Rush, Edgar Winter, Albert King and King Biscuit Boy. He has also jammed with iconic artists Jimi Hendrix and Buddy Miles, Junior Wells and Buddy Guy and John Lee Hooker. The first album he recorded with his seminal band The Ugly Ducklings (Somewhere Outside) was voted #72 in "The Top 100 Canadian Albums" for the book of the same name, and the first single he recorded (Nothin'), which debuted the night he opened for The Rolling Stones, was voted #33 in "The Top 100 Canadian Singles", for the book of the same name. This is his story and the story of The Ugly Ducklings and all of the musicians he has played with, who share his passion and dedication to music.